The Archive
of Place

The Nature | History | Society series is devoted to the publication of high-quality scholarship in environmental history and allied fields. Its broad compass is signalled by its title: nature because it takes the natural world seriously; history because it aims to foster work that has temporal depth; and society because its essential concern is with the interface between nature and society, broadly conceived. The series is avowedly interdisciplinary and is open to the work of anthropologists, ecologists, historians, geographers, literary scholars, political scientists, sociologists, and others whose interests resonate with its mandate. It offers a timely outlet for lively, innovative, and well-written work on the interaction of people and nature through time in North America.

General Editor: Graeme Wynn, University of British Columbia

Claire Elizabeth Campbell, *Shaped by the West Wind: Nature and History*

Tina Loo, *States of Nature: Conserving Canada's Wildlife in the Twentieth Century*

Jamie Benidickson, *The Culture of Flushing: A Social and Legal History of Sewage*

John Sandlos, *Hunters at the Margin: Native People and Wildlife Conservation in the Northwest Territories*

James Murton, *Creating a Modern Countryside: Liberalism and Land Resettlement in British Columbia*

NATURE | HISTORY | SOCIETY

The Archive
of Place

Unearthing the Pasts of
the Chilcotin Plateau

WILLIAM J. TURKEL

FOREWORD BY GRAEME WYNN

UBC Press • Vancouver • Toronto

15 14 13 12 11 10 09 08 07   5 4 3 2 1

Library and Archives Canada Cataloguing in Publication Data

Turkel, William J. (William Joseph), 1967-
   The archive of place : unearthing the pasts of the Chilcotin Plateau / William J. Turkel ; foreword by Graeme Wynn.

   (Nature, history, society ; 1713-6687)
   Includes bibliographical references and index.

   ISBN 978-0-7748-1376-1

   1. Human ecology – British Columbia – Chilcotin Plateau – History. 2. Indians of North America – British Columbia – Chilcotin Plateau – History. 3. Material culture – British Columbia – Chilcotin Plateau. 4. Chilcotin Plateau (B.C.) – Race relations – History. 5. Chilcotin Plateau (B.C.) – Historiography. 6. Chilcotin Plateau (B.C.) – History. 7. Human ecology – British Columbia – History – Case studies. 8. Ethnohistory – British Columbia – Case Studies. I. Title. II. Series.

QL84.26.N6S22 2007   971.1'75   C2007-902155-7

Canadä

UBC Press gratefully acknowledges the financial support for our publishing program of the Government of Canada through the Book Publishing Industry Development Program (BPIDP), and of the Canada Council for the Arts, and the British Columbia Arts Council.

This book has been published with the help of a grant from the Canadian Federation for the Humanities and Social Sciences, through the Aid to Scholarly Publications Programme, using funds provided by the Social Sciences and Humanities Research Council of Canada.

The author acknowledges the assistance of the J.B. Smallman Publication Fund and the Faculty of Social Science, University of Western Ontario.

UBC Press
The University of British Columbia
2029 West Mall
Vancouver, BC V6T 1Z2
604-822-5959 / Fax: 604-822-6083
www.ubcpress.ca

For Juliet, and in memory of J. Charles Wyse, 1966-98

Contents

Putting Things in Their Place

by Graeme Wynn

I N THE SIXTH BOOK OF *de Architectura*, written in the first century BC, Marcus Vitruvius Pollio wrote of the Greek philosopher Aristippus, who was shipwrecked off the island of Rhodes. Upon landing on the beach, he found some lines drawn in the sand. Recognizing their geometrical form, he urged hope upon his companions, crying out according to one translation from the Latin, "Be of good courage, I see marks of civilization," and in another, "Let us be of good cheer, for I see the traces of man."[1]

Two thousand years later, Clarence Glacken, a geographer from the University of California, Berkeley, drew the title of his magnum opus from this incident. Thirty years in gestation, *Traces on the Rhodian Shore* is a remarkably erudite study of nature and culture in Western thought from ancient times to the end of the eighteenth century.[2] Yet *Traces* has little to do with the sorts of material inscriptions on the landscape that buoyed the spirits of Aristippus. Although Glacken insisted that his interest in the relations between culture and the environment grew from personal observations of the immensely diverse entanglements of land and life in different parts of the world, observations which prompted him to ponder the circumstances that kindle human creativity, he expected readers to regard his work as "exclusively a product of the library." Indeed, *Traces* explores "man's place in nature" through an impressively wide-ranging engagement with ancient, medieval, and early-modern written sources. It says very little about material settings and the marks that humans make on the surface of the earth as it maps expressions of three interlocking ideas: the idea of a designed earth; the idea of environmental influence; and the idea of humans as geographical agents. It is at once a work of geography and intellectual history, and it stands, in retrospect, as an early contribution to the emerging field of environmental history, marking out both the possibilities and the value of investigating the ways in which humans have thought about the world.

In the pages that follow, William Turkel follows the trail blazed by the Greek philosopher and the Berkeley geographer by proclaiming his interest in the marks and traces – the indexical signs – that humans impose on the landscape. In some sense, the Chilcotin Plateau of British Columbia is Turkel's island of Rhodes, and ideas about nature and culture lie as close to the centre of his concerns as they did to Clarence Glacken's project. But Turkel comes deliberately to the Chilcotin, as a scholar seeking to integrate and extend various perspectives on the past rather than as a shipwrecked traveller. He sees the plateau as an intellectual challenge rather than as an intelligible sanctuary and (as a scholar shaped by his turn-of-the-millennium context) he is reluctant to accept the distinction between nature and culture that Glacken recognized as a "dichotomy that has plagued the history of geographical thought" but found impossible to resolve on account of its deep involvement with other histories of ideas.

For Turkel, the Chilcotin is neither simply a stage on which humans have left their marks, nor merely a locale in which to examine the perceptions of particular individuals. It is, rather, a setting in which to examine the complicated entanglements of these two things, an exemplar of the larger point that "every place is an archive" and a vehicle for reflection upon historical practice. It is about history and memory, about the relations between historical consciousness and the materiality of place, and about doing historical research "in the field" rather than in libraries and archives. *The Archive of Place*, Turkel tells readers in his preface, "is about the ways in which people interpret material traces to reconstruct past events." It is thus both a history of a place (an environmental history, Turkel would say) and a study of the practices involved in writing about past places. It begins in the belief (derived from the phenomenologically-oriented philosopher of place Edward S. Casey) that "places gather" a vast range of things – from animate and inanimate entities, through experience, histories, languages, and thoughts, to legends and practices – and rests on the conviction (borrowed most immediately from environmental historian William Cronon) that scholars should recount how they come to understand the world as well as provide narratives about it.[3] Thus, *The Archive of Place* seeks to historicize the act of place making and place the process of constructing the past under critical scrutiny. The result is an unusual and arresting book that reveals a good deal about the Chilcotin as it elucidates how people create, deploy, and contest evidence in the search for a usable past.[4]

To appreciate this book's contribution, it is necessary to put it in its place, to understand what it does, and does not, do because many others have sought to understand places through traces by interpreting ordinary landscapes and engaging in "archival fieldwork," although rarely from the precise standpoint adopted by Turkel.[5] Here it is well to remember, as Donald Meinig has observed so eloquently, that deciphering the material evidence of human imprints on the earth – or "reading the landscape" – is "a humane art, unrestricted to any profession, unbounded by any field, unlimited in its challenges and pleasures." In this context, the writings of American J.B. Jackson and Englishman W.G. Hoskins immediately spring to mind as superlative examples of the craft of landscape interpretation. Very different in background and temperament, engaged in understanding very different parts of the world, and endowed with "exceptionally seeing eye[s]" focused on different interpretive horizons, these two independent-minded scholars did much to advance interest in the rich historical record given material expression in the complex, ever-changing tangle of features (from hedgerows to field patterns and from farmhouses and churches to trailer parks and roadside strip malls) that set localities apart and give character to places.[6]

Both Hoskins and Jackson sought to uncover "the logic" behind landscapes that they understood as "a series of [human] compositions of varying magnitude" or as "living design[s]" adorning the face of the earth in reflection of human actions, aspirations, and beliefs. The former, a local historian, sought "truth in the details of this particular house, this lane, this hedge, by means of the most meticulous work in field and archive." The latter, a broad thinker fascinated by aerial photographs, tended to view places from more remote vantage points, and to assess them more quickly as he sought meaning in classes of things: kinds of dwellings, patterns of features, and plans of settlements. Hoskins, concluded Donald Meinig in a sympathetic and illuminating comparison of the work of these two influential figures, was "engaged in a skilled detective work of exact dating from scraps of evidence," while Jackson undertook "interpretive work" in search of "general meaning" inspired by a "keen sense of culture history." For Hoskins, landscape interpretation was a distinct form of historical practice, an approach directed to addressing fundamental historical problems. His work was necessarily conducted at the local or micro-scale of particular localities, but he was firm in the belief that the material traces left in the landscape by humans reflected the societies and environments (the worlds of ideas, technologies, beliefs, and biophysical surroundings) in which they lived, and that they were best understood through and alongside other written and otherwise recorded remnants of human endeavour.[7]

For Jackson, by contrast, encouraging landscape appreciation was a form of activism. Much of the magazine *Landscape,* which Jackson founded in 1951 and edited and contributed to for seventeen years thereafter, was devoted to commentary on the problems facing residents of rural and smalltown America as technological and social change swept across the country. It reflected Jackson's rejection of the modernist era's "one world-ism" in favour of a "less didactic" understanding of economy and society, in all their dynamic variety, at the local scale. "What we need," he wrote in a 1953 commentary on E.A. Gutkind's *Our World from the Air,*

> is not an aerial perspective of the globe but an aerial perspective of our own backyard. It is no use telling us the world is our home and that we should love it, until we have learned to love our own corner of it, until we have learned what that corner possesses in the way of beauty and potentiality for happiness. Otherwise, we can only look upon the foreign landscape as Dr. Gutkind does: not as an inhabitant, but as a kind of global social worker, bereft of all sense of wonder, but very much aware of what is wrong and how to right it.[8]

In a narrower disciplinary vein, generations of geographers have plowed somewhat parallel, although often less clearly articulated, furrows. The roots of this concern are buried deep in the mists of time. Some see the tradition of geographical fieldwork (inherent in which is a concern with the "look of the land") beginning with Odysseus; others find more recent and robust antecedents in the work of the great cosmographer Alexander von Humboldt. A third, more diffuse, precursor can be found in the common expectation, in late-nineteenth-century German geography, that graduate students would produce an initial dissertation on a local topic (involving direct engagement with the particularities of a specific locality) and a subsequent *Habilitationschrift* on a distant part of the world. Inspired in the first part by Pestalozzi's educational reforms, which valued local knowledge or *Heimatskunde,* and in the second by Goethe's celebration of the medieval *Wanderjahre* tradition as well as a commitment to self-development in German education, these impetuses undoubtedly encouraged an emphasis on field investigation and place-based studies among

twentieth-century American geographers. So too did the strong field tradition defined by the earth scientists Nathaniel Southgate Shaler and John
Wesley Powell, as they surveyed and assessed the physiography and resource potential of the American west and reflected on human-environment
relations in this area. Together, these influences were carried forward by
the influential geomorphologist William Morris Davis, the young Carl
Sauer, and others, leading to the emergence by the late 1920s of a distinctly
American form of cultural geography involving "careful studies of landscapes and economy based on archives and detailed fieldwork."[9]

Characterizing even this more narrowly defined band of work in histori-
cal/cultural geography is no easy task. In 1925, when Carl Sauer wrote
"The Morphology of Landscape," which is often regarded as the basic
foundational statement of American cultural geography, he had been ad-
vocating fieldwork for a decade and he was defining an approach in
explicit opposition to prevailing views that the physical environment
determined individual development and behaviour, and thus the cultures
in which people lived. Critical of the untested presuppositions upon which
environmental determinism rested, and cognizant of peoples' capacity to
act willfully, Sauer reversed the equation of environmental determinism
and made culture a driving force of environmental change. With the aid
of a simple but powerful heuristic model, he envisaged cultural landscapes
(constituted by the material traces of human endeavour, such as fences,
field patterns, dwelling forms, and so on) as products of the encounter
between human culture (a shared set of beliefs, attitudes, behaviours, and
technologies) and the physical environment (vegetation, soils, climate,
etc.) over time. In this schema, people of different cultures coming into
the same physical environment would produce very different cultural landscapes as their conceptions of "the good life," their appraisals of their setting and their capacities (and desires) to alter it would differ. By the same
token, people from the same culture colonizing markedly different settings would not produce identical new landscapes because they would have
to adjust their practices to work with different biophysical resources.[10]

Half a century on, Sauer's conceptual framework was roundly criticized
by scholars whose intellectual contexts were very different from those in
which Sauer wrote. Some took him to task for his "super organic" view
of culture, which he regarded (as did most of the leading anthropologists
of his day) as static and "given" rather than as the ever-changing product of
the ongoing dialectic between individuals and societal norms that those
who studied social worlds in the latter part of the twentieth century con-
ceived it to be.[11] Others were discomfited by what they regarded as Sauer's

rigid distinction between nature and culture and by his failure to avoid that age-old dichotomy, although a more sympathetic reading of his conceptual scheme might suggest that the cultural landscape fashioned by humans in encounter with the biophysical world was at least a hybrid creation. Be this as it may, for decades after his relocation from Chicago to Berkeley in 1925, Sauer continued to develop and extend his geographical practice, which bore few signs of intellectual constraint by his "morphology model" and engaged generations of graduate students in exploratory trips in which "interrogating landscapes was more important than either explaining them or interpreting them."[12]

Meanwhile, others embarked on different courses of geographical inquiry and carried the mainstream of the discipline away from both landscape studies and the investigation of human-environment relations. By the 1960s, much of the "fieldwork" undertaken by geographers was governed by a positivistic paradigm and directed to the systematic collection of neatly ordered data through the use of surveys, questionnaires, and enumeration schemes. The cluttered, disorderly world that confronts the senses and challenges the understanding of those who relish its everyday diversity and complexity was ultimately reduced to abstractions and even regarded as "naughty" for its failure to conform to the interpretations, designs, and models applied by scholars.[13] Some continued to "get out into ... [the world], look hard at it, ask questions about it, and grapple with the conundrums so presented," and attempted to decipher the jumbled record of human traces in the landscape by joining field observations in interrogative conversation with data from ethnographic, archival, or archeological sources to understand the "intersection of people, land and space in the past." But by the 1980s, fewer and fewer geographers were inclined to "take the world as it is."[14] Reflecting the cultural turn then coursing through the social sciences, a new generation of geographers thought of landscapes as texts but rejected the possibility of mimetic ("accurate"/"objective") representations of the world and, more generally, the realist assumptions that underlay field-based inquiry. Critical of earlier efforts to observe, describe, classify, and map material artifacts in order to identify cultural regions and trace the diffusion of cultural traits, they sought to understand landscapes through interpretive metaphors that implicated "a web of social processes and intersubjective meanings."[15] The field, reflected the English historical geographer Felix Driver in 2000, "is not just 'there'; it is produced and reproduced through both physical movement across a landscape and other sorts of cultural work in a variety of sites."[16]

In this context, it is perhaps hardly surprising that William Turkel found the task of understanding the Chilcotin unexpectedly challenging. Trained in psychology and linguistics before beginning doctoral work in history, in anthropology, and in the Science, Technology and Society Program of the Massachusetts Institute of Technology and then becoming interested in environmental history, he was relatively unfamiliar with both the fading traditions of archival fieldwork and landscape interpretation and the new cultural geography outlined above.[17] Initially, he thought, ambitiously, to write an account of the sparsely settled plateau that lay to the west of one of his childhood homes. He contemplated a deep and thorough study that would allow him to narrate the story of these acres in west central British Columbia through 300 million years. Quickly he discovered that records of and knowledge about this territory were fragmentary and uneven. Historians and anthropologists had written about the Chilcotin and its peoples, but relatively sparsely. Archival holdings about the place were tantalizingly incomplete. Archeologists had excavated a few sites and their reports threw light on facets of the past beyond the reach of written records as they helped piece together the picture of population migrations into and through the area thousands of years ago. Scientists specialized in several disciplines, from paleobotany to glaciology and geology, had deciphered the record of drifting continents, the collision and accretion of fragments of crustal materials (terranes) and the patterns of volcanic activity that produced the particular configuration of the western edge of the continent. They had traced the scouring and deposition of surficial materials by massive ice sheets, detailed the colonization of the area by various flora and fauna as climate changed over the millennia, and so on. Foresters, hydrologists, agricultural scientists, wildlife managers, and others had addressed many of the problems confronting those who lived in and utilized the area and its resources in the latter part of the twentieth century.

Yet the question remained: How to make sense of this disparate and patchy corpus of information? Perhaps the answer lay in and on the land itself. Armed with a digital camera and a GPS (Global Positioning System) receiver, Turkel took himself to the Chilcotin and travelled its highways and byways for a week, taking 3,500 pictures of "everything," from cliffs and clouds to power lines and abandoned cabins, from mining operations to log-hauling trucks, and from cows to alpacas. Precisely located through association with data from the GPS, each image could be plotted and entered in a Geographical Information System (GIS). Thus the features of the landscape were enumerated, inventoried, and catalogued. Through the magic of technology, Turkel was able to "revisit" this remote tract of British Columbia from afar. Sitting in his offices in Cambridge, Massachusetts, and London, Ontario, he could browse in GIS map layers, click through photographs, remind himself what the Chilcotin was like, and see things that he had missed when he was there. Information accumulated, but it was hard to make sense of it. With so many disparate fragments to hand, and so many different kinds of evidence to wrestle into some kind of order, Turkel began to wonder about the value of the materials he had collected. He, like others at similar points in their inquiries, was troubled by a seemingly simple query: "So what?" At one scale, he confronted the historians' age-old challenge of finding a story against which to measure the significance of particular pieces of information. At another, he asked himself why people should care about what he might have to say about this place.

Answering these questions meant making choices. The past of the Chilcotin – represented by the archival fragments and material traces that Turkel encountered and assembled – was open to interpretation. Speculate, for a moment, about the ways in which devoted students of Hoskins, Jackson, and Sauer might have attempted to make sense of this evidence and this place. In an effort to emulate Hoskins, one might have treated the landscape of the Chilcotin as a palimpsest. Typically, this might have entailed close scrutiny of its material features, an effort to establish, as precisely as possible, the dates of and reasons for their creation (and alteration), and the development of a chronological account of the changes made to the area through time. Another, following Jackson, might have seen the Chilcotin landscape as a reflection of contemporary society and read from it a range of arresting claims about the ways in which scenes along "three hundred miles of back road to nowhere much" revealed the local peoples' efforts to "make the earth over in the image of some heaven."[18] A third, working in the spirit of Carl Sauer, might have identified the distinctive characteristics of the Chilcotin at different periods of time as expressions of different cultures, and marked the ways in which indigenous people, transient gold-seekers, ranchers, mining interests, and other groups utilized and thus shaped the landscape in markedly varied ways. Stretching the point, we might say that students embracing these distinct perspectives would treat landscape as history, as ideology, and as cultural product, respectively.

In the end, none of these approaches appealed to Turkel. Influenced by the French sociologist of science Bruno Latour and more broadly by the late-twentieth-century intellectual movement known as post-structuralism (succinctly described as "a set of theoretical positions, which have at their core a self-reflexive discourse which is aware of the tentativeness, the slipperiness, the ambiguity and the complex interrelations of texts and meanings"), Turkel came to conclude that his attention was skewed.[19] Landscapes were important not as mirrors of history, ideology, or culture per se, but because the material traces that humans inscribed upon them endured and carried the stories that societies told about themselves through time. Places were archives of memory. Fixated on fragments and worrying about his readers, he had failed to see this. Now he recognized that the issues important to him were those framed by people who were actively engaged in reconstructing and reinterpreting the past of the Chilcotin.

Geologists, archeologists, First Nations people, anthropologist, historians, resource managers, and others, Turkel came to understand, were interested in the rocks, the human occupants, the organic life, and the other facets of this place because they were (and are) stakeholders in its future. They each sought, in different ways, to make the past usable for their particular present. As a consequence, the pasts that they produced were more or less deep, were framed and emphasized differently, and were sometimes incommensurable, as they reflected and fed into the concerns of those who constructed them. Stakeholders read the material traces of the past in the same way as Aristippus interpreted those geometrical marks on the beach – as indexical signs, things that signified "something else by virtue of a causal or physical connection between the two" (page 66 herein) – but, viewing them from different vantage points, they wove them into different stories and were often led into contention, as they asserted the primacy of their narrative over those of others. An appreciation of this provided Turkel with the basic structure of his book. Three struggles joined in the last decades of the twentieth century but rooted in the past of the Chilcotin – one over property rights, another over the creation of a heritage trail, and a third over prevailing interpretations of British Columbia history – allowed him to explore others' stories about this place, stories that lead him inexorably to the conclusion (page 227 herein) that "The different ways a place is imagined do as much to shape the understanding of what happened there in the past as any physical trace ever could."

The Archive of Place is, then, both a gathering of stories about a place in time and a study of representations, partial, contingent, and purposeful. It explores the complicated relationship between historical consciousness and the materiality of place and it reminds us that the Chilcotin is a repository of ideologies that have changed over time. Like all parts of the earth's surface, this one, Turkel tells us, is constituted by the accretion within it of things new and old, things familiar and strange, things that are tangible and things that are not. Thoughts, memories, dreams, disappointments, penchants, and prejudices are as important parts of this landscape, this archive, as the material traces left upon it by the actions of humans, their animals, and their machines. In light of this, Turkel would urge environmental and other historians to think anew about the practice of their craft. By paying more attention to the ways in which others have constructed stories about places past, by tacking back and forth between their own reading of sources and the ways in which others have understood them, by telling "not just stories about nature but stories about stories about nature," he would suggest that they have the means to bring their work more fully into the mainstream of current concerns.[20] In this lies both the challenge and the freshness of Turkel's work. In the final analysis, *The Archive of Place* is a manifesto, encouraging scholars to find new ways of thinking about venerable concerns. To do this, it draws attention to, and tells us a good deal about, a little-known, even out-of-the-way place, but its crucial message echoes that attributed to the French novelist Marcel Proust, who observed that "The real voyage of discovery consists not in seeking new landscapes but in having new eyes."[21]

Preface

THE ARCHIVE OF PLACE is about the ways in which people interpret material traces to reconstruct past events, the conditions under which such interpretation takes place, and the role this interpretation plays in historical consciousness and social memory. The book consists of three case studies from the Chilcotin plateau in the west-central part of present-day British Columbia. In each case study, a conflict in the mid-1990s over the meaning of the past for the present provided the occasion for underlying stories to surface. As different groups struggled to control the fate of the region and its resources, they invoked very different understandings of its past to justify their actions. In many cases, their beliefs about the region's history were informed, directly or indirectly, by physical evidence found in the place itself.

Material traces of past events are commonplace. Seeing a footprint in the mud, we may infer that someone walked by after the last rainfall, when the ground was soft. We readily distinguish the tracks of a child from those of an adult, human tracks from those made by other animals, or bicycle tracks from those of motorcycles or cars. In certain settings it becomes important to be able to infer more from tracks, and some people specialize in these more intensive kinds of reading. Hunters or wildlife biologists, for example, can readily distinguish the characteristically round hoofprints and telltale dewclaw marks of a caribou from the more pointed and elongate tracks of a moose. Forensic investigators can determine the size of a shoe and its manufacturer from footprints and can make reliable predictions about the weight, height, and gait of the wearer as well.[1]

But tracks are not the only material trace of the past. In fact, every single aspect of our environment bears some physical or causal connection to past events. Every *thing* has a history, and our ability to reconstruct the past of anything is limited only by the knowledge that we bring to bear and by our ability to detect or discriminate or identify or measure the trace. Blood contaminating a shoe print may be invisible to the naked eye, but if the print is sprayed with a chemical reagent called luminol, the blood will glow in the dark. The blood itself may be matched to a particular animal by the proteins that it contains. If it is human blood, it can be matched to a group of people (according to the ABO system of blood groups) based on antigen-antibody reactions or matched to a particular individual by DNA testing. What is made of such evidence, however, is rarely straightforward. Different people may have a stake in the outcome, and this is reflected in the conclusions that they draw. In a sense, the idea that different interpreters will draw different conclusions from the same material evidence is merely a corollary of the historian's methodological dictum that one should, as E.H. Carr put it, "study the historian before you begin to study the facts."[2]

Part 1 of *The Archive of Place,* "Deep Time in the Present," focuses on a case in which contemporary stakeholders presented their interpretations of different material traces of the past while arguing over the fate of a copper-gold **porphyry** deposit and a nearby lake. In the 1990s, a mining company and other proponents of an open-pit mine found themselves in conflict with other companies over mining claims, with the government and anglers over fisheries, with environmentalists over conservation, and with First Nations over land claims. As the estimated value of the potential mine increased, each of these groups tried to determine the future of the region, in part by reconstructing its past. The only way for the mining companies to find out how much the mine might be worth was to reconstruct the geological history of the ore deposit. The postglacial history of the lake and its population of rainbow trout became important for individuals and groups who wished to preserve a natural fishery. The ecological history of the region guided environmental groups in their decisions about which areas they should fight the hardest to conserve. Archaeological studies corroborated the traditional patterns of indigenous land use, which played an important role in the legal case for Aboriginal land claims. For each of these stakeholders, the key to the Chilcotin past lay in physical evidence found in the place itself, evidence that typically had to be gathered and interpreted by specialists from many different disciplines. Since these studies cost something (and often were very expensive), they were only undertaken by groups that expected to see some benefit in return. Much of the argument in this first part of the book focuses on the ways in which people reconstructing the past from physical evidence use that reconstruction to bolster claims about property rights, which in turn form a key element of the region's political economy.

There are further dimensions to the relationship between material traces and historical consciousness, however, and the idea that every place is an archive of these traces becomes progressively complicated over the course of the book. Part 2, "The Horizon of Experience," is concerned with the creation of a heritage trail to commemorate the accomplishments of the eighteenth-century explorer Alexander Mackenzie. In 1793, an expedition led by Mackenzie skirted the northern edge of the Chilcotin and ended at the Pacific Ocean. Mackenzie and some of his men became the first non-Aboriginal people to make the voyage across the continent north of Mexico. When some groups tried to celebrate and re-enact the voyage on its bicentennial, there was conflict over the role that the explorer did, or should, play in history. Canadian nationalists felt that the accomplishments of Mackenzie had been inexplicably overlooked, and those of the American explorers Meriwether Lewis and William Clark celebrated excessively; they felt it was time to rectify this historiographical oversight and relegate the American explorers to the category of "also-rans" in a race across the continent. To federalists, who feared that the Québécois might be about to split the country apart with their demands for separation, Mackenzie was a symbol of Canadian unity, one of the reasons the country stretched from sea to sea. But the Mackenzie story also contained many elements that called for revision. Two members of the expedition were Aboriginal guides from the east, and Mackenzie and his men made constant use of other Aboriginal guides and informants and followed a longstanding network of Aboriginal trails the whole way. The First Nations took a variety of positions on Mackenzie, the most extreme being that he was a harbinger of genocide. In this they were joined by some politicians on the left, who saw the opportunity to advance a program of democratic socialism.[3]

Each side in the debate about the significance of the explorer for Canadian history, identity, and unity was supported by attempts to reconstruct the route that Mackenzie followed using his surveying notes, maps and artifacts, and especially physical evidence found on the trails themselves. Federal and provincial governments, non-governmental organizations, and First Nations commissioned studies of the system of overland trails in a struggle to define a particular place and its role in history. One of the outcomes of these studies was a new appreciation for the fact that this system of trails underlay networks of trade and exchange that made the Chilcotin "coextensive with the disk of the world" over its long period of human occupation. The accomplishments of a few centuries were thus confronted with those of nine millennia. The argument in Part 2 focuses on the ways in which historical consciousness and social memory depend on the materiality of landscape. The sheer profusion of physical evidence from the past to be found in any place makes it impossible for an individual or group to limit the stories that landscape can tell.[4]

In the historiography of British Columbia, the Chilcotin has often been portrayed as a landscape of darkness, resistance, and violence, and the Tsilhqot'in, the indigenous people who live there, as essentially truculent. Part 3, "Shadowed Ground," explores the ways in which a place becomes a repository not only of the material traces of its past, but also of particular ideologies. It begins with a discussion of reburial. When an Aboriginal cemetery was accidentally unearthed during construction in the 1970s, the human remains were unceremoniously dumped with waste from the building site. When some presumably Aboriginal bones were discovered in a similar situation in the 1990s, however, their ultimate fate became a matter of widespread dispute and negotiation for seventeen months. Reburial is one way people attempt to physically correct their historical relationship with a place and with their ancestors. It is an attempt, if you will, to rewrite the archive of place. The change in attitudes toward reburial in the late twentieth century signalled a radical revision of long-held ideas about Chilcotin history and a dismantling of retroactive historical justification for contemporary racism.

Part 3 traces the history of the region from the time of Mackenzie and the fur trade to the 1990s. In the late 1850s there was a massive influx of non-indigenous people into the interior in search of gold and attendant profits, and a British colony was created. Although the newcomers had little knowledge of the past of the place or its Aboriginal occupants, they were largely responsible for creating its archival record. One of the first challenges they faced, to the authority of their government and to their identity as colonial subjects, was a series of killings in and at the edges of the Chilcotin. This became a defining moment in subsequent historiography. The events of the Chilcotin War (as it came to be known) coloured the ways the Chilcotin was imagined for the next century, feeding into a frontier myth that portrayed the actions of Euro-Canadian settlers as having a civilizing and beneficent effect on Aboriginal people. By the 1970s, the hegemony of this colonial view was beginning to break down. The death of a Tsilhqot'in man during an encounter with the RCMP became a flashpoint for reform of the relationship between the justice system and Aboriginal people. In the 1990s, a government commission was established to investigate how Aboriginal people had been treated by the police, Crown prosecutors, probation officers, and counsellors of the family courts. This provided a forum in which many of the cherished interpretations of British Columbia history, both popular and scholarly, could be called into question.

Together, the three parts of *The Archive of Place* trace the end, which occurred roughly between the 1970s and the 1990s, of a complex of ideas that governed relationships between Aboriginal and non-Aboriginal people. From the mid-nineteenth century to the 1970s, prevailing views of Aboriginal people denied their agency in a wide variety of social, legal, political, and economic contexts. A common assumption was that Aboriginal rights in British Columbia were extinguished by the establishment of colonial government or the subsequent regulatory activities of its successors. Where Aboriginal rights were acknowledged to exist, they were held to be usufructuary and not to include title to the land. Historically, Aboriginal people were portrayed as a part of nature, discovered by non-Aboriginal explorers and tamed by the settlers who came in their wake. In contemporary portraits they were often brutalized. By the 1990s, Aboriginal people and their supporters had disrupted the status quo. Aboriginal title was a legal fact, although its ramifications were unclear. Aboriginal people were agents in a revised history and a force to be reckoned with in contemporary politics. Although the details of the story are specific to this place, in many ways it parallels simultaneous changes elsewhere in the world.

The focus on a particular place, on the physical traces of its past, and on the different ways in which the past has been reconstructed and fought over makes it possible to build on the strengths of intersecting historiographical traditions like environmental history, the history of science, and ethnohistory. As a result, this book is both an environmental history and a historical study of the quotidian practices that are analogous to doing environmental history. It takes as its subject the ways people retrieve the past from a place and the reasons they choose to learn some things and not others. By historicizing this activity, however, it forces the recognition that the environmental sciences may provide a wealth of historical information, but they do not provide a unitary or authoritative account against which all other accounts must be judged. In this way, the narrative tries to pull the concerns of environmental history more into the mainstream of historical revision. As a history of science, the emphasis is on work in the field, on situations in which the products of science are not judged in a rarefied world of theory but, rather, in settings where, for example, people who want to dig mines come face to face with others who would rather cut trees, graze cattle, fish, or simply admire the beauty of nature. The work also draws on the literature of ethnohistory, which has redirected attention to indigenous people and to the ways they have been excluded from narratives and representations of the past. Indigenous people do play a significant role in each of the contests described here, but ethnological concepts and categories are given no more claim to final authority than any other kind of knowledge.

One central idea in this work is that of *clues,* drawn in large part from Carlo Ginzburg's essay of the same name and reworked. This is evident in the subject matter: the ways historians and other interpreters use latent or seemingly insignificant traces to draw wide-ranging conclusions about an external and knowable (but opaque) reality. It is perhaps less obvious, but no less important, that the narrative is also shaped by the application of what Ginzburg called the "evidential paradigm," in that it focuses on individual cases precisely because they are individual, manipulates scale as an experimental technique, and uses **abduction** to infer causes from their effects.[5]

The Archive of Place explores the ways in which usable pasts are drawn from the material substance of a particular place, typically under conditions of conflict. As with any historiographical encounter, these pasts are never fixed, depending instead on the interests, biases, and abilities of their historians. Taken in conjunction, these stories about the past characterize the people living in a particular place at a particular moment, their aspirations and anxieties, their image of who they are and where they came from, their sense of being exactly where and when they are. That moment – that binding of history and memory and landscape – constitutes the present. The physical traces of the past lie all around, manifest to a greater or lesser degree, ready to be incorporated into what comes next.

Acknowledgments

I'D LIKE TO THANK my colleagues and students at the University of Western Ontario, who have provided a congenial place to think about, talk about, and do history. Alan MacEachern, in particular, has been very generous with his good ideas, wide-ranging curiosity, and wry sense of humour. My fellow founders of *NiCHE: Network in Canadian History and Environment* have been similarly generous, and I'd like to thank each of them, too: Colin Coates, Stéphane Castonguay, and Matthew Evenden. I'm grateful to Julie Cruikshank, Pat Dunae, J.R. McNeill, and Carolyn Podruchny for closely reading the manuscript and offering valuable feedback and support. The Nature|History|Society team at UBC Press were also wonderful. My thanks especially to Graeme Wynn and Randy Schmidt, as well as to Darcy Cullen and copy editor Audrey McClellan.

I began work on this book at MIT. I couldn't have asked for better friends and mentors than Harriet Ritvo, Deborah Fitzgerald, and Shep Krech, or better classmates than the members of the P, X & Y group, especially Shane Hamilton, Dave Lucsko, Jenny Smith, and Anya Zilberstein. I am grateful for the funding I received at MIT as a Mellon Fellow for the Sawyer Seminar and as the John S. Hennessy Fellow in Environmental Studies. I was also very fortunate to participate in the Modern Times, Rural Places seminar, where I had a chance to meet scholars in the field and discuss research ideas with them. Way back, Marcel Fortin started me along the path to history, and Serkan Oray was with me when the atoms started turning into bits.

Research and fieldwork in BC was made downright comfortable by family, in-laws, friends, and helpful strangers. I was assisted by working scientists, archivists, librarians, and curators around North America and received much intelligent feedback from conference and workshop participants.

To prepare the glossary I relied on *The Oxford Companion to the Earth* edited by Paul L. Hancock and Brian J. Skinner, *Geoarchaeology* by George Rapp Jr. and Christopher L. Hill, and *Environmental Archaeology* by Dina F. Dincauze.

Last but certainly not least, I owe the greatest debt to my wife and best friend Juliet Armstrong, who has provided love, support, and companionship every step of the way. *Singe!*

Part 1

Deep Time in the Present

I

Fish Lake

AS YOU LEAVE WILLIAMS LAKE, heading west on Highway 20, you pass the stampede grounds, the sawmill and lumber yards of Lignum, a small alpaca farm, a few trailer courts, and houses here and there. It doesn't take long to leave the outskirts of town and find yourself in the midst of land with little sign of human activity. The highway passes under power lines and swings south to parallel the Fraser River. Stands of Douglas fir and lodgepole and ponderosa pine give way at lower elevations to grassland, much of which is irrigated for hay by local cattle ranchers, particularly on the benches above the river. The highway drops to the Sheep Creek bridge and then slowly climbs the hill on the opposite side of the river via a series of switchbacks. At the end of each switchback is a steep gravel "runaway lane." These give truckers hauling logs down the hill somewhere to turn if their brakes fail. At 760 metres above sea level, you reach the top of the hill and the Chilcotin plateau opens out in front of you. The land has just enough relief that you can almost always see the shadows of clouds moving slowly over the earth.

The Chilcotin is a long way from the part of British Columbia where most people live, the metropolitan region around Vancouver and Victoria. It's a long way from the leisure-centred urban society that has given BC a reputation throughout Canada as "lotus land." Newcomers to the Chilcotin have often written about the journey west on Highway 20 as if it were possible to travel back in time by following the road. The landmarks that most North Americans have come to take for granted, like supermarkets and fast-food restaurants, are simply not there. Most of the Chilcotin plateau is out of the range of cellphone service. The only stores to be found are few and far between. In those general stores you can buy kerosene lamps, horseshoes, washboards, nails, deer- and moose-hide moccasins made by Aboriginal people, coils of rope, haywire, saddles, and chaps. Caught up in the novelty of the wares, it is easy for a traveller to overlook the electricity and refrigeration.[1]

If you follow Highway 20 across the plateau and through the Coast Mountains to Bella Coola on the Pacific Ocean, you will travel along what local historian Diana French called "three hundred miles of back road to nowhere much." You will pass the occasional logging truck or recreational vehicle and, less frequently, the kind of battered pickup truck favoured by locals. About halfway along the road, the pavement ends; most of the rest is gravel. If you make it to the far edge of the plateau, you face "The Hill." For ten kilometres the road drops through a series of hairpin curves at an 18 percent grade, often narrowing to one lane. People who make regular trips down The Hill advocate travelling with doors unlocked and seatbelts off so you can jump clear if the vehicle starts to go over the edge. It sounds like hyperbole, but even in the dark you can see the cars that have gone over. Not everyone makes it to The Hill. Flat tires and blowouts are common as you negotiate "mudbogs," "fun rollers," "washboard road," and "loonshit." Paul St. Pierre, ex-MP and local humorist, wrote that "loonshit was a gumbo; it was undetectable when dry but when thoroughly soaked in water a patch of it took on the character of molasses mixed with glue. All men encountered loonshit sooner or later in that country and all but the strongest wept when they did."[2]

Behind the obviously untrue claim that a trip into the Chilcotin is a trip into the past lies a deeper truth. The sense that people have of occupying a particular place in time is supported by their lived experience in a world of familiar artifacts and landmarks. Things that you find in Williams Lake, like a Tim Hortons doughnut shop or a working cellphone, are traces of the recent past. If time travel were possible, you could use the existence of a Tim Hortons in your vicinity to figure out *when* you were – sometime after the franchise was established in the mid-1960s. Other landmarks and artifacts could be used to refine your estimate. Are people smoking cigarettes? Eating burgers out of Styrofoam cartons? Listening to Anne Murray or the Tragically Hip? Wearing mullet haircuts? Driving hybrid electric cars? Of course, most people don't need to see a hybrid car to know that Y2K has come and gone. But the very substance of a place is composed of stuff from the past and legible traces of past events. These constantly cue memory and provide a sense of history.

Without these obvious connections between a place and the present moment, history and memory cease to be grounded, and it becomes possible to imagine or pretend that this is some other time.[3]

The tourist returns home after a few weeks in the Chilcotin, but what about the people who live there? They have a stake in its future. Many of them depend for their livelihoods on grazing cattle, logging, mining, or guiding and outfitting rich foreigners who want to take home a moose. More frequently now, they cater to ecotourists and advertise their lodges with words like "harmony" and "healing." Despite the outsider's perception that these people are living in the past, they are not. But the landscape is familiar to them and reflects a distant time. Each bend in the road takes on the shading of memory, of stories heard or half-remembered. That's the place where the truck broke down a few winters ago; they're clear-cutting the hill on the other side of that lake; isn't that the place where that Indian guy got killed in the seventies? To the people who live in the Chilcotin, as for people anywhere, the landscape holds much of their past, and they have a stake in that too.

A DIVISION OF INTERPRETIVE LABOUR

To say that a place is full of traces of its past is not to say that those traces are obvious or easily read. Much of the physical evidence of the past is muddled, latent, difficult to decipher. Often it requires experience or special training or expensive equipment. As a consequence, in cases where it is important to reconstruct the past from its material traces, the interpretive labour is divided. Zoogeographers specialize in figuring out the origins of animal populations and their geographic distributions. They can tell you, for example, that moose entered what is now British Columbia about ten thousand years ago from the north, after the ice sheets of the last ice age melted, and that they competed successfully against the slightly larger stag-moose for habitat. The latter are now extinct. The records of the fur trade show that moose were hunted by indigenous people in the Chilcotin in the 1830s. Then, for some reason, the moose may have disappeared in the central interior of the province until the 1900s. They began to reappear in numbers in the early twentieth century.[4]

At this point, the reconstruction of the history of past distributions of moose becomes entangled with the threads of memory, oral tradition, and folklore. One account suggests that moose first appeared around Charlotte Lake, at the edge of the Coast Mountains, in 1914 and soon became so bold and numerous that ranchers had to arm themselves for protection during the rutting and calving seasons. In *Three against the Wilderness,* Eric Collier provided another, more fanciful version of "how the moose first came to the Chilcotin." He said that an Aboriginal man hunting around Riske Creek on the eastern edge of the plateau in 1916 saw an animal that he had never seen before and shot it. The oldest member of his group, "reckoned to be 106 years old," couldn't identify the animal, and the riddle was finally solved by an Englishman at the trading post, who had seen moose in northeastern British Columbia at the turn of the century. In 1931, the zoologist Ian McTaggart Cowan was told that moose had only arrived in the Chilcotin in the mid-1920s and that there was no word for the animal in the Tsilhqot'in language. Other evidence, however, suggests that the animals may have been present in the Chilcotin the whole time, but that their numbers were much lower. By the 1950s they were so plentiful in the area that groups of them spent the winters at local ranches, feeding with the cattle and becoming tame enough to pet. As with any kind of history, this story about what happened in the past emerges from conflicting accounts and evidence that can be read in more than one way. There is no univocal story about how moose came to be in the Chilcotin.[5]

The work of zoogeographers depends on the work of other interpretive specialists who reconstruct the history of different aspects of the environment. Paleobotanists, for example, can tell us about the past vegetation of the region. Around fifteen thousand years ago, plant life began to return to recently deglaciated land in the wake of the melting ice sheets (see Appendix A). The coastal lowlands were free of ice relatively early. They were initially vegetated by willow and soapberry, and later by lodgepole pine. Over the course of the next two millennia, alder, true fir, spruce, and ferns moved into the area. The interior remained dry and cold and was covered with ice in many places. Cattails, sedges, and bulrushes from the south moved rapidly into moist deglaciated land, to be replaced gradually by aspens and pines. The uplands were more sparsely covered with sage and perennial herbs. Since different plants thrive or decline in different climates, vegetation is one clue to the prevailing conditions at a given time. Paleoclimatologists thus have much to learn from paleobotanists, and vice versa.[6]

Between nine and ten thousand years ago, summer solar radiation peaked at levels 8 to 15 percent greater than today's, while winter solar radiation was about 10 percent less than today's. This heated the centre of the North American continent and increased the contrast between land and ocean temperatures in the summer, which in turn affected the way atmospheric and oceanic circulation redistributed heat from the equator (which always receives more solar energy) to the poles. The East Pacific subtropical high-pressure system expanded, resulting in summer drought in what is now British Columbia. In the interior, vast areas of steppe grassland developed, spreading as far north as Pantage Lake near the Blackwater River and extending to elevations over fifteen hundred metres. These grasslands were zoned by altitude, with sage in the valleys and on the lower slopes and grasses and forbs at higher elevations. Plants from the prairies and the Great Basin (in what is now eastern Oregon and southern Idaho) were able to spread as far north as central Yukon. By about four thousand years ago, the climate was again becoming cooler and wetter. Interior grasslands retreated, replaced by forests of pine and alder. Today, grasses give way to trees at elevations around seven hundred to a thousand metres, and the northernmost edge of the grasslands ends right where you cross the Sheep Creek bridge on your way into the Chilcotin.[7]

The landscape that we are most familiar with – the built environment of highways and houses and fences and irrigated fields – is the most recent addition to any place. Often, more seemingly natural features of the landscape, like rivers and forests, are also relatively recent. Beneath the surface of this familiar environment are layers or strata that are older, often much older, and glaciologists and geologists reconstruct their history (see Appendix B). In British Columbia, much of the lay of the land is the result of the events of the last ice age, known as the Wisconsin, which began with a cooling of the yearly average climate about twenty-five to thirty thousand years ago. Ice sheets spread across as much as a third of the world's surface, including what is now Canada and the northern United States and much of northern Europe. At first the ice accumulated as small glaciers on mountains and in alpine valleys. Each of these ice streams flowed separately, sculpting characteristic landforms by erosion.[8]

In the Chilcotin, many of these glacial landforms can be seen around the Fraser River in the area east of Taseko Lake. The Churn Creek valley near Gang Ranch, for example, is U-shaped in cross-section, which shows that it is a glacial trough created by the action of moving ice and not by flowing water, which creates valleys that are V-shaped. The amphitheatre-shaped depressions on Yalakom and Hogback mountains, known as cirques, are also characteristic of early stage glaciation and were formed as slowly moving glacial ice carried away the rock broken by the action of frost. In places in the Coast Mountains to the west, the steep walls of three or more cirques intersect to form a horn, a high pyramidal peak. The newly formed ice in alpine valleys blocked drainage, allowing proglacial lakes to form. In the Camelsfoot Range, what is now the Fraser River was dammed, and a glacial lake formed in the valleys of the river and its major tributaries. The ice continued to accumulate, overriding glacial lakes and rising to the point where individual glaciers coalesced and the thickness of the ice exceeded the local relief. As the ice accumulated, the movement of the sheet was governed less by the topography of the land and more by variations in climate. The lower mountains east of Taseko Lake have typically rounded and domed summits where they were overridden by the ice sheet. Higher serrate peaks in a few places emerged from the ice as so-called nunataks, surrounded but not overridden. For a few hardy species, these nunataks served as refuges, where they could live through the glaciation. Everywhere else, life was swept away by the advancing ice. At their maximum, the ice sheets of the last glaciation were massive, so huge that they spread under their own weight and depressed the surface of the land relative to sea level. Thousands of years after the ice melted, the land was still rebounding. The ice sheets were also dynamic, fed by snow that fell over their interiors and reduced by melting along their margins. Over the ocean, blocks of ice would occasionally calve from the sheet. As the climate warmed, the peripheries of the ice sheets melted. Areas in the centre of the ice downwasted, that is, melted on top, allowing the uplands to emerge first and again dividing the sheet into separate glaciers in valleys. Proglacial lakes formed as stagnant ice blocked drainage and meltwater accumulated. Life returned from the nunataks and from refuges beyond the edges of the ice sheets.[9]

THE MOSAIC OF SUSPECT TERRANES

On a geologist's time scale, the events of the past ten or twenty thousand years are very recent. Below the built environment, and below the trees, grass, soil, and glacial till, lie rock strata that are really old. Often, the deeper you go, the older the strata you will find, and people sometimes speak in terms of "time depth" or "deep time." As there are for other parts of the Chilcotin landscape, there are specialists to reconstruct the events of the very long-term past, and they have written accounts of how the Chilcotin itself was created. These are no more certain or uncontested than any other stories about the past of this place, but much of the controversy can be glossed over in the interests of getting a thumbnail sketch of the events of deep time to serve as a background for the case study that follows.

At the end of the Permian period, 250 million years ago, this place did not yet exist (see Appendix B). At the time, almost all of the world's continental crust was clumped in a single mass, known as Pangaea. The portion of the ancestral continent that would become North America did not extend as far west as it does today. Instead, somewhere east of where the Rocky Mountains now are, it gradually sloped into a continental shelf under the sea. For more than a billion years, long periods of erosion had led to the slow downwasting of the continent, depositing layer after layer of sediment on the shelf and exposing the "basement" rocks of the continental shield. Marine life was abundant, particularly in the warm, shallow waters over the continental shelf. By this time, plants had been living on land for 150 million years, drawing carbon dioxide out of the atmosphere and building some of the carbon into their tissues. In the atmosphere, carbon dioxide absorbed some of the sun's energy that was reflected from the earth and thus contributed to global warming. As the plants died, however, plant debris accumulated, forming peats and eventually coal, which trapped carbon. This slow buildup of organic material eventually reduced the overall amount of atmospheric carbon dioxide. This, in turn, initiated a shift in global temperature from generally hot and humid conditions to generally cold and arid ones. As the Permian period drew to a close, massive ice sheets accumulated around Pangaea's south pole, drawing down the global sea level and exposing the continental shelf. This put an end to most marine life. Corals, foraminifera, trilobites, brachiopods, bryozoans, crinoids, ammonoids – all were eradicated, or nearly so, by the most severe extinction event of the past 570 million years. Somewhere between 90 and 95 percent of marine invertebrates, and half of the vascular plants, perished.[10]

By the late Triassic, 230 million years ago, the eastern margin of the Pacific Ocean had become a subduction zone. According to the theory of plate tectonics, the framework that is now used to envision the dynamics of the earth's crustal structure, rigid plates float on fluid rock known as the mantle, sliding alongside one another and deforming when they collide. The oceans, like the continents, sit on plates, but oceanic plates are stronger and denser than continental plates. When the two converge, the oceanic plate bends, sliding beneath the continental plate, which crumples above it. This process is known as subduction and is accompanied by two characteristic assemblages of rock. At the point where the oceanic plate meets the continental crust, pieces of the ocean floor are scraped off into what is known as the subduction complex. One to two hundred kilometres away from this point on the overriding plate, magma (molten rock) rises through the continental crust to form another assemblage, a volcanic arc.[11]

Starting in the middle of the Jurassic, about 180 million years ago, Pangaea began to break up. The North American continental fragment moved northwest, the oceanic plate subducting beneath it. During subduction, the continental mainland slid into island arcs on the oceanic plate, and these pieces of crust accreted to the mainland. The western edge of North America became a vast mosaic of accumulated pieces of crust, known as terranes, each with a geological history that was different from that of the continental core. The subduction of the oceanic plate under North America also built the Cordillera, the massive collection of mountain ranges that run along the western edge of the continent. On a regional scale, the crust folded and faulted. In what is now central British Columbia, a subduction complex called the Cache Creek terrane was uplifted as this mountain building took place, bringing pieces of oceanic crust and fossils of extinct foraminifera to the surface. The identification of these marine protozoa provided geologists with the first evidence that the mountains of western Canada were composed of "exotic" or "suspect" terranes. Stikinia, another terrane that was once a volcanic island arc, accreted to the west of the Cache Creek terrane. The central portion of British Columbia continued to be uplifted as more terranes, the Alexander and Wrangellia, docked to the west. Since that time, the western edge of the Americas has been one of the most tectonically active places in the world. Accretion of terranes and mountain building was accompanied by strong metamorphism as changes in temperature and pressure caused the rocks to recrystallize. It was also accompanied by granitic intrusion when massive flows of magma cooled beneath the surface to form enormous bodies of granite. The overall result was a broad, plateau-like region in the central part of what is now British Columbia, bounded on the west by rugged Coast Mountains rising in a sharply defined front, and on the east by high ranges rising into the Rocky Mountains.[12]

In the Cretaceous period, beginning about 135 million years ago, climates became more seasonal and varied than they had been earlier. Fossil plants from the time are more clearly distinguishable as variants from low and high latitudes, suggesting a sharper temperature gradient. Angiosperms (flowering plants) appeared for the first time in the form of broad-leaved trees and shrubs, and they spread rapidly. Within about 50 million years they dominated many of the floras of the world; today, angiosperms make up most of the world's vegetation. Sediments formed during the Cretaceous show evidence of **Milankovitch cycles**, probably indicating short-term fluctuations of climate. The Cretaceous was also a time when many different forms of life, both terrestrial and marine, progressively disappeared, for reasons that are still debated. Some combination of factors including climate change, cosmic radiation, extensive volcanic activity, and the impact of a massive asteroid was responsible for another mass extinction event, the best-known victims being, of course, the dinosaurs that vanished about 65 million years ago.[13]

The extinction of the dinosaurs left new ecological niches in North America, and these were rapidly colonized by diversifying mammals, birds, fish, insects, and flowering plants. It took about half a million years for the placental animals to begin to diversify, but after that the process took off. The most spectacular spread of organisms into new habitats occurred among the ancient hoofed mammals, which developed fifty new genera every million years, filling the continent with a diverse collection of animals. In what is now British Columbia, coastal mammals included small whales and a large, four-footed amphibian, the desmostylid, which probably occupied much the same niche that walruses and seals do now. A creature the size of an otter, but which was more closely related to bears, lived along the shore eating molluscs. In the interior, huge herbivores known as titanotheres lived in herds. About two metres at the shoulder, they had humped backs and a pair of bladelike horns at the ends of their snouts. Smaller mammals included rodents, rabbits, rabbit-sized deerlike animals, and marsupials.[14]

During the Eocene, beginning 53 million years ago, the oceanic and continental plates along the edge of what is now British Columbia ceased to converge with subduction and began to slide past one another in a transform fault. This ended the collision of terranes. Tectonic forces continued to pull the continental crust northwards, and the crust relaxed now that it was no longer being compressed. This led to extensive volcanic activity in the interior. Lava flowed into low-lying areas, damming rivers and creating plateaus where lakes formed. Assemblages of fish, insects, and plants were preserved in the sediments of these lakes, which allowed their ecology to be reconstructed in some detail. The dawn redwood, a broad-leaved, deciduous conifer, grew in low, wet areas. Bundles of its needles and leafy twigs often fell into the shallow waters at the edge of Eocene lakes. Soft-shelled turtles, juvenile suckers, trout-perches, and salmonids swam among water lilies, loosestrife, and water plantain, pursued by predatory bowfins. Larger fish, like trout and adult suckers, lived in deeper waters. In some fossil deposits, the fish bones are partially dissolved, as if they had passed through the digestive system of a bird or other predator. The plants in the interior thrived in a temperate climate, suggesting that the area was cooler than the warm temperate to subtropical conditions that prevailed at the time in what is now the western United States. Conditions in the interior also became distinct from those in the Coast Mountains to the west, which were gradually being uplifted. This was, in part, a consequence of the relaxation of the crust, which allowed it to become hotter and more buoyant.[15]

By about 23 million years ago, at the beginning of the Miocene, the central part of what is now British Columbia had a moderate relief of 500 to 650 metres, with lower-lying areas filled in by flat or gently dipping lavas and sediments. In places, erosion had cut channels of up to a few hundred metres in depth, and these had been gradually filling with sediment. Lava erupting from vents and fissures during the middle and late Miocene covered the interior with more than 25,000 square kilometres of flat-lying basalts, creating the vast interior plateau of which the Chilcotin is a part. These lava flows formed the characteristic landform of the Chilcotin today – a gently rolling plateau bounded on one side by a steep, rocky cliff and on the other by a deeply incised valley. In the same period, the continental crust moved slowly westwards over a particularly hot plume rising from the mantle. Lava flowing out onto the surface above this "hot spot" built up a broad, round volcano. As the crust moved, the volcano was carried to the west, and a newer one was built up to the east. In this way, a series of volcanic ranges formed a trail across the Chilcotin – first the Rainbow Range, then the Ilgachuz and Itcha ranges, and finally some recent volcanoes near Nazko. The Miocene climate of the Chilcotin was cool and temperate, closer to the modern climate than Eocene climates had been, but still warmer and wetter than it is today. Overall, the flora was similar to the oak-hickory-beech-elm forests that are now found east of the Mississippi River. Conifers grew in the uplands. The warmer, wetter conditions in the interior suggest that the Coast Mountains did not yet form the extensive rain shadow they do today. This is confirmed by studies that show the land surface of the Coast Mountains has risen more than two kilometres in the past 10 million years.[16]

In the last 1.6 million years, known as the Quaternary period, human beings evolved in Africa. This period has been a time of major climatic alterations and ice ages. During successive episodes of glaciation, the upper half of North America was repeatedly buried by massive ice sheets, each scouring away most of the evidence left by the landforms, flora, and fauna of the preceding period. Each time, plants and animals recolonized the area after the ice retreated. The Wisconsin glaciation that ended about ten thousand years ago was only the latest in a series of more than twenty such shifts in climate that have occurred in the last 2.5 million years. It was different from the preceding glaciations in one respect, however. When the plants and animals returned to North America, human beings were among the colonists for the first time.[17]

AIRBORNE SURVEYS

The reason the geological history of the Chilcotin is known in such detail is that people have found it worth their while to reconstruct it. The Chilcotin economy depends primarily on resource extraction, and this invariably leads to a struggle among contemporary stakeholders because the choice to exploit one kind of resource often precludes the development of others. There is usually a lot of money at stake, and efficient exploitation of the resource, be it a mineral deposit, forest, fishery, grassland, or potential hydroelectric dam, depends on having as complete a knowledge as possible of its attributes. This is where the division of interpretive labour comes in. Geologists, zoogeographers, and other kinds of specialists are needed to determine whether or not a given resource has the attributes that will make it lucrative and cost-effective to extract. Exploitation and exploration go hand in hand. This interpretive labour often involves the reconstruction of the history of the resource: in order to determine what something is or what attributes it has, it is useful to know where it came from. Underlying stories thus emerge in the contest over the fate of the land and its resources as stakeholders search for a usable past, one that will justify their actions. This can be seen in the case study that follows, which examines the role of the division of interpretive labour in the political economy of resource extraction at a particular moment in the ever-changing relationship between the Chilcotin landscape, its stakeholders, and the stories they tell about its past.

One day in the Indian summer of 1993, a small twin-prop plane flew over Redstone heading due west. An observer on the ground might have first noticed the long stinger attached to the plane's fuselage. Even more unusual, perhaps, was the way the plane was flying: low, but always the same distance from the ground. In the days that followed there were more flights, always east to west, always at the same, precise altitude. Successive flight paths were shifted north or south by exactly eight hundred metres. If you were there in Redstone when the drone of the airplane overrode the snapping of grasshoppers, the rustle of wind in the grass, the rumble of big rigs on Highway 20, you might have concluded that someone was systematically scanning the Chilcotin plateau. You would have been right.[18]

The flights were funded by the Geological Survey of Canada, the BC Geological Survey, and some interests in the private sector as part of an effort to assess mineral potential in the region. Much of the plateau is covered by forests, glacial drift, and lava flows that obstruct prospecting. By taking to the air with extremely sensitive magnetic detectors, the surveyors were able to map the boundaries of obscured geological features, to see through, as it were, the trees, glacial deposits, and lava to the subsurface below. They were taking advantage of the fact that the earth's magnetic field varies in a measurable way from place to place. After measuring the total magnetic field and subtracting the components generated inside the earth (i.e., in the molten core), they were left with what are called magnetic anomalies at the surface (or crust), deviations from the background. These anomalies depended in part on the presence of magnetic minerals in the rock below.[19]

The minerals to be found in rock bear many traces of the conditions of their origin. For example, both igneous and metamorphic rocks can be created in great heat, the former as molten rock cools, the latter when some pre-existing rock is subject to heat or pressure or both. As the temperature of hot rock falls below a certain point, molecules of ferromagnetic materials such as magnetite (Fe_3O_4) and **hematite** (Fe_2O_3) align with the earth's magnetic field, preserving a record of the field's direction in the substance of the mineral. This is known as remanent magnetization. The principle is similar to that used in an ordinary audiotape: the magnetic record persists in the rocks and can be read with the right instrumentation. The "playback" is more complicated than a tape recorder, however, especially if you want to read the magnetic record from about three hundred metres above. To detect the minute magnetic fluctuations of rock from a low-flying airplane, the geological surveyors used an instrument known as an optically pumped magnetometer. In this device, polarized light from a cesium vapour lamp is passed through a low-pressure cell of cesium vapour and measured with a photocell. The system is exquisitely sensitive to magnetic fields.[20]

Aeromagnetic surveying provided a rapid means of mapping features of geological interest across the Chilcotin plateau, which was one of the last blank spots on the 1992 magnetic anomaly map of Canada. Two faults lying to the southwest of Redstone, the Yalakom and Tchaikazan, showed up clearly as magnetic anomalies in the new survey. Faults are fractures in the earth's crust, places where the energy generated by the movement of the massive plates that comprise the surface of the earth displaces the edges of the crust with respect to one another. When you stand on one side of the Yalakom fault system, corresponding rocks on the other side have been displaced to the right by more than one hundred kilometres. In fact, the existence of the Yalakom fault was well-known before the aeromagnetic survey took place. Topographical features in the area are aligned along the fault, and the **lineament** can be seen in aerial photographs.[21]

Radiometric dating from another 1993 survey also corroborated the presence of the Yalakom fault. Southwest of the fracture, the rocks are igneous and can be dated to the late Triassic period; they originated a little over 200 million years before present (212-208 **Ma BP**). To the northeast, the rocks are metamorphic and date from the middle to late Jurassic at the earliest, perhaps 160 Ma BP. The sides of the fault were sliding with respect to each other even more recently, for a period of about 37 million years (83.5-46.5 Ma BP), cutting all rock units older than about 65 million years. In order to date the rocks in the area of the Yalakom fault, survey geologists took samples of a mineral called zircon. When zircon is created, it does not contain any lead but it does contain the unstable uranium isotope ^{238}U. As zircon ages, the unstable uranium isotopes decay into stable lead isotopes (^{206}Pb). Since the rate of radioactive decay is accurately known, the geologists used the concentrations of uranium and lead isotopes in zircon samples to date the rocks containing the mineral.[22]

Magnetic and radioactive properties of particular minerals are just two of the non-obvious ways that any place stores a record of past events. They are unwritten sources that can be used to reconstruct a history of rocks, including their creation and perturbation by subsequent geological processes. Geological exploration is done for many reasons, of course, one of the most common being the potential for profit. For example, in 1949, the fledgling aeromagnetic program of the Geological Survey of Canada discovered a massive magnetite body in an area of Ontario that had previously been thought not to contain valuable minerals. Profits from the resulting mine "more than covered the cost of the entire aeromagnetic program" to 1993. There are always costs associated with learning something, but there are often benefits, too. It is simply not possible to know in advance whether there will be a net gain or loss.[23]

To an expert in magnetometry, the fact that the Chilcotin survey was flown at an altitude of 305 metres would immediately suggest that the motivation for the flights was primarily commercial. Flights around this altitude are ideal for detecting magnetic fluctuations caused by mineral or ore deposits. Presentation of the 1993 survey data emphasized geological features that might be of economic significance. South of Redstone near the Yalakom fault, for example, geologists found a "significant gold anomaly" in the glacial drift lying along the edge of an aeromagnetic anomaly, one of a number of "mapped and possibly unmapped features which [might] be important loci for mineral deposits." Four kilometres north of Yalakom fault, also lying on the flank of a magnetic anomaly, was Fish Lake, a **porphyry** copper-gold deposit that the surveyors and the general public were already well aware of.[24]

In fact, another airborne survey of 1993 centred on the region around Fish Lake. An environmental consulting company was contracted to do a "helicopter-mounted reconnaissance-level survey." Over the space of three days in May, the survey crew flew the helicopter along the lines of a grid measuring about thirty by fifty kilometres. Every 2.5 kilometres, the helicopter dipped down and the person doing the sampling – securely attached to the hovering helicopter by a couple of safety lines – leaned out to snip off one of the pine tree tops. These samples were passed on to the Geological Survey of Canada in Ottawa. There, biogeochemists first dried the plant tissues, then burned them and tested the ash for concentrations of various metals, including copper and gold. Finally, these concentrations were plotted on a map showing where each sample was obtained. The logic of the study was to use the trees to amplify the geochemical signature of the substrate they were growing on. As the pines grew, they extended their roots deep into the soil, the glacial drift, and, in places, the bedrock. Drawing water and nutrients up through this root system, the trees also extracted materials that they didn't need for growth, such as copper and gold, and these became concentrated in the tree tops, twig ends, and bark. Concentrations of metal in the trees could thus serve as a sign of concentrations of metal in the ground below.[25]

THE FISH LAKE PORPHYRY DEPOSIT

It is not possible to completely know the three-dimensional structure of the earth's crust, so geologists have to infer the structure from surface characteristics; outcrops; core samples; measurements of gravity, radioactivity, and magnetism; and whatever else is known or surmised about the geological history of the region. Specimens of porphyry taken from the Fish Lake area were readily identified because they consisted of a fine-grained groundmass speckled with large, distinct crystals. Most of the crystals were copper and gold; some were molybdenum, silver, and zinc. Each of the metals was an important commodity, and if there were enough copper and gold in the Fish Lake deposit, it might be profitable to mine it. Preliminary exploration suggested that the deposit was a large ovaloid. By 1992, it had been measured to be almost a cubic kilometre: 853 metres north-south by 1,310 metres east-west by 823 metres deep. The full extent of the deposit is still not known. There is a possibility that it extends farther north, west, or southwest.[26]

Companies that wish to extract the commodities in porphyry deposits must first make an effort to reconstruct the history of those deposits. In general, porphyry deposits are created in places where two of the earth's tectonic plates are colliding, and a slab of dense oceanic crust is subducted. As the subducted slab descends, the temperature and pressure increase, causing it to melt. The surface crust of the oceanic slab contains water, which is released into the overlying crust. This released water lowers the melting temperature of the overlying material, and magma is formed and rises. Sometimes the magma makes it to the surface and is erupted as lava from a volcano. If the magma cools and crystallizes before reaching the surface, however, the resulting body of igneous rock is known as a pluton.

Porphyries are closely associated with plutons and are thought to occur under the following conditions. When the magma created by the subduc-tion of oceanic crust begins to rise, the pressure drops. This reduction in pressure causes the dissolved water in the magma to separate. At the same time, the magma begins to form the crystals that will later be found in the porphyry. The separation of the water further cools the magma, which speeds crystallization and forces more water from the magma. Since the outer surface of the body cools more rapidly than the interior, a carapace is created around the magma. Pressure builds up in this carapace and even-tually shatters it, allowing hot fluids to be released upwards to circulate around the solidified porphyry and surrounding host rock. The process continues cyclically until the entire body has solidified. As the magma crystallizes, trace metals are forced out along with the water and become concentrated in it. They are typically found in a zone around the intrusive body. The Fish Lake porphyry was created in the late Cretaceous (around 80 Ma BP), when the terranes that make up central British Columbia had already docked, and the accretion of Wrangellia and the Alexander terrane farther west caused uplift, faulting, metamorphism, and granitic intrusion in the Coast Range. Near Fish Lake, movement at the Yalakom fault was accompanied by volcanism and the emplacement of plutonic bodies into older marine sedimentary rocks and non-marine volcanic rocks. Subse-quently covered by Miocene lava flows (23-5.3 Ma BP), the Fish Lake deposit was exposed as those lavas eroded.[27]

In the second half of the twentieth century, porphyry deposits were an important source of ore in a province where mining had always played a central role in economic growth. Mining led to the first large influx of non-Aboriginal people during the Fraser and Cariboo gold rushes of the late 1850s and early 1860s, and to the creation of a British colony on the mainland west of the Rocky Mountains. Most of the readily accessible deposits of gold were exhausted by the 1880s, and prospectors turned their attention to the corridors created by the newly completed Canadian Pacific Railroad. Over the next few decades, silver, lead, zinc, and copper were discovered in various places, and mines and smelters were opened. Rising demand in world markets propelled mining booms. When the demand for a particular mineral dropped, the mines closed, leaving ghost towns. This pattern of boom and bust recurred throughout the twentieth century. Production of silver, lead, zinc, and copper increased into the 1930s, while gold production declined. High production of lead and copper gave way in the 1940s and 1950s to high production of lead and zinc. Ready capital and new mining technology were put to work after the Second World War to satisfy a high demand for industrial minerals. Mining efforts were now directed at lower-grade ores (such as porphyry deposits), and open pits replaced underground mines. These new forms of production entailed new economic arrangements: increasingly, the minerals were shipped overseas under long-term contractual arrangements. Copper became valuable again in the 1960s and remained so through the 1980s, a period that also saw the increasing value of metallurgical coal, which was used for steel, primarily in the manufacture of Japanese automobiles. Coal production led the mining output of British Columbia in the 1990s, followed by silver, copper, and building materials like sand, gravel, and the burned lime and clay used for cement. Throughout most of the twentieth century, mining was the second-most-important industry in British Columbia after forestry.[28]

Economic cycles influenced mining activity at many different temporal scales, including both longer-term expansion and collapse of whole industries, and shorter-term periods of exploration and neglect in specific regions. A close look at prospecting activity at Fish Lake reveals something of the mutual contextualization and mutual determination of exploration and exploitation. In the early 1930s, gold production increased in both volume and value in British Columbia. Two prospectors following "Indian pack-trails" located the debris from ore, known as "float," and followed it to a gold-bearing zone near Fish Lake. In the late 1950s, another prospector investigated gold-silver-copper zones northeast of the Fish Lake deposit. The potential for copper porphyry in the area was recognized in 1960 by a geologist for the Phelps Dodge Corporation. At the time, however, yearly average producer prices for copper were hovering around thirty cents Canadian per pound, and the results from drilling studies were not encouraging. Phelps Dodge let its claim lapse. When the price of copper jumped to fifty-four cents per pound in 1966, Taseko Mines Limited was able to restake the claim that Phelps Dodge had held. New mineral exploration in the Fish Lake area was undertaken every time the price for copper rose, and it stopped every time the price fell (see Figure 1). Between 1966 and 1969, the price rose to sixty-seven cents per pound. In 1969, Taseko Mines drilled some holes in areas where the ore was not exposed and discovered better-grade copper than Phelps Dodge had found. Taseko Mines optioned the property to the Nittetsu Mining Company of Tokyo. In 1970, Nittetsu submitted a report to the **BC Department of Mines and Petroleum Resources** on **induced polarization** studies in the region.[29]

The price of copper fell abruptly from 1969 to 1972, and no surveying was done during this time. Between 1972 and 1974, the price of copper again jumped, this time from forty-five to eighty-five cents a pound. As the price of copper was rising, Taseko Mines optioned the property to Houston-based Quintana Minerals Corporation. In 1974, Quintana submitted the results of a drilling study to the provincial government. Over the next few years, Quintana continued to do drilling studies in the area. The price of copper fell to fifty-eight cents per pound in 1975 and then began to rise again, hitting $1.09 by 1979. That year, Cominco Limited acquired from Taseko Mines the option of earning 80 percent interest in the Fish Lake property if Cominco developed it. Cominco had an engineering firm do an economic evaluation and drilled 168 holes for sampling. When the price of copper fell from a high of $1.15 per pound in 1980, dropping to eighty cents per pound in 1982 and remaining relatively low through 1986, no surveys were made. Frustrated with the lack of progress at Fish Lake, Taseko Mines tried to terminate its agreement with Cominco in 1985. Between 1986 and 1989, the price of copper rose from eighty-six cents per pound to $1.50, setting off a flurry of surveying activity. Cominco won a 1988 lawsuit against Taseko Mines, and when the price of copper peaked the following year, it submitted a report to the ministry on almost six hundred samples that were drilled from twelve holes and assayed for gold and copper. The following year, as the price of copper was already falling, Taseko Mines submitted a report on the assay of 3,466 samples for gold and copper.[30]

High mineral prices also stimulated government surveying. In 1989 the BC Ministry of Energy, Mines and Petroleum Resources reported that

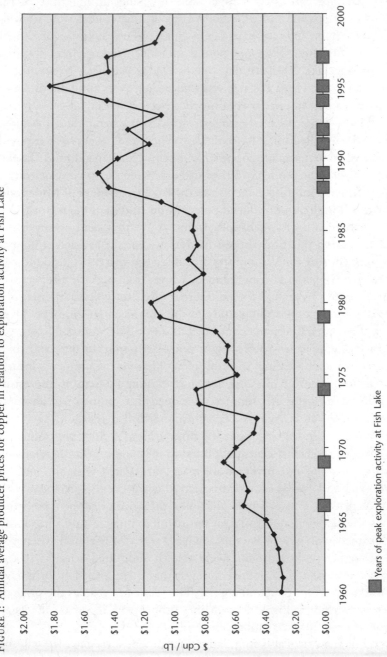

FIGURE 1: Annual average producer prices for copper in relation to exploration activity at Fish Lake

■ Years of peak exploration activity at Fish Lake

SOURCE: Price data from the BC Ministry of Energy and Mines, "BC Producer Prices – Annual Averages – 1901 to 2000," Victoria, 2000.

there was a renewed interest in copper exploration projects triggered by record copper prices. The field program of the Geological Survey Branch expanded, with forty-two concurrent geological and geochemical mapping projects in the province. A team of seven geologists, led by Dr. Cathie Hickson, was dispatched to survey the Chilcotin-Nechako basin and to compose a geological history of the region. "We're not here prospecting," she said. "We're providing the groundwork for (resource) companies to come and look harder" (parentheses in original). By 1991, as Hickson's team was surveying near Fish Lake, demand for minerals had slowed, and metal prices were consequently dropping. The relative strength of the Canadian dollar also reduced exports at a time when foreign sales accounted for 80 percent of a provincial industry producing more than $1.5 billion Canadian. In this context, the ministry stressed the exploration of "several promising deposits," including large open-pit copper-gold properties in the central interior of the province. The Geological Survey Branch focused on planning for the next decade, starting new field studies and mapping projects in "hot" regions with copper-gold porphyry deposits.[31]

THE DELINEATION OF PROPERTY RIGHTS

It probably comes as no surprise that exploration for particular minerals is closely tied to the value of those minerals. The fact that geological knowledge is accumulated in fits and starts that are closely related to economic cycles shows that, in this case at least, "history matters," that this interpretation of material traces must be historicized. The explanation that prospecting is stimulated by the increasing value of mineral resources still raises the question of *why*. Why should individuals or institutions be motivated to learn more about particular entities or places as their value increases? When geological surveyors painstakingly recorded and studied magnetic fluctuations, dated and assayed samples, mapped outcroppings, and did a hundred other scientific things besides, there is no question that they added to our knowledge of the geology of the Chilcotin. This activity was expensive, however, and it is still necessary to explain why it was undertaken at all.

One explanation for the activity of surveying arises from an economic theory of property rights. According to this account, entities have a number of attributes that can never be completely measured or known. The copper content of the Fish Lake deposit, for example, was inferred from samples but could not be known with certainty. Since it is costly to

measure the attributes of any entity, it is impossible to delineate property
rights fully, and there is always the danger that property may be appropri-
ated by others. In the 1980s, Cominco and Taseko Mines both owned
rights to the property at Fish Lake. As the value of copper rose, both companies were willing to spend money to obtain more information about the
attributes of the property. If either had been unwilling to spend the money,
the other company would have been in a position to exploit the advantage
provided by its additional information. It could, for example, have sold its
rights in the property for more than they were worth or bought rights at
a discount. In fact, some of the rights to the property were in the public
domain. Any individual or institution that was willing and able to allocate
enough resources to learn more about the property than Cominco or Taseko
Mines would have had the advantage. According to this theory, rather
than being constant, property rights are a function of the resources that
people commit to protect them, the resources others spend to capture them,
and the resources that the government allocates to protect a given distribution of rights. (Note that this theory is concerned only with describing
property rights in an economic sense – there are obvious discrepancies
with legal and moral conceptions of property rights.) Not all scientific
activity or geological surveying is undertaken to defend or capture property rights, but this perspective helps to explain the conflict over the Fish
Lake deposit.[32]

Taseko Mines appealed the court's 1988 decision in favour of Cominco,
but it lost the appeal in 1990. Although the company served Cominco
with another termination notice, it feared that the Fish Lake property
would remain tied up in the courts indefinitely and decided to bring in
some outside help. Robert Hunter and Robert Dickenson, along with two
colleagues, were allowed to take 51 percent control of the company in return
for investing $1 million each. The previous year, Hunter and Dickenson
had sold a junior mining concern with an interest in a property at Mount
Milligan in northern British Columbia to a senior company for $180 mil-
lion. The founders of Taseko Mines hoped that the two men would be
able to do something similar with their own company. Hunter and Dickenson entered into a new agreement with Cominco, and Taseko Mines'
stock, which had traded around a dollar for the previous decade, rose to
four dollars. The increased stock price reflected the new confidence that
investors had in the company, and this confidence reflected, in turn, the
value of clarifying legal property rights. Neither Cominco nor Taseko Mines
would have been willing to enter into a new agreement without the added
information about the property that geological exploration had given them.[33]

In 1991, Taseko Mines began a program of drilling to get a better estimate of the amount of subsurface ore on the property. Estimates rose from
1.9 billion pounds of copper to 3.4 billion at a time when the price of copper seemed to be going up. This would be enough to keep the mine in
operation for twenty-five to thirty years. Jeff Franzen, the company director, said, "That makes it probably the largest undeveloped copper deposit
in North America." In December, Taseko Mines reported on a four-month-
long, $350,000 project to assess the mining characteristics of the Fish Lake
deposit, including its environmental aspects. The engineering consulting
firm that it employed concluded that the low sulphide and high carbonate content of the ore and waste products would not lead to acid mine
drainage in the tailings or waste dump areas of the mine. When Franzen
was asked whether the mine might conflict with a proposal for a park near
Chilko Lake, he said that he thought not; the proposed park would be on
the west side of the Taseko River, and the proposed mine on the east side.
The fate of the proposed park would eventually become bound up with
the fate of Fish Lake, however, although perhaps not in a manner the
Taseko Mines management could have foreseen.[34]

THE CHILKO LAKE PARK PROPOSAL

By the 1990s, there had been pressure for a park near Chilko Lake for about
sixty years. It was triggered by an earlier proposal to use the lake for hydroelectric power. In the early 1920s, Richard Preston Bishop did exploratory
surveys for the provincial government in the Chilko Lake region, trying to
determine the relative difference in elevation between the lake and Bute
Inlet on the Strait of Georgia. In his 1922 report to the surveyor general,
Bishop suggested that a tunnel connecting Chilko Lake through the Coast
Range to the strait might be used to generate hydroelectric power. Seven
years later, a Water Rights Branch surveyor in the Department of Lands
was sent to Chilko Lake to search for locations to build the tunnel. The
New York Times later reported that British Columbia could potentially
realize the greatest amount of water power in Canada, with a possible 1.2
million horsepower from a Taseko-Chilko-Homathko project that would
reroute the water from Chilko Lake west into the ocean via the Homathko
River and Bute Inlet instead of following its current course east into the
Chilko, Chilcotin, and Fraser rivers. If such a tunnel were built, it would
follow a route that businessmen in the nineteenth century had imagined
using for a road to connect the coast and interior. (This road was never

built, for reasons discussed in Part 3.) The hydroelectric project was opposed by a group of people whose livelihood depended on another of British Columbia's natural resources, the salmon run. Diverting the water from Chilko Lake would destroy a fair amount of the province's productive spawning ground.[35]

In 1924, the Geological Survey of Canada sent an expedition to Chilko Lake led by Victor Dolmage, a hard-rock mining geologist and chief of the BC division of the federal survey. Bishop accompanied the team to do topographic mapping. In his published report, Dolmage wrote that "this large stretch of country, though only 140 miles from Vancouver, as the crow flies, is for the most part uninhabited and to some extent not even explored." He mentioned a number of ranching families in the area, a few prospectors and a few trappers, and "several families of Indians in Nemaia valley." Although "it would be difficult to imagine a more delightful camping ground than the shores of Chilko Lake," Dolmage thought that gold could be profitably produced in the area, and its geology suggested that more mineral deposits would be found. A decade later, the Vancouver Natural History Society evidently agreed with Dolmage's assessment of the scenic value of the region and proposed that Chilko Lake be turned into a park. Dolmage, now in private practice, wrote that "mining men view with alarm the number of requests pressed upon our government to set aside large sections of the province for park reserves." He was concerned about park advocates who pitted tourism against mining and argued that "a mine tucked away in the hills will not mar the beauty of more than a few acres" (this was before the heyday of open-pit mining). Besides, Dolmage, said, mining was a better influence on citizenship. He found the idea of using "guests as a source of revenue ... a bit repulsive" and argued that the tipping system of tourism might turn Canadians into "a nation of porters."[36]

The park at Chilko Lake remained no more than a proposal for half a century. In 1976, an interagency committee of the provincial government published a report called *Chilcotin Wilderness Park Study* in which it recommended that Chilko Lake be designated a Class A park. Under the terms of the *Park Act* of 1965, a Class A park was Crown land that was protected from any use of land or natural resources that did not "preserve or maintain the recreational values of the park involved." The following year, the government studied plans for a proposed 2-million-acre park around Chilko and Taseko lakes. If such a park were established, it would put an end to the proposed hydroelectric power project and would also interfere with mining properties and Aboriginal land claims. In 1982, a team put together by the Ministry of Lands, Parks and Housing concluded that "protection and special management of the natural features and values [of Chilko Lake was] more important than optimizing the development of all resource values in the area." In 1991, a Chilko Lake Study Team was assembled to investigate. It was chaired by three representatives, one each from BC Parks, the Ministry of Energy, Mines and Petroleum Resources, and the Nemiah Valley Indian Band. After fifty-four years, a park had still not been established.[37]

Geological surveyors and prospectors had been working in the region intermittently since the days of Richard Preston Bishop and Victor Dolmage. In a 1987 report on geological fieldwork near Chilko Lake, Graeme McLaren suggested that the varied geology of the area offered potential for new mineral discoveries of a number of different kinds. This was due to the variety of ore-forming environments that had arisen during the geological history of the region. The proportion of elements that make up any part of the earth's crust are fixed when the crust is in a crystalline state. When there is magma or fluid, however, material can be dissolved and transported. Changes in temperature, pressure, or chemical environment cause the material to precipitate, forming mineral deposits. At a depth of at least a few kilometres and temperatures ranging from 400 to 600 degrees Celsius, these deposits are usually porphyries, but in carbonate rocks adjacent to porphyry deposits, another kind of mineralization can occur, leading to what are known as skarn deposits. Closer to the surface, and at lower temperatures, vein deposits can form when rising fluids carry precious and base metals into faults and fractures in the surrounding rock. McLaren noted that all three kinds of mineral deposit (porphyry, skarn, and vein) were represented in the region of Chilko Lake. Copper-bearing skarn deposits on the western side of the lake had been known since the 1920s. More recently, veins of mercury, copper, and arsenic had also been discovered near the lake. Northwest of the lake, other veins were found to contain gold, silver, antimony, and arsenic. McLaren recommended that "further mapping and prospecting of structural zones and related intrusives [was] warranted in the Chilko Lake region." In 1990, as the proposed park began to look more likely, the provincial Ministry of Energy, Mines and Petroleum Resources published a 117-page assessment by McLaren of the mineral resources of the Chilko Lake planning area.[38]

Other stakeholders had different ideas about what should be done with Chilko Lake. The Federation of Mountain Clubs of BC, in an "educational report" of 1991, complained that the status of the proposed park was "still in limbo while mineral exploration continue[d] with little regulation."

The report described the region as one of "gentle" wilderness, ideal for hiking or horseback touring. Chilko Lake was described as a "jewel" in the Chilcotin, its spectacular scenery a draw for people interested in camping, fishing, hunting, mountaineering, and skiing. The Chilko River, draining the lake to the north, was noted to be a world-class rafting lake and the site of an important salmon run. The environmental group complained that mineral exploration roads had been constructed without regard for traditional trails or the adverse effect on wildlife populations, and that an open-pit mine might be located at the trail head in the Tchaikazan Valley. The group recommended that the best way to manage the area – until such time as the federal government settled the land claims of the Nemiah Indian Band – was to establish a Class A park. This park "should be managed as a roadless area with the aim of preserving wilderness and the visual and aesthetic integrity of the mountain ranges and valleys. At the same time, traditional resource use activities, including Aboriginal trap lines, hunting and guide-outfitting, should be permitted to continue, provided these do not threaten the viability of wildlife populations nor conflict excessively with other recreational users." Depending on how its boundaries were drawn, the proposed park might or might not include Fish Lake.[39]

INFORMATION COSTS

In 1992, the annual average producer price for copper rose from $1.16 to $1.30 per pound. Not only was the value of copper rising, but the costs of acquiring information about the area near Fish Lake were falling with each study of the region. In their efforts to defend their own property rights and to secure capital from investors, companies like Taseko Mines were forced to release information for which they had paid a great deal. The government also spent money to learn more about Fish Lake in an effort to generate revenue and to protect a particular regime of property rights. The information produced by the government and by the mining companies was available to the public at a very low relative cost. As a consequence, other companies entered the fray. In 1992, a corporation called Pioneer Metals conducted an induced polarization study of its own property adjoining Fish Lake to the north. It found a magnetically anomalous zone covering more than a kilometre. Assays of samples taken from this zone yielded a significant proportion of copper. Encouraged by these results, Pioneer Metals proposed to follow up with "systematic geophysical, geochemical and geological surveys followed by diamond drilling."

Thirty-two kilometres to the north of Fish Lake, the Verdstone Gold Corporation was also exploring for gold and copper by digging trenches. By April of the following year, it was able to report promising results.[40]

Elsewhere in the province, the feasibility of porphyry mining was called into question when the mining company Placer Dome decided not to go ahead with a copper-gold porphyry project at Mount Milligan because the expected return of the project was not high enough to cover capital investment. Initial cost estimates for Mount Milligan had failed to take into account the environmental problems raised by the disposal of tailings. Taseko Mines was still exploring at Fish Lake, however, and planned to raise $10 million for a new program of drilling. In March 1992, Robert Hunter, the chairman of the company, announced that it had begun trading on the NASDAQ electronic stock exchange and that three rigs were drilling "to delineate the ultimate size of the Fish Lake gold-copper deposit." Hunter added that Taseko Mines was considering adding additional drills and planned to release assay results as the studies were completed. Besides the drilling, the company also intended to set up a pilot plant for metallurgical work and to begin the process of obtaining environmental permits. Once it had all the necessary information in hand, the company could evaluate the economic feasibility of the proposed mine. In June, Taseko Mines announced that drilling at Fish Lake had shown that the deposit was at least twice the size estimated earlier and "remained open to extension in all directions." The *Northern Miner* ("North America's Mining Newspaper") picked up the story a week later and added that "Taseko hopes to find a buyer." By the end of the month, the company had completed final closing of its private placement – that is, it had sold its stock to a small number of private investors and was no longer open to new investment. It had raised $7.24 million and was moving a fourth drill rig to Fish Lake. Drilling continued through the summer and fall, and Taseko Mines announced that "it is clear that the Fish Lake deposit ranks among the largest deposits of its kind in the world." Over the summer, Taseko Mines also began to collect information about the site that would later help it plan a mine. The company set up a meteorological station to record temperature, precipitation, and accumulation of snowfall and snow pack.[41]

Members of the public were invited to visit Taseko Mine's Fish Lake exploration site in July of that year. Company representatives were on hand to answer questions about environmental and financial impacts and to explain the processes of exploration and mining. The visitors were allowed to see the drill at work removing core samples and to pore over the samples in wooden boxes at a sorting table. People sat in the sun at

picnic tables, ate barbecue, and drank soda. They were told that Taseko
Mines was spending $800,000 per month to test the samples and that the
mine, if it were built, would employ six hundred people for two years in
its construction and four hundred directly in its operation. It would run
for fifteen years and provide another eight hundred jobs indirectly. The
company circulated a questionnaire to gauge the mood of the attendees.
Of the 175 people present, 50 filled out questionnaires; 86 percent of them
claimed to be in favour of the mine, 14 percent were undecided, "and no
one was opposed."[42]

The company's decision to bring the public to the Fish Lake site and to
emphasize the potential for employment that the mine offered seems relatively straightforward. After all, in a province where economic survival
depended on the exploitation of natural resources, the public might be
expected to cheer more than a thousand new jobs ... especially relatively
high-paying, unionized jobs. But why should Taseko Mines, or any other
resource company for that matter, care what the general public thought
about Fish Lake? This move in the company's public relations campaign
signalled its awareness that at least some of the rights to Fish Lake were
in the public domain. The fate of the region would not be determined
solely by those with legal title, but rather as the outcome of a contest of
stakeholders. Scientific study would play a key role in this struggle as institutions sent representatives to consult the archive of place, to find information that might increase their chances of capturing some of the rights
to Fish Lake that had not yet been delineated.

By late 1992, Taseko Mines estimated that the deposit contained 5.6 billion pounds of copper and 14.8 million ounces of gold, and the company
was claiming that Fish Lake would "significantly add to the rebuilding of
Canada's rapidly depleting metal reserve inventory." Taseko managers were
also predicting that all but two of British Columbia's open-pit mines would
close by the year 2000, as ore reserves were depleted. In early 1993, the
Northern Miner reported on ongoing exploration projects in British Columbia, including Fish Lake. By March, Taseko Mines had brought in two independent engineering firms to study the mineable reserves of the deposit
and the metallurgical properties of samples taken from it. They then
reported the production costs for progressively deeper pit designs. These
ranged from 164 million tons of ore, processed at a ratio of 0.8 units of
waste to one unit of ore and yielding a production cost of less than fifteen
cents per pound, up to 895 million tons at a waste-to-ore ratio of 2.11:1 and
a production cost of less than forty-one cents per pound. At the time, the
average production cost per pound in North American open-pit copper

mines was in the range of fifty to sixty cents in Canadian currency. The results were better than Taseko Mines had predicted; the deposit was now thought to contain 6.2 billion pounds of copper and 17.3 million ounces of gold. The metallurgical test work also yielded significantly better results than Taseko Mines had reported to date. The company now thought the deposit was "capable of sustaining a world class mine for 30 to 40 years." It planned to hire another consulting firm to conduct a prefeasibility study of the project and to enter into the formal process of obtaining mine production permits from the province of British Columbia. This would be complicated by the fact that the province had recently adopted the goal of sustainable development.[43]

Standardization, Sustainable Development, and CORE

In 1987, the World Commission on Environment and Development released a report entitled *Our Common Future,* which defined sustainable development as "development which meets the needs of the present without compromising the ability of future generations to meet their own needs." This agenda was adopted internationally and served as one of the contexts for mining-related activities in British Columbia in the early 1990s. One measure of the prevailing interest in sustainable development was the Canadian Wilderness Charter, created by the World Wildlife Fund for its national endangered spaces campaign in 1989. Within five years, the charter had been signed by half a million Canadians.[44]

British Columbia's NDP government, elected under Mike Harcourt in 1991, was committed to significant environmental reform but faced the problem of acquiring and deploying information about natural resource use in the province. The government's goal was to enforce an allocation of property rights that was congruent with its program of democratic socialism. In order to balance the interests of stakeholders, including its own, the government needed to be able to integrate information about different resource entities, and this process was greatly facilitated by standardization.

Economic historians have long recognized that standardization reduces the costs of doing business – or, to put it another way, it lowers transaction costs. In this case, standardization simultaneously lowered transaction costs, which allowed new stakeholders to enter the contest over Fish Lake, and created a "market" in which information from different stakeholders (including the results of scientific studies) could be assigned relative value and exchanged. Historians of science have argued that standardization also plays an important epistemological role by facilitating the spread of techniques from the settings in which they are initially developed. This allows things that first work in one particular laboratory or setting to work in the outside world and thus appear to be universally true or valid. Here we see the interplay of both epistemological and economic factors, the perceived truth of particular statements about the Chilcotin being due, in part, to their commodification as they entered into economic exchanges.[45]

In 1991, in response to a recommendation from the Forest Resources Commission, the government established the Resources Inventory Committee in order to make an inventory of all renewable forest resources using systems that were standardized and compatible. Task forces working in a number of areas – aquatic ecosystems, atmosphere, coastal areas, culture, land use, earth sciences, and terrestrial ecosystems – tried to develop procedures and standards that would allow cost-effective data collection and exchange. The committee members were drawn from provincial, federal, private sector, and Aboriginal agencies. In early 1992, the province announced major funding to implement the Resources Inventory Committee's integration standards throughout the government. Participating ministries included Aboriginal Affairs; Agriculture, Fisheries and Food; Energy, Mines and Petroleum Resources; Environment, Lands and Parks; Forests and Tourism. Seeing an opportunity to shape the terms of contests over natural resources and land use, environmental non-governmental organizations (NGOs) encouraged their members to volunteer for task forces that were developing standards and methodologies.[46]

While the benefits of standardization were clear, the government ministries faced significant costs when they tried to combine their data, as a single spatial example will show. Geographer Nadine Schuurman argues that "people disagree about the definition of the boundaries of spatial objects, and even more strongly about how to put them in categories." In other words, spatial consciousness is every bit as contested as historical consciousness. In British Columbia, both the Ministry of Forests and the Ministry of Sustainable Resource Management have extensive information about vegetation in the Cariboo-Chilcotin region. The foresters who work for the former, however, are interested in commercially viable timber. They measure things like the height and diameter of fir trees. The wildlife biologists of the latter ministry are more concerned with vegetation as habitat. They measure things like the density of the forest canopy, which has an effect on snow cover and thus on wildlife survival. The degree to which a particular region is considered "forested" thus depends on whether it was measured by foresters or wildlife biologists and whether the measurements were intended for forest management or to protect habitat for mule deer grazing. Each of the ministries brought its own data into the standardization process, but it also brought its own epistemology.[47]

Starting in 1992, the province adopted a new strategic land-use planning framework for Crown land that tried to balance the interests of various stakeholders in a process of shared decision making based on the collection of standardized data. An independent commission, the Commission on Resources and the Environment (CORE), was established to incorporate sustainability, an ethic of land use, a process for conflict resolution, planning at the regional level, and community consensus into discussions of land use. The Cariboo-Chilcotin, long a site of intense land-use conflicts, was chosen as one of three regions to undergo the CORE planning process. By the spring of 1993, the provincial Ministry of Energy, Mines and Petroleum Resources was expressing its concern about the future of the mining industry and the reduction in funding for geological exploration. The ministry was determined to participate in the CORE process. The problem, however, was that geologists could not predict where the next mineable deposit would be found, at least not with fine enough resolution to let them identify lands that should be set aside for mining in a strategic planning framework. The best they could do was indicate areas with high degrees of mineralization and try to get other stakeholders to accept exploration and prospecting activities that had little environmental impact. One of the ministry's priorities was to continue to fund exploration so that the results could be used as inputs to the CORE process.[48]

Around the same time, in spring 1993, a dozen environmental groups, including the BC Wildlife Federation, the Sierra Club, and the World Wildlife Fund Canada, joined forces to create an umbrella organization that they called the Environmental Mining Council of BC. The new organization indicated an interest in working with companies in the mining sector to negotiate projects that would be economically viable and yet maintain the quality of the environment. The director of the Environmental Mining Council said that by forming the council, members hoped to "avoid the hostility and turmoil that has paralysed forestry/environmental interactions in this province for years." The new president of the Mining Association of BC was skeptical but willing to talk to anyone who promoted both mining and environmental protection. The Environmental Mining Council suggested that it would be a good idea to start with a test case in the pre-development stage to see if environmental and mining groups could co-operate. The project the council had in mind was Fish Lake.[49]

An Uphill Battle

In 1993, things became more difficult for Taseko Mines. The Fish Lake deposit was valued at $182 million, and buyers continued to express interest in it. An independent firm concluded that the project would be economically viable and that Taseko Mines should proceed to detailed prefeasibility planning. Despite the news, Taseko Mines' shares fell as the price of copper slumped, and analysts predicted that a deposit as low grade as Fish Lake would not be developed until the price of metals rose. Capital costs to start a mine at Fish Lake were estimated to exceed Cdn$600 million. Analysts also pointed out that Taseko Mines chairman Robert Hunter had been involved in the sale of Mount Milligan, another low-grade copper-gold deposit that had later been written off by the company that purchased it because a mine there turned out to be economically infeasible. Weak copper prices forced other mines in the area – like Gibraltar Mines, thirty-two kilometres north of Williams Lake – to temporarily suspend operations. The city of Williams Lake, crucially dependent on logging, ranching, and mining, urged the Ministry of Energy, Mines and Petroleum Resources to use Fish Lake as a model project, a "cooperative partnership between the provincial government and the mining industry." City councillors thought the ministry should try to speed up the regulatory process. Companies outside British Columbia were wary of working in the province because of "the uncertainty of tenure, compensation, and high taxation." Funding for geological exploration fell.[50]

Taseko Mines did not have the luxury of pulling support from the Fish Lake project when the going got tough. It continued to do mine planning and environmental baseline studies throughout the year. As the company was most worried about potential acid rock drainage from the mine, its scientists did extensive testing to show that this would not be a problem at Fish Lake, and the company promised to continue testing throughout the project. It noted that "alterations to the geography and topography of the mine development area would occur with the development of a large open-pit mine of the scale proposed. However, a Reclamation and Abandonment Plan to be developed with and approved by the provincial government before commencement of production will address the reclamation of the areas of development to the most natural state possible." In late August 1993, the company filed the pre-application for a mine development certificate with the province. This document, the first of two in the mine-permitting process, reviewed technical, environmental, and socioeconomic aspects of the proposed mine. It would be used by government agencies to determine what information they needed in the second document, the application for a mine development certificate. Taseko Mines also redoubled its efforts to enrol the support of various other stakeholders. It discussed the project with representatives of First Nations groups and showed them around the site. It also showed the site to senior representatives of the major environmental groups in British Columbia: the BC Wildlife Federation, BC World Wildlife Fund, the East Kootenay Environmental Society, the Canadian Parks and Wilderness Society, and Earthlife Canada. And it continued to court allies in the city of Williams Lake. In September, the company announced that it had awarded a contract for a detailed prefeasibility study to Kilborn Engineering Pacific Limited. The study, which the company expected by year end, would evaluate all aspects of the project "including geology, ore reserves, mining, metallurgy, processing, concentrate handling, tailings disposal, infrastructure, ancillary facilities and environmental requirements."[51]

Resource companies were increasingly required to be sensitive to the environment. In September 1993, the World Wildlife Fund reported that British Columbia had "earned a grade of 'B+' for its wilderness protection efforts in the Fourth Annual Endangered Spaces Progress Report." Apparently the province had learned its lessons well over the preceding year, since its grade was up from a "B–." Nevertheless, the World Wildlife Fund took a stern tone, warning British Columbia – and the other provinces, which were even more truant – that Canadian wilderness was "disappearing at a rate of one acre every 15 seconds."[52] Unfortunately, the group didn't specify how much of Canada actually consisted of "wilderness," so it was difficult to determine when it would all be gone – by the year 3062 in any event.[53]

The British Columbia government signalled its willingness to work with the environmental group by targeting unprotected natural regions for safeguarding through the CORE process. In the Cariboo-Chilcotin Land Use Strategy, the regional implementation of CORE, a draft proposal for a park around Chilko Lake was approved by consensus for integration into strategic land-use discussions. The draft divided the area into two zones: the first consisted of 230,000 protected hectares around Chilko Lake; the second was a 45,000-hectare transition zone running east of Chilko to provincial forest. Heartened by the outcome of the regional CORE process, the World Wildlife Fund specified a three-item "action agenda" for the province to work on in 1994. One of the action items was the preservation of the Chilko Lake area.[54]

Taseko Mines continued to work on the Fish Lake project as 1993 drew to a close. At the beginning of November, the company reported that it expected to have its mine development certificate by the end of the following year. Once it had the certificate in hand, it could find a senior mining firm to form a partnership with. The earliest that construction could begin would be late 1995. At a public review, Taseko Mines told the residents of Williams Lake that the mine at Fish Lake would employ 375 people directly and provide 400 indirect jobs. This was down a bit from the earlier numbers of 400 direct and 800 indirect jobs, but it would still be a welcome boost to the city's economy. A new road was planned that would allow the company to bus employees to the site from Williams Lake rather than have them living in mining camps. They would work four days in and then have four days out. Ore concentrate would be trucked in containers to Williams Lake and shipped by rail to Vancouver. In December, Taseko Mines announced an agreement with Cominco that would allow Taseko the exclusive right to purchase Cominco's residual interest in the Fish Lake project. Taseko Mines expected the agreement to improve its negotiating position with senior mining companies in the search for a partner. From Cominco's point of view, the new agreement increased the likelihood that Cominco would see at least some money from its interest in Fish Lake. Robert Stone, chief financial officer at Cominco, said that "this deal reflects [TML's] optimism about the potential of the resource." He didn't say whether Cominco shared that optimism. At the time, Taseko Mines had spent $14 million on exploration and was hoping to find a partner to share development costs estimated at $390 million.[55]

In the Clear?

The following year, 1994, turned out to be much better for Taseko Mines than the previous one had been. It was an optimistic time, a time when many uncertainties for the company were resolved, beginning with the impact that the Chilko Lake park proposal would have on the Fish Lake property. On 13 January 1994, Premier Mike Harcourt announced the creation of BC's fifth-largest park, the 233,240-hectare Tŝ'il?os Park surrounding Chilko Lake. Crown land inside the park's boundaries was permanently designated Class A parkland. The park was the third major preserve that the Harcourt government had created, part of a plan to double the amount of protected area in BC from 6 percent to 12 percent by the year 2000. Enthusiasts compared the scenery of the park to Nepal, to the Peruvian Andes, and, closer to home, to Lake Louise in Banff National

Park, Canada's first national park and a UNESCO World Heritage Site since 1984. The World Wildlife Fund pointed to Tŝ'il?os Park as a successful example of conservation based on consensus and praised the provincial government for its vision in balancing the needs and interests of people living in the region with those of future generations. Creation of the park had advanced the goal of maintaining biodiversity by protecting some part of each of the province's different natural regions. It had also contributed to the conservation of California bighorn sheep, mountain goats, grizzly bears, bald eagles, and sockeye salmon. The Taseko Management Zone, fifty thousand hectares of land adjacent to the park, had been allocated to be used for forestry, mining, and ranching in ways that complemented the park. Fortunately for Taseko Mines, the Fish Lake deposit lay in this zone.[56]

In March 1994, Taseko Mines completed its transaction with Cominco and now owned 100 percent of the Fish Lake property. The prefeasibility studies conducted by Kilborn Engineering Pacific were nearing completion. The projected mine would have a life of thirty-one years and a strip ratio of 1.57 units of waste to 1 unit of ore. It would produce 3.5 billion pounds of copper and 9.4 million ounces of gold, milling at a rate of 66,000 tons per day in a pit that would eventually be more than two kilometres in diameter. As spring rolled into summer, things started to look better for miners in British Columbia, at least from the perspective of the ministry in Victoria. The mines minister reported that exploration spending had increased by 20 percent. There was a new $13.5 million provincial government program called Explore BC that provided financial assistance in amounts up to $10,000 to prospectors working in the province over the summer. By late May, more than a hundred applications had been sent in for Explore BC funding. The new provincial budget included a $100 million program to revitalize the mining industry over the next five years.[57]

The view on the ground was less rosy. Don Carter, former president of the Cariboo Mining Association, was reported to be "mad as hell" at the bureaucracy and "exorbitant" taxes that made life difficult for individual miners. "When I first came here, you could file a notice to work a site and then work on it," Carter said. "There were no problems. Over the years the government has pandered to the mostly city-dwelling voting public. They don't seem to realize that mining brings in huge amounts of tax revenue for them." Many of the changes that were occurring in the political economy of mining and mineral exploration in the 1990s simultaneously raised transaction costs for individual stakeholders with few resources, while lowering them for institutional stakeholders with many resources. In a single day on his placer operation, Carter could see as many as seven inspectors representing government ministries in charge of environment, fisheries, worker's compensation, and water quality. From Carter's perspective, dealing with each of the inspectors took time that could have been more profitably spent mining. From the perspective of the ministries, however, the newly integrated and standardized system of data collection meant that the information gathered by one ministry was available to all. The cost for a governmental institution to enter the contest for the future of a particular region was greatly reduced.[58]

Larger mining companies could readily deal with the bureaucracy that entangled individual miners. Pioneer Metals Corporation, for example, which had found a magnetic anomaly on its property adjoining the Fish Lake deposit and performed some encouraging assays, followed up with a program of exploration. In November 1993, it reported anomalous concentrations of gold and copper in the soil, noting that its property had "the same geophysical and geochemical signature as Taseko Mines' Fish Lake deposit and [was] underlain by a portion of the same Eocene [53-36.5 Ma BP] quartz diorite intrusion." The physical evidence pointed to the same kind of mineralization as had already been discovered at Fish Lake. In March 1994, the company began a three-hole diamond drilling program on the property. By May, Pioneer Metals could report that it had discovered "a large sulphide system with rock alteration and geochemical anomalies which are typical porphyry gold-copper deposit indicators." The company suspected that it had discovered an extension of the Fish Lake deposit that had been shifted north by a fault. Although assays from the drilled samples did not contain enough precious metal to be considered ore, the company was encouraged by the results and decided to continue drilling and to begin other kinds of exploration, including more induced polarization studies, magnetometer and **very-low-frequency electromagnetic surveys**, and **petrographic analysis**. In September, Pioneer Mines reported that petrographic analysis of core samples from the property confirmed the presence of a copper-gold porphyry. The magnetometer survey had discovered two new, very strong, magnetic anomalies that were to be the focus for the next stage of drilling. The company was planning to spend $100,000 to $150,000 on the drilling, beginning in April 1995.[59]

The fall of 1994 was an optimistic time for mining and mineral exploration in British Columbia. Improved copper and gold prices allowed existing mines to reopen, and mine development certificates were issued for a number of new projects. Exploration expenditures were estimated to be $85 million for the year, mostly concentrated in areas where mineral

#401   2012-03-02 9:30AM

Item(s) checked out to p13194926.

TITLE: The archive of place : unearthing

BARCODE: 39345016856068

DUE DATE: 12-05-11

TITLE: Traditions of the Chilcotin India

BARCODE: 39345001835101

DUE DATE: 12-05-11

TITLE: Chiwid

BARCODE: 39345011227463

DUE DATE: 12-05-11

TITLE: Beyond inclusion : transforming t

BARCODE: 39345016108452

DUE DATE: 12-05-11

Due date in YY-MM-DD format

resources were known to exist and where the geoscience results indicated the probable discovery of more. The BC Ministry of Energy, Mines and Petroleum Resources predicted that the annual solid mineral production in the province would be valued at $2.56 billion, a 10 percent increase from the previous year. Of that, copper production would account for 31 percent, about $792 million. The ministry gave the new Explore BC program some of the credit for the rebound in exploration expenditures and concluded by saying that "the development of a number of copper porphyries are advancing, reaffirming that B.C. is a good place to locate large copper deposits. The province is well poised to benefit from the increases in copper prices, an excellent geoscience database, a favourable government attitude to resource development, a stable economy, and a highly skilled and flexible work force."[60]

The Lake and the Rainbow Trout

In the meantime, Taseko Mines faced new opposition over the Fish Lake proposal. In the summer of 1994, the company estimated that it would need about eight months to find a senior mining company to take the Fish Lake deposit to production. It was planning to submit its application for the mine development certificate by the fall and to start the mine in the second half of 1997. In July 1994, however, the BC Ministry of Environment, Lands and Parks objected to the proposal. One aspect of the Fish Lake plan that had received almost no publicity to that time was the fact that it called for Fish Lake itself to be drained. The mine would then dump 1,709 million metric tons of waste rock and 793 million metric tons of tailings into the former lake site and the river that drained into it. The provincial fisheries ministry noted that the mine plan included no way to mitigate impacts on the lake and that it was "unlikely that the unique characteristics of the Fish Lake ecosystem could ever be replaced through remediation efforts at the site following mine closure." Furthermore, the lake was home to a self-sustaining population of unique rainbow trout. Under the federal law of the time, it was illegal to "carry on any work or undertaking that results in the harmful alteration, disruption or destruction of fish habitat." The federal Department of Fisheries and Oceans interpreted this statute to mean that any fish habitat loss must be balanced by the creation of other habitat so that there would be no net loss. The department concluded that the Fish Lake "proposal, implemented according to the current mine plan, would result in the permanent loss of fish habitat, resulting in the loss of a wild rainbow trout stock," and that there seemed to be no viable habitat compensation plan.[61]

The Liberal Party critic for energy and mines, Don Jarvis, faulted the provincial government's consensus-based mine-permitting process, saying that it was too slow: "The development process is too onerous. There are little bureaucrats all over the place. It's costing us too much money. Typical bureaucrats only make a decision when 10 other people agree with them." Jarvis thought that Taseko Mines should be able to fill in the "puddle" and relocate the indigenous trout to nearby streams. Mike Harcourt, the NDP premier, disagreed. He said that there would be a new, streamlined permitting process in 1995, one that had been developed in consultation with representatives of both the mining industry and environmental groups. He noted that the provincial government had approved incentives for mineral exploration. From the perspective of Taseko Mines, the real problem lay with the federal fisheries department, which did not recognize the CORE process. According to the company, the people of the Cariboo-Chilcotin saw mining as an acceptable use of the Fish Lake area, but the "feds" in Ottawa did not. "Any fish habitat we impact, we will replace or enhance elsewhere," Taseko Mines management promised. "We will eliminate Fish Creek and take a creek that has no fish value and enhance it. We have spent time and money looking at other spots that don't have fish and we will make them viable fishing spots." Philip Mayfield, the MP for the Cariboo-Chilcotin, agreed with the company, saying, "We must be good stewards of the resource, but there has to be a solution where we can get the minerals out." Taseko Mines had expected to have a mine development certificate in hand by this time. Now things weren't looking so good.[62]

In January 1995, the province decided to pull the plug on Alcan Aluminum's $1.3 billion Kemano II power project on the Nechako River in northern BC, citing its potential damage to salmon fisheries. The effect on investment was immediate. Spending by resource companies "cratered," analysts said, because the companies no longer felt that titles were secure in the province. Although Kemano II was not a mining project as such, the province's decision was expected to jeopardize investment in copper-gold properties like Taseko Mines' Fish Lake. In March, resource companies banded together to form the BC Coalition of Coalitions to fight "preservationist pressures on our resource industries and resource communities." The Victoria headquarters of the coalition was to serve as a base of operations and "a centre for communications, networking, media work, [and] arranging meetings with government." The effect of such a centre would be to lower transaction costs for resource companies. It would now be easier for them to get access to BC politicians, to enrol the support of the public, and to share mining-related information.[63]

The mining industry's Coalition of Coalitions seemed to be something of a rearguard action. On the twenty-fifth anniversary of Earth Day the following month, the province was awarded a grade of "A–" by the World Wildlife Fund. Among other things, the environmental group cited the establishment of Tŝ'il?os Park in its commendation of the BC government. Resource companies in general, and Taseko Mines in particular, waited warily to see what the outcome would be. Taseko Mines had proposed a number of plans to compensate for the loss of Fish Lake, which the company said accounted for only 0.08 percent of the angling in the area. It offered to stock other barren lakes with the rainbow trout from Fish Lake, to provide a heritage fund to enhance fisheries, or to buy a private lake and put it into the public domain. There was no way, however, that it could proceed with the mine without draining Fish Lake. Ross Banner, the contract project director, said, "We've spent $41 million on studies. Some environmental group from California can call up and scuttle those millions of dollars for a $1.25 phone call." Still the company waited. As far as Taseko Mines was concerned, the government's decision should have been clear. The Fish Lake project would provide $82 million of revenue for the province each year the mine was in production. Taseko Mines continued to look for a buyer for the project.[64]

One group of stakeholders that became more proactive as a result of the greening of BC politics was the Environmental Mining Council of BC, the network of environmental groups that had suggested collaborating on Fish Lake with the mining industry in 1993. Its members were concerned that rising mineral commodity prices would lead to an increase in exploration and the opening or expansion of large open-pit operations. Among other things, the Environmental Mining Council stressed the need to prevent acid mine drainage and habitat destruction and to encourage environmentally sensitive geological exploration. The council organized an intensive weekend training session to teach members of Aboriginal, community, and environmental NGOs how to deal with "strategic, legal, and technical problems faced by citizens concerned about mining-related eco-impacts." Participants at the seminar included members from twenty environmental groups, six First Nations, and two major mining unions. One of the outcomes of the meeting was the decision to create "an active network for sharing good information on technical issues, company track records, and larger policy and legal questions." Creation of such a network greatly lowered transaction costs for the environmentalists, just as the provincial government's efforts to create a standardized data repository and the mining industry's Coalition of Coalitions lowered their respective transaction costs. Mining interests – colloquially "the browns" – responded to this new green threat with a public relations campaign. The Mining Association of BC and the BC Chamber of Mines spent somewhere between $500,000 and $1 million to produce radio and TV ads, to compile a database of 30,000 people that it would target directly, and to publish a *Voter's Guide to Mining Issues* that was sent to each of the people on the database. The *Voter's Guide* rejected the stance that the Environmental Mining Council had taken – namely, that mining and mineral exploration could be done in an environmentally sensitive way. Instead, the guide asked "which is more important, economic development or environmental protection? ... Should we maintain strict protection of wilderness areas that could hurt our chances for economic growth and jobs?"[65]

The Environmental Assessment Acts

On 30 June 1995, the provincial government introduced a new *Environmental Assessment Act*. Before this date, a company wishing to start a new mining project needed only the mine development certificate covered by the *Mine Development Assessment Act*. Now there was a standardized process to review the environmental impact of all major projects involving "energy, mining, water management, waste disposal, food processing, transportation [or] tourism." The only thing excluded was forestry. The process was designed to entail more stages of review for more complicated projects. A simple project could be jointly approved after application to the minister of Environment, Lands and Parks and the minister for the department responsible for the project domain (for example, Energy, Mines and Petroleum Resources.) A more complicated project might require a project report that could then be jointly approved by the two ministers. A still more complicated project would have to pass the first two steps and undergo a public hearing before being submitted to the cabinet for a decision. The project could, of course, be rejected at each of the three stages. The Fish Lake project had not yet received a development certificate when the new law came into effect, so it was moved into the new review process. Internal e-mail from the Environmental Assessment Office suggests that officials there sided with Taseko Mines in the matter of the troublesome trout: "The technical fisheries staff on both sides have already made their views known – they consider the project unacceptable ... In my view, the only way to move the project is to set up the project committee and get on with it." From the perspective of the Environmental Assessment Office, the project was going ahead. From the perspective of the federal Department of Fisheries and Oceans, it was not. According to federal biologist Lee Nikl, the department had made a "definitive answer technically; anything beyond that [was] political." The provincial environment minister hoped to have things both ways. While members of his own ministry opposed the project, he blamed the delay on the federal department. Taseko Mines apparently felt that the project would eventually go ahead and retained Toronto Dominion Securities to help it introduce the project "to a select group of growth oriented senior international mining companies for financing and acquisition."[66]

At the end of July, the project director at the Environmental Assessment Office said that he expected to form a Fish Lake project committee to write the report for the first stage of the review process. Based on that report, it was possible the ministers would jointly decide to accept the project. Taseko Mines thought it was about time that its proposal was approved. "We've really had an erosion of share value," a company manager told a reporter from the *Williams Lake Advocate*. The project committee was made up of representatives from provincial agencies, local government, federal government, and First Nations. It had to deal with a number of different stakeholders who were taking very different positions. It also had to respond to the provincial fisheries ministry and the federal fisheries department, both of which objected to destroying the lake and moving the fish. It had to deal with the BC Wildlife Federation, which opposed the project but might be brought on board if the compensation package were right – if, for example, Taseko Mines purchased a private lake to be brought into the public domain. And the committee had to deal with David Zirnhelt, the Cariboo-South MLA, who favoured moving the fish to a similar lake. After all, as Zirnhelt said, "no one is going to pretend that an advanced civilization is going to leave everything as it is. You don't get a chance at a mine every day. There are thousands of lakes in the Chilcotin." The city of Williams Lake was happy with the proposal as it stood, but the local Tsilhqot'in group, the Nemiah Indian Band, claimed the land around Fish Lake, and its concerns still had not been dealt with. The project committee had its work cut out for it.[67]

At the end of September, the federal government decided that the Fish Lake project came under the jurisdiction of the *Canadian Environmental Assessment Act* as well as the provincial act. This decision meant that the objections of the federal Department of Fisheries and Oceans gained new weight. According to the department, the habitat at Fish Lake fell into the "Class One" category. It provided the fish with places to spawn, feed, and winter. Ordinarily, such habitat could not be destroyed in return for compensation unless the department exercised its own discretion, and, in the words of one of the department officials, "there [were] no reasonable grounds for applying discretion in this case." The department was wary of setting a precedent that would make it more difficult to manage fish habitat in the future. Without approval from the department, the project could not pass the Canadian review process and would be stopped. On 19 October 1995, the department wrote to the provincial ministry to say that it did not intend to authorize the Fish Lake project.[68]

The rainbow trout in Fish Lake were rapidly becoming more valuable. As a consequence, various stakeholders began to spend money to learn more about the attributes of the fish and their habitat. Taseko Mines began studying the Nuntsi Lakes, forty kilometres north of Fish Lake, as a potential habitat to which it could move the rainbow trout. The Nuntsi Lakes were isolated from Taseko River by a waterfall, which served as a barrier to fish migration. Fish Lake was similarly isolated. The company tested the pH (the degree of acidity or alkalinity), electrical conductivity, water chemistry, and biological productivity of the Nuntsi Lakes. In all of these respects, Taseko Mines argued, some of the Nuntsi lakes were like Fish Lake, and the rainbow trout should thrive there. The federal Department of Fisheries and Oceans did not find Taseko's arguments persuasive and refused to put the project back on the table unless the province were to revise its own assessment of the value of the fishery and habitat at Fish Lake.[69]

This move upped the ante for the provincial ministry. The situation for the provincial government was complicated. The popularity of the NDP had recently fallen, and premier Mike Harcourt resigned in November 1995 as a result of a political scandal. Environmental groups directed their efforts toward the federal government. In a press conference, Nobel laureate and UBC professor Michael Smith presented the federal government with a letter urging it to protect habitat as the key way to maintain biological diversity. The letter was co-signed by two hundred Canadian scientists, including such luminaries as E.C. Pielou and David Suzuki. At the time, British Columbia scientists were making a similar argument in the scientific literature.[70]

This gave the management of Taseko Mines a new idea. Suppose they could show that the rainbow trout had been introduced to the lake in the twentieth century as part of a stocking plan? That would greatly reduce the putative contribution that the fish were making to the biodiversity of the province. It didn't matter that the archives of the provincial Ministry of Environment, Lands and Parks did not have any record of Fish Lake ever having been stocked. Taseko Mines would put its faith in the archive of place instead. It hired Triton Environmental Consultants to do a genetic study of the rainbow trout in Fish Lake.[71]

2

Prosperity Gold

I N NOVEMBER 1995, Taseko Mines managers decided that the last thing they wanted the Fish Lake deposit to be associated with in peoples' minds was fish, so they officially changed the name of the property to Prosperity Gold. Then they awaited the results of the trout genetics study that they had commissioned. The provincial Ministry of Environment, Lands and Parks did not like the new direction that Taseko Mines was taking. Ministry scientists argued that the genetic techniques were limited, and even if the company were to find no genetic difference between Fish Lake trout and other trout in the province, this did not make the fish "expendable or replaceable." Furthermore, the genetic uniqueness of the fish was only one factor that made the lake significant. According to the ministry, the lake was a "pristine and isolated system" that provided "unique fishing opportunities."[1]

In the autumn of 1996, Taseko Mines received some unpleasant news from Triton Environmental Consultants. The results of the study showed that the population of rainbow trout in Fish Lake had "very unusual" genetic characteristics and was "a group of unique origin." Since the trout had evidently not been put in the lake by human beings in the twentieth century, where had they come from? Fourteen thousand years earlier, the area near Fish Lake was buried under six hundred metres of ice, hardly a suitable habitat for trout. After the ice sheets melted, trout returned to what is now British Columbia from two directions. One group migrated from the south and the east; the other came from Beringia, the land bridge that connected northeastern Asia and northwestern North America during the last glaciation. Zoogeographers inferred that the trout came from two different directions by studying the distribution of a nematode parasite that attacks the swim bladders of lake trout. The range of the parasite is limited to basins in the northwestern part of the continent, suggesting that populations of trout that migrated into North America from Beringia have never been in contact with populations of trout that migrated from the south and east. If they had been in contact, the parasite would have spread to the latter groups. The trout in Fish Lake had come from the south and east. Since fish cannot travel overland, at one time there must have been an all-water route that allowed the trout to reach Fish Lake. By the twentieth century, this route was no longer in evidence; a waterfall between Fish Lake and the Taseko River blocked fish migration. So how did the fish get into the lake? The most likely explanation was that they had travelled through a series of lakes and streams that formed as the ice sheets melted and then later disappeared. Residual ice left during melting dammed the flow of meltwater and diverted it along new channels. Temporary lakes also formed along the edges of the ice sheets, some lasting centuries. The topology of these proglacial lakes and streams changed constantly, connecting some drainage basins for a time and then separating them. At some point during this process, the trout were able to move into the area that would later become Fish Lake. When the ice had finally melted and current drainage patterns were established, the trout could no longer leave. They were genetically isolated from other trout populations in the watershed.[2]

THE TSILHQOT'IN

The fact that the Fish Lake trout were genetically unique wasn't the only bad news Taseko Mines received that year. In January 1996, the company learned that the Tsilhqot'in elders, band chiefs, and councillors had met at the Stone reserve and voted unanimously to oppose the mining project. According to Joe Alphonse, fisheries director for the Tsilhqot'in National Government, the Tsilhqot'in people had the same objection to the project as the federal and provincial fisheries personnel: there would be no way to compensate for the loss of the lake or to replace it once it was gone. They were also concerned about the impact the mine would have on drinking water from the Taseko and Chilko rivers, on salmon habitat, and on the deer and moose populations, which would suffer from the increased access allowed by new roads into the area. In a press release, the Tsilhqot'in National

Government said that "it was in their best interest to protect what they consider[ed] to be their land, and that they [had] sole jurisdiction over the area in question." Needless to say, other stakeholders did not want to recognize the sole authority of the Tsilhqot'in people. The MLA, David Zirnhelt, responded by stating that the government's "position is there is no veto by First Nations, and their rights will be considered as with all resource developments." At the time, the government did not have any treaties in place with the Tsilhqot'in.[3]

The First Nations, as Canadian indigenous people called themselves in the late twentieth century, were the descendents of the people who had entered what is now British Columbia more than ten thousand years earlier. In western Canada, their political relationship to various governments was shaped by terms that had originally been set by the British. In 1763, when the British and the French signed the Treaty of Paris at the conclusion of the Seven Years' War, France renounced claim to any territory in North America that lay east of the Mississippi River. The British Royal Proclamation of 7 October 1763 declared that the lands west of the Appalachian highlands were to be an Indian Territory, reserved for the use of the indigenous people who occupied them. The proclamation also set the terms by which these lands could be alienated from Aboriginal people. In a formal council, representatives of the Crown and of the Aboriginal groups concerned would agree on the terms of a land sale and record these terms in a treaty. West of the Rocky Mountains, however, only a few land cession agreements had been made between the Hudson's Bay Company (HBC) and Aboriginal people before BC joined Confederation in 1871. Five years later, the federal government turned over to the provincial government the task of settling Aboriginal land claims and creating reserves. The new province did not recognize Aboriginal title, however, and saw no need to extinguish it with treaties. Aboriginal demand for treaties intensified to such a point that the federal government decided in 1927 to make it illegal to raise funds for land claims. This quelled the demands for Aboriginal title until the restriction was lifted in 1951. In the mid-1990s, there were still no treaties in place for BC, with the exception of an agreement (Treaty 8) that covered an area in the northeastern corner of the province.[4]

The Tsilhqot'in were descendents of people who had been living on the plateau that bore their name for millennia. Every Euro-Canadian trader, surveyor, missionary, and miner who entered the region had to interact with them in one way or another. Because there were so few non-indigenous settlers in the area, particularly on the edges of the plateau, the traditional Tsilhqot'in way of life altered only gradually. Things began to change more rapidly beginning in the 1950s. For one thing, the politically conservative Social Credit government that ran the province for more than thirty years (1952-72, 1975-86) focused on expanding the use of British Columbia's natural resources. This was a period of extensive highway construction and rapid expansion of local air transportation. Massive hydroelectric developments provided a surplus of power; their construction could only be justified by the further construction of mines, smelters, pulp and paper mills, and cement works to consume the power. In the words of W.A.C. Bennett, premier of the province for two decades after 1952, BC was "the last economic frontier of North America." The Tsilhqot'in were seeing increasing numbers of outsiders who came to hunt, fish, camp, log, prospect, ranch, and go four-wheeling.[5]

On 23 August 1989, the Xeni Gwet'in, the Tsilhqot'in people of Nemiah Valley, declared a portion of the surrounding territory to be the "Nemiah Aboriginal Wilderness Preserve" and prohibited commercial logging and road building, mining and mining exploration, and flooding and dam construction on Chilko, Taseko, and Tatlayoko lakes. The declaration went on to state that "this is the spiritual and economic homeland of our people. We will continue in perpetuity: a) to have and exercise our traditional rights of hunting, fishing, trapping, gathering, and natural resources; b) to carry on our traditional ranching way of life; c) to practise our traditional native medicine, religion, sacred, and spiritual ways." The Xeni Gwet'in also signalled their willingness to share the preserve with non-Aboriginal people for recreational purposes (subject to a system of permits) and to defend Aboriginal rights to the best of their ability.[6]

The Nemiah Declaration was supported by a number of environmental groups, including the Western Canada Wilderness Committee and the Federation of Mountain Clubs of British Columbia. It played a key role in the process that eventually resulted in the creation of Tŝ'il?os Park at the beginning of 1994. The name of the new park, Tŝ'il?os, was the traditional Xeni Gwet'in name for the mountain that had been renamed Mount Tatlow in honour of a provincial minister of finance who was thrown from his horse and killed in 1910. The fact that the park was given a Tsilhqot'in name rather than an English one signalled both the changing sensibility of the 1990s and the role the Xeni Gwet'in were to play in the park. The plan for the park specified that the Xeni Gwet'in would be "important players in the management of the park and their traditional home." Culturally significant sites in the park would be identified by archaeological and heritage studies so that they could be protected. Tsilhqot'in naming even extended to some of the management structures of the park. The subcommittee composed of Xeni representatives and members from the provincial parks ministry was called Tŝ'il?os Gwa Najegwaghaten, a Tsilh-qot'in phrase meaning "People working together for Tŝ'il?os." Xeni elders worked with representatives on this committee to guide the direction of the park. However, creation of the park did not prejudge any Aboriginal rights or title that the Xeni Gwet'in might have, and, unlike the original Nemiah Aboriginal Wilderness Preserve, Tŝ'il?os Park did not include Fish Lake within its boundaries.[7]

THE POLARIZATION OF STAKEHOLDER POSITIONS

Taseko Mines worked through 1996 to move the Prosperity Gold project forward. In March it secured $5.37 million from corporate and individual investors that allowed it to collect baseline data required under the provincial and federal environmental assessment acts. The company also continued to delineate the ore body with new drilling studies. The mining industry as a whole was chafing under the provincial leadership of the NDP. An election was anticipated in the first half of 1996, and the industry was planning to take political action. In the previous four years, the number of jobs in mining had dropped from fourteen thousand to ten thousand, and annual exploration expenditures were reported to be down from more than $100 million to about $50 million. Considering that mining was the second-largest industry in British Columbia, with gross revenues over $3 billion, industry representatives thought it was about time that voters started asking their candidates what they would be willing to do for mining in the province.[8]

Perhaps because a provincial government regime change was anticipated, 1996 was a time of polarization for the stakeholders in Fish Lake. Anglers were convinced that the mine was "inevitable" and were determined to get funding "to enhance or bring into production as many barren lakes as possible" for sport fishing. The Mining Association of BC solidified the industry's hold on the city of Williams Lake by naming it the "Mining Community of the Year." The city was commended for "supporting responsible mineral exploration and mining development." In a news release, the association president said that "political and business leaders in Williams Lake have been extremely supportive of the Prosperity Project ... but it won't just be the people of Williams Lake who benefit from a project as significant as Prosperity – it'll be the whole province." Taseko Mines attempted to win the favour of the federal fisheries department

with a new plan to create fish habitat in nearby Wasp Lake and Big Onion
Lake. The company's idea was to connect the two lakes to the Taseko River
and create stream channels that would support spawning for rainbow trout.
But the Department of Fisheries and Oceans wasn't swayed. It held to its
original position that there could be no compensation for loss of Class
One habitat. The department added, rather unhelpfully, that it would consider mine plans that did not affect Fish Lake. Taseko Mines complained
that the federal department was unwilling to consider the data the company had collected and that the department's behaviour didn't "seem democratic." The chief of the federal department's habitat management office
for the Fraser River watershed replied by saying that "the ultimate decision always lay with the federal government." The federal and provincial
governments were meanwhile trying to strengthen their own positions by
combining their two different environmental assessment processes into
one. News about Fish Lake had become more polarized, too. One reporter
described the conflict as being "between fish and jobs."[9]

As lines were being drawn, the Tsilhqot'in people's opposition to the
Prosperity project sharpened. At the end of July, Chief Roger William of
the Xeni Gwet'in said that the band might be willing to deal with Taseko
Mines if the traditional lifestyle of the Xeni Gwet'in was not threatened
and if band members received some share of the expected prosperity. They
wanted "jobs, royalties, and a say in the mine's management." Since the
project might affect other Tsilhqot'in groups, however, an agreement had
to be reached with the Tsilhqot'in National Government, and at the end
of August, that government repeated its earlier objections to the project.
In addition to the impact on traditional hunting and fishing and the pollution of their drinking water, the leaders cited other concerns. The influx
of miners and support personnel would cause "devastating" social problems for the band.

The Tsilhqot'in may also have felt a particular affinity for the fish, and
not only because the rainbow trout in Fish Lake were genetically unique.
Since the lake was one of the few in the province that had not been
stocked, the fish were native to the lake in the same way that the Tsilhqot'in people were native to the Chilcotin. The Tsilhqot'in National Government felt that traditional use studies of the area were "laughable" and
began to conduct its own. At the end of the month, the Tsilhqot'in
National Government sent a letter to Taseko Mines expressing its demands. It ordered the company to vacate the Fish Lake area by 30 September 1996: "You are to restore the area to its condition before your illegal
explorations were begun. You are to pack up and leave." Taseko Mines

tried to schedule a conference with the Tsilhqot'in National Government, but the Tsilhqot'in leaders refused to meet. They said they had a "solemn duty" to protect the wildlife of the area, and they did not recognize claims or exploration permits issued by the BC government. As the end of the month drew near, the Tsilhqot'in chiefs stated that no mine could be developed until a treaty was in place between the federal government and the Tsilhqot'in National Government. As the legal basis for their demands, they cited the landmark cases of *Sparrow* and *Delgamuukw*.[10]

SPARROW AND DELGAMUUKW

On 26 May 1984, Ronald Sparrow, a member of the Musqueam Indian band of the BC lower mainland, was charged under section 61(1) of the *Fisheries Act*. He was using a drift net that was forty-five fathoms in length, even though the band's food-fishing licence, issued by the federal Department of Fisheries and Oceans, limited drift nets to twenty-five fathoms. Sparrow admitted to using the long net but claimed that he was exercising his Aboriginal right to fish and that the net length restriction was inconsistent with section 35(1) of the *Constitution Act* of 1982, which stated that "the existing aboriginal and treaty rights of the aboriginal peoples of Canada are hereby recognized and affirmed." The provincial judge who first heard the case ruled that the Aboriginal right to fish was governed by the *Fisheries Act* and a person could not claim an Aboriginal right that was not based on a treaty. Since the Musqueam did not have a treaty, Sparrow was appealing to a right exercised by the Musqueam people before Europeans came to North America. According to the Crown, however, that right no longer existed because of "extinguishment by regulation," and Sparrow was convicted of the offence. An appeal to the County Court of Vancouver was rejected on grounds similar to those invoked by the provincial court. Sparrow appealed to the British Columbia Court of Appeal, which overturned the ruling that the Aboriginal right was extinguished by regulation. Instead, it found that "the aboriginal right which the Musqueam had was, subject to conservation measures, the right to take fish for food and for the ceremonial purposes of the band ... It has never been a fixed right, and it has always taken its form from the circumstances in which it has existed. If the interests of the Indians and other Canadians in the fishery are to be protected then reasonable regulations to ensure the proper management and conservation of the resource must be continued." In the judgment of the Court of Appeal, the conviction of Sparrow could not stand, because

it was based on an erroneous view of the law, but the facts were insuffi-
cient for an acquittal. The case went on to the Supreme Court of Canada,
where it was the first to deal with section 35 of the *Constitution Act*. In its
decision, the Supreme Court rejected two extreme positions. The first was
the Crown's claim that all Aboriginal rights and treaties were subject to
regulation. The second was Sparrow's claim that Aboriginal rights could
only be regulated by the First Nations themselves. On 31 May 1990, the
Supreme Court unanimously decided to overturn the original conviction
of Ronald Sparrow. The attorney general of Canada chose not to hold a
new trial, and Sparrow's involvement ended. The importance of the case
lay in the Supreme Court's ruling that section 35 of the Constitution limited the federal government's ability to put into effect laws or policies that
might infringe on Aboriginal rights. The court held that "the government
is required to bear the burden of justifying any legislation that has some
negative effect on any aboriginal right protected under section 35(1)." It
also held that the government needed to reconcile "federal powers with
federal duties."[11]

The *Delgamuukw* case also began in 1984. The Wet'suwet'en and
Gitxsan First Nations of northwestern BC were frustrated because the
province, which held the title to Crown land in their traditional territories, would not participate in the federal land-claims process. The Gitxsan
and the Wet'suwet'en took the province to court, claiming ownership of
the land and jurisdiction over 133 individual territories, covering a total of
fifty-eight thousand square kilometres. The province's defence was that
the colonial government of BC had extinguished all Aboriginal land rights
by law before the province joined the Confederation. The First Nations
lost the case and appealed. The Court of Appeal unanimously decided that
Aboriginal interests in the land had not been extinguished by the colonial
government. The case went to the Supreme Court of British Columbia,
where the province argued that Aboriginal title was not a right to the land,
but a right to pursue traditional activities. According to the 1991 judgment
of the Honourable Chief Justice Allan McEachern, Aboriginal interests in
the land "were rights to live in their villages and to occupy adjacent lands
for the purpose of gathering the products of the lands and waters for ceremonial purposes. These aboriginal interests did not include ownership of
or jurisdiction over the territory." McEachern's blunt dismissal of Aboriginal claims to ownership and jurisdiction meant that the case would surely
go to the Supreme Court of Canada (the outcome of that appeal is discussed later in this chapter). McEachern also ruled, however, that the unilateral extinguishment of Aboriginal title created "a legally enforceable

fiduciary, a trust-like duty or obligation upon the Crown to ensure there will be no arbitrary interference with aboriginal subsistence practices."[12]

THE QUESTION OF TSILHQOT'IN TITLE

To the Tsilhqot'in, the implications of *Sparrow* and *Delgamuukw* were that both the federal and provincial governments had a duty to see that their traditional interests in, and uses of, Fish Lake were protected. However, the tenure of the provincial NDP, the mainstream political party most likely to side with the First Nations, was uncertain. It was also not clear what would happen when *Delgamuukw* went to the Supreme Court of Canada. If Aboriginal people were found to have a right to the land, and not merely to traditional activities of hunting, fishing, and gathering, then the Tsilhqot'in's legal position would be strengthened.

In the spring of 1996, the NDP was trailing the Liberal Party opposition in provincial opinion polls. Glen Clark, who had been elected leader of the party after Mike Harcourt resigned, decided to call a general election anyway. The NDP won again. There wouldn't be a regime change just yet.

Taseko Mines redoubled its efforts at Fish Lake. In February 1997, it announced that "excellent results" were coming in from the $13.5 million work programs that were ongoing at the Prosperity site. The company was redrilling to confirm that the ore reserve contained the amount of gold and copper that earlier studies had predicted. Other teams worked on the engineering aspects of the mine, finding answers to such questions as: How should the pit be excavated? Where would site facilities like rock dumps and tailings impoundments be located? How should they design the mill? They constructed pilot plants and did environmental and socio-economic projections. All told, fifty people were employed at the site, working full time on a mine that did not yet exist. It was the largest exploration program in the province that year. In its annual report, Taseko Mines predicted that the Prosperity mine/mill complex would produce a thousand new jobs for local and Aboriginal people, giving communities in the Cariboo-Chilcotin more stability and a higher standard of living. It emphasized the fact that the mine would be producing two different metals, which would insulate revenues from a sudden fall in producer price for either of them. Furthermore, "detailed cost engineering" showed that cash costs of metal production at Prosperity would rank "within the lowest quartile of the world's producers of gold or copper." The company also noted that it had been making field surveys and continuously monitoring the climate, physiography, water, fisheries, vegetation, and wildlife in the area for five years to facilitate the process of environmental assessment. The annual report emphasized Taseko's role in building consensus among stakeholders. Managers hoped that Prosperity would "set a new standard for the mining industry in the realm of open, informed decision making that respects environmental, economic and social concerns." There was no mention in the annual report of what, if anything, could stall the project or stop it altogether. As far as the company was concerned, the Prosperity complex would eventually be built, and BC would be better for it.[13]

At the time, environmental groups expressed concern about the provincial environmental assessment process, although they thought that it was a great improvement over earlier processes. Their primary objection was to the vaguely specified requirement that the public be consulted. The standard approach taken by resource companies was simply to hold an occasional "open house." According to an environmental caucus that reviewed the process, "the walk-through sessions which typif[ied] the open house format [were] more a corporate public relations tool than an effective means of delivering information to the public or garnering substantive public feedback." The caucus thought it would be better to force the resource companies to hold structured community meetings where they would actually get feedback. Furthermore, for public input to be meaningful, there needed to be a source of funding for people who wished to intervene in the assessment process. Taseko Mines had spent a lot of money on the Prosperity project by this point: $28.7 million to acquire the rights and $20.3 million on exploration and development. The total, $49 million, was far more than could be matched by concerned citizens, First Nations, local environmentalists, anglers, or other groups that might not want to see the mine go ahead. The public perception of the environmental assessment process was that it was not possible to recommend against a project, only to approve it or mitigate its effects. The environmental caucus saw this as a failing in the assessment process; it believed the public should know that a project could be rejected and that the provincial Environmental Assessment Office was not biased toward developers.[14]

The environmentalists were probably right to be concerned about the public's ability to veto the Prosperity project. In June 1997, the federal Department of Fisheries and Oceans contacted the provincial ministry to let it know that the department was willing to again become involved in the environmental review of the project. Taseko Mines felt that things were "finally back on track" and that it would be "afforded due process."

Bruce Jenkins, the company's director of environmental affairs, dismissed the loss of the rainbow trout in Fish Lake by referring to the economic value of sport fishing there, which was estimated to bring in about $20,000 a year. In the first four years of construction, the resource company would spend about $860 million. "You don't have to be a rocket scientist to realize from an economic standpoint this is a no-brainer decision," he said. If he knew of other standpoints besides the economic one, he refrained from mentioning them. In September, Taseko Mines opened the Prosperity Project community office, a storefront location in Williams Lake, to "inform" the public of its mine proposal. People began "drifting into" the office hours before it officially opened. Bruce Jenkins said that the strong response to the opening of the office signalled a strong community interest in the project. In the office, visitors could view three different versions of the proposed mine and give their input. If they were unable to visit the office in person, they could mail in letters or send faxes. If they had questions that couldn't be answered by office personnel, Taseko Mines offered to bring in people who could answer the questions. The company stressed the novelty of giving the public a say in the design of a mining project. At the time, mine proposals were being evaluated by a new joint provincial-federal environmental assessment process.[15]

In the fall of 1997, gold prices were near a twelve-year low and shares in gold-mining concerns were doing poorly. Taseko Mines continued to work on the Prosperity project, which consisted of 196 mineral claims and nine placer claims covering about eighty-five square kilometres. The company was finalizing a computer model of the geology of the copper-gold porphyry at Fish Lake, based on 123,414 metres of drilling in 248 holes. Fifty metric tons of sample ore from the deposit had been put through a pilot mill to confirm the amount of gold and copper that would be recovered and for use in environmental analyses. The company was also working on environmental and socio-economic studies to present to the government and to local stakeholders. Bulk commodities for the mine would be shipped from Vancouver to Williams Lake by rail and trucked to the site. Copper concentrates would go in the opposite direction. Personnel, goods, and services would come from the city of Williams Lake. A standard power line would connect the mine to existing high-voltage transmission lines 124 kilometres to the east. A natural gas pipeline could also be constructed to connect the site to an existing pipeline ninety kilometres to the northeast. At the time, the company was considering three alternatives for the open-pit mine, two for the storage of waste rock, and three for the storage of tailings. One of the proposals would protect Fish

Lake at the cost of affecting two watersheds and leaving much of the ore in the ground. Another would also affect two watersheds but would attempt to preserve about two-thirds of the lake with a dam. The third would fill in Fish Lake, but its impact would be limited to one watershed. According to Dennis Deans, the company's manager of Aboriginal and government affairs, Fish Lake wasn't that good for fishing because the fish were "small and sometimes contaminated." In October, the company announced that it hoped to be producing ore by the middle of 2001. Throughout the winter it offered information seminars at the community office in Williams Lake, explaining development options, water quality, and fisheries to visitors in front of posters that were titled, "The Road to Prosperity."[16]

One of the attendees at the first Taseko Mines information seminar was Chief Roger William of the Xeni Gwet'in. He told the others in attendance that the project did not have the approval of the Xeni Gwet'in or of the Tsilhqot'in National Government, and that they could not allow it to go ahead. "If any mine extraction is going to be done, it is going to be by natives out there," William told the meeting. Since the Tsilhqot'in did not yet have a treaty with the government, they felt that the land was still theirs; they couldn't be given jobs by the company in compensation. They had more troubling concerns, however. Members of the Secwepemc First Nation (formerly known as Shuswap) had been asked to participate in the Fish Lake decision-making process, in an area that the Tsilhqot'in considered to be their own traditional territory. There were many economies of scale in the contest of stakeholders fighting over Fish Lake. If the interests of the First Nations could be divided, it would be much easier to evade their concerns.[17]

By the end of 1997, however, Taseko Mines faced the one thing that could surely halt the Prosperity project indefinitely. Not the claims of rival mining concerns, the foot-dragging of the feds, the provincial government's apparent need to coddle environmentalists, the environmentalists' desire to preserve rainbow trout, the anglers' wish to catch and release them, or even the indigenous people's belief that they were the sole owners and proprietors of the land. Instead, by the end of 1997, it was clear that the economies of Thailand, Malaysia, Hong Kong, Korea, and Japan had all suffered sharp downturns. The demand for copper and gold dropped, and producer prices fell with it. Mines around the province were revising profit margins, downsizing, closing. As the Asian markets changed for the worse, the provincial economy did too. Worldwide, the falling price of gold threatened the economic feasibility of 40 percent of all gold mines.[18]

At the end of 1997, the situation of resource companies with respect to the rights of First Nations also changed significantly. In the case of *Delgamuukw v. British Columbia,* the Supreme Court of Canada ruled that Aboriginal title did exist in BC after all, and that it was a right to the land, not merely to traditional practices of hunting, fishing, or gathering. In cases where the First Nations held the title to land, they could exclude others from it, use it for pleasure or business, and extract resources. This meant, for example, that First Nations could engage in mining, even if that had never been a traditional activity. The judgment was the most important decision yet made on Aboriginal title in Canada. It held that Aboriginal title was a communal right and not an individual one, so decisions about the land had to be made by the whole community. Lands covered by Aboriginal title could only be sold to the federal government. They could not be used in ways that were irreconcilable with the First Nation's continuing relationship to the land. Like other Aboriginal rights, Aboriginal title was protected under section 35 of the *Constitution Act* of 1982, the highest authority in Canada. Since Aboriginal title was a constitutional right, the government had to meet stringent constitutional tests in order to justify infringing on it. It had to consult with the affected Aboriginal groups before acting and might have to pay them compensation afterwards. The key question after the Supreme Court's ruling in *Delgamuukw* was which lands in BC were covered by Aboriginal title. At the end of 1997, nobody knew the answer. It would either be determined in the courts, one case at a time, or negotiated in treaties.[19]

The Tsilhqot'in National Government acted on the *Delgamuukw* decision immediately. It sent a letter to the provincial government citing the case as justification for a demand that BC "cease and desist from further processing of land-related tenure application and all processes involved with alienating lands and water" in Tsilhqot'in territory. The Tsilhqot'ins' immediate target was the forest industry, which had, between 1984 and 1994, generated nearly half a billion dollars in revenue for the provincial government in the Cariboo forest region alone. Much of the traditional territory of the Tsilhqot'in people lay within this area. The Tsilhqot'in also indicated that they would hold provincial employees "professionally and privately accountable" for any unilateral or arbitrary transactions. The proximate cause of the letter was an attempt by a local rancher to buy some unsurveyed Crown land to use for a hayfield. Tsilhqot'in tribal council members said they were not interested in blocking the rancher; in fact, they thought that he would be better provided for by the Tsilhqot'in than he was by the provincial government. The tone of the letter was firm: "In the past it has been the fiduciary obligation of Crown Government to act in the interests of the Indian people of Canada. Now it is also a legal requirement. Please avoid unnecessary unpleasantness by taking both of these responsibilities seriously." The reporter who covered the story for the *Vancouver Sun,* one of the province's two major daily newspapers, took the threat of "unpleasantness" as an allusion to the Chilcotin War of 1864 (discussed in Part 3 of this book). "Considered among the toughest and most militant of BC's aboriginal nations," the reporter wrote, "the Tsilhqot'in are one of the few native Indian groups in Canadian history to actually fight a war in defence of their territorial sovereignty."[20]

PLANS FOR THE MINE/MILL COMPLEX

The Tsilhqot'in thought that the Prosperity project should not go forward until they had resolved their dispute with the Secwepemc over the boundaries of traditional territory, but it is not clear if Taseko Mines thought the Tsilhqot'in National Government had the ability to stop the project at Fish Lake. In its report to the US Securities and Exchange Commission, the company wrote that, "although work to date is encouraging, there can be no assurance that a commercially mineable ore body exists on the Registrant's Prosperity Property." In order for commercial mining to proceed, the company needed to complete "a comprehensive feasibility study, possibly further associated exploration and other work that conclude[d] that a potential mine [was] likely to be economic." It would also need "significant capital funding and the required mine permits."[21]

In any event, the company continued to perform socio-economic and environmental studies. Recalling its earlier misstep with the rainbow trout, Taseko Mines commissioned Madrone, an independent environmental consulting company, to study the wildlife and vegetation around Fish Lake. The consultants were to determine which, if any, of the local species were on the provincial red ("endangered") or blue ("vulnerable") lists. The Madrone biologists made maps of vegetation from aerial photos and double-checked them on the ground. Douglas fir grew on the south-facing slopes, at least in places where it had not been clear-cut by loggers. In well-drained gravels, the predominant tree was the lodgepole pine; in poorly drained glacial till, spruce. The biologists flipped over logs to find salamanders and scooped up frogs' eggs in nets. They used audio detectors to locate bats and fine mesh to trap them – and discovered that the bats "all had really sharp teeth." They scouted the wetlands for migrating birds and counted beaver and muskrat in the winter. Mule deer and mountain goats were not common in the area. Cougars and caribou were not encountered at all. The Madrone consultants found no endangered or vulnerable reptiles or amphibians, and few mammals of any kind. They did find two blue-listed birds in the area during their fall migrations, the great blue heron and the red-necked phalarope. They also found a comparatively rare plant. The results of the environmental studies were released at another of Taseko Mines' information seminars, along with a draft report of the Prosperity project specifications.[22]

As part of the joint federal-provincial environmental review, Taseko Mines was required to release a report on the project to the public. At the end of February 1998, the company presented a synopsis of the report to about a hundred people in Williams Lake and made copies available at the public library and on the Internet. The public had three weeks to respond. At the time, various environmental groups were working on initiatives to make it easier for members of the public to oppose mining projects. The Sierra Legal Defence Fund soon released its sixty-six-page report *Digging Up Trouble: The Legacy of Mining in British Columbia.* In that report, the section on the Prosperity project was subtitled "Development at Any Cost." The Environmental Mining Council of BC was working on a database and geographic information system (GIS) to help the public "track mining companies, projects, organizations, and impacts on an international basis." In Williams Lake, however, the public was told that the purpose of the review was to "comment on whether the document is fair and reasonable to Taseko." The city's Chamber of Commerce was worried that the federal Department of Fisheries and Oceans would block the project. Ken Wilson, the president of the chamber, said that its members had doubts that Fish Lake was actually a Class One habitat, as the federal department claimed. Some people were saying that the rainbow trout from Fish Lake had lice on them and thus weren't suitable for eating. The chamber was soliciting its members to use the public review process as a lobby in favour of the mine.[23]

The Environmental Assessment Office received numerous letters about the project from the public in March 1998. A handful of individuals seemed to be against it, as was the Tatlayoko Think Tank, a husband-and-wife advocacy team operating out of the tiny Chilcotin community of Tatlayoko Lake. One guide-outfitter expressed his concern about the mine. Most individuals wrote in support of the project, however, and against the stance that the federal fisheries department was taking. One person was in favour of a mine but didn't like the company's preferred development option. One was in favour of a mine but wanted the rainbow trout to be relocated to another body of water. The Alexis Creek Community Club wanted a mine, as did the Williams Lake Downtown Business Association. Local businesses like Jerry's Auto Centre, Highlands Irrigation, and Western Equipment Limited also wanted to see the proposal go ahead. A representative from the Industrial, Wood and Allied Workers of Canada wanted to meet with the federal fisheries minister and his departmental personnel. By the end of the public review period, the federal department appeared to be softening. A representative said that the department was willing to consider options that did not involve draining Fish Lake, and even if the federal government did oppose the project, it would still be possible for the federal minister to set up an independent panel to review the decision. This wasn't good enough for Williams Lake. The mayor wrote to the Environmental Assessment Office to indicate the city's support for the project, and city council also sent letters to the premier and the federal fisheries minister in an attempt to pressure the federal Department of Fisheries and Oceans to "take an open approach." The position of the Williams Lake Chamber of Commerce was that the role of environmental review was "not to judge whether mining [was] an appropriate activity for this area, but to ensure the mine design and mining methods used [would] minimize environmental impact." Despite the hope of environmental groups that the project would be halted at this point, the federal-provincial environmental review committee reached the decision that Taseko Mines and the federal Department of Fisheries and Oceans could agree to disagree. Everyone would save face, and an independent study of the impact on fish habitat would be conducted. In the meantime, the mine review could go on. The final decision would lie with the federal and provincial ministers. In the aftermath of the environmental review process, the president of the BC Mining Association blamed the federal government for driving away investment when the province could really use an "economic boost."[24]

In the spring of 1999, Taseko Mines released a project development plan for Prosperity to the public. The company had started with ninety-five "reasonable" alternatives and determined that five of these were technically feasible for the Fish Lake site. Each of the five development plans specified where mine facilities would be located and how they would be built, where transmission lines and access roads would go, and how the company would operate the mine and manage the local environment. The company first settled on the best ways to provide access and power to the site. After discussions with local stakeholders, Taseko Mines chose an access road that would approach from the north, building on the existing

Whitewater Road and Highway 20. There were eleven possible corridors for the 230-kilovolt transmission line that the mine and mill complex would require. The one that was chosen, connecting the site with a new switching station near Dog Creek to the northeast, was the shortest, and it avoided Aboriginal settlements and protected areas. The access road and transmission line were common to each of the five development options. The first option located tailings and waste rock storage north of Fish Lake, mitigating the effects on the lake but affecting fish habitat in Tete Angela Creek to the north. The second option would also have an impact on Tete Angela Creek and would involve the partial loss of Fish Lake, too. Its main advantage over the first option was that it allowed more ore to be extracted. The third option was Taseko's original plan. Fish Lake would be eliminated, but the waste rock and tailings could be stored in such a way that no other watershed would be affected. The fourth and fifth options were provided by the federal Department of Fisheries and Oceans. Both limited the impact to one watershed and mitigated the effect on Fish Lake. They differed mainly in the amount of ore that could be extracted.[25]

In all cases, the design of the mine/mill complex would be conventional. Ore would be blasted from the edges of an open pit and loaded onto trucks. The trucks would haul the ore to a facility where the rock could be crushed and carried on a conveyor belt to a device known as a SAG (semi-autogenous grinding) mill. In the SAG mill, the crushed rock would be mixed with water and ground to small pebbles. The pebbles, in turn, would be fed into a ball mill, where they would be ground into a fine sand. This mixture of sand and water, known as a slurry, would be pumped into tanks, and chemical reagents would be added to make sulphide minerals float to the top. Since gold and copper are bound to sulphide minerals, this step would concentrate the gold and copper at the top of the tanks as the waste rock sank to the bottom. Tailings – the mixture of waste rock, water, and chemicals – would be pumped through pipes or ditches to an impoundment pond surrounded by earthen dams. Further flotation steps would increase the concentration of precious metals. A final dewatering step would force remaining water out of the concentrate, which could then be trucked to Williams Lake and shipped by rail to the coast.[26]

Such a complex would have extensive power requirements, estimated at as much as 16 percent of the total operating costs of the mine over its lifetime. The cost of power was one of the key factors determining the profitability, or lack thereof, of existing mines in the province, and there had been bitter complaints the previous year that Americans could buy power from BC Hydro at a cheaper rate than the Gibraltar mine near

Williams Lake could. In December 1998, the BC government and Taseko
Mines signed an agreement that would provide electrical power to the
Prosperity project at a reduced rate. The agreement was part of a provincial initiative called "Power for Jobs," which used surplus hydroelectric
power to "encourage investment, job creation and regional economic development." The program was administered by the BC Ministry of Energy
and Mines. Taseko management took the agreement as a sign that "the
government had clearly indicated its willingness to work in partnership
with mining companies to attract quantum growth in BC investment." At
the time, the company was also meeting with representatives from concentrate buyers, the wharves in Vancouver, and BC Rail to discuss shipping costs.[27]

Taseko Mines explained to the public that it used a process called "multiple account evaluation" to help decide which of the available development options was the best one. Based on this process, management was
able to rule out the first, second, and fifth options. The first and fifth
options left almost 20 percent of the ore in the ground. The first and second options affected more than one watershed. The company was left with
two real contenders: its original plan and one of the proposals put forward
by the federal fisheries department. Comparing the two, Taseko Mines
determined that its plan was better than that of the feds. For one thing, it
was safer. It also contained a less risky habitat compensation plan than the
federal proposal, which required the fish to "be physically moved from
lake to stream and back again every year for at least 60 years." The Taseko
plan would provide better recreational fishing during operations and after
Prosperity closed. It was more financially sound, better for the community, and less likely to result in the mine closing prematurely if metal prices
dropped. By April 1999, the federal fisheries department had a new set of
guidelines for the compensation of lost fish habitat, and Taseko Mines was
trying to figure out how it would affect the Prosperity project.[28]

Other than compensation for the rainbow trout, the only outstanding
issues left for the company to deal with were the claims of the Tsilhqot'in
people. Chief Roger William of the Xeni Gwet'in had begun to participate
in the Prosperity project meetings, even though the Tsilhqot'in National
Government was still opposed to the mine. His band was concerned about
logging in the area and with employment. While the chair of the Tsilhqot'in National Government was asking Taseko Mines "what part of 'no'
don't you understand?" Chief William was quoted as saying, "If all our
concerns can be met and we can all work together, why not?" The following month, Taseko Mines managers announced that they had chosen their

original design from the five options. The review process, they said, made them more confident of their decision. The company had not ceased its exploration, and the end of exploring, apparently, was to arrive where it had started.[29]

THE EXTERNAL COSTS OF MINING

The fact that a proposed mine could create such controversy was due, in part, to the external costs of mining: the social and environmental costs that would be paid by everyone and not borne solely by the mining companies. These costs are a factor in any large-scale resource extraction industry and were not specific to the Fish Lake project. Nevertheless, it is important to understand what was at stake for people who were not in a position to make money directly from the mine. The external costs of mining were incurred at every stage of the process, from preliminary exploration to management of the site after the mine closed.

The impacts of mining exploration were funnelled in such a way that many large areas were mildly affected while fewer and smaller regions came under increasing pressure. Preliminary airborne and ground-based surveying (like the 1993 airborne surveys of the interior plateau) focused on geochemical and geophysical properties of vast regions. Other than the disruptive noise of low-flying aircraft, this kind of surveying was relatively benign. However, preliminary surveying could lead to legal alienation of the land from other measures that might protect it. More intensive exploration was reserved for a few areas that seemed particularly promising. In those places, claims were staked, vegetation and surface soils stripped, lines cut, roads built, trenches dug, holes drilled, and samples extracted for bulk testing. Local habitat was disrupted, and the new roads gave more hunters and anglers access to wildlife. The runoff from thousands of kilometres of poorly built roads loaded streams with sediment and killed fish and other aquatic organisms. Fuel and oil leaked out of equipment. Spawning was disrupted at stream crossings, and roads tended to be arrayed in a grid, rather than following contours or circumnavigating ecologically sensitive regions.

Some places were subject to even deeper scrutiny. In those places, the overburden (the vegetation and soil above the bedrock) was dug, blasted, or bulldozed out of the way so extensive drilling could be done to delineate the ore reserves below. Occasionally the drills hit reservoirs of natural fluids, like brine or natural gas, which were brought to the surface and washed into local streams. The noise of blasting and the operation of heavy equipment was loud and prolonged. Exploration camps were set up, concentrating garbage and human waste. If there was a major discovery, exploration rushes were still a possibility. When diamonds were discovered in the Barren Lands of the Northwest Territories in the mid-1990s, for example, 20 million hectares were rapidly staked by mining concerns.

A handful of the most promising sites, like the copper-gold porphyry at Fish Lake, were deemed worthy of a new mine. In those places, development further concentrated the impact of mining. The construction of "all-weather" roads, which could potentially be used year-round, allowed more access to more people. More access meant interruption of animal migration routes, interference with mating and calving, and depletion of traditional Aboriginal hunting or trapping grounds. The compaction of roads disrupted the flow of groundwater, and runoff from road surfaces increased erosion, flooding, pollution, and the siltation of spawning beds. Although supporters of mining claimed that mines were temporary and had a small ecological footprint, this was not strictly true. The mine itself was merely a node in a network that included transportation routes; the infrastructure needed to generate and deliver energy; piles of waste rock and ponds for tailings; and mills, smelters, and refineries.

The most significant long-term environmental impact of a new mine was the creation of waste rock, which had the potential to pollute fresh water through a process called "acid mine drainage." Waste rock and tailings accumulated as ore was extracted, crushed, ground, and passed through various flotation steps. Technological advances in mining multiplied this waste because it had become more profitable to mine low-grade ore. In Canada, the average grade of copper being mined was under 1 percent. (The grade of the Prosperity deposit was 0.22 percent.) This meant that more than ninety-nine metric tons of waste rock were produced for each metric ton of copper. The waste rock contained acid-generating sulphides and heavy metals. Sulphides stored above ground, exposed to air and water, would react with them to form sulphuric acid. If the water became acidic enough, a naturally occurring bacterium known as *Thiobacillus ferroxidans* would find the habitat to its liking, and it would also begin oxidizing the sulphides to sulphuric acid. This greatly accelerated a process that otherwise took a fairly long time. Acid production could go on for decades or centuries, with the acid seeping into the water and polluting it. Other heavy metals in the waste rock could also leach out when the rock came into contact with water, particularly acidic water. Arsenic, cadmium, cobalt, copper, lead, silver, and zinc could all accumulate in plants and animals.

If the amount of metal was "sublethal" – not enough to kill the organism – it would be passed up the food chain to the next consumer, which concentrated an exponentially greater amount of it. Acid mine drainage was one of the potential problems with a mine/mill complex at Fish Lake. The province of British Columbia had regulations to prevent pollution from mining and to manage the impact of mine waste. Unfortunately, provincial and federal budgets were too limited to effectively monitor and enforce compliance with the law. Inadequate waste management and violation of water quality were ongoing problems at many mines. The fact that the industry wanted to "deregulate" mining worried environmental groups. If it were deregulated, how could the industry be held accountable for its waste?

Because minerals are a nonrenewable resource, when the ore gives out, the mine shuts down. The local community suffers most from the boom and bust of mining activity. The workforce is often brought in from outside the community, especially for the highest-paying, highly skilled jobs. The influx of people typically causes housing shortages. Miners suffer from high occupational hazards; some people think an increase in lung cancer is the result of arsenic emitted from copper smelters. When metal prices drop, workers are laid off. Mine closure can turn a vibrant community into a ghost town. It has happened repeatedly in BC in the past 150 years. When the mine is finally closed and the disturbed areas reseeded or replanted with vegetation, the new growth will sometimes fail. Often the costs of cleanup are passed on to the taxpayers.[30]

At the turn of the millennium, many people were cautious of incurring the long-term costs of large-scale resource development. John Turner, the country's former prime minister and the legal representative for the World Wildlife Fund in Canada, said in 1997, "The geography and wildness of this land has shaped us all, it is part of what it means to be Canadian and it must not be lost in a reckless rush for industrial resources." Ironically, mining, the very thing that Victor Dolmage once believed could preserve Canadian identity, was now thought to be endangering it. But in a way, both Dolmage and Turner were right. Fifty-two kilometres north of Vancouver, at Britannia Beach on Howe Sound, the Britannia Mining and Smelting Company operated a copper mine from 1904 to 1974. The mine's fortunes rose and fell with the price of copper. By 1929 it was the largest copper producer in the British Commonwealth. Thirty years later it had seven employees and went into liquidation. After another surge of activity, the mine was finally closed in 1974 and was turned into the BC Museum of Mining the following year. Over its seventy-year lifetime, the

mine employed 60,000 people. Now visitors are led on tours by interpreters dressed as miners, and the museum pays its way by collecting fees
for admission and by selling rock kits and fragments of mammoth tusk
and dinosaur eggs. Thanks to British Columbia's reputation as "Hollywood
North," the site has been repeatedly used as a set for TV shows like *The
X-Files* and for more than thirty motion pictures to date. British Columbia may not have become a land of porters, as Dolmage feared, but it has
become the kind of place where it is possible to play a miner on TV rather
than actually being one in a real mine. The companies that owned and
operated the Britannia mine are long gone, contributing almost nothing
to cleaning up the site. An underwater pipe now discharges acid mine
drainage into Howe Sound, putting up to a metric ton of copper into the
ocean each day. Bivalves in the water eighteen kilometres away have elevated copper and zinc levels. According to the Sierra Legal Defence Fund,
the Britannia mine site is now "the largest point source of heavy metal pollution on the North American continent," a "legal no-man's land." If it is
ever cleaned up, it will almost surely be at the taxpayers' expense.[31]

THE DECISION

And what of the proposed mine at Fish Lake? In the provincial election of
May 2001, the NDP was defeated by the Liberal Party under Gordon
Campbell, who campaigned on a platform of tax cuts. That summer, the
provincial government began its program to "rethink government." In the
future, programs or services would have to pass three tests. First, did they
serve a "compelling public interest?" Second, were they affordable? Third,
did they reflect "a legitimate and essential role for the provincial government?" Environmental groups were worried. Acts that governed water
purity, standards for food storage and production, waste disposal, disease
control, pollution, air and water emissions, protection of fish and wildlife,
and cleanup of contaminated sites would all come under review. Budget
cuts were announced for the ministries responsible for water, land, and air
protection; sustainable resource management; and forestry. A quarter to a
third of the jobs in each of those ministries were eliminated. The political
climate seemed to favour a new mine. At the end of December 2002, the
executive director of the Environmental Assessment Office ordered Taseko
Mines to produce additional information about the Prosperity project by
30 April 2004 in order to obtain an environmental assessment certificate.
Would the company finally construct the mine/mill complex at Fish Lake?[32]

On 17 February 2003, Taseko Mines released its annual information form to the Canadian Securities Administrators. After a lengthy description of the Prosperity project – including its location, access, and infrastructure; the history of exploration and drilling; title settlements; geology; history of sampling; prefeasibility work; and detailed engineering work – the report got to the bottom line: the economics of operating a hypothetical mine at Fish Lake. Using long-term average price projections, the company determined the pre-tax discounted cash-flow rate of return (DCFROR) for the project and tested its sensitivity to unforeseen changes. The DCFROR would be most sensitive to changes in the US/Canadian currency exchange rate, but it would also be sensitive to gold and copper variables and to changes in operating cost. Taseko Mines concluded that "these rates of return are not sufficient to justify construction of a mine at the Prosperity Project given current copper and gold prices." The company would focus its energies instead on a project with "some likelihood for near term feasibility."[33]

CONCLUSION: THE INTERPRETATION OF INDEXICAL SIGNS

Every place is an archive, one that bears material traces of the past in the very substance of the place. These traces can take many forms. The chemical composition of rock, the orientation of magnetic particles, the layers of sediment or strata, the radioactive decay of various elements, the geographical relationship of volcanic arcs to pieces of oceanic crust, the co-occurrence of particular fossils, the genes of plants and animals, the dissolution of bone surfaces, the acidity or alkalinity of a liquid, the concentrations of metal in living tissue, the presence of roads or bore holes or piles of waste rock ... with the appropriate knowledge, each of these kinds of physical evidence can be used to make inferences about the past.

In the terminology of C.S. Peirce, each of these is an "indexical sign," something that signifies something else by virtue of a causal or physical connection between the two. When Robinson Crusoe "was exceedingly surpriz'd with the Print of a Man's naked Foot on the Shore," it was because he was able to infer the activity of other human beings on an island he thought uninhabited. The footprint served as an "index" of human presence in that place in the recent past. If Crusoe hadn't been there to see the footprint, it would still be there, but it wouldn't signify anything. In order to function as an indexical sign, there had to be an interpreter to infer or observe the connection between the material trace and the events that gave rise to it. Since those events necessarily occurred in the past, every time Crusoe interpreted an indexical sign, he became conscious of some small part of the history of the island. When he saw one of the signs of his own activity, such as the stumps of the trees he cut down, he was simultaneously conscious of the present landscape, his memory of altering it, and the history of that place, of which he was a part. As Crusoe explored the island, he continually made use of this very human ability to decipher indexical signs and to reconstruct the past. When he returned to a heap of grapes that he had gathered earlier, for example, he "found them all spread about, trod to Pieces; and dragg'd about some here, some there, and Abundance eaten and devour'd: By this [he] concluded, there were some wild Creatures therabouts, which had done this; but what they were, [he] knew not." The limits of Crusoe's knowledge limited the inferences that he could make about the past of his island.[34]

As Marx noted in *Capital*, Crusoe, "like a good Englishman," kept a set of account books to keep track of the labour required to produce various kinds of useful product. Political economists were fond of stories like *Robinson Crusoe*, Marx argued, because the relations between Crusoe's labour and the use-value of various products was "simple and transparent." The story could serve as a basis for the study of political economy. What would happen as more people were added to the island and they became dependent upon one another? Division of labour had obvious economic advantages, but it raised many questions that Crusoe did not have to face. How would labour be valued relative to other inputs? How would goods and services be exchanged? How would property rights be allocated?[35]

The addition of more people to Crusoe's island would also allow a division of interpretive labour to arise. It would now be possible for different individuals to specialize in the interpretation of particular kinds of indexical signs. One person might excel in the interpretation of medical symptoms: pains, rashes, pulses. Another might be able to track animals by their spoor – by broken branches, prints, tufts of fur, piles of dung, and drops of blood. This division of labour would also raise questions of political economy. How would various acts of interpretation be valued or exchanged? Who would pay for them? What role would they play in the delineation of property rights?[36]

Most of the indexical signs that played a role in the contest over the fate of Fish Lake were abstruse and required the services of highly trained specialists, mostly scientists, to decipher them. The act of producing representations of these material traces was not free. It cost something to take an aerial photograph, make a topographic map, draw a stratigraphic column, plot the variations of a magnetic field. It cost something to circulate the representations, to accumulate them, to consume them. Every time someone looked at one of the representations, interpreted it, explained it to someone else, made a copy of it, moved it from one place to another, put it into storage, or retrieved it, it cost something. This activity was paid for by various stakeholders and was valued relative to other kinds of work. The interpretation of physical evidence played every bit as much of a role in the political economy of the struggle over Fish Lake as did any other kind of work.[37]

In retrospect, perhaps it isn't surprising that Taseko Mines managed to overcome the interests of the opposing stakeholders and go as far as it wanted with its original mine design. Between 1990 and 1995, the company spent more than $40 million on the exploration of this one little place so far removed from the country's urban centres. To put that figure into perspective, it is about two-thirds as much as the total amount spent on earth sciences over the same period by the Natural Sciences and Engineering Research Council (NSERC), the main funding body for academic science and engineering in Canada. Taseko Mines was willing and able to commit far more resources than any of the other stakeholders with an interest in Fish Lake. And yet, this huge outlay did not make the company completely invincible. As the Taseko Mines project director bitterly noted in 1995, the company's $40 million expenditure could be balanced by the $1.25 phone call of some California environmentalists.[38]

There was obviously an economics at work, but not a simple-minded accounting of red and black ink or of the "bottom line." In some ways, the story was similar to that of another struggle of 1995, the proposed fiftieth-anniversary exhibit at the Smithsonian Institution that was going to juxtapose the *Enola Gay* and the ground-level effects of atomic bombing in Japan. After a very different conflict of stakeholders, that exhibit was scrapped. As John Dower later described it, even after spending more than a million dollars restoring the Superfortress fuselage, "the icons of the narrative of victimization – small objects intimately associated with the individuals killed by the atomic bombs – threatened to overpower" it. The most powerful of these was a schoolgirl's lunch box "containing carbonized rice and peas," which belonged to a child whose corpse was never found. "To those who cherished heroic narrative," Dower wrote, "it quickly became obvious that, for many visitors, this pathetic little container from near ground zero might carry far more emotional weight than the gigantic fuselage in the preceding room." Although the historiographical and emotional stakes in Fish Lake were nothing like those of the Smithsonian exhibit, it was still the case that the millions of dollars that Taseko Mines had already spent, and the billions that the potential mine might generate, were very nearly balanced in value by some trout. Clearly there was a strange economy at work.[39]

But why should there even be a struggle of stakeholders in the first place? In the case of Fish Lake, debate continually focused on what economists call "social costs." When the actions of one economic actor impose costs on another, who should pay? In an influential paper, Ronald Coase argued that if transaction costs are zero, which is the assumption of standard economic theory, then, irrespective of the initial assignment of rights, the parties will negotiate an arrangement that maximizes wealth. According to Coase, what are traded on the market are not physical entities, as many economists assume, but rather rights to perform certain actions. Here is a schematic example. Suppose a mine is built that will cause $1 million damage to a sport fishery downstream. The damage can be prevented if the mining company spends $800,000 on a tailings impoundment. Suppose further that the managers of the fishery can also prevent the damage by diverting one of the streams at a cost of $200,000. It is clearly most efficient for the damage to be prevented by the managers of the fishery. The mining company will be willing to pay the fishery any amount up to $800,000 to divert the stream. The fishery will be willing to take any amount over $200,000 to do so. So says the Coase theorem. In the world of zero transaction costs, the company will build its mine and not bother with an expensive tailings impoundment. The managers of the fishery will divert the stream to prevent damage to their fish and will receive some amount of compensation between $200,000 and $800,000 from the mining company to do so. Coase's point, however, is that transaction costs are never zero. We should study the real world instead, where we can't know the future effects of our actions, where it always costs something to learn about the past or the present and we can't know everything, and where it also costs to enter into legal arrangements or to make exchanges.[40]

These real-world costs arose time and again in the struggle over the fate of Fish Lake. None of the stakeholders had any knowledge of the relevant future costs of their actions. How much would habitat destruction cost in the long run? What would be the future value of a genetically unique population of rainbow trout? What would biodiversity be worth in the future? What would copper be worth in the future? How much would it cost Taseko Mines if the Tsilhqot'in gained the rights to the land? How much would it cost the Tsilhqot'in if Taseko Mines built the mine? How much environmental damage would the mine cause in the form of acid mine drainage? What would the mine's impact be on other important resource industries in the area, like forestry, salmon fishing, and ranching? What would be the impact on tourism? None of the stakeholders had complete knowledge of the attributes of any of the entities involved either. How big was the ore body? Where did it lie? What was the grade of copper and gold it contained? Were there other, richer, undiscovered bodies of ore in the vicinity? Were the rainbow trout the only genetically unique species that would be disturbed by a mine? Were there archaeological sites that would have to be protected?

The fact that people are constantly confronted with the bounds of their knowledge and of their ability to figure things out means that they have to have some way to decide what to learn and when to learn it. As in the case of Fish Lake, these decisions are sometimes motivated by the increasing value of a place or the entities in it, or by the attributes of the place and its entities. Then information costs are incurred as a way to gain rights or to keep them from being seized by other stakeholders. There were many examples of this in the struggle over Fish Lake. Stakeholders learned more about the porphyry as copper and gold prices increased. They discovered an attribute of a population of rainbow trout when they attempted to show that the fish did not have the attribute. This shows, incidentally, that the relationship goes both ways – that increasing knowledge can sometimes increase value. The stakeholders learned more about nearby fish habitats as the value of the trout increased. They learned more about the attributes of other species in the vicinity, too.

One of the distinguishing characteristics of environmental history is that it starts from the premise that human actions and environmental constraints are mutually determining and historically specific. Indeed, this is often taken to be the definition of the discipline. The key environmental entities in the struggle over Fish Lake, the porphyry and the rainbow trout, both had natural histories of their own. This meant that their valuable attributes were contingent on the sequence of events that led to their being in the Chilcotin in the late twentieth century. To know those attributes, it was first necessary for people to reconstruct the histories of the ore deposit and the fish. The natural history of the porphyry unfolded in geological time and had to be reconstructed by geologists. The natural history of the population of rainbow trout unfolded in glacial time and had to be reconstructed by glaciologists, zoogeographers, and geneticists. Human activity around Fish Lake unfolded on a number of time scales, and this history also played a role in the contest. Archaeologists reconstructed millennia of Aboriginal life before written records and corroborated this with the oral traditions of Aboriginal groups. Understanding this so-called prehistory was crucial to the establishment of Aboriginal rights in cases like *Sparrow* and *Delgamuukw*. Over much shorter periods, the history of mining, ranching, logging, fishing, and recreation also shaped people's opinions about proper and improper uses of the area.[41]

By focusing on the contest of stakeholders in a particular place and adopting their temporal frames of reference, it becomes possible to see things that might have been obscured if the analysis was limited to a single time scale. As the lines between natural history, prehistory, and history blurred, the nuances of place became more clear. Places are always intensely particular, and this shapes the lives of the people who dwell there. As Clifford Geertz said, "No one lives in the world in general." The particular struggle over Fish Lake was unique to a particular place at a particular moment. But the more general point is true of every place. The constant interpretation of indexical signs enters into the flow of activity by which people make sense of the past, of the world, of their place in it, and of their relationships to one another.[42]

PART 2

THE HORIZON OF EXPERIENCE

3

Mackenzie

FOUR STONES THAT CAN STILL BE SEEN near the Chilcotin River are all that remain of Lendix'tcux (Dog-Husband) and his sons. To Tsilh-qot'in people with the knowledge to interpret them, these stones are material testimony of the doings of the transformers, animal/supernatural beings who changed themselves and the country during myth time. Evidence for the power of transformers like Lendix'tcux is everywhere in the Chilcotin landscape. To the south near Konni Lake, a husband and wife named Tŝ'il?os and ?Eniyud once lived with their six children. One day, after fighting with her husband, ?Eniyud threw her baby onto his lap. Tŝ'il?os, the baby, and two of the children turned into rock. They can still be seen above Xeni Lake today. ?Eniyud and her three remaining children headed toward Tatlayoko valley, planting wild potatoes along the way. Patches of these potatoes are still there, and on the far side of Tatlayoko Lake, one can see ?Eniyud, who also turned to stone. According to Xeni Gwet'in elders, both Tŝ'il?os and ?Eniyud are able to change the weather and must be treated with respect. The Chilcotin sky reminds the elders of three young men who gave their blind grandmother a piece of rotten wood to eat, telling her that it was caribou liver. For their lack of respect, the men were turned into stars, as were the moose they hunted and the dogs that accompanied them. The old woman herself became the morning star, searching for her grandsons with a lamp. These traces in the landscape both cue memory of the doings in myth time and provide evidence for the truth of the stories. The stories themselves are entertaining, to be sure, but they also teach lessons about nature, proper behaviour, and morality.[1]

Places are multivocal. They remind the heirs of a different tradition of different stories. At Chezacut, for example, there is a massive tractor-style steam engine, now long disused and sinking slowly into the earth. It was made in Ontario in the early twentieth century by the Sawyer Massey Company and marketed in a way that would play on the nationalism of rural customers: "Made in Canada for Canadians." Arthur Knoll brought the engine into the country under its own steam by way of Ashcroft and the Gang Ranch. It required a licensed steam engineer to operate it, and it was fuelled by an Aboriginal man who hauled firewood alongside with a team and wagon. When Felix Scallon wanted to build a bridge and farmhouse at Big Creek, he borrowed the engine to power a sawmill and hired an engineer to run it. The doings of the pioneers have taken on an epic quality for some of their descendents, and the tumbledown Russell fences and collapsed log cabins serve as reminders of a time when ordinary people were more heroic and the country was wilder. To someone who knows the history of ranching in the Chilcotin, a cow branded with a chevron is an instant reminder of Norman Lee, who tried to provision the miners of the Klondike gold rush. In 1898, Lee set out from Hanceville with two hundred head of cattle, drove them almost two thousand kilometres north, and butchered them at Teslin Lake, only to lose all of the meat while rafting across the lake in a storm. Nine months after setting out, he arrived in Vancouver, by his own account, "with a roll of blankets, a dog, and one dollar." A visitor who doesn't recognize the chevron brand or doesn't know the story will find a short summary on a roadside plaque erected near Lee's ranch by the government during the provincial centennial in 1967.[2]

Because the material traces of past events are everywhere in the landscape, and because they are read differently by different people, it is inevitable that disagreements will arise about the nature and role of the past in present places. Despite a professed respect for indigenous oral tradition, for example, archaeologists insist that human beings first came to the Americas after the last glaciation and that they have not always been here, as Aboriginal creationist accounts maintain. Attempts to paper over the disagreements aren't satisfactory, as when Knut Fladmark says that "in all our minds 'eternity' and 11,000 years are essentially the same," or Elizabeth Furniss says that "archaeologists' and Natives' views of Native peoples' origins are simply two different ways of looking at history" and that "neither theory is either 'true' or 'false.'" And the activities of Norman Lee are probably of less interest to a professional historian for their depiction of pioneer spirit than as an illustration of the ways the ranching industry tried to capture the economic benefits of the Cariboo and Klondike gold rushes.[3]

The groundedness of history and memory occasionally pits the interpretations of Aboriginal elders, archaeologists, pioneers, and historians against one another, particularly when the stakes appear to be high. In the case study that follows, attempts to dedicate a route in the Chilcotin to honour an explorer, a cherished symbol of Canadian unity and national identity, led to conflict among stakeholders who found evidence for very different pasts in the same place. People who were accustomed to supporting their arguments by appealing to representational evidence – the kind of evidence that is typically kept in repositories of cultural heritage like archives and libraries – found themselves at a disadvantage when using the material evidence of place. Material traces are more varied and opaque than most representations, their use limited only by the costs of specialization and the bounds of rationality. They are also fundamentally tied to particular places, giving the interpretive advantage to people who physically occupy those places. The following case study also illustrates a new truth to Mackenzie King's claim that "if some countries have too much history, then we have too much geography."[4]

A Moment of Indecision

On 23 June 1793, "after a restless night" in an Aboriginal village on the banks of the Tacoutche Tesse river (now known as the Fraser), Alexander Mackenzie met again with a group of Aboriginal people to see if he could learn more about the routes to the Pacific ocean. The previous day they had shown him trade goods that they obtained from their Aboriginal neighbours to the west: a long-bladed knife with a horn handle; brass, copper, beads, and trinkets; and an eighteen-inch bar of iron. Sharpened at one end and bound to a wooden handle, the iron could be used as an axe until it wore out. They would then recycle it into points for arrows and spikes. The pieces of brass and copper might also be used for arrowheads, but they were more likely to be fashioned into collars, armbands, and bracelets. Studying the trade goods, Mackenzie concluded that they had originally come from non-Aboriginal traders operating on the coast. It was the "favorite project of [his] own ambition" to "penetrate across the continent of America" in order to "add new countries to the realms of British commerce." The fur-trading concern that he represented, the North West Company (NWC) of Montreal, was also determined to tap into Aboriginal trade routes and to establish an overland route to the China market. Only by doing so could it hope to remain competitive against the London-based

Hudson's Bay Company (HBC) and the American Fur Company of John Jacob Astor.[5]

Mackenzie weighed the advantages and drawbacks of various routes to salt water. He had been travelling down the Tacoutche Tesse with nine men and a dog for five days, but the Aboriginal people warned him that there were many dangerous rapids and waterfalls downstream. In six places it was impossible to travel by water at all; in others, goods had to be portaged long distances across very rugged terrain. There were at least three different Aboriginal nations along the river, each speaking a different language. Mackenzie was discouraged. He was certain that the Tacoutche Tesse was the "River of the West" that emptied into the Pacific Ocean around 46° north latitude. If it had been possible to travel down the river easily, then the NWC would have found its route to the China market. But in the opinion of his men (allowing for the possibility that Mackenzie was putting words into their mouths), "it would be absolute madness to attempt a passage through so many savage and barbarous nations." Their provisions were precariously low, their ammunition nearly expended. If the river did debouch so far south, the distance yet to travel was great. The return trip would be prolonged by the difficulties of travelling upstream and possibly by the opposition of the indigenous people. On the other hand, it was also possible to reach the ocean by travelling westward overland, but to do so, the party would have to backtrack up the river for a few days. Mackenzie was hesitant to make this "retrograde motion [which] could not fail to cool the ardor, slacken the zeal, and weaken the confidence of those, who [had] no greater inducement in the undertaking, than to follow the conductor of it."[6]

Where exactly was he? At noon the previous day he had tried to take a reading with his sextant, but the angle of the altitude of the sun was too high for his instrument. Instead, he asked one of the Aboriginal men to sketch the surrounding countryside on a large piece of bark, and the man did so, occasionally consulting with the others. If Mackenzie chose the route to the west, his informants now told him, it was only about seven days' travel from the Tacoutche Tesse to "the lake whose water is nauseous." When they finished reiterating what they had told him the previous day, one of the Aboriginal men asked him why he needed to ask these questions about the country. Didn't white men know everything in the world? Mackenzie hesitated, but "at length," as he later wrote in his journal, "I replied, that we certainly were acquainted with the principal circumstances of every part of the world; that I knew where the sea was, and where I myself then was, but that I did not exactly understand what obstacles might interrupt me in getting to it; with which he and his relations must be well acquainted, as they had so frequently surmounted them."-Mackenzie thought that this explanation had "fortunately preserved the impression in their minds, of the superiority of white people over themselves."[7]

Whether the Aboriginal people believed any such thing about the newcomers is debatable; irony would not have survived the laborious processes of translation that allowed Mackenzie to understand his informants. However misguided his explanation, though, he did gesture towards a basic difference between his approach to geography and that of the Aboriginal people, one that has become important in the historiography of science. It is clear that the Aboriginal people were every bit as capable of thinking in terms of maps and of talking about navigation as Mackenzie was. They, too, could visualize space and project it onto a small, flat surface. There was a crucial difference, however, in the ways that Aboriginal people and newcomers regarded maps. For the Aboriginal people on the Tacoutche Tesse, the creation of the map was an incidental event in their evolving relationship with a potential trade partner. Mackenzie himself had told them that they would receive great advantages from the successful completion of his mission. To the Aboriginal people, the map itself was disposable. The information that it summarized was a paltry fragment of the geographical knowledge that could be generated communally, drawing on what each person carried in his or her own head. For Mackenzie, however, the map was the sole purpose of his expedition. Before setting out, he had met the HBC surveyor Philip Turnor, who had convinced him that he was not yet sufficiently prepared to make his voyage of discovery. He did not know enough about making astronomical observations to be able to accurately determine where he was. In order to remedy this defect, Mackenzie spent a winter in England, acquiring the necessary books and instruments for surveying and learning astronomy and navigation. As he made his way across the continent, he used a compass to continually estimate the bearing of his course and recorded the distances travelled. He used a telescope to observe the moons of Jupiter and thus determined his longitude. The one thing that Mackenzie most wanted to take back to Montreal was a map of his route.[8]

MAPS

Simply to say that Mackenzie wanted to return with a map obscures many details that are crucial to understanding what was at stake. The production and use of maps by Mackenzie and his contemporaries depended on many other techniques that had been developed over long periods of time and integrated into functional and commercial networks. His meticulous journal keeping, for example, depended on his ability to write words and numbers and on the abilities of others to produce pens, papers, and inks. The practice of journal keeping was inculcated into all the fur traders, as was the ability to keep financial accounts. Mackenzie's surveying depended on his mastery of trigonometry and on his use of compass, clock, telescope, and sextant. In order to determine the latitude of his present position, he had to know first how to use a clock to find out what time it was, how to keep track of what day it was, and how to use a sextant to measure the angle between the horizon and the sun. With that information, he could then determine his position using a precompiled table. Determining longitude was still more difficult, as Mackenzie had to be able to see when the planet Jupiter eclipsed its moons. Published tables called ephemerides showed the times when each of the various moons would appear from behind the orb of the planet, so the whole system could serve as a kind of celestial clock. Comparing the local time when such an astronomical event occurred with the time that it occurred at the Royal Observatory in Greenwich allowed Mackenzie to calculate the east-west distance between the two meridians. Of little use aboard a tossing ship, the method was the mainstay of eighteenth-century explorers who travelled by land. The construction of scientific instruments, the production of ephemerides, and the printing of tables and charts, in turn, depended on other constellations of technique. The combined power of all these techniques could be brought to bear on the problem of generating a representation of the route to the Pacific that would be usable in non-local contexts. The form of choice was the map. It was small, lightweight, and flat, readily transported, and easily reproduced. It could be combined with a written text, superimposed on other kinds of representation, manipulated by geometrical transformations, and scaled at will. Most important of all, the information that it contained did not change when it was moved.[9]

Maps are the product of a particular milieu: they embody the biases, values, and preoccupations of their creators. Despite Mackenzie's daily activities of sighting, measuring, annotating, and inscribing, the fact remains that his map and those of other "voyages of discovery" were significantly based on indigenous geographical knowledge, and he and his contemporaries had a crucial reliance on Aboriginal guides. The biases of the explorers can be seen in what was left out of their maps. Places they had not visited were represented as blank spaces, hiding a fully populated, pre-existing world of human activity. A profusion of indigenous toponyms and landmarks was almost entirely left out of their sketches, to be replaced with a scattering of place names that celebrated the events of their journey or the names of their colleagues and patrons. In this way, they began to erase evidence of the bonds that connected indigenous memory to landscape and, thus, to undermine histories of place at variance with their own. As these first maps were redrawn and reworked in urban centres, the names of various Aboriginal "tribes" were sometimes marked in the blank spaces, reifying the explorers' shallow conceptions or misconceptions of human groups as cultural entities that had always inhabited that spot and no other, and suggesting that without the gumption of Euro-Canadian explorers to tie them all together, these people may well have never met one another or done anything of significance.[10]

Besides Mackenzie and his men, there were many other people in the village alongside the Tacoutche Tesse that day. One of them was a woman, who had surprised the explorers by speaking a few words of the Cree language, which was also spoken by the Aboriginal interpreters who accompanied Mackenzie. She was a Sekani, from the western side of the Rocky Mountains, who had been captured by Cree raiders and taken across the mountains to the east. After a summer with them, she managed to escape and cross back over the mountains on her own. At that point, she had been captured again, this time by a war party of Carrier from the Tacoutche Tesse, and she now lived with them on its banks. As a result of being buffeted around like this, she spoke Sekani, Cree, and Carrier and so could translate from Carrier to Cree. Mackenzie's interpreters could then translate the Cree into English for him. Four of the people at the village were Secwepemc men from downriver, who had been living with the Carrier for some time. There was also a Sekani man there. When Mackenzie questioned one of the Secwepemc men about the route down the Tacoutche Tesse, his questions had to be translated from English to Cree, Cree to Carrier, and perhaps Carrier to Secwepemc, and then the answers had to make the return trip. There were also side conversations, as Mackenzie's informant "frequently appeal[ed] to, and sometimes ask[ed] the advice of, those around him." No doubt these involved further translations into and out of other languages like Sekani, Tsilhqot'in, Stl'atl'imx, and French. This was obviously not a static world of tribes, each in its own traditional territory, but a world in flux, a place where people could travel and dwell among near and distant neighbours, willingly or not, and where multilingualism was the norm and not the exception. The arrival of Mackenzie's party did not signal a moment of "Contact" with a superior and somewhat

alien race that would forever divide time into "before" and "after." In fact,
Mackenzie wrote, "one very old man observed, that as long as he could
remember, he was told of white people to the Southward." Mackenzie and
his men were instead something very familiar: delegates from a distant
people who wanted to take part in a trade system that had been flourish-
ing for far longer than anyone could remember.[11]

The end result of Mackenzie's deliberation was to do what his Aboriginal informants suggested. He planned to retrace his steps up the river and
follow a Carrier guide west along Aboriginal trails across the plateau. Having made his decision, Mackenzie had his name and the date inscribed
into the trunk of a tree by his lieutenant, Alexander MacKay. The party
then headed back up the Tacoutche Tesse. Along the way, their canoe was
damaged when it collided with a stump in the river, and they had to camp
for four days and build another. Mackenzie found it necessary to upbraid
his men for their apparent lack of enthusiasm. By 2 July, they were approaching the point where they would leave the river. They were "most
cruelly tormented by flies, particularly the sand fly," which Mackenzie was
"disposed to consider the most tormenting insect of its size in nature."
Despite the unrest among the men, Mackenzie was also forced to put
them on short rations, "a regulation particularly offensive to a Canadian
voyager." One of their daily meals consisted of dried fish roe, pounded
and boiled with a little flour and grain. Spirits lifted when the new canoe
was finished, and Mackenzie added to the good feeling by giving the men
a dram each. On 3 July, they found a river that Mackenzie named the
"West Road," as it appeared to match the description he had been given
of the route to the coast. His men found a "good beaten path" leading up
the hill to the west. It was near this path that he met his Carrier guide.[12]

The Problem of "Ground Truth"

The interior plateau that Mackenzie crossed in the summer of 1793 has
since been explored by people who were interested, for various reasons, in
reconstructing his route and determining where he actually walked. In
doing so, they faced what people who work in remote sensing call the
problem of "ground truth." Since the process of representing a place always
necessitates a loss of information, the representation – be it a verbal
description, itinerary, photograph, map, aerial photo, satellite image, or
whatever – may or may not be calibrated with the place that it depicts in
a meaningful way. In many places along the overland route, Mackenzie's

maps and descriptions were simply not adequate for the task of finding the exact route by which he had travelled. In a sense, ground truth is the inverse problem of mapping. When Mackenzie created his maps and descriptions, he abstracted away from the richness of place to create representations that could be used in non-local contexts. These new representations greatly lowered some information costs for their users: it was now possible to gain some idea of the lay of the land in a distant place without actually visiting it, to compare representations, and to combine them to gain more information.

This process of combining representations can be seen in the successive revisions of Aaron Arrowsmith's map of America. The edition of 1790 shows a relatively detailed section of the Northwest Coast around the Queen Charlotte Islands, based on the observations of Captain James Cook. The interior west of the Rocky Mountains is completely blank. Since Cook did not discover Georgia Strait, Nootka Sound is depicted as being part of the mainland. The version of Arrowsmith's map updated to 1802 includes Captain George Vancouver's discovery of the island now named for him and Mackenzie's track to the Pacific Ocean. Later editions include information gathered by Simon Fraser, David Thompson, Meriwether Lewis, and William Clark. Symbolically, maps like Arrowsmith's could be used by the British and by chartered companies to assert sovereignty over new territory in a way that was understood by other imperial powers. But the maps themselves were not usable on the ground in the region they represented. They were too small-scale and omitted too much detail. In trying to work from the maps back to the places that they depicted, the people who were attempting to re-create Mackenzie's route faced steeply rising information costs: maps are easily transported, but places are not. In order to check a place against representations of it, they needed to visit the place itself. If they were in a place that didn't line up with the map, their only recourse was to carry on and hope that they found a place that did. They could never be certain they had arrived at a particular landmark, so they had to proceed by inference.[13]

The first sustained attempts to find signs of Mackenzie's route were undertaken in the 1870s by George Mercer Dawson and Sandford Fleming. Dawson joined the Geological Survey of Canada in 1875 and began surveying the Chilcotin that year as part of the survey's mandate to develop detailed geological knowledge of the whole country. British Columbia had been surveyed by geologists before, but not systematically over large areas. Without retracing Mackenzie's overland route, Dawson crossed it many times and roughly followed most of it. In August he travelled south along the west bank of the Fraser River from Soda Creek to Riske Creek and then west along the northern bank of the Chilcotin and Chilanko rivers to the mouth of the Homathko River. In September he visited Tatla and Tatlayoko lakes, then turned north to pick up the Nazko River and follow it downstream to the West Road River, also known as the Blackwater River. The following year, he left Quesnel in May, travelling northwest along the telegraph trail with a pack train until they hit the Euchiniko River, and then followed the river west and south to hit the West Road River. In June he followed the West Road River to Eliguk and Gatcho lakes. In July he explored the Dean River, Tanya Lakes, and the upper end of the Bella Coola valley. He then returned past the Ilgachuz Range to the West Road River. By August he was on the Entiako River, heading north toward its junction with the Nechako River.[14]

Sandford Fleming was the engineer-in-chief of the Canadian Pacific Railway, charged with the task of finding the best route for a cross-continental railroad. The survey began working in BC on 21 July 1871, the day the province joined the Dominion of Canada. In 1872, the survey found a possible route through the Chilcotin, crossing the Fraser River near Lac La Hache and following the Chilcotin and Chilanko rivers to the Homathko and from there to Bute Inlet. Additional surveying in 1874 showed that it would be easier to cross the Fraser near Williams Lake instead. In 1875, they surveyed the Nazko Valley, looking for a route from Fort George to Bute Inlet. By 1877, Fleming's team was able to suggest four different potential routes for a railroad through the Chilcotin. None of these followed Mackenzie's route exactly, but all crossed it at various points. Later surveyors took up the challenge of locating parts of Mackenzie's route, building on the findings of their predecessors. In the 1920s, parts of the route were explored by BC land surveyors Frank C. Swannell and Richard Preston Bishop (the same fellow who had surveyed Chilko Lake for its hydroelectric potential). In the 1950s, Walter Sheppe, an editor of Mackenzie's *Journal*, also travelled over part of the route.[15]

The interest in Mackenzie's actual route increased as the bicentennial of his expedition approached, and people began to propose different ways of commemorating his accomplishments. The parks departments of both the provincial and federal governments were interested in setting aside "linear historic or naturally attractive routes" for conservation and recreation, and the Mackenzie trail was thought to have particularly high potential. Despite the fact that it had often been proposed as a natural location for a major transportation corridor, most of the region had never been developed.

There were few roads anywhere in the area, and no railroads. In a preliminary report on the possibility of such a commemorative park, the federal parks department suggested that about 80 percent of the route could be traced and the rest could be chosen based on the scenery and the practicality of development.[16]

The plan drew many supporters from across the province. One of the most energetic was John Woodworth, a retired architect from Kelowna who was the executive secretary of the Alexander Mackenzie Trail Association. The association, which grew from a tiny group of volunteers in the 1970s to 250 members by the 1990s, was dedicated to creating a cross-continental heritage route in honour of Mackenzie's journey. Woodworth thought that Mackenzie was "absolutely tremendous" and that the people who had followed him and occupied the land should thank the explorer for the existence of Canada. When he heard Aboriginal groups refer disparagingly to Mackenzie as a "tourist" in their lands, he became "teed off," despite his "enormous respect" for Aboriginal people. After all, Woodworth asked, who else but Mackenzie could have travelled through the country he did and survived? Two other supporters of the trail were Hälle and Linda Flygare, who became friends and colleagues of Woodworth. Hälle Flygare was a Swedish forester who had first come to Canada on a student exchange program and spent a summer in the region of Mackenzie's overland route. He later returned, married, and became a citizen. From 1975 to 1982, Parks Canada awarded summer contracts to the Flygares to re-create the trail from Mackenzie's notes and maps and from whatever could be learned from the landscape.[17]

In 1981, John Woodworth and Hälle Flygare co-authored a trail guide based, in part, on the Flygares' work. It was published and distributed by the Alexander Mackenzie Trail Association and was popular enough to warrant an enlarged and updated second edition in 1987. Armed with the guide, hikers could now attempt to retrace Mackenzie's steps. Thanks to it, they would know enough to bring insect repellent and mosquito netting so they wouldn't be tormented, as Mackenzie and his men had been, by the ubiquitous insects. Any illusion of following in the explorer's exact footsteps would soon be dispelled, however. Twenty-four of the first thirty-one kilometres of the trail followed gravel logging roads that were too dusty to be easily walked. Hikers were encouraged to travel that section in an automobile instead. The corresponding text in the guide asked: "Are there original trail sections remaining among the clear cuts and skid roads? Exactly where did they leave the Fraser? At this date (1987) we do not know."[18]

GUIDES DON'T CARRY

On 4 July 1793, Mackenzie prepared to strike out overland. He sent MacKay and one of the Aboriginal men who had come with the expedition from the east to make two hidden caches. In the first they buried a ninety-pound bag of pemmican (a foodstuff made from dried buffalo meat and grease), two bags of wild rice, and a keg of gunpowder. In the second they put some trade goods and two bags of maize. The party had to leave their new canoe, so they also built a platform under the shade of some trees to store it until their return, and they made a box to protect whatever else they couldn't carry with them to the sea. Then they shouldered their loads. What Mackenzie had to say on the subject gives a rare glimpse of the social world of the Aboriginal trails. Each of the Canadians, he says, had a ninety-pound load, plus a gun and some ammunition. Bales of fur and goods, known as "pièces," were uniformly ninety pounds in the fur trade, although historian Carolyn Podruchny has shown that voyageurs could increase their status among one another by carrying heavier packs. Mackenzie and MacKay carried about seventy pounds each, plus arms and ammunition, and Mackenzie also had his unwieldy telescope to contend with. The Aboriginal men who accompanied the party from the east had about forty-five pounds each, besides their guns, "with which they were very much dissatisfied, and if they dared would have instantly left us. They had hitherto been very much indulged, but the moment was now arrived when indulgence was no longer practicable." A day into the journey, Mackenzie wrote: "One of my men had a violent pain in his knee, and I asked the guides to take a share of his burden, as they had nothing to carry but their beaver robes, and bows and arrows, but they could not be made to understand a word of my request." For the Aboriginal people, status was evidently inversely proportional to the size of one's burden. Like all new trade partners, Mackenzie would have to learn not to make inappropriate requests of his hosts. When he did, the uncertainties of translation could be used to avoid giving or taking offence. Mackenzie apparently didn't press the matter.[19]

In the first few days on the "well-beaten path," Mackenzie saw many signs of the extensive trade between the coast and the interior. On the evening of 4 July, his party encountered four Aboriginal men coming from the west. One of them was carrying a lance that he had bartered from Aboriginal people on the coast. They, in turn, had obtained it from non-Aboriginal traders. At the Aboriginal camp, Mackenzie saw a strip of sea otter fur, for which he traded some beads and a brass cross. He also saw many European items, including halfpence from Britain and the state of Massachusetts Bay that were hanging from the children's ears as ornaments. It is not surprising that European trade goods had reached the interior by this time. In 1778, Captain Cook anchored in Nootka Sound, on the west coast of what is now Vancouver Island, for about a month. His men traded scraps of iron and other metals for sea otter pelts, which they later sold in Canton at a profit of 1,800 percent. When Cook's journals were published in the 1780s, there was an international rush to exploit this new resource. From 1786 to 1790, more than a half a dozen ships, mostly British and American, traded on the coast and hunted sea otter each year. In 1791 there were thirteen ships, twenty-one the following year, and thirteen again the year of Mackenzie's voyage. This maritime fur trade shuffled the human geography of the coast, as Aboriginal groups vied for regions with as-yet-untapped populations of sea otters or with the strategic potential to support a lucrative position as middlemen in the trade.[20]

The maritime fur trade was traditionally portrayed by historians as a kind of "looting," in which Aboriginal people were cheated out of their furs and art objects, receiving beads and trinkets in return. More recent scholarship has called this portrayal into question. The journals of the maritime traders often praised Aboriginal traders for their skill at bargaining and their ability to get the better end of a deal, a lesson that some of the newcomers learned to their own cost. That the indigenous people should have such skills is to be expected. The networks of trade long predated the arrival of the newcomers, connecting peoples along the coast from what is now Alaska to California and reaching far inland everywhere the barrier of the coastal mountain ranges was breached. According to historian James R. Gibson, the products of Aboriginal trade included:

> mountain-goat hair "blankets" (ceremonial robes), ermine skins, copper plates, and spruceroot baskets from the Tlingits; dugout cedar canoes from the Haidas; mountain-goat horn spoons, raven rattles, dance headdresses, and oolachen ... and their oil (*ssak*, or shrowton) from the Tsimshians; mountain-goat hair and horn from the Bella Coolas, the best hunters on the coast of that animal; yellow cedarbark robes and wooden utensils from the Kwakiutls; dugout cedar canoes, shark's teeth, and dentalia shells (*Dentalium Indianorum*, or *pretiosum*) from the Nootkas; dog-hair blankets and slaves from the Coast Salishes; elk hides and slaves from the Chinooks; and tobacco, woodpecker scalps, and Monterey (abalone) "ear shells" (*Haliotis cracherodii*) from the Yuroks.[21]

And those were merely some of the products traded up and down the coast. From the interior came obsidian; furs; moose and deer hide; dried soapberries, blueberries, and Saskatoon berries; amber and jet; groundhog skin blankets; jade adze blades and stone clubs; grizzly bear claws and skin; buffalo robes; rabbit-skin robes; **camas;** and baskets. These were traded in return for coastal products like dried salmon; sea lion whiskers, teeth, meat, and skins; dried seaweed; dried and smoked shellfish; dried seal meat; dried halibut and cod; tobacco; clubs made from the jaw of the killer whale; armour; shell tools for woodworking; wood carvings; and the ubiquitous grease of the **oolichan.** To this trade, the newcomers brought iron chisels, guns, powder, ball and shot, blankets, alcohol and tobacco, copper and brass kettles and pots, cloth, sheets of copper, brass wire, knives, buttons, rice and molasses, and even feather caps and cloaks from Hawaii. The trade changed constantly according to the vagaries of supply and demand and of fashion, too. There is evidence that many of the Aboriginal art objects and artifacts that the newcomers took home with them were created specifically for the trade, like masks of labret-wearing women, wooden canoe models, and woven imitations of sailor's caps.[22]

Another way the newcomers changed the Aboriginal trade networks was by introducing viral diseases such as smallpox, measles, influenza, and mumps, diseases that require concentrated populations of hundreds of thousands of people in order to become **endemic.** With fewer people, the diseases died out until they were reintroduced from a reservoir elsewhere, at which point they spread epidemically. This is not to say that the area that is now British Columbia was a disease-free paradise before the coming of non-Aboriginal traders. It is clear to epidemiologists that human beings brought many ailments with them to the New World when they arrived after the last glaciation. Indigenous people suffered from food poisoning, fungal diseases, intestinal parasites, gastroenteritis, hepatitis and encephalitis, tuberculosis, and infections caused by **treponemal spirochetes.** But the long separation of the Old and New Worlds meant that the crowd diseases, which had become commonplace in Eurasia and Africa, were particularly lethal when introduced to indigenous American populations. These diseases often spread much faster than their non-Aboriginal hosts. In northwestern North America, there is some archaeological evidence that is consistent with the occurrence of a smallpox epidemic in the 1520s that might have caused a significant decline in the Aboriginal populations of the middle Columbia River, although other explanations are possible. In the late 1700s, there is ample contemporary documentation of smallpox outbreaks along the coast from Sitka, in the panhandle of

present-day Alaska, to what is now Washington state, and inland throughout the Columbia River basin.[23]

On 6 July 1793, Mackenzie and his men encountered a party of Aboriginal people eating "green berries and dried fish," who "had a very sickly
appearance, which might have been the consequence of disease, or that
indolence which is so natural to them, or both." The people may indeed
have been recovering from some illness. As to the charge of indolence, it
is possible that Mackenzie was still irritated by his guides' unwillingness
to bear loads for him. The fur traders often accused Aboriginal people of
being indolent. The word was, as Elizabeth Vibert explains, "freighted
with cultural meaning ... often framed in terms of inherited ideas about
the moral propriety of hard work," but was also often used to signal the
preference that some Aboriginal groups had for fishing over hunting. The
same day that Mackenzie described the Aboriginal people as indolent, he
also noted, apparently without seeing the irony, that "age seemed to be an
object of great veneration among these people, for they carried an old
woman by turns on their backs who was quite blind and infirm, from the
very advanced period of her life."[24]

Palimpsests

In the area where Mackenzie was on 6 July 1793, there is now a BC Forest
Service campground near the Blackwater Bridge. Visitors can park in a
convenient parking lot and follow well-flagged walking trails along the
sixty-metre-deep canyon to a picnic spot. The campsite doesn't provide
running water or electricity, but there are basic sanitary facilities, picnic
tables, and fire rings. Those who prefer to fish or try their hand at rafting
may do so. The Forest Service guide suggests that hikers should visit the
Alexander Mackenzie Heritage Trail, which begins two kilometres north
of the campsite, describing it as "a challenging hike for experienced hikers, and often done on horseback because it is so long. But you can certainly enjoy hiking the first stretch, and getting a taste of Canada's rich
history as you imagine Mackenzie and his aboriginal guides forging this
great landscape." The authors of the guide surely intended the word "forging" to be taken in the sense of creating something new or pressing ahead
in the face of difficulties, but its alternate reading, which suggests counter-
feiting, invention, or deception, will turn out to be particularly apposite.[25]

The landscape near the trail head is layered with traces of the years
between Mackenzie's time and our own. Crossing beneath the logging and

forest service roads of the late twentieth century are the older wagon roads. One, built by the Russian-born trader Paul Krestenuk in the 1920s, runs to the west and was used to haul goods to interior trading posts by wagon in the summer and by sleigh in wintertime. It intersects with a north-south wagon road that was built in 1910 to connect Quesnel and Prince George. When the Flygares were searching for Mackenzie's route in the 1980s, they used a 1909 map entitled "Traverse of the Cluskus Lake Trail" and found one of the square axe-hewn mileposts from that survey. A decade or two before the wagon roads were built, this spot saw even more activity. The Dominion Telegraph line was pushed through here in 1898 on its way north to Atlin and eventually the Yukon. It provided news of the Klondike gold rush to the outside world when the circuit was completed in September 1901. The telegraph trail itself was used by some of the people on their way to the goldfields, including Norman Lee on his Klondike cattle drive. He described it as "cut out eight feet wide and as straight as an arrow for miles." When the cowboys reached the telegraph trail, Lee wrote that they were passed by one or more pack trains an hour and were "surprised to see the crowds of Pilgrims flocking north." "They were evidently prepared for war," he wryly noted, "as hardly a man passed but was hung all over with six shooters and bowie knives."[26]

A quarter of a century before the Klondike gold rush, this was also a crossroads of sorts. George Dawson camped here at the end of September 1875. The Canadian Pacific Railway survey was working in the area, and Dawson moved from one of its camps to another, accompanied by a packer and an Aboriginal guide named Fanny. Along the way he met up with Aboriginal families who were camping nearby, dined with survey personnel, and tried his hand at fishing. The trails he followed were in use, although overgrown in places. In one spot, his "mule overturned & mired in getting up the river bank ... but no serious consequences." Dawson camped in the same spot the following year and once again was surrounded by activity. The BC surveyor Edgar Dewdney was camped nearby. Pack trains were going to and from Quesnel. Dawson found an Aboriginal man trapping who "explained the country to [him]" but was reluctant to act as his guide. He noted in his journal that Mackenzie had camped in the same area that he was exploring. A decade before Dawson and the railway surveyors arrived, the Collins Overland Telegraph Company pushed the first telegraph line through this spot in an attempt to connect North America to Europe via the Bering Strait and Siberia. The Collins men managed to lay 650 kilometres of cable before news of a successful trans-Atlantic link caused the project to be abandoned in 1866.[27]

In some places, these traces of the past have been effaced by later activities, like clear-cutting and road building. But where the earlier routes can be discerned, they are now protected as heritage sites. The significance of such protection is that it signals a judgment of relative value: the fact that this place was used in a certain way in the past trumps any potential use in the present, and, for the time being at least, the place is protected from future use, too. Typically, such protection is highly contested when it is conferred and subject to repeated attack thereafter. For now, parts of the Dominion and Collins telegraph trails are protected. The Alexander Mackenzie Heritage Trail is protected. In places on the Mackenzie trail, there are wooden guardrails to prevent hikers from going off the path and damaging an even older trail system, the so-called moccasin trails that Mackenzie probably really followed. These trails are protected too. In their trail guide, Woodworth and Flygare wrote that "it is a startling experience on the sandy pine needled forest floor to see a gentle indentation, 2 to 3 inches deep and 16 to 24 inches wide snaking along through windfalls, occasionally butting into a hundred year old tree trunk and emerging intact on the other side, often crisscrossed with game trails and at times buried in timber." These older trails tend to follow the **esker**, gravel banks that determined the river's course, and pass through grassy areas where depressions frequently mark the locations of former settlements overlooking the river bottom.[28]

It is not always possible to tell where Mackenzie was at various points along his route, but some of his landmarks are easily recognized today. On 8 July, Mackenzie wrote: "In this part of our journey we were surprised with the appearance of several regular basons [basins], some of them furnished with water, and the others empty; their slope from the edge to the bottom formed an angle of about forty-five degrees, and their perpendicular depth was about twelve feet. Those that contained water, discovered gravel near their edges, while the empty ones were covered with grass and herbs, among which we discovered mustard and mint." Mackenzie's "basons" are probably the glacial kettles at the foot of Titetown Lake, which were formed when isolated blocks of ice left by the retreating ice sheet melted. Two of these are to the north of the wagon road, and two are to the south. In places where Mackenzie's exact route could not be determined, the Alexander Mackenzie Heritage Trail tends to follow the old wagon roads, which for the convenience of their users passed directly through Aboriginal reserves and alongside ranch houses. Now that the wagon road has become a heritage trail, the trail guides remind hikers and horseback riders to respect the privacy and property of landowners along the route. In

the mid-1970s, a Parks Canada team estimated that the permanent population of the trail between its head near the Blackwater Bridge and the spot
where it entered the Coast Mountain range in Tweedsmuir Park was about
thirty people. In the summer, the itinerant population was much higher.
Many of the ranches along the way were changing with the times and
"turn[ing] their bunkhouses into tourist accommodations."[29]

"You Are Leaving Civilization"

... at least that's what it says in the Woodworth and Flygare guide when
you hit 82.68 kilometres from the head of the trail. The guide warns that
"it was no picnic for Alexander Mackenzie and you may well share his sen-
timents." When Mackenzie travelled through here, he and his men were
feeling the effects of short rations. On 8 July 1793, he wrote that they "now
proceeded along a very uneven country, the upper parts of which were
covered with poplars, a little under-wood, and plenty of grass: the inter-
vening vallies were watered with rivulets. From these circumstances, and
the general appearance of vegetation, I could not account for the apparent absence of animals of every kind." The following day, still finding the
country "destitute of game," Mackenzie sent off his Aboriginal guides and
all but two of his men, then cached another bag of pemmican by burying
it under the ashes of their fire to hide the disturbed ground from human eyes
and the scent of his men from non-human scavengers. That day his party
was able to kill two eagles and three grouse and to catch a few small fish.[30]

One of the management plans for the Alexander Mackenzie Heritage
Trail states that "part of the unique provincial and national significance of
the trail is the opportunity to re-live the travels of natives and early adven-
turers in an environment much the same as it was when they travelled this
forest trail." Twenty-first-century hikers may even see some of the same
kinds of animals that lived in the region when Mackenzie was there. The
fauna is characteristic of an intermediate zone between the boreal forests
to the north and the warm, dry forests and grasslands to the south. Moose
are well-adapted to the region's severe winters, as are small mammals like
the snowshoe hare, which can travel on top of the snow, and the deer
mouse, which can burrow into it. The sub-boreal forests provide habitat
and prey for black bears, wolves, lynxes, fishers, martens, and ermine.
Along the rivers and streams, one can see beaver dams; occasionally they
flood the trail. But today's traveller is much more likely to encounter
mammals that were not there in Mackenzie's time: namely, the ubiquitous

domestic cattle and horses that graze in the meadows along the trail and on the forest floor.[31]

The presence of recently introduced species may bother a sensitive hiker who is trying to experience what Mackenzie experienced in this place, but they probably won't be nearly as distracting as the constant signs of recent human presence. At 95.42 kilometres, there is an old truck wreck. At 97.29 kilometres, there is a gate built by a volunteer who used to aid travellers by using his radio phone to call bush pilots or medivac choppers, driving canoeists around falls in his jeep, and serving pie and coffee. He moved away in the 1980s. Just a few kilometres farther along the trail is the Crystal Springs campsite (109.84 km), which advertises the "Best Darn Water in the Whole Damn Country." Carry on about the same distance (122.42 km) and you come to a hay meadow, barn, and the remains of a bridge for the wagon road. Now it is just a bit farther down the trail to the Euchiniko Lakes Ranch (125 km), a big-game and fishing camp with a radio phone and cabins with beds, woodstoves, and cooking utensils. At 134.12 kilometres, an old sign tells you that you are on the "Mackenzie Grease Trail." There is an old corral at 135 kilometres.[32]

For a person who is trying to follow in Mackenzie's footsteps and re-enact his voyage of discovery, these constant reminders of past human activity might make the experience seem disappointingly unlike Mackenzie's. But that isn't the case. From his journals it is clear that Mackenzie was constantly encountering the signs of a fully inhabited world, not an empty one. On 8 July 1793, Mackenzie wrote that his guide, cheerful but "not altogether so intelligible as his predecessors in [their] service," told him that he was going to meet nine members of a group of Carrier people who lived on the north side of the West Road River. A day later, Mackenzie's party came to a spot where the water narrowed. It was evidently a well-used ford, because they found a small raft there, which they used to cross the water the next day. Continuing, they soon came to "two houses that occupied a most delightful situation, and as they contained their necessary furniture, it seemed probable that their owners intended shortly to return. Near them were several graves or tombs, to which the natives are particularly attentive, and never suffer any herbage to grow upon them." Half an hour farther down the trail, Mackenzie and his men came to two huts that were occupied by people who were fishing. There were thirteen men there, "cleanly, healthy, and agreeable in their appearance." Mackenzie's guide had "secure[d] a good reception" for him, and he learned from them that they all had been to the coast, although they disagreed on the length of time the journey took. The guide and one of

Mackenzie's interpreters took him to visit some more huts a mile away. He was given some boiled trout, about which he wrote that "the fish would have been excellent if it had not tasted of the kettle, which was made of the bark of the white spruce, and of the dried grass with which it was boiled." Mackenzie's guide was going no farther along the trail, so Mackenzie engaged two of his new hosts to lead him on to the west, giving some "trifles" to their wives and children. Returning to his men, Mackenzie and the guides took a different route, and he saw two more buildings and some structures "about fifteen feet from the ground, which appeared to [him] to be intended as magazines for winter provisions."[33]

That night Mackenzie was bothered first by flies and then by rain; the next morning they had to make their way through a "morass." The country that they were crossing "had been laid waste by fire, and the fallen trees added to the pain and perplexity of [their] way." A hiker travelling through the same area today will see the signs of more recent forest fires. Fire, often started by lightning and occasionally by people, plays a cyclical and crucial role in the ecology of the region. Afterwards, the burnt ground is colonized by fireweed and shrubs like willows and thimbleberry. These plants are succeeded by deciduous trees that can sprout from the base of the trunk, like birch, or from underground roots, like aspen. The deciduous forest may persist for a long while, but it cannot remain indefinitely because lodgepole pine seedlings are already growing on the forest floor. This is because the lodgepole pine is adapted to this fire regime; its cones open when they are heated and drop the seeds that will eventually grow into the next coniferous stand, succeeding the deciduous trees. As this coniferous stand ages, its canopy thins naturally, providing habitats for other kinds of vegetation, like pinegrass, kinnikinnick, and lichens. Since fires occur frequently, the forest is a mosaic of patches of different age. As a result, it is also a mosaic of habitats, and Aboriginal people regularly used fire as a tool to create habitats for the plant and animal species that they wanted to harvest. Different patterns of burning were used to create different landscapes – for example, to make meadows and open forests or to clear traplines and trails. Burning created places for ungulates to browse and forage, increased the production of berries and roots, and decreased the likelihood of unexpected fires near settlements. The practice of indigenous burning is well-documented throughout northwestern North America, although there is currently no specific information about its use in what is now the interior of British Columbia.[34]

It is not clear whether the fire that impeded Mackenzie's progress on 11 July 1793 was intentionally set, but he saw obvious signs of human activity along the trail for the next few days, including many recent tracks made by other people. Signs of human activity are ubiquitous along the same stretch of the trail today. At 171.94 kilometres, "E.B. and J.D." memorialized their union by carving their initials into a tree. Nearby is the Mackenzie Trail Lodge airstrip (175 km), which caters to fly-in fishermen in the summer. On a tree near the airstrip are more signs: "Anahim Lake BC, 100 mi around the mountain. Anahim Lake BC, 60 miles cross the mountain. Bella Coola BC, 191 miles." It is not much farther along the trail to the Pan Phillips Fishing Resort at 192 kilometres. The resort features a radio phone, boats, cabins, and, luxury of luxuries, toilets and running water. There is also another airstrip with signs that say "Pan Phillips *International Air Port*, World Flights Arranged!" and "Dogpatch Delivery, Weekly Service, Honeymoon Trips Arranged." Despite the exaggeration of the signs, it is possible to arrange flights to a number of places, not only to locations with bush airstrips, but also, via float plane, to many of the lakes. From a float plane, the Alexander Mackenzie Heritage Trail may look like "nature's time machine"; from the ground, however, "one memory of civilization that will stay with you ... is the regular buzz of floatplanes overhead."[35]

The Pan Phillips Fishing Resort was a natural outgrowth of a ranching venture. Working on a Wyoming ranch in the mid-1930s, Richmond Hobson came home late one night from a poker game to find Floyd (Panhandle) Phillips sitting on the bunkhouse floor amidst maps and papers. Phillips called Hobson over and said, "This detail map here has a big blank space on it." Hobson asked him if it was a map to a gold mine. "Those maps show all there is known of the south tip of a country as big as Wyoming with Montana throwed in," Phillips told him. "There's reports of a grass country in there some place that reaches as far as the eye can see. Yeah – that's my gold mine. Grass! Free grass reachin' north into unknown country. Land – lots of it – untouched – just waitin' for hungry cows, and some buckaroos that can ride and have guts enough to put her over." (At least that's how the conversation went in the novelistic account that Hobson published fifteen years later.) Phillips and Hobson headed north to create a Texas-style ranch along the Blackwater River.[36]

Unlike the plateau farther south, however, most of the Blackwater drainage is marginal for cattle ranching. The main problem that every Chilcotin rancher faces is providing enough food to carry the livestock through the portion of winter when they can't forage. The greatest cost incurred in cattle ranching is thus the cost of putting up hay for winter feeding. Near the Gang Ranch, which is almost 200 kilometres south, the winter feeding period is about a month. Near the Alexander Mackenzie

Heritage Trail, it can be about six months. When demand for beef falls, the ranches with longer winter feeding periods have to turn to other sources of income, like logging or tourism, or go out of business. Blank spots on the map notwithstanding, Hobson and Phillips soon found themselves with very marginal ranch land and had to look for supplementary sources of income. Pan Phillips was a tireless supporter of the Alexander Mackenzie Heritage Trail, campaigning for it right up until his death in 1983. A visit to the aging sod- and shake-roof structures of his Home Ranch, eight kilometres north of the trail, is now a popular side trip for hikers interested in the history of the area's ranches.[37]

To Mackenzie's Rock

Past the Pan Phillips Fishing Resort, between 197 and 199 kilometres, today's hiker comes across "cat tracks" meandering through the woods, alongside trails of wreckage left by a Caterpillar tractor with a bulldozer front end and a tanklike track. Woodworth and Flygare note that "as a bushwhacking tool ... it's a great but messy way to go. By standing on the cab you can almost see forever." From the tracks it can't be determined whether the operator was headed someplace in particular, just bulldozing for the fun of it, or lost. At this point, the trail guide signals bewilderment – in the archaic sense of the word: feeling lost in the wilderness – by showing a photograph of Hälle Flygare and an Aboriginal man looking at a map. The caption reads, "Peter Alexis shows Halle Flygare the way on the Upper Blackwater – just as Peter's ancestors showed Mackenzie."[38]

Oddly enough, Mackenzie seems to have become somewhat lost near this spot, too, or at least to have taken a route that has puzzled everyone who has subsequently tried to follow his track. On 12 July 1793, Mackenzie wrote that his guides had threatened to leave his party and he had given them gifts so they would remain with him until he could secure the services of new guides. From his description, it sounds like he had just passed Tsetzi Lake and the main Aboriginal trail leading to Bella Coola via Anahim Lake and the Hotnarko, Atnarko, and Bella Coola rivers. It is possible that his guides weren't threatening to leave him but, rather, were trying to point out that he was missing the sensible way to the coast. For whatever reason, Mackenzie passed by the main trail south and carried on to the west toward Ulgako Creek and Eliguk Lake. That evening he camped without his local guides and had to reassure his men that they "could not be at a great distance from the sea, and that there were but few natives to pass, till [they] should arrive among those, who being accustomed to visit the sea coast, and, having seen white people, would be disposed to treat [them] with kindness." Mackenzie probably felt less confident about his "dubious journey" than he let on. The following day he used somewhat more drastic measures to obtain the aid of new guides. Coming to a house on Ulgako Creek in the early morning, he went right up to it without warning, whereupon "the women and children uttered the most horrid shrieks, and the only man who appeared to be with them, escaped out of a back door." Mackenzie was able to detain the women and children. "It is impossible to describe the distress and alarm of these poor people, who believing that they were attacked by enemies, expected an immediate massacre." Eventually Mackenzie was able to calm his captives enough that his interpreters could speak with them. He learned that most of the Aboriginal group had left three days earlier on a trading journey. He told the women that he wished "that the man might be induced to return, and conduct [Mackenzie and his men] in the road to the sea." Eventually he was able to gain not only the services of the man, but also those of his father and brother. That evening, Mackenzie and his men "retired to rest, with sensations very different from those with which [they] had risen in the morning."[39]

The following day, Mackenzie's party travelled past Eliguk Lake and crossed Ulgako Creek before heading over a low mountain to Gatcho Lake. From the mountain he could see "a considerable river" (now known as the Dean) to the southeast. Although he did not know it, he was standing on a divide that separates the drainages of three rivers: the West Road, flowing east to the Fraser; the Nechako, flowing northeast to the Fraser; and the Dean, flowing west to the Pacific. That evening, he crossed the Dean River and, once again, missed two main routes to the coast. One obvious trail led west, directly downriver. The other went upriver to Anahim Lake and from there to the sea. Instead of taking either of these trails, Mackenzie's party went due south toward the mountains. On 15 July they met up with another group of interior Aboriginal people heading to the coast to trade. Mackenzie found these people very agreeable, but they were travelling too slowly for him and ultimately decided to go in a direction that Mackenzie thought was too different from his own, i.e., they decided to follow the Dean River downstream. Thinking that he was determined to cross the mountains, they pointed a pass out to him and then parted company.[40]

On 17 July 1793, Mackenzie and his men climbed a mountain and found themselves surrounded by snow that had drifted into the pass. It was so compact that they didn't sink into it, but they did see the tracks of a herd of caribou, and the Aboriginal guides and MacKenzie's hunters went in pursuit. The wind picked up "into a tempest," and it began to snow, hail, and rain. Mackenzie – who four years earlier had made a three-thousand-mile canoe voyage from Lake Athabasca to the Arctic Ocean and back – called the weather "as distressing as any [he] had ever experienced," and the men took what shelter they could on the leeward side of a huge rock. The hunters did succeed in killing one doe, which the men insisted on taking with them, even though Mackenzie wanted to cache half of the meat. They continued their march toward a mountain that Mackenzie described as "stupendous" and which is now known by that name. As they trudged forward, Stupendous Mountain "appeared to withdraw." Eventually, they reached the edge of the Bella Coola gorge, a series of timbered precipices stepping a thousand metres down to the river. For the hiker intent on re-enacting Mackenzie's voyage, the trip through what is now known as Mackenzie's Pass is the most dangerous part. To guide hikers there are a series of cairns, piles of rock 1 metre tall with a 2.3-metre wooden pole sticking out of the top of each, but the sight of these can be obscured by bad weather. The last radio phone on the westward route is almost ninety kilometres back up the trail. There is no way to go but forward, steadily descending for fifteen kilometres after the pass. At that point there is a junction of three trails, and it is not known which Mackenzie used to reach the Bella Coola valley.[41]

After he descended into the valley, Mackenzie was near the ocean. The alder and cedar trees were the largest he had ever seen. The berries were ripe, and he and his men were "sensible of an entire change in the climate." He was given a warm reception at an Aboriginal village that evening, which he later named "Friendly Village." Over the course of the next three days, Mackenzie's party made its way downstream. On 20 July, he wrote that "at about eight [they] got out of the river, which discharges itself by various channels into an arm of the sea. The tide was out, and had left a large space covered with sea-weed. The surrounding hills were involved in fog." The men saw sea otters, porpoises, eagles, gulls, and ducks. They explored the coast for a few days, frequently meeting Aboriginal groups, and then prepared to return. In his journal, Mackenzie wrote: "I now mixed up some vermilion in melted grease, and inscribed, in large characters, on the South-East face of the rock on which we slept last night, this brief memorial – 'Alexander Mackenzie, from Canada, by land, the twenty-second of July, one thousand seven hundred and ninety-three.'"[42]

"A Mari usque ad Mare"

In the summer of 1923, Richard Preston Bishop of the BC Department of Lands, who was surveying in the vicinity of Bella Coola, was asked to try to locate Mackenzie's Rock. Its position had been unknown since the last recorded sighting of it in 1836, when Mackenzie's vermilion marking was described as "partly decipherable." There were a number of factors that made Bishop's relocation of the rock a matter of inference. For one thing, given the equipment at his disposal and the constraints under which he was working, the latitude that Mackenzie gave for the rock's position was estimated to be accurate to about a mile and a half north or south. Bishop was searching for the proverbial needle in a haystack, trying to locate a rock along a three-mile stretch of rocky shore. For another thing, there were at least three discrepancies between the text of Mackenzie's *Voyage* and the footnotes that he added later. In one place, the most likely course is four miles long, but Mackenzie gave the distance as a quarter mile. In another place, a piece of land that is identified as an island, and that looks like one from the sea, is actually a peninsula. The final discrepancy, and the most troubling, is that the distance along the shore to the location of the rock given by Mackenzie is quite a bit less than the distance to the rock that Bishop decided was the most likely candidate. Bishop explained this difference by suggesting that Mackenzie forgot to record one of his courses. Having identified what he thought was the rock, Bishop proceeded to check it against the other constraints that were known from Mackenzie's journal. The rock had to be near an abandoned Aboriginal village, have a sheer face on the southeast side, be easily defended, have a southerly exposure of at least three miles, and be about three miles southwest of a cove. Bishop's candidate fit the bill, and his identification was accepted by the provincial Department of Lands, the BC Historical Association, and the Canadian Historic Sites and Monuments Board.[43]

A more permanent version of Mackenzie's message was chiselled into the face of the rock that Bishop identified. On 26 August 1927, the Canadian government unveiled a 40-foot obelisk above the rock and an inscribed plaque that reads: "This rock is the western terminus of the first journey across the continent of North America. It was made by Alexander Mackenzie of the North West Company, who, with his nine companions, arrived at this spot on the 21st July, 1793. Mackenzie, by observations, ascertained his position, spent the night here, and, after writing on the southeast face the words now cut therein, retraced his course to Lake Athabasca. This transcontinental journey preceded by more than ten years that of Lewis and Clark." On the occasion, the prime minister, William Lyon Mackenzie King, sent a letter praising Mackenzie's "courage, devotion and endurance" and said that the explorer held "an exalted place in world history."[44]

When John Woodworth began campaigning for the creation of the Alexander Mackenzie Heritage Trail as the bicentennial of the voyage approached, he invoked Mackenzie's Rock as a symbol of Canadian history and national identity. Canadians of his generation had grown up with photographs of the rock, the 1927 version, in their history textbooks and had dutifully memorized the inscription. Woodworth also cited another symbol that had been created in the aftermath of the Great War: the Canadian coat of arms. Proclaimed by King George V in November 1921, its Latin motto read "A mari usque ad mare," meaning "from sea to sea." Woodworth held up Mackenzie's voyage as a defining moment in the creation of a country that stretched across the continent, and he felt that by commemorating Mackenzie's accomplishments, he could further the cause of Canadian unity.[45]

In the political climate of the early 1990s, Canada's unity was very much in question. The governing party of Quebec, the Parti Québécois, had originally come to power in 1976 on a platform that included a promise to negotiate the province's independence from Canada. A 1980 referendum on the question of separation was rejected by 60 percent of the province's voters, and the party was defeated five years later. Although the Canadian constitution was repatriated from Britain in 1982, it was done without the support of the province of Quebec. Subsequent attempts to resolve constitutional problems through the Meech Lake Accord (1987) and the Charlottetown Accord (1992) failed to strike a balance that separatists and federalists could agree on. The Parti Québécois returned to power in 1994 and again sponsored a separatist referendum. In parts of Canada that were predominately anglophone, like BC, there was a sense that the future of the country lay in the hands of the separatists. Popular federalist sentiment found a variety of outlets, from active campaigning to the spread of bumper stickers reading "My Canada includes Quebec/Mon Canada inclut le Québec." Woodworth's association can be seen as one expression of this feeling. Renamed the Alexander Mackenzie Voyageur Route Association and dedicated to "the cause of Canadian unity," the group began by petitioning each of the six provinces, from Quebec west to BC, to formally proclaim the existence of a Mackenzie heritage trail within their own borders. Once that was accomplished, the group's members turned to the federal government for recognition of the trail as a whole. On Heritage Day in 1995, Prime Minister Jean Chrétien (himself a Québécois but opposed to separation) issued an official federal proclamation confirming the existence of a "sea to sea" route that Canadians should celebrate and protect. Events in Quebec, however, gathered momentum. In June 1995, the Parti Québécois put forward a draft bill on sovereignty, and in September it set a referendum date for the end of the following month. People on both sides followed the vote anxiously. On 31 October, a record 93.5 percent of Quebec voters turned out, and the bill was defeated by a slim 1.2 percent margin, 50.6 to 49.4 percent. It is impossible to say whether the commemoration of Alexander Mackenzie played any significant role in the defeat of the referendum. In the fall of 1995, however, John Woodworth received the country's highest award for heritage conservation. "You have to know which doors to knock on," he said. "If you've got a good cause and a feasible kind of thing, then keep phoning and phoning."[46]

The efforts of John Woodworth and his colleagues to create the Alexander Mackenzie Heritage Trail united people in different parts of the country in a particular way. The trail was a static geographic entity that could be represented on maps as a line connecting the provinces from sea to sea – a line that crucially included Quebec. But the creation of the trail also made possible a different kind of national unification, a more dynamic and performative one. Commemorators could now re-enact Mackenzie's voyage by travelling along the trail in his footsteps. By crossing the Great Divide, they would be symbolically tying the country together. Many of these re-enactments were timed to coincide with the bicentennial of Mackenzie's voyage, and none was more ambitious than the one mounted by Lakehead University in Ontario. A group of forty students from the School of Outdoor Recreation, Parks and Tourism spent four summers paddling 15,840 kilometres in a $5 million re-enactment of Mackenzie's expeditions. They were supported both by the Alexander Mackenzie Trail Association, for whom they were marking the route, and by the One Step Beyond Adventure Group, whose mission was to get Canadians to adopt the adventuresome spirit of the pioneers. The students trained in canoes in the Olympic pool at their university. En route, they camped outdoors – "No showers, no Holiday Inns" – and dressed in period costumes to do an educational "fur-trade road show" at nearby schools. They were accompanied by a coast guard boat and a supply van. During the first two years, they put on historical pageants ("a lively half-hour dramatic presentation with much audience participation") in various Canadian communities and then allowed the public to tour their encampment and look at various "authentic artifacts" from the fur trade. Over the next three years they paddled from Montreal to Winnipeg (1991), Winnipeg to Peace River (1992), and Peace River to Bella Coola (1993), timing their arrival at the Pacific to coincide with the two-hundredth anniversary of Mackenzie's arrival there.[47]

So Much for the Oolichan Festival

The British Columbia and federal governments pledged more than a million dollars to support the Lakehead student expedition and other Mackenzie bicentennial celebrations, drawing criticism from politicians on the left. Ray Skelly, for example, an NDP MP from British Columbia, objected in a speech to the House of Commons on the grounds that Mackenzie and his followers had stolen Aboriginal land, resources, and artifacts and destroyed Aboriginal society. "What is there to celebrate in genocide?" he asked. This, in turn, raised the ire of people with a more conservative perspective on the past, such as Pierre Berton, one of Canada's leading popular historians. "Of course, it is proper that history record the errors, stupidities and cruelties of the past, as well as its triumphs," Berton wrote, "Mackenzie's remarkable feat, no matter what the implications, deserves to be remembered and celebrated. I, for one, propose to help celebrate it. I certainly have no intention of letting Ray Skelly lay a guilt trip on me." But Skelly's objection was a portent of those to come.[48]

At the terminus of Mackenzie's route, the town of Bella Coola was planning a five-day Oolichan Festival to welcome the Lakehead student expedition and other bicentennial celebrants. Some of the celebrations bore a more tenuous connection to Mackenzie's accomplishments than others. The Rich Hobson Frontier Cattle Drive re-enactment, for example, involved 220 people who had each paid $650 to drive a herd of cattle in a big circle that transected the heritage trail. Timed to coincide with the Mackenzie celebrations, the cattle drive was really intended to honour the pioneering accomplishments of Rich Hobson and Pan Phillips. It included a pageant of their life and times, "campfire cowboy serenades and poetry," and rodeos and bronco-busting. The centrepiece of the Oolichan Festival was intended to be the overland arrival of the Lakehead students.[49]

The student expedition ran into trouble, however, when it reached Alexandria, the place where Mackenzie had his moment of indecision before deciding to turn west. There, student brigade organizers were told by several Aboriginal bands that the "second coming of Mackenzie [was] not welcome." This conflation of Mackenzie and Christ encapsulated a number of grievances that interior Aboriginal people had against non-Aboriginal colonists. For one thing, it invoked the legacy of the Durieu system, in which Catholic missionaries had created Aboriginal states under the hierarchical authority of the bishop, local missionary, chiefs, watchmen, and policemen, and the subsequent incarceration of Aboriginal children in residential schools, often against the will of their families. The conflation also signalled an awareness that the temporal frame of reference that had come to be used in the Chilcotin after Mackenzie's voyage marked time with respect to the incarnation of a deity on the other side of the world, rather than to the actions of Dog-Husband or one of the other transformers in myth time. And it reflected the irony that the place of Mackenzie's indecision should come to be named Alexandria in his honour and that the hundred-odd Tsilhqot'in who lived there were known as the Alexandria band. For three weeks, the students waited uncertainly for a resolution of the situation, going on day hikes to pass the time. Eventually the overland portion of their journey was cancelled, and they climbed into vans to make the trip on Highway 20 instead. Upon reaching sea level, they were again able to put their canoes in the water for the final stretch of the voyage to Mackenzie's Rock.[50]

The celebrations in Bella Coola failed to live up to the expectations of many of the participants, a sadly familiar outcome in the history of Canadian commemoration. Although the students were welcomed by the Nuxalk people, there was still concern that other First Nations might block the ceremonies. Andy Siwallace, a Nuxalk hereditary chief, tied an eagle feather in the hair of Dwayne Smith, the young man who played Mackenzie on the voyage, and told him, "You are a welcome sight. You followed in Mackenzie's footsteps from beginning to end, and we are proud of you for doing this. While you are here, you will be living in peace with us." Another hereditary chief told the students, "There are always problems with history and there are always problems with our own people, too. But there's nothing we can't do if we talk together ... because times change. We speak from our hearts, not from our mouths. Be yourselves ... and stand firm in what you believe."

Nevertheless, the organizers decided that it might insult the Aboriginal elders if the students were to sing "O Canada" at Mackenzie's Rock and tried to cancel that part of the performance. On hearing the news, a local canoeist started screaming at them: "What in the hell is this country coming to if we can't even sing our national anthem at an historic event like this? What have these kids come all this way for?" In the end, some of the students sang the anthem quietly and some didn't and the singing was drowned out by the noise of the outboard motors on the boats ferrying

most of the celebrants back to shore. Reflecting on the experience, Dwayne
Smith concluded that "Mackenzie had a vision 200 years ago as to what
he thought this country could be like, and we are supporting that vision
today of a commitment among the various cultures which make up this
country."[51]

The accomplishments of other celebrants at the Oolichan Festival were
overlooked altogether. A group of Alberta teenagers who had hiked the overland trail from Alexandria were forgotten, as were descendants of Mackenzie who had come over from Scotland, and the captain and crew of the
HMCS *Mackenzie,* a Royal Canadian Navy vessel making its last voyage
ever. Most poignant of all, perhaps, was an eighty-three-year-old Scot who
had retraced Mackenzie's steps by himself over the previous four years,
faced down storms and whitewater, been bitten and mugged, and ended
up standing on the sidelines holding his Scottish terrier.[52]

No federal politicians attended the Oolichan Festival in Bella Coola,
even though it was an election year. Despite a show of support for the celebrations in the provincial Legislative Assembly in Victoria, and funding
from both the provincial and federal governments, the commitment from
the country's politicians seemed lukewarm and ambivalent. The same uncertainty had been seen in the previous year's re-enactments and celebrations of George Vancouver's exploration of the BC coast. Mike Harcourt,
the NDP premier, said that the province had no reason to celebrate the
bicentennial of Vancouver's arrival, but his government helped to sponsor
a "Wake of the Explorers" re-enactment, and government staff members
occupied the captain's chairs of boats in the festival. One reason for the
mixed signals was that the Columbian Quincentennial of 1992 had been
the occasion of such ideological conflict that no one wanted to commit
themselves too strongly to either side of what might become a polarized
debate between supporters of the First Nations and apologists for colonization. But there were deeper questions of Canadian national identity at
stake, and uncertainties about the historical role of Mackenzie's voyage
brought a paradox into sharp relief.[53]

THE SUSPECT TERRAIN OF THE CULTURAL MOSAIC

The English version of the national anthem celebrates Canada as "our
home and native land," but in a nation created primarily by immigrant
settlers and their descendents, it has always been difficult for Canadians to
draw a line between natives and newcomers. When the Historic Sites and

Monuments Board was created in 1919, it held a nationwide competition to determine the best design for a standard tablet to be placed on monuments such as the one at Mackenzie's Rock. The winning design was created by a sculptor named Major Ernest Forbery and made much use of botanical emblems. The border consisted of pine cones and needles to symbolize the northern climate. Maple leaves below a crown signified Canada, a British dominion and member of the Empire. Other plants signified the "principal races from which Canadians are descended": the rose (English), thistle (Scottish), shamrock (Irish), lily (French), and leek (Welsh). The absence of any emblem to represent indigenous people was not thought significant enough to warrant comment when M.H. Long gave a presidential address on the Historic Sites and Monuments Board to the Canadian Historical Association in 1954.[54]

But sensibilities were changing, due in part to the determination of French-Canadians not to be assimilated into anglophone society. The viability of the Canadian confederation depended on recognizing the coexistence of "two nations," sociologist Anthony H. Richmond argues, and "given the basic and necessary commitment to dualism in Canada, it is not surprising that the representatives of other ethnic groups should also aspire to the preservation of their languages and cultures as a constitutional right." When the *Canadian Charter of Rights and Freedoms* was framed as part of the *Constitution Act* (1982), article 27 stated that "this Charter shall be interpreted in a manner consistent with the preservation and enhancement of the multicultural heritage of Canadians." The accompanying commentary noted that "Canadians are proud that this country has not become a melting pot, but has maintained its multicultural character." In 1996, for the first time, the national census allowed people to write their own ethnic origins into four blank spaces rather than picking from pre-given categories like "Irish" or "French." The most common response to the question of ethnic origins on the 1996 census was "Canadian," which meant that the 1996 data could not be meaningfully compared with earlier censuses that had tried to block that response. The freedom to choose one's own ethnic category also led to a multiplication of composites, like "East Indian and Portuguese," "Irish, French, Canadian, and Métis," and so on. This recognition of the multiplicity of ancestral roots reflected Canada's ideology of the "cultural mosaic," which respected the diverse historical cultural identities of immigrants.[55]

While the cultural mosaic was a source of great pride to Canadians, it forced them to adopt a historical relativism that engendered fears that they were not as patriotic as their American neighbours. Questions about the

historical importance of Mackenzie brought these fears to the fore, especially when he was compared, implicitly or explicitly, to Lewis and Clark.
One of the reasons Bishop was motivated to locate Mackenzie's Rock in
the 1920s was that he was concerned people did not know that Mackenzie had made the first crossing of the continent and that both Thomas
Jefferson and Meriwether Lewis had read Mackenzie's *Voyages* and been
inspired by it. "All good Canadians are well aware of this," he said in a
speech in Victoria, "but the fact is apparently by no means universally recognized. Fiske, in 'The Discovery of America,' solemnly announces that
the continent was first crossed by Lewis and Clark, whose expeditions
reached the Columbia some twelve years later ... It is hard to understand
how so learned and impartial an historian as Fiske should make such a
mistake; possibly his sources of information were influenced by some of
the disputes which arose in connection with the various international
boundary questions in this part of the world."[56]

If he had lived to see it, Bishop would no doubt have been disappointed
to read the claim made by American popular historian Stephen Ambrose
in 1996 in *Newsweek* that Lewis was "the first white man to cross the Continental Divide." Bishop's intellectual heir, John Woodworth, wrote to the
magazine to correct Ambrose, noting that "an earlier claim was painted on
a rock near Bella Coola, B.C." In reply, *Newsweek* editors said that "Mr.
Ambrose's article reflects U.S. history" and he was referring to United
States territory. The Lakehead student re-enactment of the Mackenzie
voyage only served to confirm fears about Canadian patriotism. En route,
the students were consistently misidentified by Canadian schoolchildren
as "Abe Lincoln," "Daniel Boone," and "Davy Crockett," which horrified
patriotic commentators. As the celebration of the Lewis and Clark bicentennial began in 2003, some Canadian comparisons of the relative accomplishments of Mackenzie vis-à-vis Lewis and Clark became more extreme.
In an article that ran in newspapers in a number of major Canadian cities,
Vancouver Sun columnist Stephen Hume claimed that the "lionized" American explorers were the "also-rans" of continental exploration, and their
"exploits pale[d] by comparison" with those of Samuel Hearne, Alexander
Mackenzie, David Thompson, and Simon Fraser. Such views were, of
course, considerably less nuanced than those presented in the historical
literature of either Canada or the United States, but they probably struck
a chord in many of their readers.[57]

In their attempt to memorialize Alexander Mackenzie, Canadians faced
the question of how to celebrate the historical accomplishments of a particular individual or group in the country's cultural mosaic while not

alienating the others. The answer they settled on was to dedicate a place in his honour, in this case the heritage trail. Such a form of commemoration had many advantages. The trail bore an obvious physical association with Mackenzie's expedition, serving as an indexical sign of the voyage. In the face of political separatism, it was used symbolically to unite the country in both static representations and dynamic performances. It served to remind American patriots of Mackenzie's precedence in continental crossing and to attract tourists in search of adventure or outdoor recreation. Besides the tourists' dollars, people who lived along the trail gained a sense of pride in the historical importance of their region. By choosing to dedicate such a place, however, the proponents of the heritage trail also raised new problems. For one thing, it was impossible to know exactly where Mackenzie had travelled. In marking out *the* Alexander Mackenzie Heritage Trail, the trail's designers occasionally had to resign themselves to guessing which of a number of possible routes the explorer probably took and were faced with the uncomfortable knowledge that they were reifying something that they could not be certain of. A more political problem raised by the heritage trail was that connections between history and landscape are multivalent and difficult to read. Places don't speak for themselves about their past; rather, their pasts emerge from the interpretive activities of many people. Having dedicated the heritage trail to Mackenzie, its proponents found that its historical meaning remained open and contested.[58]

4

Grease Trails

IN 1993, THE ULKATCHO INDIAN BAND of Anahim Lake published a booklet entitled *Ulkatcho: Stories of the Grease Trail*. Timed to coincide with the Mackenzie bicentennial, and funded in part by the provincial Ministry of Government Services' Sea to Sea project, the book presented an Aboriginal perspective on the trail network, with stories told by Ulkatcho and Nuxalk elders in sidebars. "For the past 200 years," it began, "native people of British Columbia have found themselves in the unfortunate position of having been 'discovered' by Europeans." People of European background downplayed the activities of Aboriginal people, and "in order to take over the land, the importance of the land to native people ha[d] been ignored. In its place, the accomplishments of 'white' people ha[d] been emphasized." The introduction to the booklet went on to state that the history that people were taught in school was not necessarily correct, and that stories could be told from different points of view. The grease trail had been an integral part of Nuxalk and southern Carrier culture and history before the newcomers arrived, and its use went back thousands of years. Mackenzie's accomplishments, while noteworthy, had been allowed to eclipse those of Aboriginal people: "Mackenzie, after all, only walked down the trail once." Ulkatcho elder Henry Jack was quoted as saying, "This has always been our trail. I used to climb that tree across the trail from my father's cabin when I was a boy. I still trap along the trail today. My grandfather, Baptiste Stillas, used this trail all his life. You can still see the stumps of the trees he cut to build his barn, long before I was born. Now they want to give this trail to Mackenzie."[1]

For the people of Ulkatcho, as for their Aboriginal neighbours through-out the Chilcotin, memory is everywhere anchored in the landscape, along the grease trails and rivers, of course, but also in the meadows and forests between. For them, there is a not a single trail that connects the Fraser with the coast or that unites provinces east and west; rather, there is a dense, lived mesh of trails and a cyclicity and seasonality of travel. Traditional Aboriginal calendars in the interior started in the winter, in the moon named for ice. In the grasslands along the Fraser River, the deer began to rut, the males circling one another warily before locking antlers in a contest to determine which of them would mate. For people across the interior plateau, this was a time to enter subterranean houses. Deer and other animals, including sheep, elk, hare, and grouse, were hunted, as weather permitted, to supplement caches of stored food. Some interior groups wintered with friends and kin on the coast in villages like Bella Coola; for the rest, the following moon was a time to stay at home, a time of the first real cold. Occasionally it was possible to ice-fish the lakes for whitefish, trout, and suckers, but more frequently diets consisted of dried salmon and meat, roots, and berries. The sun turned in midwinter, the time of the big moon, and animals like mink, marten, weasel, fisher, rabbits, lynx, coyote, and fox were trapped for their plush winter coats. It was a good time to sew buckskin and to visit. By the following moon, food stores were running low. Along the Fraser near Lillooet, the snow would already be disappearing in the chinook winds, and a few spring roots could be dug. Farther north and west, the snow crusted over and began to darken with windblown debris. This made travel easier, and it became possible to run down game on foot as hooves broke through the crust when snowshoes did not. With the beginning of spring, bears came out of hibernation. By the end of the moon, most of the people had emerged from their winter houses as well. People began to disperse throughout band territories to hunt and to fish in the lakes. The snow was melting from the high ground, and the grass was growing in the valleys. By the beginning of summer, most families had moved to lake fishing stations to catch and dry trout, whitefish, and suckers. It was a time to dig potatoes, wild onions, tiger-lily bulbs, and shoots of balsamroot and cow parsnip. The summer moons were a time for berrying: strawberries and soapberries and saskatoons were gathered beside rivers and lakes. The summer also marked the beginning of the spring salmon run for some, and for others it was a time to hunt waterfowl, mountain goats, and the other ungulates that had grown fat on mountain pastures. The salmon runs occupied most people's time until the moon of the sockeye salmon and for some groups the rest of the autumn as well. Others went hunting in the fall moons and gathered pine seeds near higher-elevation base camps. For each of these activities, and for countless others, there was a trip to be made along particular trails: from Ulkatcho to Bella Coola in time for the berry harvest; from Nazko to Anahim Lake to collect obsidian; from Nemiah to Tanya Lakes to smoke salmon. And whenever and wherever people gathered, there were opportunities to trade, to teach or learn new skills, to discuss ideas, share news, tell stories, joke, flirt, and play the gambling game *lahal.*[2]

This is not to suggest that there was anything like a unified Aboriginal perspective on the grease trails. For one thing, coastal groups were more sedentary than those in the interior. They stockpiled greater surpluses and used these surpluses to support social and cultural elaboration. Aboriginal groups were further differentiated by language, ideology, religious and ceremonial practices, traditions, geographical position, access to natural resources, and so on. But there was a longstanding system of understandings, ways to negotiate with others who were not kin or did not speak the same languages; shared ideas about travel, trade, and usufruct rights; and, for those in the interior, similar ecological adaptations developed in response to similar environments.

"Native people have been living here 10,000 years," the chief of Nazko said. "There's a lot of history here. Especially around Nazko, Kluskus and Ulkatcho, where archaeologists have dug up old village sites that are very old." One of the suggestions made by the *Ulkatcho* booklet was that the Alexander Mackenzie Heritage Trail should be renamed. As things stood, there were signs along the route that said "Alexander Mackenzie Heritage Trail" in large letters, with "Nuxalk-Carrier Route" in a smaller font below. The Ulkatcho people felt that the trail network should instead be labelled with signs that said "Nuxalk-Carrier Grease Trail" in large letters. One of the many grease trails could then also have signs that were subtitled "Alexander Mackenzie Route." "Native people, after all, are not opposed to recognizing the accomplishments of others," the booklet said. "They believe, however, that such recognition should not come at the expense of proper respect for their own culture and heritage."[3]

THE FIRST SETTLERS

If one takes the really long-term perspective, the time that we live in is doubly unlikely. Glacial ages – like the Quaternary period of the past million-and-a-half-odd years – have been infrequent in the history of the earth, and interglacial periods, like the one that peaked about ten thousand years ago, occur infrequently during glacial ages (see Appendix B). Archaeologists believe that this unusual sequence of climatic conditions – ten millennia of warmth following a major glaciation – was what allowed human beings to come to the Americas (see Appendix A). At the peak of the last glaciation, mean sea level was about 120 metres lower than it is today, allowing coastal features that are now shallowly submerged to emerge. The most important of these, at least in terms of human history, was Beringia, the continental shelf that connects Siberia and Alaska. This is thought to be the route by which the ancestors of the Aboriginal people entered the Americas. The time of arrival is disputed. No human skeletal remains from the Americas have been reliably **dated** to be older than about twelve thousand years before present (BP), and most archaeologists believe that is when people first came, toward the end of the last glaciation.[4]

The traditional view was of Asian mammoth hunters who followed their prey across Beringia and southward into central Canada, probably through an "ice-free corridor" into the interior. The earliest that such a corridor could have been clear would have been about 11,000 BP. People then filled the Americas over the next thousand years by radiating from the central and southward axis of migration. This view has recently been challenged on a number of points. For one thing, it ignores the fact that the Northwest Coast was deglaciated well before the interior and would have provided a suitable habitat for human beings by 13,000 BP. Furthermore, it assumes 'that the first colonists depended on their technological skills and knowledge of animal behaviour rather than on a knowledge of geography, which implies that they followed the animals from region to region. This is not true of present-day foraging groups, which tend to be confined by their particular geography and by neighbouring peoples. Instead, some researchers now argue that it is important to think of the colonization in more ecological terms. In the Americas, major physiographical regions and large environmental zones, known as "biomes," tend to run north-south. The traditional view of unidirectional migration would have the first colonists travel through a physiographic obstacle course and cross-cut a series of environments. According to the newer model, people migrated in a number of directions at once, settling within biomes instead of moving through them.[5]

In an influential paper, archaeologist Knut Fladmark argued that people may have worked their way down "a chain of sea level **refugia**" along the southern margin of Beringia and the Pacific coast of the Americas beginning as early as 14,000 BP. There they would have easily been able to exploit rich and predictable marine and intertidal resources, like **anadro-mous** fish and shellfish. This economic adaptation, called "generalized for-aging," was well-suited to colonization. It didn't require the same rapid movement as the hunting of large mammals, and it didn't make the whole group dependent on the success of a few strong adults. Archaeological evi-dence from other parts of the world shows that human beings were able to build watercraft and navigate them near ocean shores by this time. Sub-sequent movement from the coastal zone into the western cordillera prob-ably occurred more slowly as people moved inland along rivers and adapted to interior conditions. In some places, emphasis may have been placed on the harvesting and processing of plants and seeds. In others, hunting probably became more important. The eastern coastal zone of the Amer-icas, reached by crossing the isthmus in central America and/or by round-ing Cape Horn, offered other possibilities for ecological adaptation. In this model, the interior plains of North America may have been colonized relatively late, and the archaeological evidence of mammoth predation that has been found there might indicate a relatively unique adaptation. "In other words," archaeologist E. James Dixon writes, "the spectacular and well publicized Clovis kill sites may be the least typical and the least useful sites for interpreting the peopling of the Americas and early New World adaptations." The High Arctic, the extreme northeast of North America and Greenland, was not accessible to human colonization until about five thousand years ago, and thus was colonized last.[6]

The first human occupants probably moved into what is now British Columbia around 13,000 BP. For the previous two thousand years, the cli-mate had been improving, the edges of the ice sheets were retreating, and vegetation was returning to the recently deglaciated land. In the wake of the retreating ice, freshly exposed land was unstable, and slides and floods must have been common. The increased erosion muddied streams and lakes, making poor habitat for aquatic insects and minnows that served as fish food, and thus poor spawning grounds for salmon and trout. As plant life became established, erosion decreased, and the sediment load in streams and rivers dropped. New salmon runs became established within a few centuries, providing one source of food for human inhabitants.[7]

OBSIDIAN

At many points along the Alexander Mackenzie Heritage Trail, one can find small chips of obsidian, a black volcanic glass. There is some in the mouth of an occasionally dry stream bed at 244.44 kilometres, for example, and some more at 289.51 kilometres. The sites where obsidian is found are not limited to the portion of the grease trails that Mackenzie followed, but are located throughout the trail network. The rock was brought to those places by people and used to fashion stone tools – like blades, projectile points, awls, and scrapers – leaving the chips as detritus. Geologically, obsidian arises when a silica-rich magma cools rapidly on the earth's surface. Only a handful of places in present-day BC are sources of obsidian. In every other place where obsidian is found, it is a sign of past human activity. When George Dawson was surveying near the Euchiniko Lakes in 1876, Aboriginal people told him that there was a high mountain up the Blackwater River where obsidian could be obtained. He later identified this source as Anahim Peak.[8]

In the early 1970s, archaeologists became interested in the possibility of using new technologies to substantiate indigenous oral traditions about the source of the obsidian used in various artifacts. Two of these techniques, known as **neutron activation analysis** and **X-ray fluorescence spectrometry**, allowed archaeologists to determine the concentrations of various trace elements in samples of obsidian. Since different samples of the rock contain different trace elements, the particular distribution of elements serves as a kind of "fingerprint," by which a given sample can be matched to its source. A pilot study of artifacts from present-day BC showed that the obsidian used in their manufacture came from a number of distinct sources. Thirty-two of the artifacts were made from obsidian found on the south slope of Tsitsutl Peak in the Rainbow Range and in river gravel downstream along the banks of the Dean River. The artifacts themselves were distributed in a rough ellipse centred on the source, with a 350-kilometre axis stretching from Namu on the coast in the southwest to the confluence of the Stuart and Nechako rivers in the northeast. Other groups of artifacts were traced to obsidian sources near Anahim Peak and to various lava flows at Mount Edziza in northern BC. The source of the material used in the artifacts was only part of the story; the date that each was created was another part. In some cases, the date could be inferred from the dates of surrounding material or from the morphology of the artifact itself. In others, a technique known as **obsidian hydration** was used to date the samples by determining how much water they had absorbed over time.[9]

One of the archaeologists' findings was, not surprisingly, that people tended to rely on nearby sources of obsidian rather than distant ones. Creating a map of the distribution of obsidian artifacts, they discovered a boundary in the Skeena River drainage between obsidian derived from

Mount Edziza to the north and that derived from the Rainbow Mountains and Anahim Peak to the south, which the archaeologists thought was "certainly of cultural significance," and which was reflected in a traditional boundary between Gitxsan and Carrier. Their preferred explanation for the widespread distribution of obsidian from the Rainbow Mountains was that it was due to reciprocal trade: the raw material or finished artifacts were exchanged for more perishable or intangible things that did not leave traces in the archaeological record. These may have included meat, fish, oil, tubers, seeds, berries, furs, hides, nets, shells, or feathers. And where there is trade, one can also imagine the exchange of parasites and infections, rituals and stories, slaves and spouses. In support of the trading hypothesis, archaeologists noted that there was good ethnographic evidence for it. Mackenzie's Aboriginal guides, for example, were familiar with neighbouring peoples and adjacent regions, "an indication of at least minimal interaction." An alternative explanation for the distribution of obsidian was that it was part of an "open procurement system" in which each group that wanted to make use of the resource had free access to it. This explanation was not deemed as likely as the former, because unequivocal ethnographic evidence for open procurement was difficult to find. Furthermore, the position of the Ulkatcho and Eliguk Lake village sites at the north end of the Dean River valley would have given their occupants some control over access to the obsidian there, and the location of the Anahim Lake village would have provided an analogous advantage at the south end of the valley. A third possibility, suggested by Aboriginal oral tradition, was that the sources of obsidian were controlled but that outsiders were allowed access to them. In 1967, an archaeologist was told by Ulkatcho elder Thomas Squinas that "Indians would let you go up and get a little *bes* [obsidian] but not much ... If you stayed too long Indian would run you off ... Anybody could go for *bes* to make stone tools. You didn't have to pay."[10]

Archaeologists worked in the 1970s and 1980s to clarify the location of obsidian sources and greatly extend the database of samples. Small outcrops of obsidian found in Mackenzie Pass were surrounded by flaking detritus, which showed that the sites had a long history of human use. A number of longstanding quarries and flaking stations were also located along a stream feeding into the Dean River. By the early 1990s, thirteen hundred obsidian artifacts had been tested from 180 archaeological sites in BC and adjacent areas. The picture that emerged from the distribution of these artifacts in space and time attested to millennia of human activity. The earliest known piece of obsidian was found at Namu and dated to about 9500 BP. It came from the area of Anahim Peak, 160 kilometres to the east. Two other obsidian pieces at Namu, dated between 9000 and 8000 BP, also came from the Chilcotin: one from Anahim Peak and one from Mackenzie Pass. One of the implications of this finding was that a portion of the so-called Alexander Mackenzie Heritage Trail – the part from Mackenzie Pass to the ocean – had been traversed by human beings as the ice sheets were retreating, a full ten thousand years before Mackenzie arrived. There was also evidence of similar activity in what is now Alaska, northern BC, and Oregon. In the north, obsidian from Mount Edziza was taken west down the Stikine River and then north and south along the coast. In the south, obsidian from sources in Oregon was being transported up the Columbia River and along the Pacific coast. "From this perspective," archaeologist Roy Carlson writes, "obsidian trade started in all regions of the Northwest by 9,000 years ago." Since the sources for the material were few, the routes by which it was transported tended to be long. The distribution of artifacts from all the major sources of obsidian overlapped by 6000 to 4000 BP, indicating that people were in contact over long distances. The origins of regional cultural complexes also date from this period, showing that none of the human groups was acting in a vacuum. Each was in full communication with its neighbours and had, no doubt, murkier knowledge of more distant peoples in the network. Since the obsidian had to travel great distances across linguistic and ethnic boundaries, reciprocal trade (rather than open procurement) seems like the most obvious explanation for its spread. By 4000 to 3000 BP, obsidian from Anahim had reached present-day Alberta.[11]

The Indians' New World

The ice age ended about ten thousand years ago and was followed by a climatic optimum known as the **hypsithermal**, the warmest interval in the interglacial period that we live in. For human groups in the New World, this was a time of efflorescence, a time when people who lived in areas with a poor-to-moderate resource base diversified their exploitation, and when people who lived in resource-rich areas specialized in the habitual exploitation of a few key resources. Namu, on the central coast west of the Chilcotin, was an area of very rich marine resources. Before 6000 BP, the people at Namu were fashioning tools by flaking stone. They created scrapers, points and knives, and small stone sinkers for nets or lines. They also made some objects by grinding and pecking stone, showing that they were familiar with a wide range of lithic techniques. Artifacts created over the next thousand years include long, delicate microblades fashioned from Chilcotin obsidian, which could be hafted to create spears and harpoons. The people at Namu also created a number of tools that were probably used for woodworking: gravers and drills for light work, and pebble choppers, rasps, and scrapers for heavy-duty construction. Cedar pollen does not appear in the **palynological** record until 6000 BP, so other woods must have been used for boat and house frameworks. Bone tools also appear in the archaeological record around this time. Most of them were created to help with fishing, but there are also harpoons for hunting sea mammals, bone needles for sewing skin clothing, and beaver incisors that were used as chisels. By comparing the artifacts at Namu with contemporaneous ones from elsewhere in northwestern North America, archaeologists have concluded that the people of Namu were in regular contact with peoples in the north, from whom they learned to make microblades (the technique originated in northeastern Asia and spread along the Pacific coast), and with peoples in the south, who developed a technology of pebble tools. And, of course, there was also regular trade with the interior.[12]

By about 8000 BP, people living in the Chilcotin had also learned to fashion microblades from obsidian. From their neighbours in the southern interior, they learned to make and use simple basalt scrapers, leaf-shaped knives and projectile points, and a wide range of tools from cobbles. These cobble tools could be used to drive stakes, pulverize bone, peck or grind stone, chop things, shape bone and wood, and process hides and pulpy foods. Like obsidian, the other stones used to make tools were not uniformly available but had to be quarried in a few favourable locations. Large basalt quarries were located to the east of the Fraser River in the Arrowstone Range. A glassy basalt could also be obtained at Beece Creek near Taseko Lake, at the Baezeko River north of Chezacut, and near Pantage Lake. Basalt was "typically found as cobbles in fluvial deposits along the creeks and in the glacial drift and till on the valley slopes." Chert came from outcrops near Puntzi Lake and along the lower Blackwater River. Other rocks and minerals quarried farther away but well known in the Chilcotin were jade and nephrite from the lower Fraser, steatite, ochre for paints and dyes, and copper for bracelets and jewellery.[13]

Interior peoples continually diversified their resource base for subsistence in this period, leaving many traces of their innovations. For one thing, they made more use of small animals like rabbits, birds, and rodents, whose bones began to appear in **faunal assemblages**. Their ground-stone tools could be used to mash seeds, to convert inedible cartilage and small bones into edible pulp, and to process plant starches for leaching. Their constantly improving fishing technologies allowed them to gradually exploit more of the plentiful salmon in the rivers and lakes. One piece of evidence for this comes from the remains of a hapless fellow, now known as Gore Creek man, who was trapped in mud and drowned near Kamloops about 8000 BP. An analysis of the **stable isotope ratios** in his skeleton suggests that he ate mostly meat (probably deer), but that 8 to 10 percent of his dietary protein came from marine fish like salmon and steelhead. People also began to exploit freshwater shellfish like mussels in a few places where they were abundant. Another technology that was developed in this period, to judge from the increasing number of fire-cracked rocks, was the widespread boiling of foods, which would have reduced food poisoning by killing harmful bacteria. Archaeologist Brian Hayden notes that boiling also "could have rendered edible many plants containing toxins and could have been used to extract otherwise unavailable fats, marrow, bits of meat, and other tissue from animals, as well as ... reduce calorie loss from charring."[14]

Lacking utensils that could be placed directly into the fire, early peoples developed an alternative that was still in use more than six millennia later, when Mackenzie followed the grease trails. On 16 July 1793, one of his Aboriginal hosts offered to "boil a kettle of fish roes." Mackenzie wrote that

> he took the roes out of a bag, and having bruised them between two stones, put them in water to soak. His wife then took a handful of dry grass in her hand, with which she squeezed them through her fingers; in the mean time her husband was employed in gathering wood to make a fire, for the purpose of heating stones. When she had finished her operation, she filled a watape kettle [i.e., one made by weaving the fine roots of the spruce tree] nearly full of water, and poured the roes into it. When the stones were sufficiently heated, some of them were put into the kettle, and others were thrown in from time to time, till the water was in a state of boiling; the woman also continued stirring the contents of the kettle, till they were brought to a thick consistency; the stones were then taken out, and the whole was seasoned with about a pint of strong rancid oil.

On the grease trail in 1876, the geological surveyor George Dawson also "saw the Indian women boiling up fish heads in pots about a foot square, made of wood about 3/8 inch, ingeniously bent round. The boiling accomplished by dropping heated stones into the pot, a pair of tongs composed of a couple of long sticks tied together, being used for lifting them." In order for stone boiling to be possible, interior peoples had to know how to make watertight containers. Those containers must have been flammable, or they would have been placed directly in the fire and stone boiling would not have been necessary. This implies that interior peoples knew how to make such baskets of wood, hide, or woven bark or fibre. This, in turn, implies that they also knew how to make cordage by braiding animal and vegetable fibres, which could be used for snares, fish lines, and nets as well as cooking utensils. Unfortunately, few of these materials left durable traces in the archaeological record, but the cracked and discoloured rocks that were used for stone boiling were found beside hearths in sites more than six thousand years old.[15]

On 21 June 1793, as Mackenzie was approaching, for the first time, the place that would later be named Alexandria in his honour, he was told by Aboriginal people about their neighbours "who lived in large subterraneous recesses." Over the next few days, as he and his men followed the grease trail, they became more familiar with a particular kind of house, "the roof of which alone appeared above ground." Today the remains of these houses appear in many places along the grease trails, usually as circular depressions. On Mackenzie's route, for example, there are house pits at 32.76 kilometres and more at 147.80 kilometres, protected now as heritage sites. In fact, these sites are found throughout the interior, the traces of a shift in settlement that began about four thousand years earlier. House pits at Punchaw Lake date from 3980 BP, at Tezli on the Blackwater River from 3850 BP, at Nakwantlun near Anahim Lake from 3500 BP, and at Natalkuz Lake on the headwaters of the Nechako River from 2415 BP. At the time, the climate was becoming cooler and wetter, and interior grasslands retreated, to be replaced by forests of pine, Douglas fir, and alder. People in the interior began to build a new kind of house along the rivers and creeks, a pit house in the style of their southern neighbours on the Columbia plateau and what is now northern California. Unlike earlier shelters, which were probably lightweight and portable – perhaps tents or conical huts covered with hides, slabs of bark, or woven mats – these new pit houses were permanent. They typically consisted of a circular pit, about eight to ten metres in circumference and a metre and half deep. Four posts against the wall inside the pit were used to support rafters, which rose to a square hatchway. A pyramidal roof was built of logs, poles, and bark, then covered with earth and sod. A single notched pole projected at an angle through the hatchway, serving as a ladder so that people could go in and out. The hearth was centrally located. Smoke escaped from the hatchway, which also acted as a skylight. On the edges of the hearth there were places for sleeping and for indoor work and recreation.[16]

SURPLUS AND WHAT THAT ENTAILED

Adoption of pit houses coincided with a change in the ecological adaptations of people in the interior. They now lived in semi-permanent winter villages, located beside the salmon streams that were fished in spring and fall. The stable isotope ratios of human skeletons found in the southern interior near Clinton and dated 4950 BP show that 37 to 38 percent of the protein in peoples' diet came from marine sources, and the amount was increasing: later skeletons from the area have values ranging from 40 to 60 percent. Other evidence for the heightened dependence on marine protein comes from the numbers of notched pebbles – used as net sinkers – that are found at interior sites. Much greater numbers of the shells of freshwater molluscs also appear in middens from the time. The shift from mobile camps to semi-sedentary pit house villages may have been due, in part, to the cooler, wetter climate. The climate change may also have increased the number of salmon that could be harvested in the Fraser River and its tributaries. The new emphasis on marine protein in the diet was important not only because it forced Aboriginal groups into a more sedentary way of life, but also because it committed them to a resource that fluctuated dramatically for reasons outside their control. In good years, the number of salmon available at a given point on the river might be a hundred times greater than the number available when the run failed, which happened every four years or so.[17]

Because of the life cycle of the salmon, this resource was not uniformly distributed, but rather decreased as one travelled upstream. Pacific salmon lay their eggs in the gravel beds of freshwater rivers or lakes, where the fry hatch and live for a year or two, depending on the species. They then migrate to salt water and spend their adult lives in the North Pacific Ocean and Bering Sea. Sometime between the late summer and early winter of their fourth or fifth or sixth year, again depending on the species, they return to their natal breeding grounds to spawn. No one is sure exactly how they find the place where they came into the world, although scientists do know that they can't find it if their noses are plugged. Occasionally a few stray into the wrong spot, which enables salmon to colonize new spawning grounds and maintain their genetic diversity. Before they enter fresh water, Pacific salmon stop feeding, and as a consequence they become leaner the farther upstream they have to travel. They spawn, defend their nests, and die.[18]

For human beings who depended on the salmon runs for subsistence or surplus, there was a spatial gradient in resource wealth. Farther up the river system, the runs were smaller in size and of shorter duration, and they peaked later in the year. One consequence of this gradient was that certain favoured spots became seasonal focal points for the human harvest; they also became – in recent times for certain and in the more distant past in all likelihood – sites where indigenous people worked to delineate property rights. Archaeologists note that pit house sites in the southern interior were "not only situated in an optimal area for procuring, drying, and trading salmon, but they were also strategically situated geographically to control the major southern trade routes from the coast to the interior." The important role played by these places in the Aboriginal economy can also be inferred from the massive Aboriginal "trade fairs" that eighteenth- and nineteenth-century observers witnessed at The Dalles on the lower Columbia River and at the mouth of the Nass River. People circulated through these points with novel goods and new ideas, timing their arrival to the seasonal harvest of salmon and other fish. Disc-shaped beads of coastal shells would later be found on the Peace River in northeastern British Columbia, Oregon obsidian turned up in Lillooet, and turquoise from the Southwest or Great Basin has been found in the Okanagan Valley.[19]

Archaeologists argue that by 3500 BP, the differential access to salmon allowed cultures in the southern interior (on the plateau south of present-day Williams Lake and east of Lillooet) to begin to accumulate large surpluses and thus to develop a number of institutions that resembled those of the northwest coast. Counterparts to these institutions did not develop in the northern interior, where the subsistence base was more marginal. The pit houses in the southern interior were large enough to have hearths for a number of families, and they also had bark-lined pits to store surplus salmon. Woodworking tools included wedges, nephrite chisels, and small adze blades that could be fitted to wooden handles and used to split, smooth, and facet wood. These adze blades were among a number of products made from ground nephrite and steatite that were exported to the coast. Other exports included sculptures made from the same material. Some people wore bone bracelets, pendants, or beads or marine shells obtained from their coastal trading partners. They began to bury their dead with more elaborate grave goods. The surplus of salmon was, archaeologists believe, at the root of the cultural elaboration that followed. Dried salmon provided subsistence during lean times, allowing people to become semi-sedentary. Once they had a permanent home base, they could accumulate more goods than they could carry. They could also have more children, with all of the corporate advantages that accrued from living in larger populations: increased disease resistance for the survivors, widespread division of labour, people who specialized in violence. (Of course, the relative advantages of a sedentary population should not be confused with the advantages of individuals in that population: people were often worse off than they would have been living nomadically.) The surplus of salmon could be redistributed, fuelling an increase in trade and creating status hierarchies. The rise of chiefs gave rise, in turn, to competition, displays of wealth, raiding and slavery, and ever finer gradations of social rank. Obsidian, relatively common in earlier times, is not often found in these later pit house village sites of the southern interior. Roy Carlson suggests that "its near absence is possibly an indicator of hostile relationships between the mid Fraser and the obsidian sources of the Rainbow Mountains."[20]

Around this time, people in the interior also began to make more intensive use of plant foods such as spring beauty (also known as mountain potato or Indian potato), bitterroot, wild onions, tiger lily, and balsamroot. These were collected in the spring with digging sticks and roasted in large, earthen, baking pits. Not only did they taste better that way, but they could also be stored more easily. Because the roots themselves did not survive in the archaeological record, their use has to be inferred from artifacts that did, like the earth ovens and digging sticks. In spite of their absence, the roots' importance in the subsistence of interior peoples should not be underestimated. Ethnobiologists estimate that some interior groups obtained more than half of their food energy from vegetal foods like starchy roots and bulbs. These foods were recognized in celebrations and narratives, and thus, as ethnobiologists Eugene Hunn, Nancy Turner, and David French note, "women's economic product was not symbolically discounted in the Plateau." Ethnographic evidence also suggests that this increased use of plants may have been facilitated by various burning practices. According to Stl'atl'imx elders, hillsides were burned when they got too bushy to support plants with roots or edible berries, like Saskatoon berries, gooseberries, huckleberries, blackcaps, blueberries, and raspberries. This burning was done in rotation: one hill was burned while another was harvested. After about three years, the burned hill would begin to produce large berry crops for a few years. When the plants got too old, the hillside was burned again. Although Aboriginal peoples made use of a variety of plant cultivation techniques, including transplanting, selective harvesting, weeding, pruning, turning of the soil, and burning, these activities were often de-emphasized in traditional ethnographic accounts, which tried to portray Aboriginal ways of life according to pre-established ideas of what constituted agriculture and what did not. The view that Aboriginal peoples of what is now BC did not cultivate plants is currently being revised.[21]

The Athapaskan

The world of the interior peoples was a geologically unsettled one. In 2350 BP, the volcanic complex at Mount Meager, sixty kilometres south of Taseko Lakes, erupted. Prevailing winds carried the tephra – the airborne dust, ash, and pumice – to the east, blanketing the villages and trade routes of the southern interior. On slopes near the volcano, the deposit was up to eighty metres thick. Lava and ash temporarily dammed the headwaters of the Lillooet River; when the dam collapsed, a billion cubic metres of water were released, flooding the Lillooet valley. Today, a stratum of the Mount Meager tephra can be found as far away as Alberta, 530 kilometres east of the vent.[22]

The interior volcanism was related to the subduction of an oceanic plate beneath the continental plate of North America off the coast to the west. As a result, the coast had been periodically hit by earthquakes and tsunamis for millennia. When these occurred, they frequently led to the abandonment of coastal villages, and the survivors may have sought help from their inland trading partners. Indigenous coastal people from northern California to central BC have ceremonies and oral traditions relating to seismic events. According to the Nuxalk, the western neighbours of the Tsilhqot'in, a giant supernatural being held the earth in ropes. When he adjusted his grip, or when the rope slipped in his hands, the Nuxalk could feel the tremors and performed a ceremonial earthquake dance. We don't know how the survivors responded to the Mount Meager eruption, but news and stories of it must have circulated far and wide along the trails of trade and communication.[23]

Some scholars believe that another volcanic eruption had a significant subsequent impact on the Chilcotin. Around 1250 BP, the Mount Bona volcano in the St. Elias Mountains of what is now eastern Alaska ejected more than twenty-five cubic kilometres of tephra into the air. By comparison, the better-known Krakatau eruption of 1883 ejected about twenty-one cubic kilometres of tephra. The Mount Bona tephra fell to the east, mostly in what is now the Yukon, over a "lobe" measuring about 250,000 square kilometres. The effects were drastic. Thunder, lightning, and torrential rain accompanied the tephra cloud, which darkened the land for days. Sulphuric acid damaged eyes, skin, and clothing. Ash fouled water supplies and suffocated and starved salmon and trout. Noxious gases poisoned vegetation downwind. Evidence suggests that the eruption occurred in the early winter, a time when daylight was limited and food already in short supply. The short-term psychological effects on the survivors must have been devastating. Over the longer term, the carrying capacity of the land was significantly reduced, and its human occupants had to evacuate it.[24]

This disaster may have been responsible for a sudden southward migration of Northern Athapaskan people into what is now the northern half of BC. Today's Tsilhqot'in and Carrier – as well as the Wet'suwet'en, Sekani, Tahltan, Kaska, Dunne-za, and Dene-thah – all speak Northern Athapaskan languages. There are also speakers of Athapaskan languages on the southern Oregon and northern California coasts and in the American Southwest, the Navajos and Apaches being the best known. One hypothesis is that these groups represent the southernmost limits of Athapaskan migration triggered by the volcanic eruption.[25]

There is evidence both for and against this hypothesis of rapid and late migration. The area that was covered by the tephra was reoccupied after a short time. Furthermore, recent archaeological studies in southern Yukon suggest that around 1250 BP, throwing darts were abruptly replaced by bow-and-arrow technology, and stone points were replaced by barbed antler points. Attempts to find characteristic artifacts in the archaeological record that could signal the replacement of earlier southern peoples by a wave of Athapaskan migrants have not been successful, however. Instead, the interior plateaus from Babine Lake to the northern edge of the Great Basin show a continuity of cultural elements. Indigenous people in this vast region relied on extensive trade, were spatially and ecologically oriented around rivers, built winter villages of pit houses, practised seasonal **subsistence rounds**, made variable projectile points, worked wood, and created cords by twining. This continuity predated any possible replacement of interior peoples by millennia.[26]

An alternative to the rapid-replacement hypothesis emphasizes the long-term and gradual movement of people, ideas, words, techniques, and things through a longstanding network of communication and exchange. At first, speakers of Athapaskan languages were merely new faces on the trails that tied this system together, but over time, the prevailing ethos gradually took on more and more of their way of looking at the world. Michael Krauss and Victor Golla, linguists who study Northern Athapaskan languages, argue that, in the subarctic, "intergroup communication has ordinarily been constant, and no Northern Athapaskan language or dialect was ever completely isolated from the others for long." Thus, they continue, "local dialects and languages are important as symbols of social identity, but the native expectation that these differences, even across relatively vast distances, will not be barriers to communication gives the Northern Athapaskan speaker a distinctively open and flexible perception of his social world." The spread of a dialect complex across such a large area would have facilitated trade by lowering transaction costs, a phenomenon that economic historians refer to as a "trade diaspora." Whatever the reason indigenous people in the Chilcotin came to speak Athapaskan languages, the Tsilhqot'in and Carrier themselves have no traditions of migration.[27]

Around 1000 BP, the southern interior winter villages of Pavilion, Fountain, Seton, and Lillooet, which had had populations of five hundred to a thousand people each, were abruptly abandoned. The village sites were never really reoccupied. Archaeologists have proposed a number of possible explanations for the apparent cultural collapse of the southern interior sites. Perhaps epidemic diseases were introduced by trading partners from the plains and found a receptive habitat in the dense settlements along the Fraser River. Perhaps the largest villages were destroyed during intergroup warfare, or maybe an interruption of the trade routes caused economic collapse. Alternatively, the sites may have been abandoned because the salmon runs were disrupted in some way. To select among these hypotheses, archaeologists sought further evidence in the sites themselves. The radiocarbon dates of burned beams found on the floors of the last occupied pit houses in different village sites were identical, 1080 ± 70 BP. Given the earliness of the date, the abandonment of the winter villages was probably not precipitated by diseases introduced from the Old World. There was evidence that each of the pit houses had been burned, which might seem to signal a violent end; but there was no evidence of killing, no unburied skeletons or human bones. There were no unused food stores or valuable items that might have been abandoned. Instead, the pits seem to have been deliberately filled by their occupants prior to departure, and the burning was another sign that the exodus was planned and methodical. Around the turn of the twentieth century, pit houses were burned when people moved out in order to kill the rodents and vermin that had moved into them. The people who inhabited the southern interior winter villages evidently chose to abandon them about a thousand years ago, but why?

The most likely answer was found in the sequence of **fluvial sediments** underlying steplike river terraces near the present-day town of Lillooet. Geologists expected to find a layer of gravel in the main channel of the watercourse, overlain by progressively finer sediments. Near the shallow edges of the river, where the water moved slowly, there should have been thin banks of silt and fine sand, deposited during floods, capped with an uppermost layer of windblown silt. Instead, the geologists found that the expected sequence was interrupted. In two places, a layer of relatively coarse gravel rested upon lower layers of finer gravel, sand, and silt, suggesting that long-term degradation was punctuated by brief intervals of **aggradation**. What this meant was that at least twice in the past the river had been temporarily blocked by landslides downstream. These blockages had dammed the river, forming a temporary lake in which sediments accumulated. When the landslide dams eroded, the river resumed its course, leaving the aggraded gravels as terraces. Charcoal that was buried under these relatively coarse sediments dates to the time just before the southern interior winter villages were abandoned. Archaeologists Brian Hayden and June Ryder argue that if landslides did temporarily dam the Fraser around 1000 BP, they "would have blocked all or large parts of the salmon runs, thereby destroying the economic foundations of trade, not to mention subsistence, for the vast majority of people. Indeed, after depletion of all stored food, it is necessary to postulate large-scale migration out of the area and possibly severe starvation for large numbers of people, similar to the early twentieth-century occurrence when commercial fishing and canning at the mouth of the Fraser River drastically reduced salmon runs upstream."[28]

THE GREASE

As mentioned earlier in this chapter, on 16 July 1793, Alexander Mackenzie tried a dish that an Aboriginal woman had prepared for him that was "seasoned with about a pint of strong rancid oil. The smell of this curious dish was sufficient to sicken me without tasting it, but the hunger of my people surmounted the nauseous meal." Later commentators, tasting Mackenzie's "stinking oil" for the first time as adults, tended to agree with his assessment of its smell and taste. In the 1950s, Lyn Harrington described it as "malodorous," looking "remarkably like grapefruit juice, yellow and a little murky. The pungent reek is lessened in processing, though it is still too much for white palates." Terry Glavin described his first taste in the 1980s as "indescribable, true enough, but after a moment or two it didn't seem anything near as horrible as I'd been led to expect." People who grew up eating the oil did not find it horrible, of course, and could often tell by the taste where it had come from and who made it. The oil was the most distinctive product of Aboriginal trade between the coast and the interior, and the ways in which newcomers perceived it were symptomatic of their ultimate inability to remake the system of grease trails to suit themselves.[29]

The oil, the grease of the oolichan fish, was what gave the grease trails their name. The oolichan is a smelt, a small anadromous fish that spawns in large numbers in rivers along the Pacific coast in the spring. In what is now BC, the most important oolichan fishery was in the lower reaches of the Nass River. There, and at other rivers along the coast, great numbers of the fish were caught after people performed ceremonies to communicate their respect for the oolichan. One method of catching the fish, the most elaborate, involved staking a long purselike net, facing upstream, in a shallow spot where the tide fell swiftly, carrying large numbers of fish into the net. When it was full, the net was emptied into a canoe and reset in time for the next tide. The oolichan could also be caught from canoes using dip nets and herring rakes – long slim sticks with a comb of bone points along the edge of one end. The fisher would stand in a canoe and sweep the rake through the water like a paddle, impaling numbers of the fish, which could then be shaken loose into the bottom of the boat, something that greatly impressed the first Europeans to visit the coast.[30]

Some of the oolichan were dried in the sunlight or smoked over an open fire in communal houses. They were first strung up by the gills in rows on cedar cords or thin sticks and then hung from racks. The accounts left by the non-Aboriginal traders show that oolichan were fished in very large numbers and must have served as a source of wealth for the Aboriginal groups that controlled key fishing grounds. The Hudson's Bay Company (HBC) trader P.N. Compton, for example, who was stationed at Fort Simpson near the mouth of the Nass River around 1859, later recalled seeing "an extent of four or five miles each side of the river, lined with oalahans which were being dried on posts, by the Indians." The dried fish could be kept for years and carried as a lightweight food source on overland journeys. They were nutritious, rich in iodine and in the fat-soluble vitamins A, E, and K, and full of oil. They were so oily, in fact, that they could be threaded with rush pith or cedar wicks and lit on fire like candles.[31]

The vast majority of the oolichan that were caught were not dried, however, but used to make the highly prized grease. The fish were first put for a few weeks into large bins or pits lined with evergreen boughs, known in some Aboriginal communities as "stink boxes." There the fish decomposed, making it easier to separate the oil. The young anthropologist T.F. McIlwraith, who did his fieldwork at Bella Coola in the early 1920s, noted that this decomposition was prolonged "until the disgusting smell has penetrated for miles, proving that putrefaction is well advanced." The decaying fish were then moved to large wooden cooking boxes and covered with water. Hot stones were added to bring the mixture to a simmer, and planks were laid on top to help press out the grease. The mixture might be stirred occasionally or constantly, according to the style of the person making the grease. As the grease rose to the surface, it was skimmed off and ladled into watertight wooden storage boxes that could be transported along the grease trails. The grease that was going to be used locally was kept in the stomachs or bladders of seal, mountain goat, or deer. The remainder of the fish might be wrapped in a porous mat to get a second pressing by hand, then made into fish cakes or fed to the dogs.[32]

The farther up the Pacific Coast one goes, the oilier the oolichans become. Runs are concentrated on glacier-fed rivers with distinct spring freshets. As was the case with salmon, human interaction with this natural gradient resulted in seasonal focal points in Aboriginal political economy. Indigenous groups that controlled access to the oolichan runs were able to monopolize a source of power, wealth, and prestige in the form of grease. At first, non-Aboriginal traders were bothered by the fact that some coastal Aboriginal people spent so much time on the oolichan fishery when they could have been hunting for furs. The traders soon realized that the grease was a valuable product in itself and moved to capture some of the wealth, trading it up and down the coast. At Fort Simpson in 1840, an Aboriginal trader could receive fourteen gallons of grease from the HBC for one beaver skin. In fact, many of the interior furs that made their way to the coast were paid for with grease; if the company had figured out a way to gain control of the grease trade, it would have had more control over trading in the interior. As it was, the HBC never managed to establish a monopoly in the interior because the indigenous people living there could do business with coastal groups instead of with the company. (This is discussed further in Part 3.)[33]

The Tsimshian, who fished the run at the mouth of the Nass River, operated what the HBC governor George Simpson called "the grand mart of the Coast." The Tsimshian put grease in **kerfed boxes** and packed it upriver from the lower Nass, where it was traded for obsidian and animal products like moose hide, sheep and goat horn, goat wool, and furs. At two places on the upper Nass, the Kitwanga and Cranberry rivers, grease was carried into the drainage of the Skeena River and from there east along the Bulkley and Babine rivers. Oolichan runs in the Kitimat, Kildala, Kemano, and Kitlope rivers provided surplus grease for the Haisla, who carried it up the Kitimat River to the Skeena and into the interior. They also exported directly east, from Kemano to Tahtsa Lake, and from thence to the François, Ootsa, Whitesail, and Eutsuk lakes and the Nechako River. Frank Swannell, who did land surveys in the Nechako Valley from 1909 to 1912,

found coast-made cedar boxes at François Lake, "still redolent of the grease."
The Haisla also had an overland trail from the Kitlope River south to
Nuxalk villages. The Nuxalk themselves fished the oolichan runs in the
Bella Coola, Klinaklini, Kimsquit, and Dean rivers to create surplus grease
that they could trade with their interior partners. From Kimsquit village
on the Dean Channel, there were two trails into the interior; from Bella
Coola, five. As the grease was packed up the mountains on people's backs,
it occasionally spilled, staining the rocks along the way.[34]

ULKATCHO AND THE CULLA CULLA POTLATCH HOUSE

In the summer of 1926, a small party led by surveyor Frank Swannell set
out from Bella Coola to retrace, in reverse, Mackenzie's trip on the grease
trail to Ulkatcho village. Along the way, "a whole mob of Ulkatcho Indians passed with sixty horses," and Swannell began to muse about the past
of the trail. "One wonders for how many years," he wrote, "perhaps hundreds, this annual trek has been made." From his reading, Swannell knew
that George Dawson had had a similar encounter near the same place fifty
years earlier. On 7 July 1876, Dawson wrote that he "travelled on ... to
Crossing place of Salmon R. Found there a whole tribe of Indians on their
way to Salmon House for the Annual fishery there. Men women children
dogs, & a few horses." That same day, Dawson wrote, he "saw a very old
Indian who remembers seeing the first white men who penetrated this
part of the country. Says 4 white men, with one gun (then a novelty to the
Indians) Came from E walking, & got two Indians from near Il-gatcheo
L to go on with them. The Indians returned but the white men went on
to the Sea by the Bella Coola Trail. (Can they be identified as any of the
first explorers)." Dawson was thinking of Mackenzie, of course. From his
own reading he knew that Mackenzie had had a similar encounter on 15
July 1793, when his party met a travelling group of five families. "Every
man, woman and child," Mackenzie wrote, "carried a proportionate burden, consisting of beaver coating and parchment, as well as skins of the
otter, the marten, the bear, the lynx, and dressed moose-skins. The last
they procure from the Rocky Mountain Indians. According to their account,
the people of the sea coast prefer them to any other article. Several of their
relations and friends, they said, were already gone, as well provided as
themselves, to barter with the people of the coast; who barter them in
their turn, except the dressed leather, with white people who, as they had
been informed, arrive there in large canoes."[35]

Ulkatcho, the focal point of all this activity, had been strategically positioned to control sources of obsidian. Archaeologists found evidence there for early occupation in the form of stone tools: microblades and the core they had been struck from, a drill, a projectile point, and a biface, a chert tool that had been worked on both sides. The site had taken on new strategic significance in the late eighteenth century as the balance of trading on the grease trails shifted to accommodate the maritime fur trade. At that time, a coastal-style longhouse, later known as Culla Culla House (after a Chinook Jargon expression for "bird"), was constructed there. It must have been relatively new when Mackenzie described it on 14 July 1793. The building materials were, he wrote,

> [well] prepared and finished. The timber was squared on two sides, and the bark taken off the two others; the ridge pole was also shaped in the same manner, extending about eight or ten feet beyond the gable end, and supporting a shed over the door; the end of it was carved into the similitude of a snake's head. Several hieroglyphics and figures of a similar workmanship, and painted with red earth, decorated the interior of the building. The inhabitants had left the house but a short time, and there were several bags or bundles in it, which I did not suffer to be disturbed.

When George Dawson explored the building in the summer of 1876 and photographed it, he thought that it "bore the marks of considerable antiquity." In his journal, he wrote:

> Gotcheo L., a Celebrated resort of the Indians, a building of their's existing here Known as the Culla-Culla House, or Bird House, a large Crow Carved in wood, rather neatly, & painted black, adorning one gable. The Indians tell me that the [abode?] made by Bella Coola Indians, the natives here not understanding painting & decoration so well. A curious instance of mingling of customs of two now friendly tribes. A door in each end of this Shape that at the west end being surmounted at each side by a painted collosal figure resembling a bear, more than anything else ... The inner side of the East end covered with a corresponding picture, but this time of two gigantic birds touching their bills above the door. Also in the same style. Both in red paint. Various other designs on the inner walls, some evidently secondary & added fancifully by poor artists. Among most conspicuous a red hand with claws. The Carved figure of a blackbird already mentioned stands on the head of a long snouted monster with a good row of teeth on each side, which the projecting end of the roof tree.

As with any site that is regularly occupied and used by people, Culla Culla House changed over time. When Dawson visited it, he noted that it had been "repaired for a great *potlatch* this summer." In Mackenzie's time the house had also been used for potlatching, but the institution as practised on the coast and in the interior was no more static than anything else that people have a hand in.[36]

"Potlatch" is typically taken to refer to a kind of gift exchange and is perhaps the most contested term in the discourse about the Aboriginal peoples of the Northwest Coast and their neighbours. In a recent dictionary of anthropology, potlatch is defined as "a competitive gift exchange in which contenders for social rank organize elaborate feasts that include large distributions of possessions, and sometimes their destruction, in order to enhance the giver's prestige. Rivals were expected to respond by even more elaborate ceremonies or face humiliation." Different interpreters don't agree with the emphasis on one-upmanship. An alternative definition describes the institution in terms of the display and witnessing of traditional names, ranks, hereditary privileges, and hereditary cultural possessions like masks, dances, and songs. According to this interpretation, the gifts were a form of payment to the guests, who "validated and sanctioned the status displayed and claimed."[37]

Ever since the institution was described by Franz Boas in the 1890s, anthropologists have sought to explain it by appealing to its history; its place in social, economic, and political order; its ecological function; and its symbolic meanings. The task of interpreting the potlatch is complicated by the fact that "potlatch" is not what Clifford Geertz would call an "experience-near" concept, one that represented the "native's point of view" or that came naturally to people who participated in the institution. Instead, it was used by Aboriginal people only when discussing the practice with outsiders. Interpretation is further complicated by the fact that the Canadian government outlawed the practice in 1885, and attempts to define the potlatch so that laws could be enforced or opposed multiplied the number of different meanings and the shadings of each.[38]

The past of the potlatch house at Ulkatcho is characterized by the same indeterminacy as the past practices of potlatching. Archaeologists have failed to establish the exact relationship between newer and older material elements. The stone tools that were found there, the core and microblades, are thought to date from more than fifteen hundred years ago. The problem is that they were found in the upper ten centimetres of the site, whereas objects that are obviously of European manufacture, such as fragments of glass bottles, metal buttons, and a painted clay pipe, were found as deep as eighteen centimetres below the surface. The most likely explanation is that some later human activity – perhaps digging or construction – or a non-human process like erosion, transport, and redeposition mixed the artifacts from earlier and later deposits. When such disruption has not occurred, archaeologists sometimes speak of "horizons," a technical term they use to denote the widespread spatial distribution of something with limited temporal extent. As a particular kind of artifact, for example, is used and then falls out of fashion, a layer where such artifacts can be found is gradually covered with more recent deposits. Thus, horizons often correspond to surface and subsurface layers that can be seen or imagined in cross-section as one digs into a site. This metaphor of horizons, however, as archaeologists well know, hides the complexity of the processes whereby objects "move through a trajectory from being part of a living, dynamic context to being a static accumulation or assemblage of materials." Artifacts and **ecofacts** that are deposited while people dwell in a place may eventually be buried or may remain on the surface. Their nature and distribution may provide clues to human activity or may reflect later physical and chemical changes that are the result of weathering, erosion, compaction, soil formation, and many other processes.[39]

Human activity at Ulkatcho predated the rise of the maritime fur trade in sea otter pelts in the late eighteenth century and continued long after the sea otters were pushed toward extinction and the trade collapsed. In the early nineteenth century, people at Ulkatcho adjusted their seasonal rounds to take advantage of new demand for the fur of animals like beaver, muskrat, and lynx at the North West Company (later HBC) forts at Fraser Lake, Fort George, Alexandria, and Fort Chilcotin. After the middle of the nineteenth century, they took jobs as guides and packers during the gold rush, and turned to cowboying when the gold rush ended. Sometime in the decade after George Dawson visited in 1876, they built newer buildings to the north of Culla Culla House. They continued following their seasonal rounds, however. When Indian reserve commissioner A.W. Vowell came to lay out four reserves in October 1899, many of the residents were away in the mountains. The village was abandoned in 1945, when most of the Carrier of Ulkatcho moved to Anahim Lake. The remains of many of the buildings are still there: people's homes and stores, including Paul Krestenuk's; an old church and a newer one; a house for the priest; a schoolhouse; barns, sheds, and outhouses. Ulkatcho elders remember life in the village: the summertime arrival of pack horses loaded with groceries that were traded for furs; the women cutting boards for the new church with a whipsaw; helping parents hunt groundhogs and tan their hides for blankets, and the good taste of their thick back fat, especially when smoked; going to the village school during the Second World War; the sleighs that were used to move mowing machines, hay rakes, and cook-stoves along winter trails; and the visits of surveyors, fur traders, mission-aries, government agents, ranchers, and an ethnographer.[40]

CONCLUSION: GROUND TRUTH ON THE GREASE TRAIL

In February 1985, the provincial and federal governments signed an agree-ment to establish, protect, and develop the Alexander Mackenzie Heritage Trail co-operatively. In the foreword to the document, the authors noted that the trail was intended to "accord recognition to one of the most sig-nificant feats of exploration in the world, one that had profound impact on the political and economic axis of North America." In the historical background to the agreement, they emphasized Mackenzie's precedence over Lewis and Clark and the importance of his voyage for the later estab-lishment of the Canada-US border at the 49th parallel. This emphasis on anteriority was complicated however, by the recognition that there were actually a number of "important cultural resources" in the trail corridor, including Aboriginal trade routes that had been used for millennia, dense concentrations of archaeological sites, other sites that were highly signifi-cant to contemporary Aboriginal people, historic trails and wagon roads, historic and contemporary settlement at Bella Coola, and an existing ranching community in the Blackwater valley. Furthermore, conservation of a trail raised problems of multiple jurisdictions, rights of access, and co-ordination amongst various interests.

A number of basic divisions arose in the contest of stakeholders over the fate of the proposed trail. There was national support for a heritage trail, and the idea was favoured by some regional businesses as a means of in-creasing tourism and stimulating the economy, but local residents, including Aboriginal people on reserves, feared disruption. Already there was an increase in uncontrolled use of all-terrain vehicles on the trail and frequent reports of vandalism, poaching, "wildlife harassment," and environmental damage. Increased recreational use of horses could only decrease the limited natural fodder available to residents. Other businesses, whose continued financial health depended on extracting natural resources, were concerned that protection of the trail would interfere with logging, mining, hydro-electric development, and so on. Logging operations, for example, would now have to include trail managers in decisions about road construction, harvesting, insect and fire control, and "viewshed management." The federal and provincial governments had mandates to protect the archaeological sites, so they welcomed the trail for the protection it might afford against the inroads of resource companies, but any such victory could ultimately be Pyrrhic, because having more people on the trail would surely increase the potential for site disturbance. Sport anglers and Aboriginal residents were concerned by the decrease in natural fish stocks, and parks personnel noted that some species, such as the oolichan and sockeye salmon, had "potential for interpretation." Presumably, exhibiting the uses to which they were put in the past and granting the fish heritage status might preclude other possible uses, such as creating a modern-day fishery. Environmentalists were concerned about the adverse impact on flora and fauna generally, and everyone acknowledged the "higher probability for bear-human confrontations." And, as it was everywhere else in British Columbia, the legal situation with respect to Aboriginal land claims was not clear.[41]

In an attempt to bring some semblance of order to the welter of readings and experiences of the trail, the federal-provincial agreement suggested four interpretive themes centred on Mackenzie. The first was the man himself, first to cross the Rocky Mountains and the whole continent, first to survey what is now BC, a man who gave impetus to the expansion of the fur trade and to the activities of later explorers like Simon Fraser and David Thompson. The second theme was Aboriginal prehistory and ethnology as seen through the lens of Mackenzie's journal, "one of the first and finest European accounts of early B.C.'s native culture." The importance of Mackenzie's Aboriginal guides was also to be stressed, but only insofar as they played a role in his accomplishment. The third theme was natural history. Again, Mackenzie's journal played a key role as "a benchmark for evaluating and interpreting today's landscape." Under the theme of natural history, the authors of the agreement included the trade routes themselves, as if their layout were solely a function of the sources of various natural resources and not of human agency. The final theme was "post-contact history," framed in terms of the traders, surveyors, and missionaries who followed Mackenzie, and the present-day inhabitants who exhibited his virtues of independence and self-reliance.[42]

When the creators of the heritage trail relegated the historical activities of Aboriginal people to supporting roles for non-Aboriginal colonists in their interpretive themes, they virtually guaranteed that the site would become the focus of discontent. The idea that Aboriginal people were a part of nature, waiting to be discovered by Mackenzie and civilized by those who followed him, was already in general disfavour when the document was written. The studies of sites along the trail by government archaeologists directly contradicted any such notion, showing that the system of grease trails had been evolving for nine or ten thousand years. The interpretive themes of the heritage trail failed to cohere as people fought over the meaning of the trail's past in the present because the use of place to support a particular view of the past raises difficulties that are rarely encountered in the use of other repositories of cultural heritage. As people create representations – maps, written descriptions, photographs, and so on – they create something more abstract than the referent, the thing represented. Representations are fundamentally non-local; they can be easily transported without losing congruence with the referent or with one another. Representations can be duplicated, combined, exchanged, accumulated. To use the language of economics, transaction costs are greatly reduced if one can deal with a representation of something rather than the thing itself. This has important ramifications for the ways that people understand the past. When historical consciousness is based on representations, the fight for a usable past occurs in the realm of discourse. There are serious issues of epistemology, power, and bias, to be sure, but the problems are well-known. Furthermore, the importance of facts and events in discourse lies in their particularity. They are individually unique but can be comprehensibly related to the bigger picture, to shared concerns or common experience. The idea of Alexander Mackenzie as a symbol of national unity and Canadian identity was very much based on representations: on his journal, on the motto of the Canadian coat of arms, on the map of his journey, on his message painted on a rock, and on the handsome portrait of him hanging in the National Gallery in Ottawa.[43]

When the shift was made from the symbol of Mackenzie to a trail dedicated in his honour, historical consciousness was grounded in place, and the struggle for a usable past quickly became mired. The immutability and abstractness of maps was a liability in the search for ground truth. The creators of the heritage trail were forced to admit that they often did not know where Mackenzie had actually walked, and they had to simply choose a route themselves. Every use of the trail, rather than of a representation, was subject to steeply rising transaction costs. To the extent that collective memory was anchored in material surroundings, the definite advantage in interpretation went to the people who dwelt there. Moves made in the realm of discourse could be confronted with situated action. When the Lakehead students attempted to re-enact the Mackenzie expedition for nationalist reasons, their anachronistic endeavour bogged down in the present, where occupants of the region were unwilling to let them pass. From the time of Mackenzie and before, everyone who travelled the grease trails was surrounded by the ubiquitous indexical signs of past human activity. There are no untainted passages through a place: you always leave something of yourself, and you always take something with you. And as there can be no untainted passages, there can be no pristine places either. What there are instead are muddy places, lived places, places filled with the tracks of those who have gone before.[44]

Part 3

Shadowed Ground

5

Converging towards "Banshee"

E DWARD S. CASEY has argued that, from a phenomenological stand-point "*places gather*." What he means by this aphorism is that places not only amass animate and inanimate entities, holding them in a particular configuration, but that "places also gather experiences and histories, even languages and thoughts. Think only of what it means to go back to a place you know, finding it full of memories and expectations, old things and new things, the familiar and the strange, and much more besides. What else is capable of this massively diversified holding action?"[1]

This gathering aspect of the archive of place is the subject of the case study that follows. In the decades after Mackenzie's voyage, the traders of the Hudson's Bay Company (HBC) moved into the northern interior of what is now BC in an effort to monopolize the trade of the grease trails. In this they were only partly successful. They were never able to monopolize the maritime trade, and interior Aboriginal people could take their furs to the coast if they didn't like the terms offered at interior trading posts. Furthermore, non-Aboriginals were greatly outnumbered by Aboriginal people before the mid-nineteenth century, so non-Aboriginals had to step relatively lightly. During the fur trade, the Chilcotin gathered experiences, memories, stories, and customs that were largely an outgrowth of the grease trail system. The status quo ended abruptly in the gold rush of the late 1850s, when beleaguered Aboriginal groups were confronted by tens of thousands of newcomers, and control of the region passed from the HBC to a new colonial government. One of the first challenges to colonial authority was a series of killings known variously as the

Bute Inlet or Waddington Massacre, the Chilcotin Uprising, or the Chilcotin War. In choosing what to call this event, we necessarily take a stance on how it should be interpreted: what appeared to colonists as a massacre or an uprising looks more like a war in hindsight, and that is closer to what the perpetrators intended. After being incarcerated, they told the missionary R.C. Lundin Brown that "they meant war, not murder."[2]

The Chilcotin War led people to reimagine the past of the Chilcotin and its role in the present. In mid- to late-nineteenth-century accounts, the Chilcotin was portrayed as a landscape of resistance, violence, and tragedy. It gathered a new set of stories, a reputation for darkness. In building on this version of the Chilcotin past, people recast the social relations between them into the (fantastic) form of a relationship between human being and nature, charging the landscape with affect. This affective loading of place, influenced, in turn, those who dwelt there, casting a pall over the Tsilhqot'in people. This view of Chilcotin history persisted until the 1970s, when the tragic death of a Tsilhqot'in man named Fred Quilt led people to reimagine the past of the place and its occupants. Over the next two decades, the colonial view came under attack from a variety of perspectives and rapidly disintegrated.[3]

The colonial story of the Chilcotin is about the rise of modern racism and its retroactive historical justification. It has many parallels elsewhere, as does the postcolonial revision and dismantling of the story. The details, however, are specific to this place, with its boom-and-bust cycles of resource extraction, its fraught relations between Aboriginal people and non-Aboriginals, and its distinctly Canadian setting.

HUMAN REMAINS

When Aboriginal remains were accidentally disinterred in the early 1970s, they were treated very differently than those uncovered in an analogous situation two decades later. This difference in treatment was one expression of the late-twentieth-century change in attitude that is the subject of this case study. In early 1974, as the new Boitanio Mall was being constructed in Williams Lake, a rumour began circulating through local pubs. Excavators working on the project had unearthed human bones; nobody was sure exactly how many. Williams Lake residents alerted the provincial Archaeological Sites Advisory Board, which managed to stop work in what is now the mall parking lot long enough to excavate two mounds. According to the provincial archaeologist, Boitanio Mall was located on what was probably a burial site. A number of house pits had been destroyed already in the construction; what remained were two areas that were used for storing food and working stone. After a brief salvage operation, these too were paved over. The human remains were never recovered, having been unceremoniously dumped with other excavated material near the Tastee Freeze.[4]

Twenty years later, such an outcome would have been impossible. On 12 September 1996, workers from United Concrete and Gravel found the remains of eight bodies, including that of a small child, while clearing land for a rancher's hayfield south of the Sheep Creek bridge. The workers stopped immediately. Their manager later told a *Williams Lake Tribune* reporter, "I've been digging here for 30 years. It happens quite often."[5]

The Tsilhqot'in National Government found out about the discovery a few weeks later and responded with some irritation. "It would be like me taking a backhoe into a graveyard in Williams Lake and putting up a high rise," said Ray Hance, the deputy national chief. "As far as I'm concerned this has to stop right now." Hance immediately called the provincial archaeology branch in Victoria, claiming that workers had continued digging for three days after the skeletons were found. The provincial archaeology branch denied this, however. Hance wanted to take legal action to establish a precedent, but it wasn't clear against whom: "It's an issue that we as Tsilhqot'in people can't ignore. This is going on too much. It happens every time a road is built, every time logging goes on."[6]

The provincial archaeologists claimed that the bones were probably several hundred years old and planned to use pieces of manufactured copper found at the site to date them precisely. Ray Hance, however, thought they might be no more than seventy years old. According to Tsilhqot'in oral tradition, the site where they were found was once used for sturgeon fishing and as an alternative burial ground for people who died en route from Williams Lake to the reserves. The bones were moved to the Williams Lake morgue until a decision could be made about their final resting place. As indexical signs of past human activity, the bones were still indeterminate enough to be put to different uses by different stakeholders. To the archaeologists, they represented a prehistoric find; to the Tsilhqot'in, a link with a much more immediate past. Both views had consequences for action in the present.[7]

The following June, a Liberal MLA was stripped of his post amidst allegations of conflict of interest after he contacted the archaeology branch of the culture ministry to ask about land owned by the Thompson Land and Cattle Company. Part of the land in question was the site of the burial ground, and the owner of the ranch was the MLA's father-in-law, Neil MacDonald. MacDonald defended the politician's actions, saying that he was trying to forestall a NDP-supported "attack on private land" rather than lobbying on behalf of an in-law. MacDonald complained that ranching was not very lucrative and that he could not afford to pay for an archaeological assessment every time he needed to clear some of his land. This was the second time he had been stopped because his land was thought to contain artifacts. "The thing that bothers me, and should bother everyone," MacDonald said, "is where is it going to end? ... Can any private land owner be disposed of his or her land and home by the mere allegation by someone that it is sacred land or an archaeological site?" Once again, indeterminate material traces were invoked to support opposing points of view. Near where the bodies had been found there was an area of soil darkened with charcoal. To the Tsilhqot'in National Government it was a sign of indigenous activity, but MacDonald said that it was simply the remains of slash burning from when the land was originally cleared.[8]

In October 1997, the Tsilhqot'in tried to establish the terms on which all present and future conflicts would be negotiated. At an assembly of more than five hundred Tsilhqot'in at Tl'esqox (Toosey), Chief Ervin Charleyboy read the Tsilhqot'in Declaration of Sovereignty to the federal minister of Indian Affairs. The declaration began with traditional territory, positioning the Tsilhqot'ins with respect to their Aboriginal neighbours and establishing their claims by appealing to Aboriginal language names: "Our mountains and valleys, lakes, rivers and creeks all carry names given to them by the Tsilhqot'in people ... Our territory is that which is named in our language. All living things in our country – animals, birds, insects, amphibians, reptiles, worms and flies, fish, trees, shrubs, flowers and other plants – also bear the names given to them in the language of the Tsilhqot'in." The declaration went on to trace the affinity of the Tsilhqot'in with the Dene (Athapaskan) nation and then to oppose the "history of illegal colonization of our Nation."

The first white men to enter our country did so only with our permission and when we told them to leave they left. When men settled in our country without permission, we drove them out. When the Queen of England extended to our nation the protection of her law, by including our territory in the colony of British Columbia in 1858, she did so without our knowledge or consent. When the colony joined the Dominion of Canada in 1871 it was done without our knowledge or consent. Since that time, whilst our people were suffering from the effects of European diseases, our country has been invaded and despoiled. Our people have been deceived, impoverished, oppressed, exploited, imprisoned and maligned. Our sovereignty has been encroached upon and our jurisdiction ignored. Yet we have survived and once again we thrive.[9]

The next three points of the declaration accused the federal and provincial governments of "repeated and shameless violation of their own laws and of international agreements and covenants," asserted Tsilhqot'in jurisdiction over their own territory and people, insisted on the "right to decolonize," and offered to negotiate a Tsilhqot'in constitution that would set the terms of union with Canada. The Tsilhqot'in National Government also asked the United Nations to monitor the situation "because Canada has stolen our lands and continues to have an interest in maintaining control over them. It is difficult to ask a thief to sit in judgement on his theft." The declaration then recognized non-status Tsilhqot'in as Tsilhqot'in citizens, decried the inadequacy and illegality of the reserve system, and declared that federal and provincial laws would cease to hold force in Tsilhqot'in country after a future date, to be set later. It asked for the recognition of British Columbians, other Canadians, and people around the world. The final point of the declaration was a call for respect:

To those people who have settled amongst us in our country the Tsilhqot'in Nation declares that we bear no enmity towards you, as long as you respect us: it is the policies of the governments, the courts and the churches of Canada that have done us so much harm and that now must change. We do not blame you; we ask you to understand that change must now take place for all our children. We govern according to principles of consent. We ask you to understand that what we are saying is not unique or peculiar to the Tsilhqot'in – it is happening throughout the Americas. The period or era of colonization is passing; the Fourth World is emerging.[10]

The declaration signalled the Tsilhqot'in's resolve to do things on their own terms, and this was reflected in their subsequent actions with respect to Neil MacDonald. On 14 October, Ray Hance said that the whole plateau near the Sheep Creek bridge should be declared a sacred site, including the hayfield and gravel piles. He said that his people couldn't wait any longer for a decision, so they were going to go and rebury the skeletons regardless of Macdonald's wishes: "We're not prepared to put up with any more B.S. At the same time, we feel bad for Mr. MacDonald who has lost the use of his land. We don't want to see anyone displaced from their livelihood." The BC Cattlemen's Association responded with alarm. In a letter to the premier of British Columbia, the BCCA president wrote that the association "view[ed] this matter with extreme importance and suggest[ed], at the very least, it is not being addressed with the seriousness or with the expediency it deserves. [The situation] could escalate with dire consequences." At that point, MacDonald said that he had received "six absolute zero letters from Victoria. They fill a couple of pages and don't say anything."[11]

At the end of the month, the local MLA, David Zirnhelt, released a press backgrounder saying that the province would begin negotiating with Neil MacDonald to buy his land or give him compensation of some sort. Zirnhelt's political opponents accused him of potentially creating a stand-off between the Tsilhqot'in and MacDonald by his failure to take action. In mid-November, MacDonald responded to the Tsilhqot'in's threat to rebury the bones on his land, saying, "I'll be there and I'll stop them. I'm tired of people trespassing. I'm going to make sure they don't have access to my land. No one does. It's my land." Ervin Charleyboy responded by saying, "If Neil is saying 'over my dead body,' things might get ugly. We're prepared for anything. If that's the route they want to take, so be it. We're tired of the B.S. the government has put us through." The Tsilhqot'in claimed land west of the Fraser as their traditional territory, so it was, according to them, the government that was guilty of trespass. For the first time, however, Charleyboy acknowledged another potential problem: "The origin of the bones has yet to be determined. They might be Shu-swap [i.e., Secwepemc] bones." As was the case with the rainbow trout at Fish Lake, the increasing value of the bones provided opportunities for other stakeholders to claim rights that were still in the public domain. The archaeologists would likely be willing to argue that the bones were those of Aboriginal people. It was less likely, however, that they would commit themselves to distinguishing between different Aboriginal groups. The Secwepemc thus had an opportunity to claim the skeletons, to use them to support their own version of the past, and to buttress their own land claims in the present.[12]

Zirnhelt blocked the Tsilhqot'in's plan to rebury the bones by refusing to release them until all parties were in agreement. MacDonald had granted permission for provincial archaeologists to do research on his land, to come up with a plan to rebury the remains and protect any oth-ers that might still be at the site. Even though they did not have custody of the bones, the Tsilhqot'in gathered at the site. There they met with the archaeologists to learn about how the site would be stabilized. "Because the Tsilhqot'ins and the Shuswap Indians are in disagreement about the origins of the bones, chiefs and representatives from both nations talked in front of MacDonald's property, before walking to the site," the *Williams Lake Tribune* reported. "The media was asked to stay away from the group as they spoke." If the two Aboriginal groups could find some common ground, it would be more difficult for other stakeholders to use a strategy of divide and conquer.[13]

In November, the Tsilhqot'in and the Secwepemc "verbally agreed to rebury the ancestral remains on rancher Neil MacDonald's property in a partnership." MacDonald had reversed his own position and gave the Aboriginal groups his blessing; he was even thinking of attending the burial ceremonies. "Everything is going to be done with my knowledge and cooperation," he told the *Tribune*. "I never really did change my mind. We discussed it and came up with a solution, and now we have mutual respect and understanding between all of us." Zirnhelt refused to release the bones until there was a written agreement between the Tsilhqot'in and the Secwepemc. In retrospect, this turned out to be a wise plan, as talks between the two Aboriginal groups stalled over a dispute about whose land it was and which group's reburial ceremonies would be used. The Aboriginal negotiators took the matter back to their own communities to get direction. The dispute was complicated by the fact that the Tsilhqot'in were not participating in the BC Treaty Commission process, and the commission had taken the Secwepemc's word for where territorial boundaries lay. Zirnhelt objected to the idea that the treaty process was to blame for the dispute.[14]

In late December, the skeletons were finally reburied in a traditional ceremony. The Tsilhqot'in said that there was never a question that the resolution would be peaceful, but "there was always a problem with jurisdictional interests here that everybody had to defend. Sadly the ultimate victims of this were the remains of the ancestors." But history is never about the ancestors per se, but about the relationship between their time and the present in a given place. Between the 1970s and the 1990s, the history of the Chilcotin and the accepted view of its Aboriginal people underwent a sea change. People in the 1970s would have been no more able to imagine the dispute that erupted over the Sheep Creek bones than those in the 1990s could imagine treating the Boitanio bones like construction waste. To explain how such a change in historical consciousness could occur, it is first necessary to see how the conventional account of Chilcotin history arose.[15]

DID THE TSILHQOT'IN REALLY "OPT OUT"
OF THE FUR TRADE?

From the mid-nineteenth century through much of the twentieth, the conventional view of Chilcotin history assumed that the Tsilhqot'in people violently resisted all non-Aboriginal encroachment, both before and after the gold rush. One popular history of the Chilcotin War, written by Mel Rothenburger in the 1970s, claimed that "the Hudson's Bay Company had not been able to induce them [i.e., the Tsilhqot'in] to enter the fur trade." Similarly, in the influential *Contact and Conflict,* a book that otherwise did much to bring Aboriginal people into BC historiography as agents, the historian Robin Fisher wrote that "some [Aboriginal peoples] preferred not to be involved in the trade and found it possible to exercise that choice." As an example, he used the Tsilhqot'in, who he claimed "had opted out of the fur trade." The Tsilhqot'in may have chosen to limit trade with non-Aboriginal people at interior posts, but this does not mean that they didn't participate in the fur trade or that they were exercising some kind of violent resistance against non-Aboriginal incursions into their territory. Instead they chose to trade with other Aboriginal people. The story of the Tsilhqot'in during the fur trade should be seen as a failed bid on the part of the HBC to change the **spatial ecology** of the region.[16]

After Mackenzie's voyage, his employer, the North West Company (NWC), extended its trade network across the Rocky Mountains and established a series of posts in what it called "New Caledonia," now the northern interior of BC (see Map 1). From Hudson's Hope on the Peace River, also known as Rocky Mountain Portage, a party led by Simon Fraser moved southwest to establish a post at McLeod's Lake in 1805. The following year they established posts at Stuart's Lake, which became the centre of operations in New Caledonia and was later renamed Fort St. James, and Fraser Lake. In 1807, they established Fort George, now Prince George. This last post served as a support base from which Fraser set out to explore the Tacoutche Tesse River, which both he and Alexander Mackenzie thought was the Columbia. In 1808, Fraser took a party of twenty-one NWC employees and two Aboriginal guides down the river in four canoes, reaching tidewater in July. The river turned out not to be the Columbia – it is now known as the Fraser – and, as both Mackenzie's and Fraser's Aboriginal informants had said, it was nearly impassable due to rapids and canyons. The fur traders would need to find a different way to transport goods to and from the coast.[17]

In 1812, the NWC asked John Stuart to establish a route from the post at Stuart's Lake to the Columbia River and the Pacific Ocean. If such a route could be found, the company could ship its trade goods for New Caledonia to the Pacific Coast and send furs directly from there to the China market instead of laboriously transporting the goods and furs overland between New Caledonia and Montreal. The following summer, Stuart took nine men in two canoes and descended the Stuart River to Fort George, where it joined the Fraser. They continued down the Fraser to the point just above the first bad rapids, the place where Mackenzie had

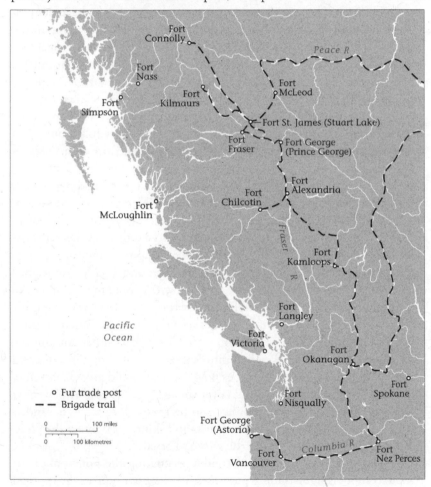

MAP 1 Fur-trade posts and brigade trails established by the North West Company.
SOURCE: Basemap data from the BC Ministry of Sustainable Resource Management.

stopped and set out overland. From here, Stuart and his men also set out overland, on horseback, south to Fort Kamloops and then to Fort Okanagan, where they could continue to the ocean in canoes. Having established the route, the NWC used it once the following year, then abandoned it because trade goods from the coast could not be distributed to New Caledonia posts before freeze-up. In 1820 the company decided to try again, working over the next few years to make the route, in John Stuart's words, "not only practicable but perfectly established."[18]

In September 1821, Fort Alexandria was established above the first rapids on the Fraser River and began operation under the management of George McDougall. The following month, three Tsilhqot'in came to the new post at Alexandria and asked McDougall to "pay them a visit in the winter." They returned home and began collecting furs for the company. In November, McDougall received a letter from John Stuart, his superior at Stuart Lake, informing him that the NWC, which he worked for, had merged with the HBC. Stuart asked McDougall to leave his post in the hands of a colleague and make "a trading excursion to the Chilk o tins." The following January, McDougall set out into the Chilcotin with fourteen men. The roads were bad and the snow was deep. The first Tsilhqot'in families they met had hardly enough salmon to share and had made all of their beaver pelts into robes, which they were wearing. The traders continued on to the next settlement, "two ground Lodges containing 9 or 10 families." There were a few furs in the lodges and enough new beaver robes that McDougall suspected that other nearby Tsilhqot'in might have some surplus furs to trade. He camped with his men and sent an Aboriginal messenger to round up some locals to trade with. Some more Tsilhqot'in arrived with a few furs, and McDougall wrote that "they very candidly told us, they had killed a number of Beaver in the Fall, purposely to trade with us, but finding we did not come and the cold weather coming on, they made all the Beaver they had into Robes." The Tsilhqot'in expressed their willingness to trade their robes if McDougall could give them something else "with which they could cover themselves." He didn't have anything that would fit the bill, however, so he returned to Fort Alexandria with a meagre thirty-seven pounds of furs and skins. "It is by far the poorest trip of its kind I ever made," he wrote to Stuart.[19]

McDougall seems to have had trouble evaluating the potential of the region to support a fur-trading post. Despite the poor returns, he thought highly of the Tsilhqot'in, "certainly a fine brave looking set of Indians." He also thought that their winter clothing showed that the territory was rich in furs, "the Men being generally well and warmly clad, with good

Chevreux, Elk, as well as some Carriboux Skins as Blankets, with good Leggings of excellent Leather, their Women, those we seen as well the Children are in general covered with good Beaver Robes, we did not see a Single Indian Man or Woman bare legged, nor with any thing of a shabby covering on their backs." The Tsilhqot'in, for their part, were very interested in the traders' ironwork, especially their traps. The account that they gave of their country was encouraging. In season there were plenty of beaver, fish, moose, and caribou. "In short if a person could believe them, their Lands abound with Milk & honey," McDougall concluded. After determining that there were about 131 Tsilhqot'in families with whom to trade, McDougall recommended that a post be established in the Chilcotin. He thought the Tsilhqot'in might also buy ammunition, since they already purchased guns from Aboriginal people near the coast.[20]

The following year, the northern council of the HBC decided to establish a post in the Chilcotin. These plans were delayed, however, when some company men were killed at Fort George and Fort St. John in 1823 and 1824. These deaths had nothing to do with the Tsilhqot'in people, but John Stuart decided to concentrate his forces at posts that were already established rather than splitting his men up to build new posts. In 1825, Stuart was succeeded by William Connolly. In the winter, Connolly made a trip to the Chilcotin to reassess the prospects for a new post and returned with six packs of beaver. Although he thought that a Chilcotin post might be advantageous to the company in the future, he hesitated to build one because the Tsilhqot'in and the Carrier were embroiled in "disputes of a most serious nature." These were triggered by a quarrel among hunters, but the more general issue seems to have been that the Carrier were using their geographic advantage to take over a lucrative position as middlemen and edge the Tsilhqot'in out of direct trade with the HBC. At this point, it had been five years since the Tsilhqot'in had requested a post in their own territory.[21]

The trouble – Connolly later referred to it as "the Chilcotin war" – started in March 1826 when four Carrier men went hunting in Tsilhqot'in territory. There was a dispute of some sort and three of the men were killed by Tsilhqot'in, while one escaped to return, seriously injured, to Fort Alexandria. The HBC traders prevented the Carrier from executing a Tsilhqot'in man at the fort in retaliation. Although the man escaped, he was later killed by a Carrier. Connolly reported that "altho' the Indians residing in the immediate neighbourhood of Alexandria only, were concerned in this war, all others attached to that post were nevertheless influenced thereby, and from an apprehension of being involved in the quarrel, retreated, on the first appearance of hostilities to the eastward of Frasers

River from where they must not return until the commencement of winter." This suggests that the other Aboriginal groups who traded at the post may have had closer kin or trading relationships with the Carrier than the Tsilhqot'in and were afraid of suffering collateral damage.[22]

The Carrier went skirmishing and lost three more men as a consequence. According to Joseph McGillivray, they then proclaimed "a War of extermination," attacked a Tsilhqot'in village, and returned to Fort Alexandria in June with five prisoners and the scalps of twelve Tsilhqot'in men, women, and children that they had killed. A party of Tsilhqot'in, meanwhile, showed up at Fort Alexandria and killed one Carrier man, perhaps in retaliation for the skirmishing. At the time, they didn't know that the Carrier had attacked one of their villages. A few weeks later, twenty-seven Tsilhqot'in appeared on the bank of the river opposite the fort. Their leader made a speech of some kind, but it was a very windy day and the traders and Carrier at the fort couldn't hear what he said. As well, the post's interpreter was away. The Tsilhqot'in left without attacking and without harming any of the company personnel they encountered. It's impossible to know if things would have turned out differently if this message had been received.

In September, about eighty Tsilhqot'in attacked Fort Alexandria. The Carrier were protected by the palisades of the fort and suffered few casualties. The Tsilhqot'in, however, were attacking from an exposed position, and many were killed or wounded. The HBC officers were afraid that they would be successful, however, and decided to arm the Carrier at the fort. A Tsilhqot'in woman who lived at Fort Alexandria, seeing that the HBC was giving arms and ammunition to the Carrier, slipped away to warn her fellows. The Tsilhqot'in decided to retreat, but they swore vengeance on the HBC traders "and threatened to cut off all white men that might thereafter fall their way." According to McGillivray, the Carrier then "raised the Scalps" of the Tsilhqot'ins they had killed, "mounted the dead bodies on Stumps" and mutilated them, and subjected the Tsilhqot'in prisoners they had taken alive to further atrocities. In early 1827, McGillivray wrote that "no overtures of a Peace by either Tribe has been made – both the Superintendant of the District and myself have sent paroles to the Chilkotins but so far no answer has been returned – and not one of that Tribe has been seen in our Neighbourhood since September 1826." The Tsilhqot'in sent proposals of peace to the Carrier by March, however, a year after the outbreak of hostilities.[23]

Despite the fact that the Tsilhqot'in may have had a grievance not only against the Carrier, but against the HBC as well, the company decided in autumn 1827 that it would proceed with building a post in the Chilcotin. Its timing couldn't have been worse. That year the salmon run completely failed, and other important food resources, like berries, were also in short supply. The traders at Fort Alexandria sent to Kamloops for twenty-five hundred salmon and obtained an additional fifteen hundred from William Connolly. With these, and thirty-five kegs of potatoes, they managed to keep from starving. The Tsilhqot'in didn't have the luxury of ordering food when their own ran out. They resorted to eating emergency foods like Black Tree lichen and, when possible, taking refuge with kin and trading partners on the coast. The famine further delayed the establishment of a post in the Chilcotin. In 1829, Connolly made yet another trip to the area, finding the Tsilhqot'in "greatly reduced in numbers" since 1825 and "in a state of utmost indigence." "The information I received from them on this occasion in regard to the resources of their country," he continued, "varied materially from that which they had formerly given. And, indeed, their appearance was sufficient to convince me that I had in that particular been deceived, they now acknowledged that their resources for subsistence were so extremely scanty and precarious that when salmon failed, which happens commonly three years out of four, they were reduced to the necessity of deserting their lands and of flying for relief to some other quarter near the sea coast." Connolly suggested that a fort would be of little use in a region where the occupants frequently had to migrate and that "the surest plan by which to draw from the Chilcotins all the benefit of which their country is susceptible, will be by attending to them by the means of Derouins [see below] and by endeavouring to make them resume the intercourse which they formerly held with Alexandria." If the company could put this plan into effect, it would remake the spatial ecology of the region by encouraging the Tsilhqot'in to become sedentary.[24]

As the fur traders extended their reach across the continent, they faced the constant problem of provisioning men who were too busy with the tasks of trade and transport to be able to feed themselves. Because of the long winter, northern rivers were only clear for canoe travel a short part of the year, and the distances that had to be covered were immense. There was no time for the men to hunt or gather food en route. Furthermore, when posts were established, the occupants quickly depleted the resources in their immediate vicinity, and most posts were located in areas where agriculture was very limited. To solve the logistical problems, the fur-trading companies had to develop elaborate food-supply networks. The long voyages made from a post to collect supplies – which is what Connolly had in mind for the Chilcotin – were known as "dérouines."[25]

This was a complicated business. Every move the HBC made could significantly alter the human geography and ecology of a region. Encouraging a group of Aboriginal people to hunt and trap instead of pursuing subsistence activities meant that those people had to be brought into the provisioning network too. The logic of killing animals for the market meant that some were driven towards local extinction, which rapidly altered food webs and natural population cycles. Unable to explain the ecological changes that they observed, some of the traders saw the working of God's will. Reflecting on his experiences at Fort Alexandria in 1834, for example, John McLean wrote,

> I have already observed that the salmon fail periodically, and the natives would consequently be reduced to the utmost distress, did not the goodness of Providence furnish them with a substitute. Rabbits are sent to supply the place of the salmon; and, singular as it may appear, these animals increase in number as the salmon decrease, until they swarm all over the country. When the salmon return, they gradually disappear, being destroyed or driven away by their greatest enemy, the lynx, which first appear in smaller, then in greater numbers; – both they and their prey disappear together. As to the *cause* that induces those animals to appear and disappear in this manner, I cannot take upon myself to explain.

Furthermore, by concentrating on the beaver, the trappers removed an animal whose activity created the ponds and lakes that provided habitat for many other species.[26]

The human consequences were every bit as complicated. There were new opportunities for indigenous groups to enter the provisioning trade, but the exchange of food, especially meat, seems to have had different cultural entailments for different peoples, providing more room for misunderstandings to arise. It also seems that Aboriginal people and newcomers had differing perspectives on scarcity and surplus, and it is often hard in retrospect to determine where on a continuum of want a particular group actually lay. In a classic article, Mary Black-Rogers analyzed the use of terms like "starving" and "starvation" in the reports and post journals of fur traders who were stationed among subarctic Algonquian and Athapaskan people. She discovered that the words were used to cover a wide range of situations, but that "starving" often meant "hunting for the belly, and not for furs." Faced with "starvation" in eastern James Bay in 1745, the Cree near the HBC's Eastmain House preferred not to trade their furs for oatmeal, expecting to be able to claim the food freely instead. Faced with "starvation" at Kamloops in the winter of 1829, some of the Aboriginal people actually died.[27]

Arthur Ray has argued that the cumulative impact of the fur trade was to change the spatial ecology of a given region in the following way. Before the arrival of the newcomers, indigenous groups moved to take advantage of seasonal surpluses. These seasonal subsistence rounds are well-documented for the Carrier, Tsilhqot'in, and other peoples of the interior, as well as for peoples in much of the rest of the continent. When fur-trading companies established trading posts, however, the food surpluses became concentrated at the nodes of a network that the company controlled, while local resources became depleted. Aboriginal groups were encouraged to settle near the posts and turn to the company when they faced privation. This is what Connolly had in mind for the Tsilhqot'in.[28]

FORT CHILCOTIN

On 1 October 1829, Connolly wrote to George McDougall, ordering him to take nine men and found a post "at the first point of woods you come to after falling on the Chilcotin River." Eight years after the Tsilhqot'in's first trip to Alexandria to request their own post, the bad blood between the Tsilhqot'in and Carrier had finally been cleared up, and the salmon run had been plentiful that year. McDougall had more knowledge of individual Tsilhqot'in than his colleagues and thus was the ideal person to become the first post manager. Connolly apologized for not being able to provide "a more efficient Interpreter ... than Baptiste Bouché Junr., but as he speaks the language perfectly supported by you I trust that he will answer tolerably well." McDougall wrote back to say that he would do as Connolly asked, but was unable "to prevail on any Indian of this place [i.e., Alexandria] to go to the *chil cotin* country."[29]

On arriving at the designated spot on the Chilcotin River, McDougall found no trees that were suitable for building and very little fuel for fires. He moved instead to "a cluster of small poplars," where he intended to build the winter huts for his men in the vicinity of present-day Redstone. He "would look round for a more convenient place" later if the company decided to keep its establishment in the area. McDougall was confronted with the Tsilhqot'in's seasonal subsistence activities right away. The "principal men are all off to the interior with their families," he wrote, "some to hunt Beaver, but the most of them to their root Grounds ... the Indians of the lake are off to the mountains, but they are expected back in

the fall, as the most of their families have remained to gather roots."
McDougall planned to obtain salmon for the subsistence of his own men,
but was uncertain how much he could get; he was glad that he had
brought supplies from Alexandria.[30]

By the end of January the following year, it was clear to Connolly that
"few if any" of the Tsilhqot'in had actually hunted for beaver over the winter and that it was unlikely they would start doing so because the task was
becoming more difficult as spring approached. He reported that "from these
premises the natural conclusion is that no advantage can accrue from the
Chilcotin Establishment during the winter, and not deeming it safe to
continue it for the summer no manner of injury can therefore arise from
withdrawing it as soon as possible." Connolly was afraid that the traders
did not know the Tsilhqot'in well enough to trust them if there was to be
no trade during the summer. The returns from the post that winter were
a meagre eight packs of beaver skins that had been hunted before the onset
of cold weather and thus were sparsely furred. Although McDougall seems
to have acquitted himself well enough, Connolly's successor, Peter Warren
Dease, suggested the following year that the problems at the Chilcotin
post were due to the fact that there was "a deficiency of Gentlemen required for the management of the Posts in the district." Dease wrote that
"the post has been for the Winter under the management of one of the
common Servants, who could not be supposed to possess that influence
or authority, nor command that respect among them necessary to incite
them to industry as a Gentleman would, indeed in general they would
entertain rather a contemptible opinion for common Servants, the scant-
iness of Returns from there will sufficiently shew this." Dease went on to
acknowledge that "other causes may have operated partly in producing the
unfavorable result of the Season, scarcity of Salmon and means of subsistence during Winter has obliged them to leave their own Lands and resort
to the neighbouring Tribes (whose means are not so limited) to escape the
horrors of Famine." George Simpson was also ambivalent about George
McDougall, calling him "a man of no principle ... A sly knowing low
Vagabond who Drinks, lies, and I dare say Steals," but noting that he was
"an excellent Trader and keen Shrewd fellow who [was] qualified to be
very useful either at a Trading Post or Depôt."[31]

Over the next few years, the company maintained contact with the Tsilhqot'in but did not try to re-occupy the post in the Chilcotin. Dease was
careful to "give them some encouragement to work in the Expectations of
having again the Post established of which they appear to be very desirous."
The Tsilhqot'in may have been getting tired of being strung along, however.

When one company man and an interpreter were sent from Fort Alexandria in September 1831, they "met a very rough reception, [the Tsilhqot'in] behaved with much insolence and used some Menaces toward them." Apparently the Tsilhqot'in didn't think that the company was serious about trading with them. When an HBC man reported from the Chilcotin at the end of December, he said that most of the beaver pelts had already been converted into winter robes, and the Tsilhqot'in weren't willing to part with them.[32]

The archival record is fragmentary, but by 1834 the company seems to have finally re-occupied Fort Chilcotin, now under the charge of the clerk William Fletcher Lane. George Simpson, governor of the HBC, was confident that there was "a prospect of this country becoming more productive that it has heretofore been, from the growing industry of that tribe, who, until lately, could not be induced to exert themselves in hunting." The returns were reasonable, but the post had to be abandoned sometime in 1835 or 1836 as conflict flared up again between the Tsilhqot'in and the Carrier. During this time, the Tsilhqot'in may have been moving to the northwest to establish more direct trading links with the Nuxalk. By 1837, Fort Chilcotin was back in business under the management of John McIntosh, who was soon replaced by the clerk William McBean.[33]

McBean's post journal for the years 1837 to 1840 is the only surviving account of daily life at Fort Chilcotin, and it, too, is fragmentary. Much of it is concerned with the company men's daily subsistence activities. On 26 October 1837, McBean reported that "as it is not likely the Bull will get any fater than he is from the cold setting in – I have shot him to day, which job occupied my two men all day." The following day they spent searching for their horses, an activity that would become familiar to Chilcotin residents of subsequent generations. Throughout the week they continued to bring home bundles of hay for their livestock. By 31 October they had accumulated 392 bundles at the post. During the coming winter there would be almost no range for their animals, and they would have to feed them hay instead. Since this winter feeding period was about four months long in the vicinity of the Chilcotin post, caring for the animals put a considerable strain on the time and energy of the men. There was little margin for error. The men would run into trouble if they tried to keep too many animals or too few.[34]

At the time, horses were relatively new in the Chilcotin. Mackenzie didn't see any in 1793 and surely would have ridden most of the way to the coast instead of walking if he could have. Simon Fraser, on the other hand, did see horses in the area in 1808, although they were scarce enough that he had difficulty obtaining them to assist with his portages. In the 1820s, the HBC perfected the brigade route that it had inherited from the NWC. Each spring, furs were shipped out of the interior from the post at Stuart's Lake (also known as Fort St. James) to Alexandria by canoes, packed from Alexandria to Okanagan by horses, and transported from Okanagan to Fort Vancouver on boats. In the summer, the traders carried trade goods into the interior in the opposite direction (see Map 1). The southbound brigade required a large supply of horses and feed at Alexandria. Posts farther along the trail to Fort Okanagan also had fresh horses, hayfields, corrals, and "horse keepers"; some of these posts would form the nuclei of gold-rush-era ranches. McBean's mention of the bull shows that the interior posts also had some cattle by the 1820s. The HBC would go on to introduce them by the thousands in the 1840s as the company strove to make interior posts self-sufficient. By committing to the use of horses for the brigade, however, the company also bound itself to the animal's biology. As the environmental historian Elliot West notes in a related context, "people tame and direct an animal's power, but they are really using the animal's ability to acquire energy. It follows that an owner must pay at least as much attention to that energy source – to the animal's food – as he does to the creature itself. The crucial relationship, in short, is not so much between people and their animals. It is between people and the things their animals eat."[35]

Besides gathering hay for winter feed, the men at Fort Chilcotin also had to spend a lot of time cutting firewood. This was noted in the post journal on 2 and 3 November 1837 and off and on thereafter through the winter. In the twentieth century, January mean daily temperatures in the Chilcotin were around −11.5 degrees Celsius with occasional cold snaps to −40 degrees or lower. The temperatures that McBean and his men faced, although not recorded, would have been a bit colder, since many of the glaciers in the province were nearing their maximum recent extent at the time. A surviving letter to McBean from Alexander Fisher hints at some interpersonal difficulties at the Chilcotin post without providing enough information to indicate what exactly was going on: Allow, one of the Tsilhqot'in chiefs, was proving to be a bit of a "scamp"; Baptiste LaPierre, one of the company men, was involved in a quarrel with the Tsilhqot'in; "contrary to Rules and Regulations," McBean's predecessor John McIntosh had taken furs without paying for them; and, Fisher advised McBean, "if under existing circumstances (the Natives' feelings not too friendly towards you) that it should happen on a Barter that an indifferent skin is presented you to make up a payment of a Gun, Blankt. or any large article of Trade for them to purchase I would not hesitate to take it for the present, but I would tell them that it was good for nothing & even say that in future, you will not take any of such kind, that you sell at a Cheap Tariff, in comparison to ... Alexa. that your Goods are good and what they give out to be so also &c." Apparently McBean had his hands full ensuring that his men survived the winter, smoothing over misunderstandings, and trying to convince the Tsilhqot'in that they should not take their business elsewhere.[36]

On 7 November 1837 McBean noted that the weather remained fine, but continued, "I regret I have not men at my disposal to take advantage of the favourable Weather and to build the men's House while the Ground is not too much frose." He came down with a severe cold the next day, and his men made "an Indian lodge into the square of the Ft. to shelter themselves from the cold & inclemency of the weather." The men continued to haul hay. On 10 November, McBean wrote, "At sundown this day Mrs Jane McBean was brought forth to bed of a male child (John) – she took ill last night." The next day saw the first snowfall of the winter. By 14 November they had finished bringing in the hay, and McBean had cause to worry. "This ... forms a total of 605 [bundles] add to which 50 close by not yet hauled is all the stock we have to feed two Milch Cows, one Calf & a Bull and now & then a horse – 1000 bundles is the less quantity that ought to have been made – The Hay Business has been done in a careless way – some of it must have been stowed in a green state as a great deal of it is spoiled & will not do for the Cattle." On 28 November, the men had to insulate their "Indian lodge" with hay and earth to keep it warm. McBean was concerned because one of his men had been having "sensual intercourse" with another man's wife in the fort. "There has been too much dirty work carried on at this Post for some years passed," he wrote, "and to put a stop to it & teach others to break Rules & Regulations of the Co. this man ought to be made an example of & should be fined according to his disent."[37]

The Tsilhqot'in were taking their trade elsewhere. This fact gradually dawned on the HBC traders, although they misinterpreted the signals at first. On 22 December 1838, Allow tried to visit McBean, but the trader had Baptiste show him to the "Indian lodge" instead,

> telling him I did not wish to be disturbed – particularly as he had no Furs to trade & only wished to pass away his time. He expected I would give him tobacco, however I was too busy to think of that ... He set off quite displeased and this day an Indian was sent to me by his order to apprise me

that he had forbidden all the Indians to hunt and that he expected we would
be off from his Lands immediately so that they might have the pleasure of
burning the Fort – stating that the whites did them no good – Could not
smoke when they wished – that the Ft. abt. this time was always destitute
of Trading goods – that we rejected their bad Furs and sold at a high Tarriff.

Instead of apologizing, McBean responded with a bit of bravado, sending
word to Allow that the Tsilhqot'in were free to trade or not, but that "I
despised his menaces and would not quit my Fort until I had received
Instructions to that effect from a Chief whose shoes he was not worthy to
pick up."[38]

McBean was then left to repent at leisure. On Christmas Day 1838, he
wrote, "Every thing quiet and not an Indian comes to the Fort. Three have
passed on their way to Long Lake seeming in a great hurry and not stop-
ping to the Ft. – a conduct very unusual – I begin to think they meditate
a blow upon the Fort – and I am badly provided to receive them as my
Fort is not fortified and destitute of a single Bastion." The men spent the
next few days moving the pickets closer together, putting more pickets up
around the bastion and cutting portholes, creating a second "rough but
Ball proof" bastion to defend the back of the fort, and so on. There was
no attack, however. Allow's speech to McBean is sometimes cited as evidence that the Tsilhqot'in were not interested in trade with the HBC. This
is belied by the fact that Allow settled his accounts with the company on
16 January and told McBean that "the natives are peaciple & well disposed
towards the Fort."[39]

In May 1839, McBean heard rumours of trouble among the Tsilhqot'in
and their neighbours and again feared that Fort Chilcotin would be
attacked. It wasn't. When the HBC men tried to create a "barrière" in July
to harvest salmon for the fort, to "no small astonishment of the Indians,"
the Tsilhqot'in responded by deliberately blocking the river downstream
so the HBC men could not get the fish. In the Aboriginal law of what is
now BC, the right to fish at a particular site was usually owned either by
individuals or by residence groups. It was too much for the HBC men to
expect that they should be able to consume such a valuable resource in the
Chilcotin, particularly as the local Aboriginal people were not obtaining
any benefit from their presence and were not being paid for the salmon.
The following summer, McBean brought dried fish with him from
Alexandria. Writing back to his superior, he noted, "Having now obtained
the first object (food) I wish next to secure the sundry Furs which the
Chilcotins have abt. them, & which from the scarcity of Goods I have

not been able to trade previous to their disposing them shortly to the Atnahyews – a Tribe whom they are in the habit of visiting & trading with annually."[40]

UNDERSTANDINGS AND MISUNDERSTANDINGS

Sometime around 1840 or 1841, William McBean was transferred and Donald McLean took his position as the manager of the Chilcotin post. The archival record for McLean's tenure at Fort Chilcotin is scanty, but McLean would later make a name for himself in the HBC by going farther than circumstances warranted. At Quesnel in 1848, for example, McLean was sent to arrest an Aboriginal manslayer. Failing to find the man, he killed his quarry's uncle instead. Such a response may have been acceptable under Aboriginal law, but the fact that two other relatives of the manslayer were also killed, a man and a baby, was not. McLean's view of the matter was that "the black, ungrateful, blood-thirsty, treacherous, and cowardly scoundrels should have prompt justice for it; hang first, and then call a jury to find them guilty or not guilty."[41]

From the beginning, McLean was not impressed with Fort Chilcotin: "The keeping up such a paltry Establishment is in my humble opinion a dead loss to the H[onorable] HB. Co. and risking the lives of people placed at it – who are little better than slaves to the Indians, being unable to keep them in check ..." McLean thought that the company should focus its energies on trade at Kluskus instead. This was a sign that the HBC was manoeuvring to cut off the Tsilhqot'in's trade with the coast. There are references to a sporadic dérouine trade to Kluskus in the journals of Fort Alexandria and Fort Chilcotin as early as 1837. At the beginning of 1843, Alexander Caulfield Anderson, then in charge of Fort Alexandria, wrote to HBC governor George Simpson to outline the strategy behind such a move:

> The objects it is proposed to attain by this measure are first the interception
> of a good many Beaver that find their way through that channel to the Sea
> Coast, from the Nas-cotin [Carrier] villages attached to Fort George and
> Alexandria ... At present the bulk of the returns ostensible yielded by the
> Chilcotins are procured at Tluz-cuz by parties sent thither ... As for the furs
> traded directly at the Chilcotin post ... they could be procured by sending
> occasionally from this place ... To maintain the [Chilcotin] post, owing to
> the evil disposition of the Chilcotin Indians ... an officer and at least two

men are necessary; a number that would suffice at Tluz-cuz, where the natives, on the contrary, are well disposed, industrious, and extremely urgent that we should settle among them.

Anderson went on to note that Kluskus was "the nucleus where all the surrounding roads unite, being directly on the track followed by Sir Alex McKenzie." Fort Chilcotin was maintained until 1844, however, with McLean still in charge. After the company had withdrawn, Anderson wrote to Simpson to tell him that "the Chilcotin trade (a mere trifle in itself) is not decreased, but on the other hand slightly improved, since the withdrawal of the Establishment." At least the Tsilhqot'in didn't have to worry about the HBC men taking their salmon any more.[42]

Far from "opting out" of the fur trade, the Tsilhqot'in did everything in their power to be a part of it. They were willing to fight with the Carrier for direct access to the HBC traders. They repeatedly expressed an interest in having a post of their own. When the company failed to establish a post year after year, brought goods that the Tsilhqot'in thought were inferior, charged high tariffs, and depreciated the furs that Aboriginal people brought in to trade ... even then some of the Tsilhqot'in persisted in dealing with the company men at the post. When the HBC traders did something outside the bounds of propriety – treating important Tsilhqot'in with a complete lack of respect, for example, or trying to capture their most valuable and unpredictable food source – the Tsilhqot'in were forced to take their business elsewhere. The HBC's ideal scenario would have been for the Tsilhqot'in to live around a post in the Chilcotin and spend all of their time harvesting fur-bearing animals in return for company-provided food and sundries. This strategy worked best in places where the HBC could establish a monopoly. In the Chilcotin, however, Aboriginal people had access to the system of grease trails that connected them to the extensive maritime trade. The Tsilhqot'in could get better terms from other Aboriginal people in other places, from the Carrier and Nuxalk at Ulkatcho and Kluskus, from the Nuxalk at Bella Coola, from the Homalco on the Southgate and Homathko rivers, from the Secwepemc along the Fraser River (see Map 2). The HBC moved to intercept this trade by focusing its attention on Kluskus, but the company ultimately failed there too. Like the traders' failed attempt to take over the trade in oolichan grease on the coast, the bid to make the Tsilhqot'in dependent on dérouines signalled a basic misunderstanding of spatial ecology, particularly in the places where interior and coastal groups met one another.[43]

The company's inability to dictate the terms of trade in the Chilcotin was one indicator of the extent to which the land-based fur trade represented a continuation of the grease trail system rather than a replacement of it. The widespread use of interpreters was another sign that, to a large extent, interaction still revolved around Aboriginal people. At the time the newcomers arrived in the late eighteenth century, the Aboriginal peoples of British Columbia spoke more than twenty-five different languages from six different language families. There is no conclusive evidence for the existence of a trading pidgin in interior BC before the arrival of the newcomers. Thus, given the state of linguistic diversity, Aboriginal peoples must have relied on bilingual or multilingual interpreters for the purposes of exchange with neighbouring groups. When fur traders arrived in the interior, they too had to rely on interpreters to help them conduct business, and the fur-trade journals are full of references to them. Alexander Mackenzie and Simon Fraser, for example, both mentioned using interpreters.

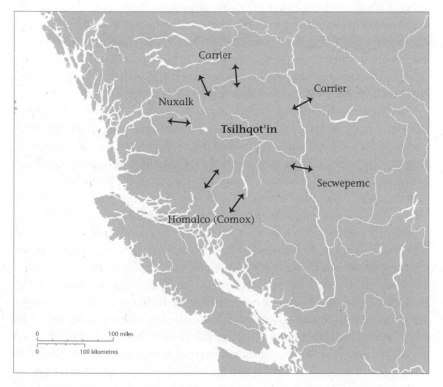

MAP 2 The Tsilhqot'in and their neighbours on the grease trail and reciprocal trading agreements.
SOURCE: Basemap data from the BC Ministry of Sustainable Resource Management.

Daniel Harmon spoke of being accompanied by his interpreter Baptiste Bouché on a number of occasions. George Simpson mentioned interpreters for particular languages and interpreters in the service of particular traders. Interpreters were also used on the brigade. William Connolly's journal of the brigade mentions the interpreters Waccan Bouché and Baptiste Lolo. Peter Warren Dease's journal of the brigade mentions the interpreters Baptiste Lolo, Wastayap Campbell, Alexis Bélanger, Joseph Porteur, J. Baptiste Lapierre, J. Baptiste D. Bouche "fils," and J. Baptiste Boucher. Because interpreters were readily available, there was no reason for a pidgin language to arise during the fur-trade period in the interior. What this means is that up until the mid-nineteenth century, newcomers to what is now interior BC tapped into a vast multilingual network of communication and exchange. The predominately indigenous people, ideas, words, techniques, and things that circulated through this network established the terms by which everyone negotiated much of their existence, including the nature of the past in particular places and its bearing on the present. Some of the non-indigenous traders may not have shared the respect for indigenous knowledge that many people profess in the twenty-first century, but they never lost an opportunity to avail themselves of it. Furthermore, many of the newcomers married into Aboriginal families and maintained very close ties to indigenous communities.[44]

Another sign of Aboriginal influence in the fur trade was the set of understandings that surrounded retaliatory vengeance. The fur-trading companies were certainly capable of exacting swift, certain, and brutal vengeance when one of their own was killed. Often this vengeance took the form of summary execution. The legal historian John Phillip Reid argues that this policy was adapted from North American Aboriginal law, whether the traders acknowledged it or not, and was thus understandable to the Aboriginal people. When the fur traders transgressed the boundaries of accepted behaviour, however, they had to step very lightly indeed to avoid catastrophe. Robin Fisher notes that when some company men were killed by Aboriginal people at Fort George in 1823, the Carrier "warned the traders that, should any wholesale killing of Indians occur, they would retaliate and would not leave a white man alive in western Caledonia." In 1828, James Douglas entered a Carrier village near Fort St. James with two accomplices and killed an Aboriginal man to avenge the earlier murder of a fur trader. Douglas, in turn, was nearly killed by the Carrier, not because he had killed the man, but because the man he killed was a guest in their village. Douglas' life was spared only through the intervention of Aboriginal people.[45]

PRIESTS AND THE PROPHET DANCE

Aboriginal people in the Chilcotin were first exposed to elements of Christian thought during the fur trade, not as the passive recipients of proselytism, but rather as the active creators of a new system of ideas. As with other cultural innovations of the time – in bartering, domestic arrangements, linguistic practices, and intergroup violence – this process was shaped by the workings of the grease trails. In the late eighteenth century, a syncretic religious movement known as the Prophet Dance arose among the Aboriginal peoples who lived on the vast plateau southeast of the Tsilhqot'in. Prophetic figures emerged in Nez Perce, Umatilla, Spokane, Yakima, Kootenai, and other groups living in what is now eastern Washington state, northeastern Oregon, northern Idaho, western Montana, and southeastern British Columbia. A common interpretation of the movement is that it was a response to crisis: historian Christopher L. Miller, for example, argues that "the conjunction of sickness with the coming of horses, guns, climatic deterioration, and near constant war put an unbearable strain on the Plateau world." The Prophet Dance spread "with amazing rapidity" along the grease trails of the interior, reaching the Tsilhqot'in and Carrier in the 1830s. HBC Trader John McLean described the cult as "a sort of religion, whose groundwork seemed to be Christianity, accompanied with some of the heathen ceremonies of the natives." It was embraced at Fort Alexandria and Fort St. James in 1834. McLean bemoaned the fact that there were no missionaries to satisfy the Carrier's request to be instructed in Christianity and feared that their conversion would be difficult. "As to the doctrines of our holy religion," he wrote, "their minds were too gross to comprehend, and their manners too corrupt to be influenced by them." In fact, the Carrier were not waiting for the traders to "give" them Christianity as McLean understood it; they were creating a form of religious life that suited their changing world. Prophets were active among the Carrier from the mid-1830s until at least the 1870s.[46]

Catholic missionaries began working on the fringes of the Tsilhqot'in's world in the 1840s. In 1842, Modeste Demers left his base at Fort Vancouver and travelled north with the HBC brigade to Fort Alexandria. He found the travel difficult: "There is a feverish atmosphere, an oppressive sun, a choking dust, a hill to climb, a ravine to cross." He spent the winter at Alexandria and had a small chapel built there. Writing to his bishop in Quebec, he said, "I have the consolation of being able to hope that the divine mercy which called me from the shores of the St. Lawrence to the midst of these immense solitudes will well know how to 'change stones into children of Abraham.'" His chapel was initially windowless, but after preaching outside in mid-winter a few times, he was able to get some animal parchment to make windows, "and there we were, comfortable, very comfortable. However, O vexatious disappointment, don't we see some miserable starved dogs begin to eat our windows? We had to set traps and catch several guilty ones to put a stop to the scandal." While stationed at Alexandria, Demers also visited the Carrier at Fort George and Fort St. James, travelling again with the traders of the HBC. Most historical accounts of the Oblates suggest that Demers did not visit the Tsilhqot'in, but the post journal for Fort Alexandria has the following entries for 6 and 27 October 1842: "After Breakfast, The Revd. Dumars accompanied by Antoine Gregoire Thaniere Laird and several Indians started for the Chilcotins" and "Mr. Dumers arrived from the Chilcotins." Even if Demers did not visit the Tsilhqot'in, some of them must have heard his preaching at Fort Alexandria or to the Secwepemc near where the city of Williams Lake is now. At Demers' request, the Secwepemc also built a small chapel and a house for the priest. Demers taught them prayers and hymns, which they taught their children. One of them was able to surprise an Oblate missionary many years later by singing the hymns he had learned as a child.[47]

In 1845, the Jesuit priest John Nobili arrived in the area and stayed for a couple of years. Nobili visited the Tsilhqot'in and made an impression on them, despite being "of a very modest stature" and perhaps "handicapped by a rather timid disposition" (according to Nobili's successor, the Oblate priest Adrian Gabriel Morice). Morice mistakenly believed that the Prophet Dance arose after Demers and Nobili left the country, thanks to "the devil [who] was to ape their ministrations and thereby bear an indirect testimony to the worth of their efforts." Nobili may not have started the Prophet Dance among the Tsilhqot'in, but his influence was still discernible sixteen years later, when a Protestant missionary named R.C. Lundin Brown went to preach to a group of them near Fort Alexandria in 1861. Brown spoke in French, which was translated into Chinook Jargon and then into Tsilhqot'in. The Tsilhqot'in listened to Brown in what he described as "that attitude of deep attention which marks an Indian audience." One man, a Tsilhqot'in named Klatsassin, seemed more attentive than the rest, never taking his eyes off the missionary. At the conclusion of Brown's sermon, Klatsassin went up to him and began to search his clothing. Brown "hardly relished this" but asked him calmly what he wanted. Klatsassin showed the missionary a crucifix tied around his own neck and told him that it was the mark of a true priest. "I had *no* crucifix,"

Brown said. "I was accordingly in danger of rejection as a false priest. I told him, however, that I was a 'King George' or English priest, not exactly like those he knew about: and that the King George priest wore no crucifix about his neck, but carried it inside his heart."[48]

THE LOTUS-EATERS

The fur trade was a continuation of the grease trail system, in part because Aboriginal peoples greatly outnumbered the newcomers. During the heyday of the maritime and land-based trades – roughly from the 1770s to the 1850s – the resident non-indigenous population of BC never rose above a thousand people. In 1824, HBC governor George Simpson wrote that there were a total of 151 officers and men in the Columbia district, which included both British Columbia and present-day Washington and Oregon. The historian Jean Barman estimates that at the time of the first census of Victoria in 1855, there were about seven hundred non-Aboriginal people on Vancouver Island and around Puget Sound, with "handfuls" of people scattered at posts throughout the interior. Aboriginal populations, on the other hand, are estimated to have been on the order of seventy to a hundred thousand persons. Robert Boyd, for example, says that the pre contact population of the Northwest Coast was at least 180,000 persons, and Wilson Duff put the Aboriginal population of BC at 70,000 in 1835. In this context, the exact numbers aren't crucial. Until the 1850s, newcomers were outnumbered by indigenous people by a ratio of seventy or a hundred to one.[49]

During the fur-trade period, distant governments slowly negotiated who would be controlling the region. In 1818, the United States and Britain agreed to a border along the 49th parallel to separate their respective territories east of the Rocky Mountains. Ownership of the territory west of the mountains, from what is now Oregon to the Alaskan panhandle, remained unclear. In subsequent decades, Americans embraced the idea that it was their "manifest destiny" to control the continent from sea to sea, and in 1838 they called for military occupation of the land west of the Rockies and north to 54°40′. If this plan had succeeded, much of what is now interior British Columbia would have been part of the United States. On the other hand, the HBC had posts throughout the region, with a centre of Pacific Slope operations at Fort Vancouver near the mouth of the Columbia River. The British thus claimed that the border should be extended along the 49th parallel as far as the Columbia River, then follow the river to the sea. If this plan had come to fruition, what is now western Washington state would have been part of Canada. The ultimate result was a compromise. In 1846, the Treaty of Washington stipulated the extension of the border along the 49th parallel to the Pacific Ocean, resulting in an American Oregon Territory south of the border and in British possessions under the stewardship of the HBC to the north.[50]

Negotiations between the US and Britain for control of the Oregon country and New Caledonia proceeded at a relatively leisurely pace because few non-indigenous people entered the area before the 1840s. Gold was discovered in California in 1848, however, triggering a rush of settlement in Oregon. By 1850 there were an estimated 13,000 non-Aboriginal settlers there. Gold was discovered in the Queen Charlotte Islands that year, and on the BC mainland shortly thereafter. The HBC tried to keep the discovery under wraps because it feared an influx of American miners and the eventual annexation of the area by the US. The company was successful until 1858. That spring as many as thirty thousand people may have headed for the lower Fraser River, most travelling through Victoria.[51]

The massive influx of people suddenly and permanently altered the demographic composition of what is now BC. It coincided with the rapid decline of many indigenous populations due to introduced epidemic diseases. Robert Boyd argues that the indigenous population of the Northwest Coast fell from over one hundred thousand in 1800 to less than sixty thousand in the 1850s. A smallpox epidemic in 1862-63 further reduced Northwest Coast Aboriginal populations to less than forty thousand. Thus, by the mid-1860s, the ratio of Aboriginal to newcomer had fallen from seventy or a hundred to one to two to one or less. This demographic shift had important consequences for the ways in which people in the 1850s and '60s imagined the past of what is now BC.[52]

The experience of the newcomers who arrived in the late 1850s was very different from the experience of the non-indigenous fur traders a generation earlier. Practically every person that the gold rushers encountered had also just arrived in the area. For each non-indigenous person who had been there during the fur trade and remembered the past of the place and its occupants – remembered the grease trail system, in other words – there were now twenty or thirty other non-indigenous people who did not. Even if these recently arrived newcomers had wanted to use fluent interpreters when they encountered Aboriginal groups, there were not nearly enough bilingual speakers to go around. Under the circumstances, communication between newcomers and Aboriginal people became sporadic and rudimentary, limited to whatever could be expressed in Chinook Jargon, a newly adopted pidgin tongue. The circumstances under which the new-comers sought out Aboriginal people were correspondingly limited: they were often in search of mining or packing labour, food, sex, or souls to save. During the gold rush, the newcomers spoke mostly to one another, and their view of the present and future was very much shaped by their shared experiences elsewhere, in the goldfields of California and Australia or in the distant marches of the British Empire. New networks of com-munication and exchange were extended along old routes, superimposed on older networks, with few points of contact.

One measure of the insularity of this newer system was provided by the coverage of the press that sprang up to report the news and doings of the gold rush. Papers like the *Victoria Daily Chronicle,* the *Daily British Colonist* (also of Victoria), and the *British Columbian* of New Westminster printed reports from the goldfields, stories and announcements about prominent local businessmen, and arrival and departure times for steamers. On 5 June 1861, the *British Colonist* noted the arrival of the steamer *Eliza Ander-son* from Puget Sound in Washington Territory carrying US mail. There had been a chance that the mail would be delayed by "Indian savages" in Washington, and the paper noted that "the laying up of the Anderson would be a great misfortune to our people as well as to residents on the Sound. It is the only regular communication that we now possess with the outer world, and if we were to lose that, we should be almost as isolated from the rest of mankind as Alexander Selkirk on his island of Juan Fer-nandez." To the extent that Aboriginal people occupied any space in the newspapers, it was in the third person, as in a letter to the editor of the *British Columbian* that opposed the "repeal of the Indian Liquor Law," which forbade selling or giving alcohol to Aboriginal people.[53]

ROUTES TO THE GOLDFIELDS

Two newly created local metropoles, Victoria and New Westminster, struggled for control of the interior hinterland during the gold rush. Vic-toria had been founded by the HBC in 1843, when the increasing number of American settlers entering Oregon was making it more difficult to use Fort Vancouver for fur-trading operations. It seemed likely that the US would gain control of the territory around the lower Columbia River, so the company decided to build a fort on the coast farther north in British territory. New Westminster, on the mainland at the mouth of the Fraser River, had been established in 1859 to serve as the capital of the colony of

British Columbia. (Vancouver Island and British Columbia were separate colonies from 1859 until they joined in 1866.) The creation of New Westminster coincided with a shift in the focus of gold-rush activity, with prospectors moving up the Fraser and beginning to explore the Thompson River. The following year, the *British Columbian* printed reports of fabulous strikes in the Cariboo. By 1863 there were estimated to be more than ten thousand people in the boom town of Barkerville, fifty kilometres east of Quesnel. The goldfields of the Cariboo were far removed from coastal shipping. To avoid paying exorbitant costs for food, clothing, mining equipment, and sundry items, the gold rushers had to have their "outfits" packed instead. James Douglas, the governor of both colonies, concentrated on establishing an efficient transportation system. The most ambitious and successful project, the Cariboo Wagon Road, linked Yale, at the head of steamboat navigation on the Fraser, with Barkerville. When it was completed in 1865, the road was over six hundred kilometres long and had cost the government more than a million dollars to construct (see Map 3).[54]

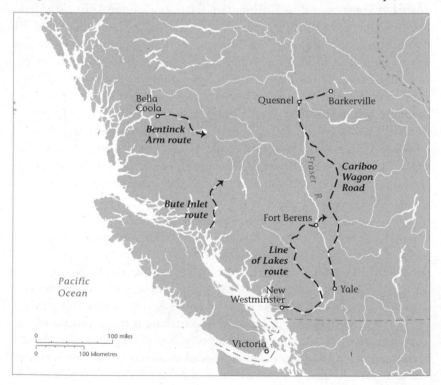

MAP 3 Gold rush routes to the Cariboo.
SOURCE: Basemap data from the BC Ministry of Sustainable Resource Management

When the focus of prospecting and mining shifted to the Cariboo, the majority of gold rushers departed from New Westminster on a steamer up the Fraser River. In order to avoid the worst of the Fraser Canyon, between Yale and Fort Berens, they took a route known as the "line of lakes." The experiences of the Englishman W. Champness and his nephew provide an example. Leaving the Fraser River at Carnarvon, they travelled up the Harrison River to Harrison Lake, then to Douglas, Lillooet Lake, Anderson River, Anderson Lake, Seton Lake, and finally Fort Berens in the Fraser Canyon. Fort Berens was a short-lived HBC post on the opposite bank of the Fraser River from Lillooet. It was also "Mile o" of the Cariboo Wagon Road. In 1862, the wagon road from Lillooet to Alexandria was under construction, but it wouldn't be completed until the following year.

At Lillooet, Champness joined a party of twenty men, who "determined to lay in a large stock of flour, bacon, and beans, and engage a team of seven horses." They "further hired the services of an experienced California packer, who undertook to accompany [them] and securely pack [their] supplies on the beasts from time to time, at a uniform charge of thirty cents (fifteen pence) per pound on the whole weight of baggage." From Lillooet, they took the brigade route across the mountains to the Thompson River, then up past Loon Lake, Green Lake, Lac La Hache, and Williams Lake. The scenery was "wild" and "magnificent," the travel slow and dangerous, the insects so numerous that their "animals would doubtless have been driven stark mad had [they] stayed long there at that time of year." The Aboriginal people, too, whom Champness occasionally encountered, were portrayed in broad-brush and conventional terms, suggesting that he had little experience with Aboriginal individuals: "The native races of British Columbia exist in a condition of even greater squalor and degradation than the other aboriginal tribes of the Far West. Many of them inhabit holes and caves; others move about and erect temporary tents or huts of bark ... They are exceedingly filthy in their mode of life, swarm with vermin, are very licentious, superstitious and cruel." After leaving Williams Lake, the trail became worse. The party's "horses were often plunged up to the belly in swamps and mud." Champness observed that "British Columbia is truly a horse-killing country."[55]

From the city of Victoria's point of view, an ideal route to the goldfields would be one that bypassed the lower mainland and New Westminster altogether. With any luck, once discovered, such a route would be shorter than the line of lakes. One possibility was to sail from Victoria to Bentinck Arm and head east overland from Bella Coola. On 24 July 1861, Ranald Macdonald and John G. Barnston wrote to Governor Douglas informing him about their attempts to find such a route. Leaving Alexandria, they crossed "an elevated table land ... studded in every direction with lakes and meadows," finding plenty of feed for their riding and pack animals. In a few places there were "some swamps which would have to be corduroyed" and some fallen timber that could be cleared with little difficulty. The only part of the road that was not level or easily travelled was a slide going into the Bella Coola valley. The Aboriginal people informed Macdonald and Barston that there were alternate routes through the coast range, which they used to travel between Bella Coola and Fraser's Lake or Fort George. Macdonald and Barnston concluded that they were "firmly convinced that if the Upper Frazer turns out to be the rich mining country that is expected, goods and provisions can be laid down by this route for as low a figure at any point of the Frazer above Alexandria, as they can now be had for at Williams Lake." This wasn't idle speculation. Ranald Macdonald, who was the Métis son of HBC trader Archibald McDonald, had been born at Fort George (Astoria) in 1824 and raised at various posts in the HBC's Columbia district. After travelling widely, he came to BC in 1858 and established a packing business that ran between Little Harrison Lake and the Fraser goldfields. He and Barnston later tried to establish the Bentinck Arm and Fraser River Road Company to pack goods along the trail they had scouted, but the company collapsed for financial reasons.[56]

Victoria newspapers continued to print new information about the Bentinck Arm route. In October, the *British Colonist* published a letter by Captain Cavendish Venables, who suggested that a long lake crossed the interior plateau tending in a southwesterly direction. If it were possible to reach the plateau by an inlet south of Bentinck Arm, it might be possible to use this lake for shipping to the Cariboo. Although the Bentinck Arm route was regularly served by Aboriginal packers, it could be unreliable. On 22 July 1862, the *British Colonist* published a piece about the "destitution and suffering" of some gold rushers who had attempted to use the route. One party had gotten through, albeit short on provisions, in fifteen days. The second group, however, ran into trouble trying to get out of the Bella Coola valley. The story was related to the newspaper "in harrowing terms" by a Mr. F. Poole, an English geologist: "At the Slide the Indians refused to pack further, and the provisions were nearly all left there, the miners depending on obtaining supplies of fish and game from the interior Indians. After leaving the Slide, two Canadians (brothers) named Linn, fell sick of the small pox and were left ... to the tender mercies of the savages. At Chilcooten Lake, two more Canadians ... fell sick of the same complaint and were left with the Chilcooten Indians. All these cases gave evidence of the disease in its worst or confluent form." The men who did not succumb to smallpox ran short of food. The newspaper went on to note that "few of the party had ever undergone privation or suffering in any form, and on these the hardship and privation endured bore most heavily." Some of the men managed to feed themselves with berries and small game, and on reaching Alexandria they "hired Indians to ... pack provisions to the starving men on the trail." No one at the fort seemed to care about the stragglers, or perhaps they didn't share Poole's estimation of their danger, but the packers did what they could to relieve them. Poole, who imagined "that some of the party left behind perished for want of food," would "not advise any person to go that way until a proper trail [had] been constructed."[57]

The colonial government was interested enough in a proper trail from Bella Coola to Alexandria that it sent Lt. Henry Spencer Palmer, a subaltern in the Royal Engineers, to survey the route in the summer of 1862. The twenty-four-year-old Palmer's letters back to Colonel Moody, the detachment commander, were casual and chatty. "And a lively journey it is!" he wrote on 16 July. "Slow work but I'm doing my best. The trail is of the vilest, simply an Indian Track, and much work to be done to get horses through. Swamps & brush of the thickest kind I ever saw hourly impede our progress & the streams, which are now very high, give us much trouble ... the evil must come to an end soon, & I am really inclined to believe that, once past the slide, I can push on rapidly." He didn't think highly of the Nuxalk, calling them "the most extortionate, inconsistent, thieving rascals [he] ever saw," and he praised the man who had had the discernment to name Bella Coola "Rascal's Village"; apparently he didn't know at the time that the appellation had been bestowed by Alexander Mackenzie.[58]

Tension between Palmer's party and the Nuxalk was heightened by the smallpox epidemic that was killing so many Aboriginal people in the area at the time. Palmer got the idea that the Aboriginal people thought he was using his sextant to have a "cloche nanitch" at "sochally tihe" – Chinook Jargon for "a good look at God" – to see whether the smallpox was going to be bad. After a misunderstanding one evening, Palmer and his men found themselves brandishing revolvers at some of the Nuxalk, who responded with a display of superior firepower. Palmer holstered his revolver and managed to talk his way out of the situation in Chinook Jargon, telling them that his "tumtum" (heart) was good. A few gifts cleared up any remaining bad feeling. "The man who was at the head of the row, is now taking my things up the river in his canoe. We are perfectly at their mercy & they extort what they like or leave your things on the bank." On

24 July, Palmer's party arrived at the "Great Slide" near the junction of the Atnarko and Talchako rivers, and he decided that he would not be able to get up out of the valley with horses. He engaged some Aboriginal people to pack for him, and they angered him by stealing his beans, pannikins, and pepper. He wanted to horsewhip them, but his better judgment prevailed – he was "utterly in their power" – and so he resorted to "coaxing" and "wheedling" instead.[59]

According to Governor Douglas, who was not favourably inclined toward the Royal Engineers, Palmer had performed with "great credit to himself and [had] done good service in fixing points and distances in the Upper Country." Arthur Johnstone Blackwood, the senior clerk for the North American Department at the Colonial Office, described Palmer as "exceedingly clever ... on the spot & faute de mieux," a possible successor to Colonel Moody. But the detachment of Royal Engineers was disbanded in July 1863, and Palmer left BC for good in the autumn.[60]

WADDINGTON'S SCHEME

The *British Colonist* continued to publish reports about the Bentinck Arm route, but there were other ways of bypassing the lower mainland. One was to sail from Victoria up Bute Inlet and then follow either the Homathko or Southgate River through the coast mountains into the Chilcotin. On 5 June 1861, the *Colonist* ran a short piece about a meeting that was held the previous evening by the Industrial Exhibition Committee to consider a project to explore a route from the head of Bute Inlet to the Cariboo goldfields. At the meeting, Alfred Waddington "made a few remarks setting out the vast benefits which would accrue to Victoria, and explained the line of country proposed to be explored." The fifty-seven-year-old Waddington was a veteran of the California gold rush, where he had been a partner in a wholesale grocery firm in San Francisco. In 1858 he opened a branch of the firm in Victoria to provision the BC gold rush and soon became "an ardent partisan of Victoria in its rivalry with New Westminster." The meeting ended with the appointment of a committee to evaluate the "scheme." The committee consisted of Waddington; J.D. Pemberton, former HBC man and surveyor general of Vancouver Island; J.W. McKay, chief trader at the HBC Thompson's River Post (Kamloops) and a man with extensive surveying and retail provisioning experience; Amor De Cosmos, journalist, politician, and veteran of the California gold rush; J.W. Trutch, engineer, surveyor, and California gold rush veteran; A.C. Anderson, ex-chief trader for the HBC and postmaster of Victoria; R. Burnaby, a civil servant recently arrived from Her Majesty's Customs Office in London, and founder of a firm of commission merchants; and P.M. Backus. About $200 was raised for the venture at the next meeting, by subscription.[61]

On 20 August, about 250 people met in Victoria to hear a report from Major William Downie, who had been commissioned by Governor Douglas to explore Bute Inlet. Sharing the stage with the speaker were two maps – one of the area surrounding Bute Inlet, and the other of Bella Coola and the Chilcotin. Downie and his partner, a Mr. McDonald, had travelled up the "Hermatsker River" (i.e., the Homathko), which empties into Bute Inlet, and turned up a small tributary, which they named after Waddington. The head of this stream was blocked by a massive icefield, which they also named after Waddington. As they were unable to climb the glacier, they returned to the Homathko and continued up the river for two more days, eventually reaching a point where waterfalls blocked further progress. They gave up on Bute Inlet and tried taking the North Bentinck Arm to the Bella Coola River, reasoning that it would be passable since a tribe of interior Aboriginal people came down it every summer to fish for salmon. There they found "perpendicular" mountains on every side of the Bella Coola valley: "The travelling was very dangerous, but Major Downie's partner was more like a goat than a man, and a jump of fifteen or twenty feet was nothing to him." They finally lost the river in "an aperture in the mountains, at a point by all odds the most miserable he had seen in British Columbia. The mountains ran straight up and down – not even a bear trail was visible – and where a bear can't get along there's a poor show for a wagon road." Downie and McDonald backtracked again, this time to try another river by which the Lillooets travelled to the coast every year, but were again blocked by canyons and falls. Downie thought the country was "too rough for cheap packing, or any packing at all." At the meeting, Downie also quelled a rumour of gold discoveries on Bute Inlet. "He had got some *black sand*," the newspaper reported, "but he did not believe there was gold enough on the whole coast of British Columbia to pay a man a dollar a day." This would have sounded pretty bad to his listeners; that summer Aboriginal packers were being paid $50 per day in the Cariboo, and individual miners reported earning $20 to $100 per day. Ever alert to the possibility of other kinds of profit, Downie's audience questioned him on the resources of Bute Inlet: timber (spruce), soil (too light for farming), weather (rainy), and salmon (plenty). The major's conclusion was that "money invested anywhere else on the coast would pay better than if put in at Bute." The audience took up a collection to defray Downie's expenses. The *British Colonist* reported that "the Major remarked that for himself he asked nothing; but he thought the expenses of his partner and the Indians should be paid." The meeting ended with three cheers for Major Downie.[62]

Downie and McDonald's failure to find a passable route to the interior from Bute Inlet did not discourage Waddington. On 1 October 1861, the *British Colonist* reported that Waddington had returned to Victoria, leaving a party of five explorers on the Price River heading into level country. The article stated that "the Indians were found to be very friendly and obliging and declared that a practicable trail to the interior really existed. They gave the party every assistance." Waddington seemed convinced that his enterprise would be ultimately successful, although he was reluctant to discuss the details of the expedition. More news of the Bute Inlet route was printed on 21 December, when one of Waddington's surveying parties returned after two months in the field. At the request of the HBC, the seven-man party had been led by the civil engineer Robert Homfray. The loss of the party's canoe in one of the rapids of the Price River had meant that they "had to endure the greatest suffering and privation on their return, and their lives were in jeopardy for more than a fortnight." They improvised rafts after they failed to make their own canoe using the tools they had managed to save: two axes and a spade that they cut into three adze blades. "Finally, when reduced to their last meal, they were rescued from what seemed certain death, by the Indians of Desolation Sound. These Indians Mr. Waddington had made the acquaintance of, some two months before, while on the steamer Henrietta, and on learning that the party had been sent by the 'old tyhee [chief] from Victoria' (as they called him) showed every kindness, took the party to their lodges on Desolation Sound, fed and kept them, and finally brought them in canoes to Victoria." The article also reported that the Bute Inlet route was practicable. Price River could be navigated by light-draught steamboats for forty miles and by boats and canoes for fifty-two, at which point there was an easy portage of about 350 yards. The distance from the head of steam navigation to Big Lake was reported to be sixty miles, and the lake itself was thirty miles long. "The distance from the lake, according to Indian report, [was] five days to Alexandria. The natives say that there is not a single mountain or swamp between the cañon and Fraser River, and claim to make trading trips to Alexandria twice a year and back by this route." The author of the newspaper article attributed the mishaps of the surveying party to the fact that they started out too late in the season, but noted that the subscribers appeared "to feel perfectly satisfied with the results."[63]

Waddington received a charter for a wagon road at the head of Bute Inlet in March 1862, and his men began construction immediately. By May they had "completed about a mile of the trail and built ten bridges and two store-houses." They had some difficulty with the Kwakwaka'wakw, but eventually secured their co-operation by promising them presents from the "Victoria tyhee," Waddington. While the men worked, the Kwakwaka'wakw fished for oolichan. Hearing that Waddington's men were at the head of the inlet, parties of Tsilhqot'in from Chilko Lake and Alexandria brought furs to trade with them, "but on obtaining information that the Euclutaus [i.e., Kwakwaka'wakw] were there, they retreated immediately and could not be prevailed on to return."[64]

As Waddington's men worked on the construction of the wagon road, a surveying party in his employ, led by Herman Otto Tiedemann, forged ahead to Alexandria – or attempted to. The party met with mishaps from the start. Its members were abandoned by their Aboriginal guides at the mouth of the Homathko. Not knowing the trail, they tried to follow along the river. In places they were reduced to crawling along the edges of the granite walls on hands and knees, eight hundred feet above the river. On the other side of Homathko canyon, they lost some of their provisions as they forded a creek and thereafter subsisted on berries, fir bark, and whatever miners and Aboriginal people in the Chilcotin were willing to give them. Tiedemann left the rest of his party at Puntzi Lake and continued on alone to Alexandria, where he wrote to Waddington. By his own account, he was "reduced to a skeleton, unable to walk." But he thought that it would be possible to build a road through the Homathko canyon if an elevated roadbed was supported on beams drilled into the canyon walls. Other people did not think so highly of Tiedemann's abilities. Lieutenant Palmer, for example, thought Tiedemann had "no business to be mapping when there [were] R.E.'s in the country." He also described him as a "humbug" who seemed "to oscillate between a desire to 'blow' about The Bute route and get up an excitement, and a desire to keep it dark and speculate pretty largely on his own account," someone who told "no two persons the same story."[65]

In August, Waddington wrote a long letter to the editor of the British Colonist, extolling the Bute Inlet route, "which must eventually become the shortest, cheapest and easiest line of communication with the northern mines." One evening at the end of the month, about 300 people gathered to hear him speak and to see a map of his proposal. According to the British Colonist, "Mr. Waddington came forward amid great applause and told how he was laughed and sneered at when he first stated his belief in the existence of a pass through the Cascade Mountains by which a practicable road could be made to the mines." At the meeting, the plateau was described as "a country more like our English parks than a wild stretch of land." Waddington proposed to form a company to build the difficult portion of the road. He would issue 500 shares at $100 each, and "for the trouble and expense which he had been to so far, all he asked was 2 per cent on the entire amount of stock taken, and to show the confidence which he felt in the undertaking, he would put his name down for $5000." After Waddington was done speaking, "Mr. C.B. Young, being called for, came forward and condemned the Bentinck Arm route, and advocated that *via* Bute Inlet, and to show his earnestness and faith in the latter, subscribed for several shares, and invited others to do the same." Two days later, the *Colonist* reported that 125 shares of the Bute Inlet Road Company had been taken up already.[66]

In November, the workmen's term of employment ended for the year. The Bute Inlet trail was reported to be ready for travel thirty miles up from the mouth of the Homathko River. A messenger had left Waddington farther up, at the mouth of the main obstacle in the Homathko canyon, at the end of October. "Mr. Waddington determined to push through as far as possible this season," the *Colonist* reported. "None of the party have as yet gone through the pass, but the Indians travel through it continually, and represent it as presenting no extraordinary difficulties. An Indian woman and two children who started in the morning came through by three o'clock p.m." By that point in the trail, there were thirty to forty separate bridges, "all built so as to be above high water mark." The report went on to add that "the Indians are very quiet and friendly, and have been of great assistance to the party in packing."[67]

In the spring and summer of 1863, Waddington suffered some setbacks. Not only was his gout bothering him, but "heavy freshets had destroyed three bridges," all of which had supposedly been built above the high-water mark. These had to be rebuilt before his men could pack supplies through to the end, where new construction was to be done. The Aboriginal packers they engaged had quit after each earning a blanket, leaving the packing labour to Waddington's men. Furthermore, although his party had managed to overcome "some considerable obstacles" and had gotten more than half of the way into the Homathko canyon, "there was still one solid obstruction which would require a good deal of blasting." Nevertheless, Waddington still had hopes of getting through the canyon before he left for the year.[68]

6

Chilcotin War

O N 5 MAY 1864, the artist Frederick Whymper abruptly returned from Bute Inlet, where he had been sketching Waddington's road to create more publicity for the enterprise. Early on the morning of 30 April, he had been awakened by friendly Aboriginal people who told him that Tim Smith, the man in charge of the ferry across the Homathko River on the Bute Inlet road, "had been murdered by the Chilcotens for refusing to give away the provisions and other property in his care." For almost a week, the rumoured death of the ferryman circulated through Victoria. On 11 May, the steamer *Emily Harris* arrived in the city with more news, and the following day the *British Colonist* published an account of "the most startling thing of the kind that has yet taken place in either colony," the killing of not only Smith, but also thirteen more of Waddington's men by Aboriginal people. According to the paper, "sixteen able bodied Indians, who had been accustomed to pack for the workmen, accompanied by a number of youths, [stole] upon twelve of the sleeping white men, and with gun, and knife, and axe, fire[d] and cut and hack[ed] at their surprised and helpless victims. Three of the men escaped with their lives, though not entirely unscathed, two having been severely wounded. The other portion of the wagon-road party, four in number, were making preparations to commence the day's work, when they were ruthlessly shot down and savagely mutilated." The *Colonist* called the killing a "treacherous massacre," said there was something "almost fiendish" about the way that it was perpetrated, and attributed its cause to "plunder." "The Indians have been hitherto treated in the kindest manner, and ... there was not the slightest indication of ill feeling amongst them prior to this murderous attack," the article reported. The paper was willing to concede that there may have been some outstanding grievances: "There have been rumors – but they are only rumors – that the Indians had on a former occasion some quarrel with the foreman of the party, Mr. Brewster. Whether this be true or not we have no means of deciding; but it would not, under any circumstance, palliate in the slightest degree the treacherous atrocity of these savages."[1]

The *Colonist* used the occasion to editorialize about "the growing insecurity of the white man's life amongst the northern savages. What between the reckless indifference to Indian life, amounting to inhumanity, of one portion of our population, and the maudlin sympathy, amounting to the encouragement of crime, of another, the Indian is actually forced into disregarding the law. When we add to these mischievous extremes, the notorious bad faith of our own Government with the Indian tribes, the great wonder is that a general warfare with the savages has not broken out long ago." That serious difficulties had been avoided to date was to the credit of Roman Catholic priests working "in the cause of civilization." The *Colonist* also called for parties of volunteers to apprehend the killers and bring them to justice by converging on them from Bute Inlet and Bentinck Arm. "It is understood that upwards of a hundred and fifty men will be organized in Victoria at once," it reported, "ready to act under the proper authorities" to set "an example – a terrible example," to keep "the savages in entire subjection."[2]

The following story emerged over the course of the next year in newspaper accounts, letters, and court records. On the morning of 29 April 1864, the Tsilhqot'in Klatsassin, accompanied by his two sons and some other Aboriginal men and women, found Tim Smith at the ferry site. Klatsassin shot Smith, and the man's body was thrown into the river, never to be recovered. The place where Smith died was later identified by a blood stain and a bullet lodged in a tree. The Tsilhqot'in then took some of the goods from the stores – including two kegs of gunpowder and thirty pounds of balls – hid some and destroyed the rest. They also chopped up the ferry skiff and cast the scow adrift, leaving a cable across the river. By doing this, they strategically cut off the main route by which the non-Aboriginal people upriver might reach the coast. They then continued on up the river. About a mile above the ferry, Klatsassin's party met a Tsilhqot'in named Telloot, who had been assisting Frederick Whymper, and a Comox known as Squinteye coming down the river from the main road camp, which was half a dozen miles farther up. Klatsassin told the men that he had killed Tim Smith. There was an argument. Telloot joined

Klatsassin's party, while Squinteye hurried down to the river's mouth to
warn Whymper. Klatsassin and his companions continued to the main camp,
where they joined the other Tsilhqot'in working there. Apparently they
joked around with the workmen after the evening meal and then sang for
part of the night.[3]

At about dawn, the Tsilhqot'in attacked the twelve workmen at the main
camp as they were sleeping, pulling down the tents to trap them, then
shooting, stabbing, and clubbing them. Nine of the non-Aboriginal men
were killed, three escaped. The Tsilhqot'in continued on about two miles
upriver to the advance camp. The four men who were working there had
already risen when the Tsilhqot'in arrived, and they found only a Comox
teen named George, who was cleaning up after the men's breakfast.
George later told the court that there were six or seven Tsilhqot'in and one
of their slaves; all had guns except the slave and one other. The Tsilhqot'in
went up the trail and shot the four workmen from the advance camp. The
bloody footprints of one led to the river's edge, where he may have jumped
in. Three of the bodies were later found. One was Brewster, the foreman
who had been rumoured to have quarrelled with the Tsilhqot'in. He had
been shot, his head smashed in, and his corpse mutilated. Neither of the
other bodies had been mutilated. The slave, who knew George, told him
to run away. Heading back down the trail, George encountered another
party of Tsilhqot'in, including Klatsassin, his son Piel (or Pierre), and Telloot. The women in the party were carrying heavy loads on their backs.
George continued to the main camp, where he saw the corpses of the
killed workmen, and to the ferry site, where he saw two of the workmen
who had escaped from the killing at the main camp. They called to him,
but he ignored them, jumped into the river, and swam across, carrying the
news down the inlet. The following day, the two workmen were joined at
the ferry site by the third survivor, who had been a sailor. He fixed a loop
to the cable across the river, and they were able to make it over to the far
bank. An hour later, they were rescued there by two French-Canadian
packers and five Aboriginal people from Bute Inlet who had heard about
the killings.[4]

Klatsassin and the other Tsilhqot'in travelled into the interior and
headed towards Anahim Lake, possibly to intercept another of Waddington's parties that was travelling via Bentinck Arm to work on the upper
end of the Bute Inlet road. One of the members of that party, a man
named McDougall, had a Tsilhqot'in common-law wife named Klymtedza. She heard of the planned attack on Waddington's men while she was
visiting her kin at Anahim Lake and warned the workmen. They dug some

defensive earthworks and waited for two days, then tried to retreat to the coast. The Tsilhqot'in ambushed them on the path, killing three of the men and possibly Klymtedza. Five of Waddington's men escaped from the ambush, although four were wounded. Some time after the killings at Anahim Lake, a settler named Manning was killed at Puntzi Lake by a Tsilhqot'in named Tahpit. Although Manning thought himself on good terms with the Tsilhqot'in, he had earlier driven them off the land that he was occupying. Manning's body, when it was later found, had also been mutilated.[5]

THE RESPONSE

The new governor of British Columbia, Frederick Seymour, had only been in the colony for two weeks when Waddington's men were killed on the Homathko River. Seymour took immediate action. He wrote to Lord Gilford, the senior officer stationed at Esquimalt, requesting assistance. He also had a letter sent to William G. Cox, the gold commissioner in the Cariboo, asking him to send an expedition from Alexandria to try to force the surrender of those responsible for the killings. On 15 May, Seymour sent Chartres Brew, the police magistrate, to Bute Inlet with twenty-eight special constables. There they found evidence of the killing of Waddington's men, including the bodies of Brewster and two others at the advance camp. Ten days later, the *British Columbian* of New Westminster posted a $250 reward from the colonial secretary "for the apprehension and conviction of every Indian or other person concerned as principal or accessory before the fact, to the murder of any of the fourteen Europeans" killed on the Homathko River. Seymour visited Bute Inlet himself between 26 May and 31 May on the Royal Navy gunboat HMS *Forward*. On 28 May, the *British Columbian* published Chartres Brew's list of twelve "Supposed Murders": Klatsassin, two young men, Telloot, Telloot's sons-in-law Jack and George, "Indian slave Chraychamum, or Bob," two "stout young men" named Lowws and Cushen, an Aboriginal man with two scars on his face, an older Aboriginal man, and one "with a very wide mouth, black moustache, and a ring in the nose." The paper also carried news of "Another Indian Massacre" – the killings of Waddington's men near Anahim Lake and of Manning at Puntzi Lake.[6]

Even in the commotion after the killings, New Westminster and Victoria continued to vie for the public perception of various routes to the goldfields. On 1 June, the *British Columbian* ran an article criticizing the Bute Inlet route. "We would not deem it worth our while to devote any more space to the discussion of the merits of a route which may now be considered defunct," it said, "were it not that a Victoria contemporary has provoked it by the insertion of the following paragraph: – 'The *Forward* had no difficulty in steaming up to the town site, and lay at the wharf during the whole time of the visit, although drawing nine feet six inches of water.'" The article went on to dispute the draft of the gunboat (which it claimed was seven feet) and emphasized the difficulty the ship had navigating the river in flood tide and the fact that it had been stuck when the tide went out. Two Royal Engineers who had seen Waddington's road "declared it to be utterly unworthy" to be called a trail: "They found a total absence of feed for animals, and upon several parts of the trail they were obliged to wade through water up to the loins." As they did so, marks on nearby trees showed them that the water level was comparatively low. The article reported that "what Mr. Waddington dignifies with the name of bridges they describe as the most inadequate and trumpery crossings, constructed in the most unworkmanlike and temporary manner, and even now falling into ruin." Waddington himself came in for the worst criticism:

> The extraordinary course, pursued by Mr. Waddington respecting this route can only be accounted for on the ground of monomania; and we would feel disposed to spare the old gentleman's feelings at the present moment, were there not too much system perceptible in his madness. The fact of his having pressed his imaginary claim on the Government for indemnification when he came up to report the massacre of his men did not say much for the depth or delicacy of his feelings, while his manoeuvers to try and induce the Government to purchase the road from him says less for his modesty.

The article held Waddington responsible for being instrumental in the death of his workmen and for starving the Aboriginal people in his employ and concluded, "Indemnify him, indeed! It would be more like the thing to hold him responsible for the expense he has been the means of entailling upon the Government."[7]

Governor Seymour's plan was to send three expeditions against the Tsilh-qot'in – from Alexandria, Bentinck Arm, and Bute Inlet – "all to converge towards Banshee [i.e., Puntzi Lake]." Seymour later explained that the Bute Inlet expedition failed "owing to the natural difficulties of the country, and ... returned after having afforded decent burial to such of the corpses of the murdered men as were found, and making a demonstration of force on the spot where the death struggles of the White men took place." The expedition from Alexandria, led by Cox, started out at fifty men and an Aboriginal boy and gathered another dozen or so volunteers en route. Seymour thought Cox's party had the best chance of capturing those responsible for the killing, but he worried that "the expense [would] be something awful" because the men had to be recruited in the Cariboo, where mining activity was in full swing. Seymour's main concern was that non-Aboriginal access to the Cariboo would be blocked by war, which would spell financial ruin for the colony. "Each day that the Chilcotens continue to range the country loaded with the spoils of the murdered white men increases the probability of an extensive rebellion," he wrote to Admiral Kingcome. Of secondary concern were the handful of English settlers in Bentinck Arm, "scattered without defence." As prompt as Seymour's actions were, things seemed to be moving too slowly for some. On 1 June, the *British Colonist* called for citizens to take matters into their own hands. That evening, 129 men stood up for vigilante justice at a public meeting in Victoria, spurred on by people like Amor de Cosmos, one of the backers of Waddington's scheme.[8]

Cox's team arrived at Puntzi Lake on 12 June and found Manning's corpse. The following day, some of his men were fired upon by Aboriginal people and one was injured. They took refuge in a hastily constructed fort. A week later, Cox wrote to the colonial secretary in New Westminster to tell him that he had so far been unable to obtain the services of the Tsilhqot'in chief Alexis, whom he had been hoping to use as a guide. Alexis and his family had apparently fled, fearing rumours that Cox's party had come to exterminate all of the Aboriginal people, regardless of their disposition. Although Cox probably didn't understand Alexis' actions, this was a perfectly reasonable response on the part of the Tsilhqot'in. The legal scholar John Phillip Reid has argued that the concept of collective liability was central to most North American Aboriginal law. It was thus perfectly reasonable for Alexis and his family to expect Cox's men to kill them if they couldn't find Klatsassin and his comrades. Reid has also argued that the officers of the HBC often incorporated the idea of collective liability into their own practices when dealing with Aboriginal people. Thus, the Tsilhqot'in may well have been basing their responses on their own history of interaction with non-Aboriginal people during the fur trade. Alexis did meet with Donald McLean at Chilcotin Forks, however, and told him that the men responsible for the killings "were lurking about the Country ranging between Bute Inlet" and Puntzi Lake.[9]

Meanwhile, having failed to enter the Chilcotin via Bute Inlet, Chartres Brew took Seymour and a party of forty volunteers to Bentinck Arm on the HMS *Sutlej*. On 15 June, the Custom House officer at Bella Coola wrote to the *British Colonist* with news of the killing of Waddington's men near Anahim Lake. On 20 June, Brew's party set out for the interior from Bella Coola. Going up the "Great Slide," they captured a Tsilhqot'in man who was shouting in the bushes near the path. They continued on to Anahim Lake, finding it deserted, and a little farther down the trail found the remains of the three members of Waddington's party who had been killed. Picking up the fresh trail of some Tsilhqot'in families, some of Brew's men followed them for many days, guided by the Tsilhqot'in man they had captured on the Great Slide. Along the way he deserted them, leaving them to make their way back without aid – and leading later commentators to suggest that he may have arranged to be "captured" so he could lead the party away from his kin.[10]

Brew and the rest of his group continued on to Puntzi Lake, where they joined Cox's men. There, they took his position, while Cox led a group of men to Tatla Lake in search of the Tsilhqot'in who had done the killing. Donald McLean, who had gone with Cox, was shot by an Aboriginal sniper on 17 July. As with Brewster and Manning, there were rumours that the Tsilhqot'in held unsettled grievances against McLean, dating from his tenure at Fort Chilcotin. On 20 July, Cox's men returned to Puntzi Lake, having seen signs of the Tsilhqot'in but having been unable to catch any of them. Cox suggested to Seymour that they wait for winter, when starvation might force the Tsilhqot'in to give up. Seymour was afraid that would look like a defeat, however, and planned to use his men to search the country. Things were still undecided when the Tsilhqot'in chief Alexis arrived. Seymour expressed his opinion that Manning should not have been allowed to be killed in Alexis' territory, but Alexis told him that the men under Klatsassin and Telloot were free to make war on the newcomers since they had renounced any connection with him, showing that Seymour's idea of the authority of a Tsilhqot'in chief was not correct. Seymour left the Chilcotin, travelling to the Cariboo before returning to New Westminster. On 8 August, Brew and his men left Puntzi for Tatlayoko, but again failed to make any contact with the Tsilhqot'in near the Homathko River. Two days later, Tahpit's son came to Puntzi Lake to negotiate the voluntary surrender of Klatsassin, Telloot, and six others.[11]

COLONIAL IDENTITY AND HISTORICAL CONSCIOUSNESS

Klatsassin and seven of his followers came peacefully to Cox's camp on 16 August 1864. Except for their knives, they were unarmed and apparently believed that Cox had promised they would remain free and be allowed to meet with Governor Seymour. They discovered that this was not to be the case when they were seized and put in irons. There had obviously been a misunderstanding of some sort; whether or not they had been intentionally deceived is not clear now. They were taken to Quesnel, where six of them were tried before Chief Justice Matthew Baillie Begbie at the end of September. Five, including Klatsassin, were found guilty, and Begbie sentenced them to be hanged. On 2 October, the Protestant missionary R.C. Lundin Brown arrived in Quesnel and was given permission to minister to the condemned men. They were executed on 26 October. The following year, another of the Tsilhqot'in involved in the war tried to make peace with the colonists. He brought hundreds of dollars' worth of furs to Bella Coola to make compensation for the killings. He, too, was seized, tried, and executed. A relative of his, who was seized along with him, was eventually pardoned, the only one of the Aboriginal people to receive clemency.[12]

The colonial perception of, and response to, the Chilcotin War was shaped by people who had little prior experience in the region: Waddington, Cox, Brew, and Begbie had all arrived in the colony in 1858, and Seymour in 1864. They attempted to make up for their lack of knowledge by consulting people who had been involved with the fur trade. One of these was a sixty-nine-year-old retired trader named John Tod. He had been with the HBC since 1811, and from 1823 was stationed at posts throughout the Columbia district, serving at Forts George, McLeod, Vancouver, Alexandria, Kamloops, Nisqually, and Victoria.[13]

On 1 June 1864, Tod wrote to a fellow former trader about the fact that the governor, Royal Navy officers, and other colonial authorities were continually visiting his house "to consult 'the old Settler' as to the course to be pursued for the capture and punishment of the murderers." The difference between the understandings of the old and new regimes, however, seems to have been too great to be easily bridged. Tod viewed the colonial response as overkill, describing volunteers "mustared by hundreds," and "prodigious quantities" of armament and ammunition, "all for the punishment of a small, but certainly determined, band, which, as You undoubtedly well remember, would have been undertaken in our time with the flintlock gun alone, and a mere handful of Fur Traders ... To one and all of these gentlemen," he continued, "it seems altogether incomprehensible how the Company's officers, in former times, always few in number – often alone and single handed – widely scattered over a country, in extent, nearly equal to Europe itself, should Yet have been able to Keep its numerous and lawless tribes of Savages in such complete subjection as they generally did – I tell them that our Sway, Such as it was, rested on a moral foundation, but tho' partaking of that character chiefly it by no means excluded a proper digree of severity, the moment it became necessary."[14]

Of course, the "sway" that Tod remembered the fur traders exercising was more a matter of negotiation and compromise on the ground than he describes in the letter, and the subjection was mutual. For their part, the colonial authorities probably viewed Tod's advice as impractical. They agreed that the response must be severe, but it could not be dispensed summarily. It had to be lawful.

The historian Tina Loo argues that the Chilcotin War was used by non-Aboriginal people as an occasion to form a colonial identity in which "a liberal notion of law – the idea of equality and equal treatment before the law – was central ... For in discussing what happened at Bute Inlet, why it happened, and what they should do about it," Loo explains, "European British Columbians revealed as much about who they thought they were as they did of the event and its perpetrators." In describing the violence of the killings and the destruction of property, colonial accounts portrayed the activity of the Tsilhqot'in as irrational and savage, defining themselves as civilized by contrast. The Aboriginal people were said to have been "impelled" to kill, suggesting that passion was not governed by reason in their essential nature. The frequently repeated claim that all had been well between Aboriginal people and newcomers only served to underscore the putative irrationality of the killings. Much was made of the Tsilhqot'in's alleged cannibalism and their physical appearance. The "natives," for colonial accounts readily generalized from a few individuals to all Aboriginal people, were also portrayed as superstitious instead of religious, covetous instead of generous, profligate instead of thrifty, fickle instead of constant. In setting up such an opposition between the supposed characteristics of Aboriginal and newcomer, the colonists were drawing on traits that had long been used to separate the civilized from the savage in western thought.[15]

Loo argues that in deciding on an appropriate response to the killings, the colonists also drew on what they knew, or thought they knew, but "it was the American rather than the Indian who served as the foil against which they structured their identity and their actions." Americans, especially those who lived in the west, were perceived as lawless, reckless, and degraded, assimilated to the Aboriginal people by a process that Begbie and his fellows called "californization." The colonists believed that "meting out justice according to the law was what separated British Columbians from Americans, and a failure to do so would surely mark the beginnings of 'californization,' and a descent into savagery." But that standard posed a problem. Since everyone was equal under the rule of law, the carefully drawn distinctions between the civilized and the savage were undermined. Loo concludes that stories about the Chilcotin War "illustrated a constant tension between two different conceptions of justice in liberal societies: one rooted in a recognition of differences (themselves constructed in part by liberalism) and in acting upon them, and the other premised on over-looking those differences as insignificant and treating everyone similarly in accordance with liberalism's universalist tendencies. Despite the peculi-arities of this particular nineteenth-century manifestation, it is a tension yet to be resolved."[16]

The colonists were forming not only a new identity in the second half of the nineteenth century, but also a new historical consciousness, one based primarily on documents instead of direct experience or oral tradi-tion. The newspapers of the gold rush period and the letters of colonial authorities make up the bulk of early written material from what is now BC. The Chilcotin War looms in these sources, perfect fodder for a press that thrived on sensationalism and one of the first real challenges to the authority of the colonial government. Given the importance of the event in terms of the ways colonists differentiated themselves from imagined Indians and Americans, its subsequent prominence in the early histories of the province was guaranteed. Furthermore, since almost all of the doc-uments expressed the colonists' view of the situation, the portrayal of the event was certain to be skewed in that direction. As Jill Lepore notes in her study of King Philip's War, "if war is, at least in part, a contest for mean-ing, can it ever be a fair fight when only one side has access to those per-fect instruments of empire, pens, paper, and printing presses?"[17]

THE CONTEXTS OF ARCHIVAL FORMATION

In the aftermath of the Chilcotin War, the mutual understandings of the fur trade, such as they were, no longer held. The Tsilhqot'in had been accustomed to a certain way of doing things; the rules of the game had now been changed without notice. Klatsassin and his accomplices were treated as subjects of the colonial government rather than as independent agents. They still faced retaliatory execution, but now they had to be tried first. Compensation for killing was no longer an option, as the Tsilhqot'in man who turned himself in at Bella Coola discovered. Aboriginal people were now expected to conform to a new place in society, to submit to a new rule of law.

For those interior Aboriginal people who were not directly involved in the Chilcotin War, the first sustained negotiations with the colonial authorities revolved around land. In the 1860s, Aboriginal land policy in the colony was set by Joseph Trutch. Trutch neither recognized Aboriginal title nor believed that Aboriginal people should have the right to use good arable or grazing land. He thus took steps to minimize the extent of Aboriginal reserves while increasing the amount of land a non-indigenous settler could acquire. In 1867, the Dominion of Canada was established and the *British North America Act* charged the federal government with responsibility for Aboriginal people and the lands reserved for them. When British Columbia entered Confederation four years later, Aboriginal people still outnumbered non-Aboriginals in the province by a ratio of about two to one, and the federal minister of public works saw the continuing importance of BC Aboriginal people "in the capacity of guides, porters and labourers." The Tsilhqot'in probably would not have accepted this characterization of their place in the new system. Their thoughts in 1872, however, were turned to land. They were afraid that they were going to be moved to small reserves and their land taken without compensation. Given Trutch's policies, this was a reasonable fear. Nevertheless, in a letter to Ottawa, Trutch denied that this was his intent.[18]

In the summer of 1872, three Tsilhqot'in chiefs met with Peter O'Reilly, a county court judge. O'Reilly assured the Tsilhqot'in that they would be protected from disturbance, that they could keep their houses and their hunting and fishing grounds, and that the Dominion government would provide them with education and assistance in agricultural development. The Tsilhqot'in had recently quarrelled with a man named John Salmon, who pre-empted land in their midst. This concerned O'Reilly, and he advised the government not to allow further pre-emption in the Chilcotin until the reserves had been laid out. He was afraid that future confrontations might be more serious. Another sign of trouble was the recent killing of a Chinese man who lived opposite Dog Creek. The Tsilhqot'in man responsible for that act was still at large. In October, Israel Wood Powell was appointed the provincial superintendent of Aboriginal affairs. Unlike his predecessor Trutch, Powell was a proponent of giving Aboriginal people land and water rights so that they could establish an economic base and eventually be assimilated into non-Aboriginal society.[19]

One of the first issues that was brought to Powell's attention was "the position of the Chilcoaten Reserve, and the desirability of some steps being at once taken to map out the Indian Reservations and throw the country open to intending settlers." The provincial government was hampered in this plan by its lack of detailed knowledge of the land lying between Bute Inlet and Alexandria. The reports of those people who did have some familiarity with the region "differ[ed] materially as to the wants of the Indians." Powell wrote to Victoria to ask for instructions regarding a reserve for the Tsilhqot'in. In the meantime, the situation worsened. On 11 January 1874, Powell sent a telegram about the Tsilhqot'in to the federal minister of the interior: "Reported Indian troubles exaggerated – great discontent however existing – revolt considered in council but overruled for present – cause apprehend injustice regarding lands have promised."[20]

Aboriginal groups elsewhere in the interior also complained of injustices done to them. At Kamloops, for example, which Powell visited in the summer of 1874, the Aboriginal people did not have enough land to graze their stock, although white settlers were allowed to lease thousands of acres around them for the same purpose. The dissatisfaction of the Aboriginal people around Kamloops and in the Okanagan to the southeast came to a head in 1877, when many settlers in the area believed that another Aboriginal war was in the offing. The Aboriginal reserve commissioners and the local Catholic missionary managed to defuse the situation. Ironically, the area was subsequently terrorized by the notorious McLean Gang of outlaws, led by some of the sons of the same Donald McLean who had been killed in the Chilcotin War.[21]

In 1883, ranchers wrote to Powell for help: "We inhabitants of Chilcotin, beg your attention with regard to the Indians resident here. There is existing a state of lawlessness among them that makes it all but impossible for us to remain in our places, owing to their depredations." The ranchers claimed to have always treated the Tsilhqot'in with justice, fairness, and generosity, and to have been repaid, for the most part, with ingratitude. About two dozen of their cattle had been killed by the Tsilhqot'in, and the ranchers had had three Tsilhqot'in men arrested and brought to trial. Those men escaped, "stealing and taking Govt blankets with them in their flight." The ranchers also complained that "for nigh eleven years too a Chilcotin has been running at large who murdered a Chinaman opposite Dog Creek." Powell wrote back to tell them that he would do what he could, but that the local magistrate "should invest one or two men with a commission" as justices of the peace.[22]

In 1883, the attorney general received a telegram saying that two Tsilhqot'in had confessed to shooting two Chinese men. These killings raise a possibility that has received little attention in the historiography of BC. We know that the activities of non-Aboriginal ranchers, missionaries, and government officials were putting pressure on the Tsilhqot'in on a variety of fronts at a time when disease and poverty were rampant. It is probable, however, that the actions of another marginal group, the Chinese, were also a source of friction, and Chinese people may have been specifically targeted as an outlet for the frustrations of some of the Tsilhqot'in.[23]

Chinese people had been in BC nearly as long as members of any other non-indigenous group, with the first arriving in the late eighteenth century during the maritime fur trade. As was the case for other non-Aboriginals, however, the bulk of them came during the Cariboo gold rush. Their numbers peaked at almost 7,000, but dwindled to 1,548 by the time of the 1871 census. Of these fifteen hundred-odd Chinese, only fifty-three were women. Chinese prospectors who remained after the gold rush tended to specialize in reworking abandoned diggings, which took them along the rivers into the Chilcotin. Like the Aboriginal people, the Chinese were under a lot of pressure. In 1875, they were deprived of the right to vote in provincial elections. They were also prevented from practising many professions and relegated to low-paying manual labour. The federal government imposed a head tax on Chinese immigrants in 1885, which prevented many of them from bringing their families into the country. By the early 1900s, they were subject to mob violence in a number of places in BC.[24]

In 1883, Justice of the Peace W.L. Meason convened a coroner's inquest to determine what had happened in the killing of the two Chinese men. Working with the testimony of a man who had escaped the assailants and with clues that they found in the place itself, the jury was able to reconstruct a predawn ambush. The similarity to events of the Chilcotin War, some two decades earlier, would have been sickeningly clear to the men viewing the cold bodies in a cold cabin on the river bank. The proceedings stated that

one of the Chinamen Pack Sing was lying on his bed, as if shot when sleeping[.] The ball went in under the left shoulder and came out at the right breast[.] We found a pistol ball which dropped out of the blankets when the body was moved. The other Chung Hang was lying on the floorr[.] The bullet entered his forehead, and was cut out (by Mr. Bowe) at his throat a large bullet. The Chinaman who escaped states. ["]Two Indians came to our cabin Friday evening 13 April and got their supper. They went away and came back in the morning early when we were still in bed and shot one the first one Pack Sing. The second one Chung Hang then jumped out of bed and looked up at the hole from where the shot had come, and said what are you doing or something of that kind, when the Indians shot him. One of the Indians was lame and used a stick to walk. The other was a little shorter in size.["] We examined the ground round the cabin and found marks of a stick as if used by a man leaning his weight on it. On level ground the stick went in about 1 ½ inches, but on the hill side it went in about 6 ½ inches. On the roof of the cabin we found marks of the stick and moccasin marks, at the place where the shooting must have been done. The hole in the roof of the cabin is about 20 x 16 inches. The Chinaman who escaped states also. ["]I got into a corner of my bunk, the upper one, and the Indians shot twice at me but did not hit me.["] We found that from the hole in the roof a weapon could not be aimed at the place the Chinaman shewed us that he was in. The Chinaman who escaped also states that after the others were killed, he found that the door was tied on the outside. We found that dirt had been scratched down from the roof on the inside where the surviving Chinaman said he had been trying to break a hole to escape through but that he heard or thought he heard the Indians outside so he ceased his work. The Chinaman also states that the two Indians when they came to the house were riding two horses one of a red colour, the other grey or white. The holes made by the stick were about 1 ¼ inches across and the holes were rounded at the bottom as if made by a stick that had been much used.[25]

The pre-dawn killings of the Chinese men matched the killings of the road builders during the Chilcotin War not only in modus operandi but also in intent. One of the killers had been living with a local rancher named Doc English for six months and had told him that he had a part in the killings. The other was a man named Twentymen. He was crippled in one leg and was the son of one of the Tsilhqot'in who had been executed in the aftermath of the Chilcotin War. (Note also the multiple resonances of Twentymen's name: Klatsassin said there were twenty-one people implicated in the killings of the Chilcotin War, and nineteen non-Aboriginal people were actually killed.) After Twentymen and his companion killed the Chinese men, they planned to kill all of the "whites" on the west side of the Fraser River. Doc English talked with all of the Tsilhqot'in leaders and, by making promises to them, managed to set them against the two killers, whom they turned in.[26]

In the 1890s, a Tsilhqot'in named Nemiah or Emia was arrested for wounding an Aboriginal man with the intent of killing him. The government agent also suspected him of killing another Chinese man, but complained that he had "not a particle of evidence that [he could] produce against him." Nemiah was later arrested and jailed at Tom Hance's ranch. He admitted to having stabbed the Aboriginal man and to having killed a Chinese man while a Tsilhqot'in boy named Quitalt was present. A letter from a rancher to the attorney general described this killing:

The Chinaman (according to my recollection of the story) was mining on the right bank of the river (Fraser) Emia & the witness who was then a small boy [Quitalt] went to his cabin had supper there. There was no one else there. In the evening or rather during the night Emia took his gun the boy knowing from his actions what he intended hid himself he heard a shot fired & afterwards saw Emia drag the dead Chinese at times by his queue to the river's edge (the recollection of which amused the Indian very much while he was telling me about it) & threw his dead body into the river. The indian at that time was without any belief in a state of future reward or punishment.

In the next half century, the killings of the Chinese by the Tsilhqot'in would come to be remembered as something very different from what they really were.[27]

RESERVES

The Tsilhqot'in faced increasing pressure from non-indigenous settlement and recreational hunting in the twentieth century. In 1904, some land speculators staked the area around Redstone, and local ranchers wrote to the Department of Lands and Works on behalf of the Tsilhqot'in. A reply to one of them said, in part, "Dear Sir, I am pleased to be able to inform you that I have succeeded in obtaining for the Indians at Redstone flat the land contiguous to their village ... you can inform Charley Boy, only make him understand that they are not going to get the whole country side." The provincial government published pamphlets that told "intending Pre-emptors" how to pre-empt land, how to purchase and lease Crown land, where the best possibilities for grazing and irrigation were, and what the various regions of the Chilcotin plateau were like. The provincial game warden's correspondence of the early 1900s included complaints made by recreational big-game hunters about animals killed by the Tsilhqot'in for subsistence. A group writing from a hotel in St. Paul, Minnesota, in 1908 said, "We have just returned from a hunting trip in the Lillooet district ... There are indications that the Chilocotins have been hunting sheep in that section which is a great pity." In his annual report of the same year, the provincial game warden repeatedly decried Aboriginal hunting: "Now that the raids of the Chilcotin Indians are more or less checked by the district having been patrolled by a Deputy Game Warden, matters are in a much more prosperous state ... From the Caribou country of Chilcotin come disastrous reports of the slaughter of Caribou by the Indians; it is said that the Ootsa Lake Indians, having cleared out the game to the north in their own country, last fall practically denuded the Itcha Mountain district to the south ... The Chilcotin Indians were ravaging the famous Bridge River country every summer; deer by the thousand and numbers of sheep and goat fell beneath their rifles, male female and young without mercy or thought of the future."[28]

The Tsilhqot'in's shift to life on reserves was, in part, both precipitated and facilitated in the 1870s and '80s by Catholic priests of a French order, the Oblates of Mary Immaculate, who returned to the Chilcotin toward the end of the gold rush. The Oblate priest Leon Fouquet tried to find the Tsilhqot'in in 1864 but was unable to do so. His colleague James Maria McGuckin met with Tsilhqot'in and Carrier at Fort Alexandria in 1867 and visited the Tsilhqot'in in the winter of 1870. "The weather was very cold," McGuckin wrote, "the trail very bad, having on it a good deal of fallen lumber besides from 6 to 15 inches of snow all the way both going and returning. At night it froze so hard that the trees were splitting with the cold." Although the Tsilhqot'in were evidently very poor, having "no houses, no provisions and the majority very nearly no clothing," McGuckin didn't interpret this poverty as a sign of sanctity but rather of savagery. Nevertheless, he was pleased with his visit to the "terrible Chilcotin." They hadn't killed him, as he feared they might, and he was able to baptize "18 children and one old woman."[29]

McGuckin returned again in 1873 to lay the groundwork for converting the Tsilhqot'in to Catholicism. One of the things he did was appoint a "captain" and "watchman" for each of the Tsilhqot'in chiefs. These roles were part of an evolving system of governance that is now known as the Durieu system, named after Paul Durieu, the bishop who directed the work of the Oblate missionaries from the 1870s onward. In the Durieu system, the captain was the chief's deputy. He administered public punishment, usually whipping, for activities that the missionaries wanted to suppress, like adultery, the consumption of alcohol, or participation in traditional feasting. The watchman's job was to discover and apprehend suspected sinners. By creating these roles, the missionaries also created a new role for the chief, subject to the missionary in a semi-theocratic hierarchy. In the late 1870s or early 1880s, a new priest, Fréderic Guertin, was assigned to the Tsilhqot'in. Unfortunately, Guertin was intimidated by the Tsilhqot'in and unable to learn their language. He wanted them to plant crops (which he doesn't seem to have realized was impossible on their land, due to frequent summer frosts, lack of precipitation, and variable soils), but they didn't have seed or equipment. He attributed their wide-spread mortality to the fact that they ate too much dried salmon and didn't exercise enough. The only adult baptisms he performed were for people on their deathbeds. In fact, one concomitant of the imposition of the Durieu system was that interior Aboriginal people were moved from pit houses to "modern" log-cabin-style houses, with both domestic and health consequences.[30]

In 1883, the Tsilhqot'in were assigned a new missionary, Adrian Morice. Morice was much more determined and forceful than Guertin had been. His new charges were soon calling him "the young priest with strong words." By conversing with a Tsilhqot'in woman in Chinook Jargon, Morice was able to learn enough of the Tsilhqot'in language over his first winter to compile a six-thousand-word vocabulary, a rudimentary grammar, and Catholic catechism, prayers, and hymns. The Tsilhqot'in saw his usefulness as a cultural broker. They asked Morice to write to the Queen to intercede for them in the case of the two Chinese men who had recently been killed by Twentymen and his accomplice. Morice promised to write to Israel Wood Powell, the superintendent of Aboriginal affairs, if it turned out to be necessary. In 1883 and 1884, Morice made long trips through the Chilcotin, setting up the Durieu apparatus where possible. He was unable to get along with his superiors, however, and was reassigned to the Fort St. James area in 1885. The Durieu system was also used by Morice's successor, François Marie Thomas, who was assigned to the region in 1897 and worked there for sixty years. The system had a long life in the Chilcotin. The last Durieu courts were held at Redstone in 1940. In addition to setting up a new political structure, Morice and the other Oblate priests were responsible for concentrating the Tsilhqot'in into villages and for pre-empting land on their behalf.[31]

The provincial government also took steps that changed Aboriginal society. The 1880 revision of the *Indian Act* allowed federal officials to replace traditional leaders with individuals they thought were more appropriate. They also redefined Aboriginal social structures by inventing a new category called "status." An individual was now either a status Indian – allowed to live on the reserve and receive government services – or non-status. Since status was given to Aboriginal men, their wives, and children, many non-Aboriginal women automatically acquired status, while those Aboriginal women who married non-status men lost it. Métis children of the former families were status, whereas those of the latter were denied the right to acquire it.[32]

THE FIRST HISTORIES

The first historical accounts of the Tsilhqot'in were written after the Chilcotin War, as non-indigenous settlement was encroaching on their territory, the church and state were working to restructure their political, domestic, and religious life, and the continued pressure of disease and poverty pushed their numbers toward an all-time low. R.C. Lundin Brown's *Klatsassan, and Other Reminiscences of Missionary Life in British Columbia* was published in London in 1873 by the Society for Promoting Christian Knowledge. Brown retailed the stereotypes that had filled the newspapers of the previous decade. The Tsilhqot'in, "like all the British Columbia Indians, [were] in a state of decadence," he wrote. "A set of men and women more squalid and repulsive I have rarely beheld. Dark faces, with big mouths, high cheek-bones, ferocious black eyes, narrow foreheads, long tangled hair black as night; their thin and sinewy frames with little on them save dirt and a piece of blanket or deer-skin." In the first few pages of his account, Brown also gloried in the power that he imagined writing gave him and other non-Aboriginals over the Tsilhqot'in. He attributed the war to a misguided member of Waddington's crew who, he said, on finding that some flour had been stolen, wrote down the names of some Tsilhqot'in and then told them that sickness would come to their country and kill them all. Brown went on:

> The Indians were much alarmed and distressed by these proceedings. They have, be it observed, a very special horror of having their names written down. They look upon paper as a very awful thing, they tremble to see the working of a pen. Writing is, they imagine, a dread mystery. By it the mighty whites seem to carry on intercourse with unseen powers. When they are writing, there's no telling what they may be doing. They may be bidding a pestilence come over the land, or ordering the rain to stay in the west, or giving directions for the salmon to remain in the ocean. Especially is the Indian appalled when he sees his own *name* put on paper. To him the name is not distinct from the person who owns it. If his name is written down, he is written down: if his name is passed over to the demons which people his hierarchy, he is sure to be bewitched and given as prey into the teeth of his invisible foes.

This seems much more likely to have been Brown's fantasy than that of the Tsilhqot'in. By the time he met them in the 1860s, they had already had more than forty years of experience with the newcomers writing things down. Surely if it were possible to work magic by writing, the Tsilhqot'in would have seen evidence of it by then.[33]

After retelling the events of the Chilcotin War, Brown described ministering to the condemned Tsilhqot'in men in the days leading up to their execution. Toward the end of his account, there is a long description of the conversation on their last night, which Brown remembered to be mostly about the future. The assimilationist picture that Brown painted for the men was evidently the best future he could imagine; we will never know what they made of it, because we have only his word for their response. In the future, he told them, "Indian children would be educated and taught to understand the mysteries of reading and writing." Families would settle down to till the soil and build houses. They would wear "respectable clothing," and each household would be headed by a patriarch "having but one wife, as the Lord had ordained." Their spiritual life would be led by Aboriginal priests. They would live in peace with other Aboriginal people and with the whites. "For the whites would not leave the land. No they had been sent here by the Great Lord of all!" Although the Aboriginal people and the fur traders had made "small account" of the land, "the Highest, the Maker of all, had other purposes for [it] ... No doubt it was painful for them to see it in the hands of strangers, but it was for the good of mankind, and for the greater glory of the land itself." God had put the gold and silver in the rocks for the British to find. They would put steamboats on every body of water and build a railway to the Atlantic, "and thus the will of the Most High would be accomplished." In Brown's view, the Tsilhqot'in's past was unimportant except for the brief moment in which they temporarily opposed the will of God. Their future, too, was nonexistent; they were truly a people without history.[34]

Oblate missionary Adrian Morice's *History of the Northern Interior of British Columbia* was published in London in 1906, after he had spent two years with the Tsilhqot'in and nineteen with the Carrier. Unlike Brown, Morice acknowledged the existence of an indigenous history that predated the arrival of the newcomers. He began with a physical description of the extent of the country, its vegetation, lakes and rivers, fish and fauna: "These, from time immemorial, have been trapped or chased by the American representatives of the human species who call themselves *Déné* (men), and are divided into four main tribes." He went on to describe the physiognomy of each of the groups, using more neutral terms than were usually deployed by his contemporaries: "the Sekanis, for instance, are slender and bony, with fairly delicate features, very small eyes, and thin lips. The Carriers are stouter and more heavily built, with coarser traits, thicker lips, and quite large eyes. The Babines and Chilcotins are shorter than the Carriers, with broader shoulders and, the former at least, with even thicker lips and flattish faces ... They have all very black and straight hair, dark eyes, small hands and feet, and a complexion of a swarthy brown." Morice then turned his attention to their social structure, noting that "none of them originally had any village chiefs in our sense of the word." Instead, they were governed by the older members of related families and, in some cases, by hereditary clan leaders. Morice also noted that the Dene held religious beliefs: about a future world, about spirits, about the power of shamans, about the proper treatment of the dead.[35]

When discussing the respective characters of the four "tribes" of Dene, however, a curious asymmetry crept into Morice's account. Here is an example: "The Sekanis are the most honest and moral; the Carriers are the proudest and most progressive; the Chilcotins are violent and none too scrupulous, while for loquacity and conservativeness the Babines have few superiors." Throughout the *History,* Morice described the Tsilhqot'in in distinctly negative terms, as when he portrayed another indigenous group as "possibly less bloodthirsty than the Chilcotins, [but] even more noisy and restless." One might argue that his assessment was based on his experience of the Tsilhqot'in people in the early 1880s. But this interpretation is not supported by Morice's own writings on the subject, which changed over time. In 1883, Morice wrote a long letter about the Tsilhqot'in to the *Missions de la Congrégation des Missionaires Oblats de Marie-Immaculée,* published in Paris. David Mulhall, author of an unflattering biography of Morice, wrote that "he included a list of their violent deeds, but he was careful to explain that in murdering certain whites, the Indians were simply defending their land, the honour of their women, and their dignity." In fact, this is the same argument that Morice makes when he discusses the specific details of the Chilcotin War in the *History.* His more negative assessment arises in contexts where he makes generalizations about the Tsilhqot'in people as a whole. In 1889, after Morice had been living with the Carrier for four years, he was still able to put a somewhat positive gloss on the Tsilhqot'in character as he perceived it. "Were I required to particularize in two words the ethic peculiarities of each tribe," he wrote in an article for the *Proceedings of the Canadian Institute,* "I would state that the Chilhχotins are the most violent and manly of the whole group; the Carriers, the proudest and most accessible to progressive ideas; the Sékanais, the most superstitious and naïve." As Morice remembered the Tsilhqot'in during successive episodes in his life, the events of the Chilcotin War took on an unwarranted significance, colouring all else.[36]

In the second chapter of the *History,* Morice turned to a chronological account, beginning in 1660 with the birth of the Carrier nobleman Na'kwoel, who around 1730 became the first of the Dene to acquire an iron axe or adze. In a footnote, Morice noted that the prevalence of iron goods among the Dene when they were first contacted by Alexander Mackenzie and Simon Fraser showed "the ease with which such goods travelled in pre-European times." The Tsilhqot'in made their first appearance in the *History* in 1745 as the perpetrators of "a most melancholy event, which was to cause a permanent change in the ethnographical map of the country." Wanting "to avenge ... the death of one of their notables," the Tsilhqot'in descended on the Carrier village Chinlac, at the confluence of the Stuart and Nechako Rivers, and "practically annihilated the whole population." Morice dwelt on the horror of the scene, the pools of blood, and two poles bearing "the bodies of the children ripped open and spitted through the out-turned ribs in exactly the same way as salmon drying in the sun." For the principal chief of the Carrier village, who had survived the attack, there was no alternative but to exact "the vengeance due to such an unprovoked crime," and, after more killing, "the affront to the Carrier tribe was thus washed out in blood."[37]

Considering that Morice earlier noted that the Tsilhqot'in were seeking vengeance for a death, it doesn't seem fair of him to call the killings at Chinlac "an unprovoked crime." In fact, Morice's account was based on Carrier oral tradition, in particular on a version that he heard from the daughter of the principal chief of Chinlac when she was about ninety years old. Subsequent accounts of the events at Chinlac have been based on Morice's and embellished. A magazine article published in 1986, for example, described the Tsilhqot'in as "hostile" and "murderous," expanded on Morice's description of the devastation at Chinlac by adding some imagined details ("the only signs of life were the scavenging ravens and jays"), and crucially attributed the abuse of a young woman to the Tsilhqot'ins, when she was actually a captive of the Carrier. In fact, there is archaeological evidence that calls some aspects of Morice's version into question. In the early 1950s, Charles Borden excavated Chinlac and found contact goods that suggested the village hadn't been abandoned after the killings in 1745, but had remained occupied until a later date, toward the end of the eighteenth century.[38]

The next time the Tsilhqot'in entered the narrative of Morice's *History* was in 1808, when Simon Fraser, descending the river that now bears his name, noted the presence of a group of Dene who lived on the western side of the river and called themselves "Chilk-hodin." "About sixty Indians were present on this occasion," Fraser wrote, "and as many more were on the opposite shore bawling to send for them, but, as their presence could be of no service to us, we thought it more advisable to dispense with their company as much as possible." Around 1830, they made an appearance again when the HBC established Fort Chilcotin "on a tributary of the Chilcotin River, which, after many trials and varying fortunes, had to be abandoned, owing to its isolation and consequent expensiveness, but especially on account of the troublesome disposition of the natives who frequented it." Morice took the California historian Hubert Howe Bancroft to task for suggesting that Fort Chilcotin was founded around the same time as Fort Alexandria (1821): "To anyone familiar with the geography of the country and the innate restiveness of the Chilcotin Indians, such a statement calls for confirmation." Later Morice described the Chilcotin in the mid-1830s as in a "chronic state of disaffection."[39]

Practically the only time the Tsilhqot'in entered Morice's *History* was to make trouble. Not only at Chinlac in 1745 and at Fort Chilcotin in the 1830s, but also during the Chilcotin War: "We have had more than once to refer to the turbulent character of the Chilcotin Indians. So late as 1864, their appearance and costume did not betray much contact with representatives of European civilization, and in the absence of all missionary influence their inner self had undoubtedly remained even more refractory to humane ideas." The last time they showed up in the *History* was at Alexandria in 1868, where they heard a Catholic bishop preaching and "profited not a little."[40]

Morice's depiction of the Tsilhqot'in people as resistant to non-indigenous "civilization" was echoed in most twentieth-century accounts. For example, in *British Columbia from the Earliest Times to the Present* (1914), F.W. Howay argued that after the initial killings at Bute Inlet, "the assassins now became promoted to the dignity of insurgents by the adhesion of the whole Chilcotin tribe ... It was reported that the Indians were combined for the purpose of killing every white man they met." Later, according to Howay, when the Tsilhqot'in saw that the government did not intend to kill them indiscriminately, but rather "to impress the Indian mind with the superiority of British law in this very respect that only the guilty can be punished ... the great chiefs became ranged on the side of law and order and engaged to assist in securing those murderers who were still at large."[41]

PLACE FETISHISM AND THE DANCING "CHINAMAN"

The first histories of British Columbia were written after the Chilcotin War, and the war coloured the imagination of events that had nothing to do with it. The Tsilhqot'in people became troublesome, restless, and violent in the retelling, responsible for atrocities at Chinlac in the late eighteenth century, responsible for the failure of Fort Chilcotin in the nineteenth. The Chilcotin, in turn, became a landscape of resistance, violence, and tragedy. This reification of human characteristics in place required a kind of forgetting. To the extent that there was a dominant mode of historical consciousness about the Chilcotin for most of the twentieth century, it was based on the myth of the frontier, on the imagined discovery of a near-empty land, the brief conflict with its wild inhabitants, its peopling by the settlers, and the subsequent establishment of colonial society. Historical details that did not accord with the myth had to be reworked in collective memory.[42]

The wildness of the Tsilhqot'in, for example, now governed the imagination of their every encounter. In local histories, the unearthing of an occasional stone tool became a sign of "earlier Indian skirmishes and wars." These might be imagined in detail, as in the following account from a 1950s compilation of Chilcotin "history and legends": "Once in the early 1880s, the Bella Coola Indians intended to attack the Chilcotins and advanced down the valley from Puntzee. The Chilcotins being prewarned by their scout were prepared. They were in ambush above the cliff now known as Battle Bluff and rolled huge rocks down on the enemy, killing many and driving them from the valley." What the Nuxalk were doing at Puntzi or what they had against the Tsilhqot'in is anyone's guess. The story is given without any supporting evidence, and if it weren't incredible enough, there are two other Battle Mountains in the province that were supposedly named after Tsilhqot'in altercations. One in Wells Gray Park, well east of Williams Lake, memorializes a battle between the Tsilhqot'in and Secwepemc around 1875 over caribou hunting grounds. The other, west of Alexis Creek, was noted by George Dawson in the 1870s and described by the ethnographer James Teit: there are a number of boulders below the mountain, "which, according to tradition, are the transformed bodies of Alexandria warriors who strayed over a cliff in the dark while on the way to attack a camp of Chilcotin who lived in the vicinity."[43]

The imagined former prevalence of inter-Aboriginal wars was used both to justify the subsequent actions of the colonial government in the Chilcotin War and to rhetorically depopulate the Chilcotin, to make it into an empty land awaiting settlement. The fact that the land policy of the colonial government had actively dispossessed Aboriginal people played no role in the myth. Instead, the myth required the land to be empty, and the logic of this requirement transposed the imagined violence

of the Tsilhqot'in people to the place itself. The beginnings of this trans-
position can be seen in the writings of the settlers of the 1920s and '30s.
Rich Hobson, who came with Pan Phillips to establish a cattle empire,
wrote that "the Anahim Lake country, its sullen forests recently echoing
the shots of explorers who had fought and died there, is a dark and for-
bidding land, jealously guarding its immense boundaries from men creep-
ing north and west from the rim of civilization." And this: "A strange hollow
loneliness seemed to reach up out of the vastness of the jackpines ... An
eerie, empty, lifeless land of monotonous sameness; uninspiring, unspec-
tacular, colorless, exuding a sinister feeling of complete isolation from the
living. A land that breathes no spirit of a past life, and gives little hope of
a future one." To Eric Collier, who titled his book *Three Against the Wilderness,* the Chilcotin was the "strange untamed" country where he and his
Métis wife and son "tasted all of summer's searing heat and winter's pen-
etrating hostility, our only neighbours the moose, bears, timber wolves
and other wild life of the muskegs and forest; some of whom seemed ever
ready to dispute our right to be there at all. There we learned to accept the
mosquitoes and deer flies that often drove us, our work horses, and saddle
stock almost crazy with their persistent thirst for blood."[44]

By the early 1950s, the mythic Chilcotin frontier was well established,
the stuff of Sunday newspaper supplements in the lower mainland and of
special editions of Williams Lake newspapers published in the summer for
tourists. "Four purple mountain ranges stand guard over this strange corner of B.C. called the Anahim," one *Vancouver Sun* article read, "which is
the land of fifty years ago ... the last frontier of the West." Inspired, no doubt,
by Hollywood westerns and the prime-time parade of the Cisco Kid, Lone
Ranger, Roy Rogers, Wild Bill Hickok, and Hopalong Cassidy across the
TV screen, the author imagined Chilcotin cowboys "riding through the
last scene of the almost-forgotten picture of free grass and open range."
Another article described the Tsilhqot'in riding on horseback or in wag-
ons from the Anahim reserve to Pigeon's store at Alexis Creek to see movies
on Saturday night. "The Indians sure love cowboy pictures and if there
is no wild west picture they just won't come," said a woman who worked
in the store. "Jungle and Tarzan pictures go over good also." This was a
clear sign to the author that Alexis Creek was "the nerve centre of a great
cattle country that is still the wild and wooly west." "The wild west comes
to life again," he wrote, "both on the screen and among the audience."
The idea that the Tsilhqot'in may have enjoyed westerns as escapist fantasy, just as everyone else did in the 1950s, doesn't seem to have occurred
to him. The onscreen antics of John Wayne and Ronald Reagan had little

to do with the day-to-day work of cowboys in the Chilcotin, Tsilhqot'in or otherwise.[45]

The RCMP officers at Alexis Creek were also caught up in the region's mythic past. When a local construction company unearthed the remains of three human bodies in a gravel bar in October 1951, one in a "well preserved sawed lumber box," the investigating officer imagined that the people had died during the Chilcotin War. He questioned "all the early settlers" and "old Indians," but none knew of a burial ground in the area. "There is no doubt there was a large encampment of Indians on the Hudson Bay Flat at that time," the Mountie wrote in his report, "and if these graves are of persons who died at that time, the Indians would refuse to reveal any information about them." On the strength of that hunch, the detachment forwarded the report to the BC Archives, "in the event that the Historical Society may be interested."[46]

In 1958, the *Williams Lake Tribune* printed the following item, with the headline "Chinaman Died While Dancing to Tune of Bullets":

> Tom Hance, the original settler at Hanceville, besides his normal job of running a ranch and store, was also justice of the peace, jailer and policeman. A story still told of Hance, the policeman, is typical of the rough and ready manner in which law was maintained in those days. The story concerns Chief Quilt of the Stoney Indian tribe. It seems there was a Chinese prospector mining on the banks of the Fraser from whom the Stonies were in the habit of cadging small things like tobacco. On one occasion, the Chinaman, probably thinking he had been generous enough, declined to give out any more gifts. The Indians were hurt and argued the point. Both sides grew louder and finally the prospector cussed his visitors out in a vigorous mixture of Cantonese, pidgen [sic] English and Siwash [almost certainly Chinook Jargon]. Still angry, the Stonies left, but after getting some distance away their indignation rose, and they decided to return with the intention of telling off the Chinaman for his parsimony. By the time the Stonies had returned to the Chinaman's cabin they were so angry the Oriental became alarmed and withdrew inside, locking his cabin door. This didn't stop the Indians. Having heard how the Barkerville miners used to make Chinese "dance" to a tune called by bullets, the Stonies climbed on the roof and began firing through the smoke opening. Just as they expected, the poor harassed Chinaman was soon hopping around in a wild effort to avoid the bullets. All might have been well, but the cabin was dark inside, and, unfortunately, a mistake was made. The Chinaman was shot and killed. After cleaning out the Chinaman's scanty stock the Stonies travelled

to Hanceville, and there Chief Quilt informed Constable Hance of the unlucky occurrence. Tom told the Chief "When the grass turns green" Chief Quilt would have to go to Ashcroft and stand trial at the assizes. Nothing more was done until spring, when, sure enough, the chief returned, and with Tom Hance, by saddle and pack horse, travelled to Ashcroft. After all the evidence had been given, and Tom Hance and the priest had testified to his good character, the court asked Chief Quilt for his statement. Through the interpreter the court was informed by Chief Quilt that, "All my life I be good Indian. Never kill white man or Indians. Only coyotes and Chinaman." He was acquitted and returned to Chilcotin with Tom Hance to spend the remainder of his years as a law abiding citizen, highly respected for his good influence over the Stony Tribe.[47]

This story, a mythologized version of the altercations between various Tsilhqot'in and Chinese people in the late nineteenth century, is a fascinating example of the ways in which events are forgotten and remade in collective memory. The claim that Barkerville miners made Chinese "dance" by shooting at their feet, for example, is pure Hollywood western. There is some basis to the story in fact: Chinese men were killed by Tsilhqot'in men firing through the smoke opening of their cabin on the banks of the Fraser river. Other details have been reconstructed. Tom Hance, although not involved in the original killings, did play a significant role in Chilcotin justice as constable, jailer, and coroner. He wasn't officially appointed as a lawman until 1895, more than a decade after the killings, but if it is a story about Chilcotin justice in the old days, then it makes sense that it be about Hance. What about Chief Quilt? The position, a hereditary one, was held by both father and son from the 1880s to the 1950s. Coincidentally, Chief Quilt was accused of perjury, on what seems to have been an unrelated matter, right around the time that Nemiah was arrested and jailed. Two missionaries wrote on Quilt's behalf, begging that he be released because the apparent perjury was actually due to the fact that depositions were taken through an interpreter who didn't understand what Quilt said. They noted that Quilt was a good Christian and an influential man in his community. He was discharged. Quilt's presence in this story would seem to be the result of confusing his name with that of Quitalt, the small boy who witnessed Nemiah killing a different Chinese man. And one element has been completely forgotten or submerged or effaced: the fact that these killings weren't a little misguided fun that ended badly, but rather the first steps toward a second Chilcotin War.[48]

The year before the dancing "Chinaman" story was published, Chilcotin rancher Edward Penrose Lee wrote about greenhorns coming from as far away as California, looking for ranches. These people "thought all they had to do was take up a good large piece of land and go into the cow business." Lee, however, had been in the Chilcotin "for close onto seventy years and it [had] gradually filled up with stockraisers and there [was] no vacant land suitable for this purpose any more." He thought the cattle industry was waning in the area and that the Aboriginal people, "on whom we depended to a large extent," could get better pay than stockraisers could afford. Such practical advice did nothing to stem the tide of articles about the Chilcotin, the "Big Country," "a wild, untamed land," a place where some Aboriginal people lived "so far out in the wilderness they have never set eyes upon a white man." Some of the prose in these articles was more purple than the mountains guarding Anahim. One piece, written in 1970, concluded that "as you drive the dusty miles along the Chilcotin Road you know that despite man's mania for raping virgin land, this is a land that will never be tamed, and where people will remain just as they are today: rugged, individualistic, proud – and free." But the darker side of the mythic frontier was about to come to the nation's attention.[49]

THE DEATH OF FRED QUILT

In 1972, *Rolling Stone* reporter Tim Cahill went to Alexis Creek to cover the story of the death of a Tsilhqot'in man named Fred Quilt. Cahill, who would later make a name for himself as an adventure travel writer, evidently felt that the story of Quilt was very much the story of a place. "For months, the corpse of Fred Quilt's burnt out pickup truck has rusted in this Canadian meadow," his piece began. "Ravens perch on the cab to scan the grasses or haggle loudly among themselves. The hundred or so white folks who live down at Alexis Creek don't care to see the truck, and they bounce their cars over this section of the road with a quick burst of speed. Local Indians shun it like bad medicine – shun it as if it were the ghost of one gloomy, frozen twilight last November." Later in the article, he wrote that "Alexis Creek is set dead in the cold green heart of British Columbia." And to describe Quilt's home, the Stone reserve: "The roads on Anahim are gravel, but the few lanes on the Stone reserve are mud and dirt. Now, in the dry season, wind-driven dust covers everything and everyone. The cabins, the people, the few cars are all the color of dust." The residents of Stone reserve, Cahill wrote, "do not dare to speak a dead man's name for fear that this will bring him back from the dead. Those who travel with the dead, they say, will join them the next day." Fred Quilt's adopted son, Robin, who was present during the events that led to his father's death, reportedly heard Quilt calling his name one night as he walked by the graveyard where the body was buried. "For three days and three nights he hid in the woods," wrote Cahill. "Now, he never walks by the burial ground, nor does he visit his father's grave."[50]

Fred Quilt, the fifty-five-year-old man whose death was causing such unrest in 1972, had had a hard life. He lived on the reserve in a small cabin covered with tar and shingles, eking out a living by raising a few head of his own cattle and by cutting hay and building fences for local ranchers. Making less than $2,000 a year, he managed to support his wife, Christine, and four adopted children. His pickup truck, one of a handful on the Stone reserve, was used both for his own work and for community errands, and was his family's most important possession. Quilt drank from time to time and had gotten into his share of altercations. He had twice been admitted to the hospital in Williams Lake, once for a concussion that he got in a fight and once for a gunshot wound in the leg.

On 30 November 1971, Fred, Christine, his adopted son Robin, Christine's sister Agnes (Robin's biological mother), and a friend named Isaac Meyers drove to Anahim reserve for the wake of a little girl. The afternoon was overcast and below freezing. The mourners stood around a large bonfire, drinking and playing the gambling game *lahal,* as was customary. At the end of the evening, Fred, Christine, Robin, and Agnes left in the pickup. At some point they stopped on the road, or possibly beside it, for reasons that are not clear. Leslie Roberts, a public health nurse, found the Quilts' truck on the road around 5:30 or 5:45 p.m., as it was getting dark. She went up to the passenger door and found Agnes, whom she knew, singing very cheerfully. A passing truck driver stopped and helped Roberts turn on the red warning flasher on her flashlight, which she then left ten or twelve feet behind the Quilts' truck. The truck driver left, and Roberts went to Alexis Creek, where she reported the incident to the RCMP. At 7 p.m., a resident of Vancouver who was driving on Highway 20 came across a flashlight beside the road with a red warning signal on. A quarter of a mile farther along he found a truck stopped on the wrong side of the road with four Aboriginal people in it. Twice he asked them in a loud voice if there was any trouble and if they needed help. He got no response. When he played his flashlight over the driver's face, he could see the man's eyes rolling. He drove to Alexis Creek and stopped someone on the street, asking them to tell the police about the incident.[51]

Eyewitnesses disagreed about what happened next. Two RCMP con-

stables later testified that they were having dinner when they received a
phone call from their commanding officer. He told them that there was a
truck blocking the road, possibly full of "drunken Indians." Although only
one of the policemen was on duty, the other agreed to accompany him in
case of trouble. They found the Quilts' truck blocking the road, everyone
in it asleep or passed out, and the hood of the vehicle cold to the touch.
When the first constable opened the door, he couldn't find any keys in the
ignition. There was a strong smell of vanilla in the cab. Quilt slumped out
onto the ground, and the policeman asked his colleague to take him to the
RCMP vehicle. The other constable lifted Quilt up by grabbing him under
the arms from behind and leaned him against the truck. Quilt grabbed the
box of his own truck, apparently resisting the constable's effort to get him
over to the police truck. When the constable pulled on him, the two men
fell and Quilt landed on his stomach. The constable helped him over to
the police car, getting vomit all over his hands and jacket. The two Mounties took the other Quilts to their vehicle. Agnes "was swearing and curs-
ing and quite belligerent about the whole thing. Most of it was in Chilcotin
and [they] didn't understand it." They tried to push the Quilts' truck off
the road, but the gearshift seemed to be jammed and they couldn't get it
into neutral. They drove the Tsilhqot'in to Anahim – Christine thanked
them for the ride as she got out – and then returned to Alexis Creek. On
the way back, they decided that the Quilts' truck was still in a potentially
dangerous position, so they set up some flares to prevent an accident and
went for towing cables. At Alexis Creek they washed up, the off-duty policeman got into uniform, and they returned to Quilt's truck. They found
that someone had moved it off the road and set it on fire. There was quite
a bit of traffic on the road, and a carful of people watching the truck burn
told them that they had found it like that a few minutes earlier. In the previous two years, four cars had been burned on Highway 20 in that area.[52]
The Quilts' account of the event was very different. While they were sleeping in their vehicle beside the road, the RCMP parked behind their truck.
A uniformed policeman pulled Quilt from his truck and threw him on
the ground. Another man, out of uniform, began screaming obscenities
and then "jumped up and down" on Fred Quilt several times, on his head,
chest, and groin. The man was wearing heavy cowboy boots with sharp
heels. The Quilts were put in the police vehicle and driven back to Anahim.
There, bleeding from a head wound and doubled over in agony, Fred Quilt
was rolled out of the RCMP vehicle into the snow in front of the church.
Laughing, the Mounties drove off. One of the Tsilhqot'in families in Anahim
helped get Fred Quilt indoors, while another man drove Christine back to

get the truck. They found it thirty-five feet from where they had left it, in flames, with the wrapper of a highway flare lying on the road. Meanwhile, Fred Quilt kept asking his son Robin, "Why didn't the police just kill me there?" A local nurse, a nun, was summoned, and Quilt told her that the police had "kicked" him. She wrapped his abdomen in an elastic bandage. Christine, returning from the truck, went to the Catholic priest and told him that the police had "jumped" on Fred Quilt. She asked him to call the provincial judge in Redstone, but the judge was not available. The following morning, Christine called Leslie Roberts, the Alexis Creek public health nurse. Quilt told her that the police had "jumped up and down" on him. She called for an ambulance, which arrived that evening around 6 p.m. Quilt refused to ride in it, as it was carrying a dead Aboriginal child to Williams Lake for an autopsy, and he was unable to sit up. The ambulance returned for Quilt the following day around 1 p.m. and took him to the hospital in Williams Lake. He was pronounced dead at 4:20 p.m. on 30 November, about 48 hours after the encounter with the policemen.[53]

An Inquest, and Another

Dave Stockand, the only reporter to show up at a Vancouver press conference convened by an Aboriginal group called the Fred Quilt Committee, found that its members had "taken affidavits from witnesses, drawn maps, and prepared what amounted to a legal brief." Impressed, he wrote up the story from the Aboriginal point of view. It appeared with a banner headline on the front page of the Saturday edition of the *Vancouver Sun*. The following year he told Tim Cahill that he was "still bloody astounded by the story. What separates Quilt from any number of other similar Indian injustices is that it wouldn't bloody go away. It's taken major coverage for nearly nine months and it's still going on." As the controversy gained momentum, the Fred Quilt Committee gathered evidence of other injustices toward Aboriginal people. During the same winter that Quilt died, a man was thrown out of a pub far from his home and froze to death, but no charges were laid. The autopsy of another man, hit by a train, revealed that he was dead on the tracks before the train came, but police didn't investigate. Farther north, another Aboriginal man was thrown out of a bar, his back broken, and he, too, froze to death, but no charges were laid. Finally, a baby froze to death in a house after the oil dealer refused to extend credit to an Aboriginal family, but no charges were laid. A couple of years earlier, an Aboriginal girl named Rosemary Roper had been found naked and dead at a garbage dump near Lac La Hache after a night in the company of three white boys. One was acquitted on reduced charges of manslaughter; the other two were each sentenced to a year of jail time. The perceived inadequacy of the sentencing led to an outcry.[54]

In mid-January 1972, a coroner's inquest into the death of Fred Quilt was held in Williams Lake. The coroner, who was also the manager of the local medical clinic, a justice of the peace, and an ex-RCMP officer, supervised the selection of the jury. Jury members were chosen by the Williams Lake RCMP detachment. One of the jurors lived in a house with two members of the RCMP; another, the jury foreman, was an auxiliary RCMP officer himself. The rest of the jury were also white and male. The two Mounties involved in the incident were subpoenaed and had their expenses covered by the government. The investigation was headed by a friend of theirs, a senior RCMP officer. Although there were Aboriginal witnesses to the events, only non-Aboriginal witnesses were interviewed by the police. No Aboriginal witnesses were subpoenaed. The ones who attended the inquest, including Fred's wife, Christine, had to hitchhike into town and pay their own way.

When Christine took the stand, her story was so different from that of the Mounties that the coroner asked her if she knew what it meant to tell the truth. She was examined by Gunnar Eggertson, who represented the RCMP and the Department of Justice. Eggertson repeatedly tried to force Christine to make eye contact with him and asked her if someone had put words into her mouth. Many of the Tsilhqot'in couldn't speak English, and some had never been to Williams Lake. Matters were complicated by people in the courtroom bursting into laughter during Aboriginal testimony. The testimony of the surgeon who performed the autopsy was treated with more respect but with apparent incomprehension. Dr. Han Choo Lee testified that Quilt's bowel had probably been transected by a kick, certainly by a sharp external blow of some sort that occurred around the time the Quilts encountered the Mounties. He had to tear a piece of paper in half to demonstrate to the court what a "transection" was. After three and a half hours, the jury returned a verdict of accidental death by peritonitis and absolved the Mounties of blame. An hour of their deliberation was taken up with an argument over the correct spelling of "peritonitis."[55]

After the first inquest there was a "series of protests and demonstrations." By late January 1972, the provincial attorney general was receiving regular telegrams – from the Fred Quilt Committee and Aboriginal leaders, the United Fishermen and Allied Workers Union, the Canadian Public Employees Union Local 1004, the Native Indian Committee of the BC Conference of United Churches, and so on – calling for an investigation into the inquest and asking whether it was possible for charges to be laid against the police officers involved in the incident. The Fred Quilt Committee, which orchestrated the campaign, made sure that copies of the telegrams were sent to Dave Stockand, and his article, headlined "Demands Grow for Inquest Probe," was published in the *Vancouver Sun*. Questions were raised in the provincial legislative assembly. Ernie LeCours, Social Credit MLA for Richmond (who would later be known as a "self-styled maverick" and someone "who fought very hard for the little men and little women of the Province"), took the opportunity on 21 January to push for an Aboriginal court case-worker program. Referring facetiously to Quilt as "the gentleman who was the victim of an accident recently in the Cariboo country ... who happened to be an Indian," LeCours stated: "In view of my past experience with some members of police forces – and I say some members and I emphasize a small number of them – I am very suspicious of what takes place at times, especially on dark roads at night. I urge the Hon. Attorney General to make every effort to investigate this case very thoroughly and ensure that justice is done." The following day, a *Vancouver Sun* editorial called for an investigation by the attorney general. On 27 January, W.L. Hartley, MLA for Yale-Lillooet, raised the matter again in the legislative assembly, suggesting that there had been "either a gross miscarriage of justice or a gross misinterpretation by the Press of what ha[d] gone on." Hartley went on to say that he had been contacted by "various native organizations," as had the attorney general. The history of Canada and of the province, he argued, had given Aboriginal people reason to question the non-Aboriginal sense of justice. It was time to "make it abundantly clear that all Canadians will stand equal before the law." Hartley, too, called for a program of government-funded Aboriginal case-workers for the courts and asked that the attorney general order the chief coroner to review the Fred Quilt case and the subsequent inquest: "I think this is a fair question and it's something the Attorney General could stand up and be prepared to deal with now – not six months from now when all the damage of innuendo and rumour has gone on through the media for weeks and weeks."[56]

The attorney general responded to the growing pressure by asking Glen McDonald, the chief coroner, to review the evidence. Some felt that this was a stalling tactic; as a potential candidate for the premiership of the province, the attorney general was not about to endanger his chances by doing anything as unpopular as investigating the RCMP. However, MLAs continued to raise troubling questions. On 14 February, L. Nimsick (Kootenay) asked what progress had been made in the Quilt investigation: "What about the transcript that was taken on the evidence at this review? Why is it not made public? Why is it not released? I think it should be released unless there's something that's being hid." It wasn't only the Aboriginal people of BC and the rest of the country who had to be satisfied on the matter, Nimsick said, but "a lot of other people throughout the province" as well. The attorney general began receiving telegrams again, including messages from the BC Social Workers Union and the BC Civil Liberties Union. The latter group told him that it did "not intend to let [the] matter drop into oblivion." The Legal Committee of the Human Rights Council of BC reviewed the transcript of the original inquest and found it wanting. In a report issued by the chairman, the legal committee described the coroner's attitude as one of "paternal racism" and the testimony of the Mounties as "unusually sparse and lack[ing] detail." A July article in *Maclean's,* Canada's national news magazine, described cases in which members of the RCMP had falsified evidence, perjured themselves, ignored the rights of suspects, and met bureaucratic quotas by targeting Aboriginal people.[57]

The BC Supreme Court quashed the proceedings and findings of the first inquest because of the association between the RCMP and the coroner's jury. In July, the attorney general finally called for another inquest, one that would have what he called "the appearance of impartiality." The venue was moved from Williams Lake to the larger town of Kamloops, which then had a population of around forty thousand. A judge was put in charge of the proceedings, and he set up a lottery system for jury selection that ensured there would be two Aboriginal people and four non-Aboriginals; as it happened, there were also two women on the jury. The Quilt estate chose Harry Rankin to be its lawyer. Rankin was an alderman in the city of Vancouver, known by his supporters as the "People's Champion," and rebuked by opponents for his close ties to the Communist Party. He had a long record of fighting for unpopular civil rights cases. Before the second inquest, he told a group of Aboriginal people that fighting the Fred Quilt case all the way would make their lives "a hundred times easier." "Brutal racist police will realize they can't move you as easily," Rankin said. "They know you'll be watching." Over a hundred members of the public attended the inquest, some wearing small placards around their necks that read "Fred Quilt is Dead – Why?" Outside the Kamloops courthouse, fifty to sixty members of the Fred Quilt Committee kept a peaceful vigil.[58]

At the inquest, RCMP corporal Robert Holland entered as evidence forty colour photographs of Fred Quilt's body, taken the night that he died. The *Vancouver Sun* reported that "Holland said the photographs showed some marks which he did not notice on the body when he took them and added he has come across this in previous cases. Holland: 'There is a tendency to pick up certain things on film which at the time are not visible to the naked eye.'" When asked why he didn't order that the Quilt's truck be impounded so that the cause of the fire could be determined, Holland explained that this was the duty of the investigating officer. The cowboy boots worn by the officer who was alleged to have jumped on Quilt were also entered into evidence, although they had been worn after the event and thus had no forensic value. Holland agreed with Rankin that the boots should have been tested for shirt fibres or other evidence, but said, again, that it was not his responsibility at the time, and too late to do so by the time they came into his possession. The on-duty officer who went to the scene was asked why he didn't push Quilt's truck off the road with the RCMP vehicle (against policy) and why he had to return to Alexis Creek for towing equipment (because the winch on the police truck had recently broken and someone had borrowed the towing cables from it a few days earlier). Rankin then asked him why he didn't impound the Quilt's truck. "For what?" the officer asked. "Possibly bloodstains, possibly vomit, possibly alcohol, possibly fingerprints, possibly anything," Rankin replied.[59]

The jury asked to see the original police report for the incident, but the RCMP refused, saying that it wasn't their policy to produce documents. This brought opposition from the Quilts' attorney, from the representative of the provincial attorney general, and from the judge presiding over the inquest, who told them, "This is not some secret document." The RCMP eventually produced the report. "[Leslie Roberts] to office, advising that there was a pickup truck with a load of drunks in it smack in the middle of the road at the above location," it read. "Patrolled to scene, where the vehicle, belonging to Christine Quilt, was found right in the middle of the road with the four occupants extremely intoxicated on vanilla." The remainder was quite brief – a sketch of what the RCMP officers had already testified, with no information about a possible injury to Fred Quilt. At the inquest, the police testified that they didn't know there were any allegations against them until notified by the Williams Lake coroner a few days after Quilt's death.[60]

The RCMP were again represented by Gunnar Eggertson. The Tsilh-qot'in nicknamed him "Gopher" because he repeatedly sprang to his feet, shouting "objection," and then sat down again just as quickly. The RCMP team's strategy was, first, to question the autopsy results and, second, to impugn Christine Quilt's testimony and character. To achieve the first end, they called the former head of pathology at Vancouver General and St. Paul's hospitals. He testified that the force required to transect a bowel was too great to have been applied externally and suggested that Dr. Lee must have accidentally severed the bowel himself during a hasty autopsy. He said that Lee should have been suspicious of his own diagnosis and tried to confirm it by taking a section of the gastrointestinal tract for microscopic examination. There was no other case in the medical literature where the small bowel was severed closer than fifteen centimetres from the point where it enters the large bowel, but Lee claimed Quilt's small bowel had been severed within five centimetres of the large bowel. The pathologist also expressed his disbelief that a Mountie would jump up and down on a supine person. A diagnostic radiologist testified that the X-rays taken just before Quilt's death were not consistent with Dr. Lee's conclusions. A third physician claimed that Lee's autopsy contained a number of features that didn't "fit in with the usual and accepted practice": it mentioned no bruises or distinctive marks, no tissue was taken from the lung to confirm or deny pneumonia, no tissue was taken from the bowel, and it mentioned no injuries to other organs, although such injuries certainly would have been expected if Quilt had died from a transection of the bowel. The third physician also testified that peritonitis was usually caused by appendicitis, the implication being that Quilt contracted the condition around the time he was being moved to the RCMP vehicle and died of it two days later. To undermine Christine Quilt's testimony, the RCMP lawyers asked her if she bought artificial vanilla extract (an inexpensive and disreputable means of getting drunk), which she denied doing. They then brought in the owner of the local general store, whose credit receipts showed that Christine had, in fact, bought seventeen bottles of vanilla extract between 5 November and 21 December, three of them on the day of the incident.[61]

The jury was doubtful enough about what had actually happened to return an open verdict. On 3 August it found that Quilt's death was due to "unnatural causes," the injuries sustained during his encounter with the RCMP that perforated his small bowel and led to his subsequent death by peritonitis. They refused to attribute blame for Quilt's death to anyone, however, citing his failure to avail himself of ambulance service and medical help as a contributing factor. As a consequence, criminal charges were not laid against the police officers in question, and the matter petered out without really being laid to rest.[62]

LOOKING BACK AT THE WAR

The 1970s were a time of renewed interest in the Chilcotin War, "the best documented instance of conflict between Indians and whites in British Columbia." In 1972, Edward S. Hewlett finished a master's thesis on the event at the University of British Columbia; the same year, the magazine *Canadian Frontier* published a short article on the war by Garnet Basque. A revised version of Hewlett's thesis was published in the journal *BC Studies* in 1973 and remains the most complete and authoritative account in the literature. The magazine *Canada West* ran a short article in 1976, and two years later Mel Rothenburger's popular history, *The Chilcotin War,* was published.[63]

The Chilcotin War was the only book-length treatment of the event and was used as a history text in some interior schools. In his introduction to the book, Rothenburger suggested that "modern Indian-White confrontations" in Canada were the result of a history of "improper or non-existent Indian policy perpetrated through the decades." The Chilcotin War was symptomatic of that deficiency, and "by coincidence it was the Chilcotins who became the accidental cause of the intensification of efforts by modern B.C. Indians to regain what they consider[ed] to be their rights." The accidental cause that he had in mind was, of course, the death of Fred Quilt. While Rothenburger seemed to accept the exoneration of the policemen accused of purposely inflicting the injuries that caused Quilt's death, he also implied that a better knowledge of the past could illuminate such modern problems. The aftermath of Fred Quilt's death provided people with an occasion to think about the meanings of the Chilcotin War for the present.[64]

Rothenburger was the great-great-grandson of Donald McLean, the former HBC trader who was killed in the conflict. According to the cover blurbs, *The Chilcotin War* was a somewhat lurid account of "the true story of a defiant chief's fight to save his land from white civilization," which promised to relate "the terrifying events of one of the bloodiest chapters in British Columbia's history." The painting commissioned for the cover of the book showed the bloodiest scene of the conflict, when twelve non-Aboriginal men were killed in their sleep on the morning of 30 April 1864. In the painting there are six white tents, with three standing on either side of a clearing in the woods at dawn. The central figure of the image is a screaming Aboriginal man in motion, one leg upraised. Over his shoulder he is swinging a double-bladed axe with both hands; he also has an unsheathed Bowie knife tucked into his belt. Directly in the path of the axe is a blond man, just emerging from his tent. He, too, appears to be screaming, but with fear rather than blood lust, and he has an arm raised defensively. The background of the image, against which the axe stands out, is a row of tall conifers; in the foreground, directly beneath the axe, there is a single stump. Taken together, the trees and stump provide a context in which the use of the axe as a tool appears to be natural, but its use as a weapon seems unnatural. Behind the attacking Aboriginal man there is another, perhaps egging him on. He is brandishing a Bowie knife in one hand and raising a rifle overhead with the other. In the background, Aboriginal men are firing into the other tents with rifles. Most are standing; one is down on one knee, aiming. Given how little we know about the exact details of that day, most of it had to be imagined by the artist. Some of the clothing of the attackers seems more appropriate to the Aboriginal cultures of the prairies than to those of interior BC. And one thing we do know from the accounts of those non-Aboriginal men who escaped the killing is that the tents were pulled down over the sleepers to trap them long enough that they could be clubbed, stabbed, or shot. For the attackers, who wished to sustain as few casualties as possible, this was an eminently practical move. The artist chose not to represent it, however. Perhaps he felt that the resulting image would be too hard to interpret, or that the deaths of the non-Aboriginal men would seem too ignominious.[65]

In many ways, *The Chilcotin War* fit a pattern identified by Margaret Atwood in her 1972 book *Survival*. She argued that Canadian poems and stories dwell on survival and obstacles to survival. "Nature" is a force that maims and kills. Winter is the only true season. Protagonists often freeze to death or drown or go crazy in the bush, and even when they don't, they can find themselves in situations where life itself becomes a threat to life. Canadian stories are often stories about victims. Rothenburger not only exaggerated and reworked traditional accounts of the killings to bring them more into line with the frontier myth, but he also perpetuated the fetishization of the Chilcotin as shadowed ground. Although *The Chilcotin War* was framed as a study of conflict between peoples, it retailed many of the familiar tropes of people victimized by hostile nature. In Rothenburger's retelling, the Aboriginal people were slaves to their essential character and thus coded as wild, uncivilized. This was nature in the guise of a determinant: the nature of the "haggard-looking" Tsilhqot'in could be read in "a certain latent ferocity in their appearance" and the fact that "the squaws had flattish foreheads purposely deformed in infancy." Both sexes "often smeared their faces and bodies with a sort of sooty grease," went about "in various states of nudity," and had "tangled black hair." Throughout the book they lived up to their savage portrayal, making "animal-like gasping whoops," "mutilating ... corpses and celebrating on the plunder," and practising cannibalism. On one Sunday, several of them were discovered "roaring drunk, screaming, stumbling around, and generally getting out of hand" after drinking adulterated whiskey, a concoction that was "enough to drive any poor Indian foolish enough to drink it mad for a few hours, or kill him." Rothenburger was not entirely to blame for attributing individual characteristics to Tsilhqot'in people as a whole; this was also a characteristic of the colonial accounts that he was presumably drawing upon.[66]

In *The Chilcotin War,* the "whites" were not wild and thus did not have an essential character as such. Rothenburger made no corresponding attempt to portray their physiognomy as a group, although he did describe some non-Aboriginal individuals. His forebear, Donald McLean, for example, was "tall, muscular, and handsome with long curly hair, mustache and bushy sideburns." In keeping with such a noble mien, McLean was also "a devoted family man and an efficient administrator," a man with "a reputation for his fairness and wide knowledge of English law," "a fine citizen and a gentleman," intelligent, aggressive, tough, "confident," "ever wary," "highly respected," and ultimately a "fallen hero." (To be fair to Rothenburger, an earlier book of his was about some of his more disreputable ancestors – the sons of Donald McLean who became outlaws.) In situations where the actions of non-Aboriginal people threatened their own lives, it was the result of individual foible: someone "accidentally setting off a forest fire on a small island," a fellow who accidentally shot his compatriot through the wrist, or another "unfortunate victim" who accidentally shot himself through the leg. Or this: "Back at camp three of the volunteers were sitting on their haunches peering intently at the ground. One of them had a magnifying glass in his hand, playing it on some of the spilled gunpowder. Suddenly there was a blast and the three men were knocked over on their backs. Except for a few burned whiskers they weren't hurt."[67]

Nature also acted as a direct cause in *The Chilcotin War.* A hostile and often anthropomorphized landscape presented obstacles that could kill the unwary and the unprepared. The terrain was "treacherous," a "mountain suddenly closed in," or a "river weaved drunkenly back and forth between the mountain ridges." "The snow-streaked walls of rock reached upward like gothic buttresses," "magnificent obstacles of Nature" impeding the work of Waddington, who wanted to build a road into the interior, to "break the back of the Cascade range." Forests were "thick timber strewn with windfalls and prickly thickets." A recent burn was "dead land," an "eery" "black swath of burned out forest." The upland plateau had "stunted firs, sparser brush and grass grasping sandy soil." In the low-lands one might find a "swampy delta," "quagmire," or "a swamp, where the volunteers thrashed around up to their thighs in mud and water, and horses became mired." Weather could endanger life, as snow loads caused makeshift bridges to collapse; the flooding that followed days of heavy rain stranded people, made river crossings dangerous, and raised the spectre of death by drowning. Disease also took its toll as non-Aboriginal people suffered from repeated outbreaks of dysentery, and a smallpox epidemic decimated Aboriginal populations. Rothenburger imagined the horror of the non-Aboriginal people encountering Aboriginal villages hit by small-pox: the smell of decaying corpses, the wolves eating the unburied dead, the starvation that followed for survivors. Taking a page directly from his nineteenth-century sources, Rothenburger blamed smallpox for the "de-generation" of the Nuxalk.[68]

Faced with such a hostile land, people in *The Chilcotin War* did not fare well. A surveying party was lost in the woods, abandoned by a guide "that left the hapless party to its own resources. After 23 days in the mountains, they made it back ... living skeletons. In the last few days before reaching safety, the only food they had had was a wood rat and an old leather purse which they cooked. One of the men was so weak he could barely stand and had he not been packed on the back of a Chilcotin Indian the last sev-eral miles he probably would not have survived." Aboriginal labourers also faced starvation in the spring – or at least that's how it seemed to non-indigenous observers – and the non-Aboriginals eventually had the idea of waiting for winter to starve their Aboriginal opponents into submission. Such a notion was consonant with the garrison mentality displayed by Rothenburger's protagonists as they, for example, dug protective earth-works to hole up in or barricaded themselves in a store for weeks. They were dogged by suicide, both apparent and attempted.[69]

Life after Oka

The Chilcotin War was one expression of a point of view that was already coming under attack in the late 1970s. A decade earlier, Pierre Trudeau had become Canada's prime minister by campaigning for a "just society" and had made Len Marchand, an Okanagan man from Kamloops, the first Aboriginal federal cabinet minister. The National Indian Brotherhood (NIB) was formed at the same time to resolve the problems of Aboriginal people in the context of Aboriginal culture. One of the ideas the NIB promoted was that Aboriginal peoples constituted a potential "fourth world," which would take its place alongside the other three. In 1969 the Trudeau government released a white paper that suggested abolishing Aboriginal rights and treaties and integrating Aboriginal people into the just society. According to this view, Aboriginal people would simply be one ethnic group among many in Canada's multicultural makeup. Aboriginal leaders objected, and the paper was withdrawn the following year. On 31 January 1973, the decision of the Supreme Court of Canada recognized the existence of Aboriginal title with its decision in the landmark case of *Calder v. Attorney General of British Columbia,* which provided the impetus for federal claims policy.

BC politics also swung briefly to the left, with an NDP government in power from 1972 to 1975. The Fred Quilt case thus came to national attention during a period in which Aboriginal people were working to assert their political agency, and non-Aboriginal people in government positions were relatively receptive to their plight. In 1975, the Dene of the Northwest Territories declared their right to be regarded as a nation by themselves and by the rest of the world. The Dene Declaration would serve as a model for other similar declarations, including the Tsilhqot'in Declaration of Sovereignty in 1997. The numbers of Aboriginal and Métis people were climbing; in 1982 there were more than 75,000 in BC.

The Canadian Constitution, which recognized existing Aboriginal rights and treaties, was repatriated from Britain in 1982. The same year, the National Indian Brotherhood was reorganized into the Assembly of First Nations (AFN), giving Aboriginal self-government new impetus. Some BC interior Aboriginal groups worked hard to address problems of alcoholism in their communities, and many pressed for land claims. For the time being, however, the province refused to acknowledge its own role in the land-claims process, which produced a stalemate. In 1985, an amendment to the *Indian Act* known as Bill C-31 allowed Aboriginal women who had married non-Aboriginal men to regain their own status and status for some of their children. Aboriginal people continued to play a more prominent role in questions of land use. The Xeni Gwet'in Tsilhqot'in's role in the establishment of Tŝ'il?os Park was one example of the changing sensibility, as was the Supreme Court decision in *Sparrow.* As the 1980s came to a close, however, a new crisis led some non-Aboriginal people in BC to rethink their historical relationship with Aboriginal people. In a sense, they were retracing the steps that their ancestors had taken, reimagining the Aboriginal "other" as a way of forming a new, postcolonial identity and a new sense of the shared past of Aboriginal and non-Aboriginal people.[70]

In the winter of 1989-90, the Quebec town of Oka planned to extend its nine-hole golf course to eighteen holes by cutting a fairway into a stand of trees that the Mohawks in the adjacent community of Kanesatake claimed as sacred ground. The legal status of the land, which included a cemetery, had been in dispute for almost forty years, but the town had finally cleared the obstacles to development. Or so it thought. In March 1990, the Mohawks set up a barricade across the access road and then strung barbed wire through the trees. Masked men began to patrol with rifles. The town responded by getting a court order at the end of June to have the barricade removed. The Mohawks dug in, however, and on 11 July shot a police officer. Within a few hours, there were about a thousand police officers on the other side of the barricade. They blockaded the Mohawks with sandbags and took steps to cut off their food, water, and electricity. The confrontation was now the subject of live television coverage across the nation. The fact that many of the Mohawks were non-combatants, and some were children or elders, triggered a wave of support for them. Kahnawake, a larger neighbouring Mohawk community, block-aded itself too, shutting down two major highways and a commuter route into Montreal. The presence of TV reporters behind the barricades meant that the Mohawks' point of view was being broadcast nationally. By mid-August there was a plan to begin negotiations under the supervision of an international team of observers. In the meantime, anti-Mohawk demon-strators, frustrated by the road closures, began throwing firebombs and rocks at the police. About fourteen hundred members of the Canadian Armed Forces replaced the local police, Quebec Provincial Police, and RCMP, bringing armoured personnel carriers and heavy weapons with them. When negotiations broke down, the army announced plans to forcibly remove the barricades. The Mohawks began negotiating with the army and reached an agreement to clear the commuter route. The towns remained blockaded, and the army began using low-flying helicopters and searchlights at night to intimidate the Mohawks. Media coverage was not sympathetic to this "psychological warfare" or to the seizure of film and videotape and the interrogation of reporters. At the end of September, the Mohawks surrendered. When it became clear the following year that the cost of the seventy-eight day standoff was over $200 million, commenta-tors noted that the figure was about ten times the amount the federal gov-ernment budgeted annually for land claims.[71]

There was a growing perception that Aboriginal people were being mis-treated by the justice system. An article that appeared in Ottawa and Cal-gary newspapers during August 1991 presented five troubling case studies.

In 1991, Leo Lachance was shot by the owner of a gun store / pawnshop in Prince Albert, Saskatchewan, as he walked out the door. The store owner later pleaded guilty to manslaughter and received a four-year sentence, a much shorter term than Aboriginal people were getting for comparable crimes. The judge stated that the fact the store owner was also the president of the local neo-Nazi group had nothing to do with the killing. When Minnie Sutherland was hit by a car in 1988, a passerby asked a police officer to call an ambulance. Thinking that she was a "lying drunk," the policeman refused. Minnie died in the Ottawa General Hospital ten days later from a skull fracture. In 1998 J.J. Harper, wrongly identified as a car thief, was shot in the chest by a Winnipeg police officer. The internal review cleared the police officer of wrongdoing, but the case went on to become a prominent part of Manitoba's Aboriginal Justice Inquiry. In Sydney, Nova Scotia, Donald Marshall served eleven years for a murder he didn't commit. A royal commission later concluded that he was the prime suspect in the case because he was Aboriginal. He was acquitted in 1983. The fifth case mentioned in the article was the death of Fred Quilt in 1971.[72]

JUSTICE INQUIRY AND REPARATIONS

In 1992, in response to complaints about the treatment of Aboriginal people by the justice system in BC, the attorney general asked Judge Anthony Sarich to look into the matter to see if a full inquiry was warranted. After meeting with Aboriginal representatives in the Cariboo-Chilcotin and hearing a number of "disturbing allegations," Sarich advised the attorney general that such an inquiry should be made. On 1 October 1992, the Cariboo-Chilcotin Justice Inquiry was formalized, and Sarich was made commissioner. In the first phase of the inquiry, the commission would hear complaints from Aboriginal people in the area. In the second phase, it would ask for written and oral submissions from both Aboriginal and non-Aboriginal people in order to evaluate the complaints from the first phase and propose solutions where possible. It soon became clear to Sarich that he could not hold the hearings in an urban courthouse; "the Commission had to go out to the people, and this it did." He found that many of his informants were fearful of testifying, cynical about the commission's power to do anything, or hesitant to expose "some of their own people in compromising situations." "Once underway," he noted in his report, "the hearings were attended by all community members at the site of the hearings, from toddlers in 'jolly jumpers' to elders who needed assistance in and out of the premises. Even a stray dog would come in from time to time to check out the proceedings and perhaps get a scratch or two behind the ear. Nearly every witness who came forward testified in front of the residents of his or her own community and knew that what he or she said would live with him or her." The report went on to say that people brought up "two other matters of much significance to them": the residential schools and the Chilcotin War. According to Sarich's report,

> in every village, the people maintained that the chiefs who were hanged at Quesnel Mouth in 1864 as murderers were, in fact, leaders of a war party defending their land and their people. Much has been written but little is known with any certainty of the facts that led to the trial of those chiefs before Judge Matthew B. Begbie. The people of the Chilcotin have long memories. They hold the memory of those chiefs in high esteem and cite the effect of smallpox on their ancestors, the incursions onto their land, and the treatment of their people by the road builders hired by Alfred Penderill Waddington as justification for the war. Many natives consider the trial and subsequent hanging as a political event in a deliberate process of colonization.[73]

The vast majority of the complaints that the commission heard in the first phase of the inquiry were directed at the police. In rural, unincorporated areas, the police answered to no one except the attorney general, and personnel were transferred as frequently as every two years, making it difficult for officers to form any attachment to the community they were serving. Since the RCMP was a federal force, it could not be disciplined by provincial authorities. The organization also had a policy of refusing to reveal what kind of discipline it imposed on its officers, if any. The report said that "the estrangement from the communities, the structure of the force, its policies and training [had] helped to create a dehumanizing relationship between natives and the police." Added to that was the fact that police officers tended to share the negative attitudes of the non-Aboriginal communities from which they were drawn, the commonsense racism that postulated the inferiority and dependence of Aboriginal people.[74]

The Sarich Commission categorized the 179 complaints it heard into recurring patterns of conduct: inappropriate reactions, abuse of authority, invasion of privacy, use of excessive force, lack of communication. Sometimes the police treated Aboriginal people with indifference, arrogance, or disrespect. Sometimes the police failed to react when they could have, especially when dealing with missing or lost individuals. There were many cases in which they clearly abused their authority. In one instance,

an Aboriginal man was stopped on the Sheep Creek bridge because a
police officer suspected he had stolen the bicycle that he was riding. The
officer handcuffed him to the bridge and then responded to another call,
leaving him there for over an hour. The bicycle was not stolen. Another
man claimed to have been held in custody for three days on suspicion of
theft; there were no police records of the event. There were many cases of
the police invading Aboriginal people's privacy, as when an officer entered
an Aboriginal man's home without a warrant and awakened him by putting a gun to his head. The police were also accused of using excessive
force, both at the time of arrest and later, in detention cells. In many inci-
dents they refused to provide information to Aboriginal people, either because of apparent insensitivity or indifference. To mitigate the findings
somewhat, Sarich observed that "in many instances, the police become the
flash point for reaction to repeated humiliation and rejection of the native
people by other segments of non-native society."[75]

The commission also identified a "cultural lacuna" between the Canadian court process, with its "concepts of guilt and innocence, standards
of proof and examination and cross-examination of witnesses," and the
consensus-based system of conflict resolution in Aboriginal communities.
This was problematic because "in a great number of cases that came before
the inquiry the complainants stated that they did not understand what
happened in court." One of the more poignant examples in the commission's report – and one that would later affect its recommendations – was
"Incident #096": "Elderly woman escorted through court building in
handcuffs & terrified because of lack of comprehension of process and
irrational fear of hanging." The submission that Judge Cunliffe Barnett
made to the commission after practising for more than twenty years at
Alexis Creek cast the woman's "irrational" fear in a different light. "I believe when a Chilcotin person appears before a court in 1993," he said, "the
judge encounters the ghost of Begbie J. He bent the rules to permit the
judicial execution of men who were not criminals. It is very difficult for a
Chilcotin person to have faith in our justice system."[76]

The key problem that Sarich faced was what to do about the allegations
against the police. Early in the proceedings he discovered that Aboriginal
people would be intimidated by having to testify in front of the officers
concerned, so he followed an alternate procedure. In the report he said
that "officers whose conduct could have constituted a criminal act were
informed of as much detail as was available of the complaint made against
them and were invited rather than compelled to come before the Commission to answer. If the officers failed to come forward, I felt free to draw

whatever inferences were appropriate from their failure to testify. Once this procedure was set, only one of a considerable number of invited officers gave evidence." The upshot of this was that the Aboriginal complaints remained, for the most part, unanswered. Sarich noted that "the purpose of the inquiry was not to establish with the certainty of a criminal trial the truth of allegations made by the native people, but to determine why they made those allegations."[77]

CONCLUSION: REMEMBERING AND FORGETTING

The Sarich Commission made a number of recommendations: to begin negotiations over land claims and the preservation of natural resources; to set up a treatment centre for alcohol abuse in consultation with Aboriginal people; to monitor security guards more carefully; to provide interpreters; to train emergency and forensic personnel in cultural concerns and the imperatives of Aboriginal people; to provide financial support for programs like the Aboriginal law centre; to create Aboriginal police forces for communities that wanted them; to train peacekeepers to work in particular societies; to integrate the RCMP into the communities that they served; to use surveillance cameras to monitor police activities; to establish a public process for complaints against the RCMP; to have court officers like justices of the peace drawn from each Aboriginal community; and so on.[78]

One of the recommendations of the Sarich Commission was novel, however, in that it directly addressed the negotiation of historical consciousness and the present-day perception of the Chilcotin War: "Many natives still feel that the trial and hangings were more a showpiece to impress the natives than an honest search for the truth. Whatever the correct version, that episode of history has left a wound in the body of Chilcotin society. It is time to heal that wound." Sarich recommended that Victoria grant a posthumous pardon to the Tsilhqot'in men who were executed, locate their remains and rebury them, and erect a suitable memorial.[79]

In 1993, the UBC Museum of Anthropology asked artist Judith Williams to create an exhibit that would be, in part, about the Chilcotin War. The following year the museum exhibited her installation "High Slack." It allowed visitors to go from one station to another "from which one could look at the native/white/landscape concurrence from different viewpoints." Williams intended the exhibit to explore "the issue of parallel realities" and wanted to provide the descendents of the Tsilhqot'in with a chance to comment on her portrayal of history. Together with the curator of the museum and a colleague, Williams organized a symposium on the Chilcotin War and the Cariboo-Chilcotin Justice Inquiry. It was held at the UBC First Nations House of Learning, and 150 people gathered for the meeting on 19 November 1994. In the course of the symposium, Tsilhqot'in chief Thomas Billyboy told the participants that "the names of people involved in the war are in, and of, the land, come about through people's lives, and were themselves powerful." Judge Cunliffe Barnett recommended that the hanged men be pardoned. The attorney general's representative argued that it was not clear which level of government should be making the apology, and "members of the audience told him they wanted the graves, now under a hospital parking lot, marked, that they wanted a full pardon from the minister of justice, and their own police force. They suggested that the Sarich inquiry was just a big show." Toward the end of the day, another speaker rose to provide a dissenting opinion. "My name is Mel Rothenburger," he said. "There is a lot of talk about apologies, and I want to know, who will apologize for the shooting of my grandfather in the back?" The reception was frosty. Williams had named the exhibit to refer to the time when the tide has risen to its highest point but not yet begun to ebb, and she meant it "as a metaphor for a pause in ideological currents, a time to collect ourselves and perceive, not just what we have been taught to see and know, but to imagine what might be if our socially-acquired filters evaporated." No one would be apologizing for Donald McLean's death any time soon.[80]

In August the following year, a group of Aboriginal activists and sympathizers seized land overlooking Gustafsen Lake west of 100 Mile House, claiming its spiritual importance for their sundance ceremonies. The land was legally owned by a local rancher named Lyall James. In the late 1980s, James had allowed Percy Rosette, a Secwepemc man "who lived on the fringes of his community, the village of Alkali Lake," to use the land for summer ceremonies, provided that he and his followers did not build any permanent structures. The nineteenth-century sundance tradition that Rosette practiced had been revived in the mid-1970s as Aboriginal communities struggled to combat social problems such as alcoholism. The Alkali Lake reserve had served as a national inspiration by becoming one of the first "dry" Aboriginal communities, and it seems Rosette became interested in the sundance tradition around this time. The first sundance ceremonies were conducted at Gustafsen Lake in the summer of 1988. By 1990, the larger North American community of sundance practitioners had come to regard Gustafsen Lake as a power site. Peaceful celebrations were conducted there every year until 1994. During this time, Rosette and his followers took to warning local hunters and anglers of the danger of being in proximity to such a sacred place, a caution that doesn't seem to have been received particularly well by local non-Aboriginal people. At the time, Rosette was also distancing himself from the local Aboriginal leadership.[81]

In 1995, the sundancers fenced off a couple of square kilometres of the land, breaking the agreement with Lyall James. James obtained an eviction notice, but instead of waiting for the RCMP to serve it, he decided to try to evict the sundancers with the aid of some of his cowboys. Rumours of an Oka-like standoff spread. The sundancers began calling themselves the "Defenders of the Shuswap Nation," although it is not clear how many of them had any affiliation with the Secwepemc. They were joined by a number of non-Aboriginal activists. Eventually matters escalated into an armed confrontation with the RCMP. Fortunately no one was killed, and the final "defenders" surrendered in mid-September. After Oka, armed conflicts with non-Aboriginal people and the government had become a conceivable strategy, although a seemingly ineffective one. Eighteen people were later charged with a variety of offences, resulting in twenty-one convictions and thirty-nine acquittals. The maximum prison term received by those convicted was four and a half years. The standoff at Gustafsen Lake served mainly to dramatize the tense relations between Aboriginal and non-Aboriginal people during a time when they were renegotiating their relationships with one another. The future, as always, remained unknowable.[82]

The first histories of what is now British Columbia were written in the aftermath of the Chilcotin War. They were written by people who had little knowledge of what had happened there before the arrival of the newcomers. For the most part, the authors of these texts were concerned with legitimating their own presence and authority. Many of them had little direct experience with Aboriginal people and drew on the commonsense understandings of the day instead. Subsequent authors, emphasizing the archival record, tended to repeat earlier claims or to look for evidence of their truth in other settings. In the late nineteenth and early twentieth centuries, as the Aboriginal people of the interior suffered the effects of introduced diseases, disruption of traditional lifeways, resettlement, and so on, their presence as actors in historical accounts was gradually erased, and the place itself, the landscape, took on the negative characteristics attributed to them. With the growth of interest in Aboriginal history in the 1960s and 1970s, the Aboriginal people were put back into the story, but some earlier misconceptions were retained. One of these misconceptions – that the Tsilhqot'in had opted out of the fur trade as a form of resistance – is not supported by the archival record, but rather reflects earlier prejudices.

Between the 1970s and the 1990s, this longstanding view of BC's past, the "colonial" view, began to break up. The position occupied by the Tsilhqot'in around the time of Fred Quilt's death and the position that they occupied after the justice inquiry two decades later were very different. Beginning in the 1990s, they had far more perceived power to oppose the activities of the government and of large corporations. A series of landmark legal decisions gave them wide-ranging power in disputes over land claims. Prominent non-Aboriginal people were willing to acknowledge the past damages inflicted on Aboriginal people by the government and religious organizations and to try to redress the wrongs. Although they were still treated as inferior in many settings, interior Aboriginal people were gaining a new measure of respect. This change could be seen in many settings: in 1974, Aboriginal remains were unceremoniously dumped with construction waste; in 1996, their accidental exhumation triggered two years of negotiation among a variety of stakeholders. When the Sheep Creek bones were finally laid to rest, it was an occasion for living Tsilhqot'in and Secwepemc to re-establish connections with their ancestors and with the land where they were buried.[83]

In response to the Sarich Commission's report, the attorney general eventually issued an apology for the hangings of the Tsilhqot'in men and announced funding for an archaeological excavation to ensure that the men's bodies were properly buried. On 26 October 1999, 135 years to the day after the hanging of Klatsassin and his collaborators, the Tsilhqot'in Ervin Charleyboy unveiled a plaque on the lawn of the hospital in Quesnel. It bears Klatsassin's last words in both English and Tsilhqot'in: "We meant war, not murder!" Speaking at the event, Charleyboy said, "It's good to look to the past to be proud of who we are today. Then we need to forget about the past and look forward to where we are going, to lead our people." Old narratives of the past might be forgotten, but every trail into the future leads back to this place, into an archive that continually accumulates the traces of its past. Where the people in the Chilcotin end up will depend, in part, on how they read the signs along the trail.[84]

Afterword

IN HIS COLLECTION OF SHORT STORIES about the Chilcotin, *Smith and Other Events,* Paul St. Pierre tells about ten-year-old Sherwood, who rode out by himself on a big bay horse and failed to return home to the ranch by supper time. His mother, Norah, is worried; the beans boil over on the woodstove and she goes repeatedly to the door as midnight approaches. Smith, his father, pretends less concern. They finally decide to go in search of Sherwood when his saddle horse returns without him, but at that point the boy walks up whistling, with his chaps over his shoulder. Over a plate of beans, Norah tells Sherwood she was worried. Smith admits he was surprised when the horse came home before the boy. Sherwood tells them that his horse startled and he went over its head:

> Smith wanted to hear more. Sherwood, sensing this, took his time in answering ...
> "I was trottin' old Bud and he never saw the bear until we was almost on top of him. So when he stopped, I kept goin', right over his head."
> "... Yeah ..."
> "Old Bud, he went one way. The bear went 'woof' and he went the other way."
> "What did you do, Sherwood?" said Norah.
> Sherwood considered his answer before delivering it. "I just sat there in the trail feelin' lonely," he said.[1]

The original idea for *The Archive of Place* was to narrate the environmental history of one place — a place with a very shallow archival record, unfamiliar and far from urban centres – over the past 300 million years. The story was to consist of three parts covering vastly different time scales: the geological, the glacial, and the recent past, and these parts were meant to correspond loosely to natural history, prehistory, and recorded history. If we take the bear, the horse, and the boy as metonyms, St. Pierre's anecdote shows the problem with such a tripartite division: the three really belong together in a single story.

Here, the different time scales and different approaches to the past have been kept together as much as possible. The account of the collision of terranes and eruption of lavas that created the Chilcotin was narrated as part of the story about modern-day prospectors in search of mineral wealth deposited millions of years earlier. Likewise, the account of the paleo-Indians crossing into the Americas and creating extensive networks of exchange well before the domestication of the horse was juxtaposed with accounts of people in the twentieth century negotiating some of the same trails on horseback and negotiating the meaning of the trails in time frames long and short. So, too, the account of the historical activities of ranchers and Aboriginal people was part and parcel of the story of their modern descendents' attempts to re-create a shared past more in line with changing sensibilities.[2]

The decision to try and keep these stories together was based on a consideration of the historical actors in the late twentieth century. These people were willing to invest a lot of time, energy, and other resources in various attempts to recover the Chilcotin past from the traces that they found there. As with any historical endeavour, the most basic question that can be posed is "so what?" Why did they care about figuring out what had happened 80 million years ago, or 10,000, or 135? Again, as with any historical endeavour, the answer was to be found in the present. These people were in search of usable past.

The narrative of *The Archive of Place* still ended up in three parts, but the final structure was based on observed effects and inferred causes rather than on scale or historiographical approach. In the first part, it was clear that people were willing to learn more about an out-of-the-way place as its relative value increased. But why should that be the case? By inference, because they were attempting to delineate property rights. In the second part, an attempt to commemorate the activities of an eighteenth-century explorer fizzled. Why? Again, by inference, because the commemorators ran into the problem of ground truth while trying to use place itself as a warrant for historical belief. In the third part, commonsense racism and an imagined landscape of violence were traced to a historiographical tradition of retroactive justification and a contemporaneous process of place fetishism.

Over the course of the work, the idea of place as archive becomes progressively more complex. The first part is relatively direct: people recover material traces of the past from the place to buttress particular points of view. In the second part, material traces play a more ambiguous role. Representations always underdetermine the things represented, and any attempt to make things more concrete invariably leads to unexpected difficulties. In the third part, the archival nature of place is phenomenological. Places gather stories, attitudes, opinions, and practices in a way that cannot be measured by instruments. The different ways a place is imagined do as much to shape the understanding of what happened there in the past as any physical trace ever could.

APPENDIX A

Glacial Time

Archaeological Period	Climatic Period	Paleoclimate	Uncalibrated ^{14}C Dates	Events in Central British Columbia
Late	Neoglaciation	Warm/Dry		200 BP. Euro-Canadian fur traders. 640–130 BP. Little Ice Age. 1000 BP. Abandonment of southern interior pit house winter villages. 1300 BP. Eruption of White River volcano, Athapaskan migration?
		Slightly Cooler / Wetter	5000 BP– Present	1800 BP. Little Climatic Optimum. 2350 BP. Mount Meager eruption. 2500 BP. Intensified plant-food collection. Use of earthen ovens. 3500 BP. Intensified fishing. Storage of surplus salmon. Export of nephrite products. 4000 BP. First pit houses. Area of grasslands reduced.
Middle	Hypsithermal	Slightly Warmer / Drier	10,000– 6000 BP	5500 BP. Increasing importance of salmon. 6000 BP. Stone boiling to cook food.
		Warmer / Drier		8000–7000 BP. Increasing moisture. Trees expand downslope. 9000–8000 BP. Obsidian quarried in Chilcotin. Indigenous trade networks. Grasslands at maximum level. 9000 BP. Human occupation at Namu. 10,000–9,000 BP. Summer solar radiation peaks.
Early	Wisconsin Glaciation	Cool / Moist		11,000–10,000 BP. Aspen and pine forests in uplands. 11,500 BP. Pioneer grasslands in south-central interior. 13,000 BP. Suitable human habitat on Northwest Coast.
		Cold	30,000– 11,000 BP	18,000 BP. Peak of glaciation. Beringia occupied.

NOTE: Periodization is adapted from E.C. Pielou, *After the Ice Age: The Return of Life to Glaciated North America* (Chicago: University of Chicago Press, 1991); Richard J. Hebda, "Interior Grasslands Past and Future," *Cordillera* (1996): 344-46; Knut R. Fladmark, *British Columbia Prehistory* (Ottawa: National Museum of Man, 1986); Arnould H. Stryd and Mike K. Rousseau, "Early Prehistory of the Mid Fraser-Thompson River Area," in *Early Human Occupation in British Columbia*, ed. Roy L. Carlson and Luke Dalla Bona (Vancouver: UBC Press, 1996), 177-204.

APPENDIX B

Geological Time

Eratherm	System	Series	Geochronometry (Ma BP)	Events in Central British Columbia
Cenozoic	Quaternary	Holocene	0.1–Present	9000 BP. Latest date for beginning of human occupation. 30,000–9000 BP. Last major glaciation (Wisconsin).
		Pleistocene	1.6–0.1	1.6–0.1 Ma BP. Period of ice ages. Major rivers acquire present courses.
	Neogene	Pliocene	5.3–1.6	5.3–3.3 Ma BP. Uplift.
		Miocene	23–5.3	23–1.6 Ma BP. Basalt flows. Shield volcanoes formed.
	Paleogene	Oligocene	36.5–23	53–36.5 Ma BP. Period of volcanism. Adaptive radiation of mammals, birds, fish, insects, flowering plants.
		Eocene	53–36.5	
		Paleocene	65–53	
Mesozoic	Cretaceous		135–65	65 Ma BP. Extinction of dinosaurs. 80 Ma BP. Fish Lake deposit formed. 83.5–46.5 Ma BP. Yalakom fault formed. 100 Ma BP. Cascade terranes thrust over Cache Creek and Stikinia. Rise of flowering plants.
	Jurassic		205–135	152–95 Ma BP. Wrangellia and Alexander terranes dock. Coast Range formed. Uplift. 180 Ma BP. Stikinia thrust under Cache Creek terrane.
	Triassic		250–205	
Paleozoic	Permian		290–250	250 Ma BP. Mass extinctions.

NOTE: Dates are expressed in millions of years before present (Ma BP), except where otherwise indicated. Divisions of geological time are from the global rock-stratigraphic chart in Paul L. Hancock and Brian J. Skinner, eds., *The Oxford Companion to the Earth* (Oxford: Oxford University Press, 2000), Appendix 1a.

Glossary

abduction   A method of inferring the best explanation for a given set of observations. In 1878, C.S. Peirce distinguished between three kinds of reasoning, using a beanbag as an example: (1) Deduction – All the beans from this bag are white, and these beans are from this bag, therefore these beans are white. (2) Induction – These beans are from this bag, and these beans are white, therefore all the beans from this bag are white. (3) Abduction – All the beans from this bag are white, and these beans are white, therefore these beans are from this bag.[1]

aggradation and degradation   When landforms are built up by the deposit of sediments or cut down by their removal.

anadromous   Fish (like many salmonids) that live in the sea for the greater portion of their lives and enter salt water only to spawn.

BC Department of Mines and Petroleum Resources   The ministry responsible for mining and geological surveying in BC changed its name many times. It was established in 1899 as the Department of Mines and subsequently became the Department of Mines and Petroleum Resources (1960), the Ministry of Mines and Petroleum Resources (1976), and the Ministry of Energy, Mines and Petroleum Resources (1978). It was disestablished in 1996, with most of its functions absorbed by a new Ministry of Employment and Investment. In 1998 the Ministry of Energy and Mines regained its independence, and it is now once again called the Ministry of Energy, Mines and Petroleum Resources.[2]

BP   Before present.

camas *Camassia quamash* (Pursh) Greene, a "herbaceous perennial with glutinous bulbs about the size of daffodil bulbs." A staple food for Aboriginal people of the Northwest Coast and their trading partners.[3]

dated In the literature, dates expressed in "thousands of years before present" are assumed, by convention, to be uncalibrated radiocarbon dates (^{14}C dates) unless otherwise stated. These dates cannot be assumed to be "calendar years before present" until they are calibrated by cross-dating them with a reliable indicator of elapsed calendar years, like the tree rings of bristlecone pines. In this study, the date cited is the one given by the author. In cases where it was necessary to determine a calibrated date range for an individual uncalibrated date, the 95 percent confidence interval was calculated with OxCal. Calibrated date ranges given for uncalibrated date ranges are the upper and lower ends of the 95 percent confidence intervals for the upper and lower individual dates, respectively.[4]

ecofacts Organic and environmental remains (such as seeds, grains, and pollen of plants, eggshells, animal skeletons) that are non-artifactual but which have been found alongside evidence of human activity in archaeological sites and which are presumed to have cultural relevance.

endemic/epidemic An endemic disease is one that is always present in a given population to a greater or lesser degree. It is typically contracted in childhood, after which survivors are immune to reinfection. An epidemic disease prevails widely for a short time and then dies out until it is reintroduced.

esker A long body of sand and gravel deposited by water flowing under a glacier. When the glacier melts, a snakelike ridge remains.

faunal assemblage The collection of animal bones found at an archaeological site. It is used to support inferences about paleoenvironments, diet, subsistence strategies, and resource acquisition and exploitation.

fluvial sediments Sediments transported and deposited by a stream or running water. Depending on the slope of the watercourse, the amount and frequency of discharge, and the amount and size of the sediment load, a river channel may take various forms: straight, meandering, braided, or anastomosing. (This last is characterized by channels that occasionally intersect, creating islands between them.) Each of these kinds of river channels deposit sediments in a predictable geometry.

hematite Iron oxide (Fe_2O_3). When powdered, it is a vivid red colour (hence its name, which means "bloodlike") and is often used as a pigment.

hypsithermal The Holocene period, including the postglacial climatic optimum, goes by many names, including "the hypsithermal," "the altithermal," and "the xerothermic." In keeping with the earlier literature on

British Columbian prehistory, "hypsithermal" is used in this book to denote the period between about 10,500 to 10,000 BP and 7000 to 6000 BP.[5]

induced polarization   A kind of surveying that relies on the same principles as an ordinary metal detector. A varying electrical current is created, producing a fluctuating magnetic field. This field is passed over a region that contains hidden conductive materials. The magnetic field induces currents in the conductive materials, and those induced currents produce secondary magnetic fields. The secondary magnetic fields can then be detected, providing information about the hidden materials.

kerfed boxes   Also known as bentwood boxes, these were made by many indigenous groups of the Northwest Coast. "The box maker started with a wide, thin board split from a cedar log. He cut three transverse kerfs (grooves), spaced according to the box's ultimate dimensions. To soften the wood for bending, he steamed it over a fire covered with wet moss or seaweed, or soaked it in a creek for several days, weighing it down with rocks. When the board was pliable enough, he bent it carefully along the kerfs to make a square or rectangular box, and pegged or sewed the ends together, usually with spruce or cedar root. The box maker then attached a flanged board to the bottom with pegs and sewed it tightly enough to make the box watertight. Finally, he fitted the box with a lid. Bent-wood boxes were used for boiling or steaming food, or for storing berries, fish, oil and other products."[6]

lineament   A large-scale linear feature, such as a fault, that controls the alignment of valleys, ridges, and other topographic features for long distances. Lineaments can extend for more than a thousand kilometres and be tens or hundreds of kilometres wide. There are more than twenty major lineaments in British Columbia.

Ma   Millions of years.

Milankovitch cycles   Over time, the earth's orbit around the sun is thought to change in eccentricity (the degree to which the orbit is circular or elliptical), inclination (the angle at which the earth's axis is tilted from the plane of the orbit), and the precession of the equinoxes (a "wobble" in the earth's axis of rotation). The combined effect of these orbital changes causes different parts of the earth to receive different amounts of solar energy over time, and thus leads to climatic fluctuation.

neutron activation analysis   A kind of analysis used to determine trace-element concentrations in a sample of rock. The sample is bombarded with slow neutrons in a nuclear reactor, which causes unstable compounds to form and emit gamma rays. These rays are measured with a spectrometer to determine the concentration of elements in the sample.

obsidian hydration   As a sample of obsidian absorbs water, it forms a hydration "rind." The thickness of the rind can be used to determine the age of the sample, assuming that obsidian hydrates at a given rate. If the rock is fractured and a new surface is exposed (e.g., when the material is flaked to create a stone tool), that fresh exposure can also be dated.

oolichan   (Spelled in a variety of ways: eulachon, hoolican, oolican, ooligan, uthlecan, etc., and also known as candlefish or shrow.) The small anadromous smelt, *Thaleichthys pacificus,* that enters river mouths from San Francisco Bay, California, to Bristol Bay, Alaska, in large numbers every spring to spawn.

palynology   The study of pollen, spores, and other microbotanical remains that have been preserved in the layers of sediment at the bottom of lakes and ponds, in peat deposits and rock strata, and in the annual accumulation of ice on glaciers. The dates and distribution of such material allow palynologists to reconstruct past environments.

petrographic analysis   A kind of analysis for determining the mineral components of a rock sample. A microscope is used to examine sections of rock that are very thin – about thirty micrometres or 40 percent of the width of a hair – and transparent. As polarized light is passed through the rock section, various colours appear, and the refractive index can be measured. The refractive index is a measure of how light is bent when it passes from one medium, the air, into another, the rock.

porphyry   A fine-grained igneous rock with distinct embedded crystals.

radiometric dating   Chemical elements like uranium or lead can exist in more than one form. These other forms are known as the isotopes of that element. Unstable isotopes are said to be radioactive; they are subject to decay, by which they become the isotope of another element, emitting radiation in the process. Since the rate of decay is accurately known, the age of a sample can be inferred from the relative concentrations of unstable and stable isotopes in the material.

refugia   A location that escaped the changes the surrounding area underwent, thus allowing for the survival of species that became extinct elsewhere.

spatial ecology   The study of "the fundamental effects of space on the dynamics of individual species and on the structure, dynamics, diversity, and stability of multispecies communities."[7]

stable isotope ratios   The tissues of living plants and animals are composed of elements like carbon, nitrogen, and hydrogen, which naturally occur in more than one form, known as the isotopes of those elements. Carbon has three isotopes, two of which, ^{12}C and ^{13}C, are stable. (^{14}C

is unstable and is used in radiometric dating.) These stable isotopes of carbon are incorporated into plant tissues from atmospheric carbon dioxide during photosynthesis. Different plants have different biochemical pathways for photosynthesis, and this causes them to make use of different amounts of ^{12}C and ^{13}C. When plants are eaten by humans and other animals, this carbon is incorporated into their own tissues, including bone. It is thus possible to analyze human remains to determine what kinds of plants a particular group of people ate. Nitrogen isotope ratios in bone can also be used to infer prehistoric (or nonhuman) diets because different kinds of plants obtain nitrogen in different ways. Some plants derive their nitrogen from decayed plant matter in the soil; others can fix nitrogen directly from the atmosphere. These different strategies result in different ratios of the nitrogen isotopes ^{14}N and ^{15}N. Nitrogen isotope ratios are particularly useful for distinguishing marine- versus terrestrial-based diets.

subsistence round Systematic movement to take advantage of resources that fluctuate seasonally.

treponemal spirochetes Bacteria responsible for a variety of non-sexually-transmitted infections, such as bejel, yaws, and pinta, and the sexually-transmitted disease syphilis.

very-low-frequency electromagnetic surveys This kind of surveying relies on electromagnetic induction, the same principal used in induced polarization. The use of very low frequencies allows the instrument to penetrate the ground to depths greater than a few tens of metres, revealing information about the size, shape, orientation, and conductivity of subsurface features.

x-ray fluorescence spectrometry A technique for determining the concentration of trace elements in a sample by passing an x-ray through it. The irradiated sample emits a fluorescent spectrum that is characteristic of the elements that it contains.

Notes

1 The Texts of Vitruvius on Lacus Curtius (a website developed by Bill Thayer) being *The Architecture of Marcus Vitruvius Pollio*, translated by Joseph Gwilt (London: Priestley and Weale, 1826), http://penelope.uchicago.edu/Thayer/E/Roman/Texts/Vitruvius/home.html; and The Project Gutenberg EBook of Ten Books on Architecture, by Vitruvius, being Vitruvius, *The Ten Books on Architecture*, translated by Morris Hicky Morgan (Cambridge, MA: Harvard University Press, 1914), 167, http://www.gutenberg.org/etext/20239.

2 Clarence J. Glacken, *Traces on the Rhodian Shore: Nature and Culture in Western Thought from Ancient Times to the End of the Eighteenth Century* (Berkeley and Los Angeles: University of California Press, 1967); quotations in this and the following paragraph are from pages xi, x.

3 Edward S. Casey, *Getting Back into Place: Toward a Renewed Understanding of the Place-World* (Bloomington and Indianapolis: Indiana University Press, 1993) and Edward S. Casey, *The Fate of Place: A Philosophical History* (Berkeley: University of California Press, 1997). See also Thomas Brockelman, "Lost in Place? On the Virtues and Vices of Edward Casey's Anti-Modernism," *Humanitas* 16, 1 (2003): 36-55. William Cronon, "A Place for Stories: Nature, History and Narrative," *Journal of American History* 78, 4 (1992): 1347-76; Cronon's well-known injunction encouraged environmental historians to tell "not just stories about nature, but stories about stories about nature" (1375).

4 This phrasing echoes one of Turkel's own reflections on this issue in "Every Place Is an Archive: Environmental History and the Interpretation of Physical Evidence," *Rethinking History* 10, 2 (2006): 259-76.

5 Donald W. Meinig, ed., *The Interpretation of Ordinary Landscapes: Geographical Essays* (New York: Oxford, 1979) and Cole Harris, "Archival fieldwork," *Geographical Review* 91, 1-2 (2001): 328-34 were the examples I had in mind as I wrote this. The special double issue of *Geographical Review* in which the Harris paper appeared was devoted to "Doing Fieldwork."

6 The "exceptionally seeing eye" phrase is from a review of W.G. Hoskins, *The Making of the English Landscape,* in the *English Historical Review* 71 (1956), 327, cited by Donald Meinig, "Reading the Landscape: An Appreciation of W.G. Hoskins and J.B. Jackson," in Meinig, ed., *The Interpretation,* 199.

7 The interpretations offered in this and the following paragraph depend in large part upon Meinig, "Reading the Landscape"; quotes above from pages 197, 213, 233.

8 *Landscape* 3 (Summer 1953): 28-29, quoted in Meinig, "Reading the Landscape," 317, from which the other quotations and larger arguments of this paragraph are drawn.

9 This highly abbreviated genealogy draws in the first instance on Kent Mathewson, "Between 'in Camp' and 'Out of Bounds': Notes on the History of Fieldwork in American Geography," *Geographical Review* 91, 1-2 (2001): 215-24. The final quotation comes from an assessment of the impact of one of Sauer's monographs, published in 1927, and can be found in P.P. Karan, "Regional Studies in Kentucky and American Geography," in *The Evolution of Geographic Thought in America: A Kentucky Road,* ed. W.A Bladen and P.P. Karan (Dubuque, IO; Kendall/Hunt Publishing, 1983), 97. See also David N. Livingstone, *Nathaniel Southgate Shaler and the Culture of American Science* (Tuscaloosa: University of Alabama Press, 1987); Donald Worster, *A River Running West: The Life of John Wesley Powell* (Oxford and New York: Oxford University Press, 2001); Richard J. Chorley, A.J. Dunn, and R.P. Beckinsale, *History of the Study of Landforms: or, The Development of Geomorphology,* vol. 2: *The Life and Work of William Morris Davis* (London: Methuen/New York: Wiley, 1964); Kent Mathewson and Martin S. Kenzer, eds., *Culture, Land, and Legacy: Perspectives on Carl O. Sauer and Berkeley School Geography* (Baton Rouge, LA: Geoscience Publications, Department of Geography and Anthropology, Louisiana State University, 2003); Robert C. West, *Carl Sauer's Fieldwork in Latin America* (Ann Arbor, MI: Published for Department of Geography, Syracuse University by University Microfilms International, 1979).

10 Carl O. Sauer, "The Morphology of Landscape," [1925] in John Leighly, ed., *Land and life: A Selection from the Writings of Carl Ortwin Sauer* (Berkeley: University of California Press, 1963), 315-50.

11 James Duncan, "The Superorganic in American Cultural Geography," *Annals of the Association of American Geographers* 70, 2 (1980): 181-98.

12 Mathewson, "Between 'in Camp' and 'Out of Bounds'," 222.

13 On this general point, see R.A. Rundstrom and M.S. Kenzer, "The Decline of Field Work in Human Geography," *Professional Geographer* 41, 3 (1989): 294-303; Matthew Sparke, "Displacing the Field in Fieldwork: Masculinity, Metaphor and Space," in *BodySpace: Destabilizing Geographies of Gender and Sexuality,* ed. Nancy Duncan (London and New York: Routledge, 1996), 294-303; Barbara A. Kennedy, "A Naughty World," *Transactions: Institute of British Geographers* n.s., 4, 4 (1979): 550-58; and Nicholas J. Clifford, "Editorial: Physical Geography – The Naughty World Revisited," *Transactions: Institute of British Geographers* n.s., 26, 4 (2001): 387-89.

14 Harris, "Archival Fieldwork," 328.

15 James Duncan and David Ley, "Introduction: Representing the Place of Culture," in *Place/Culture/Representation,* ed. James Duncan and David Ley (London and New York; Routledge, 1993), 11. See also Trevor J. Barnes and James Duncan, eds., *Writing Worlds: Discourse, Text and Metaphor in the Representation of Landscape* (London and New York: Routledge, 1992).

16 Felix Driver, "Editorial: Field-work in Geography," *Transactions: Institute of British Geographers* n.s., 25, 3 (2000): 267-68.

17 This commentary is drawn from material herein, from discussions with Turkel, from Turkel, "Every Place Is an Archive," and from William J. Turkel, "Augmenting Places with Sources," unpublished paper.

18 The "back road to nowhere much" phrase is from local historian Diana French and is quoted by Turkel, herein, on page 4; the "make the earth over" phrase is from J.B. Jackson, "Human, All Too Human Geography," *Landscape* 2 (Autumn 1952): 5-7, quoted in Meinig, "Reading the Landscape," 229.

19 John Lye, "Some Post-Structural assumptions," posted at http://www.brocku.ca/english/courses/4F70/poststruct.html (accessed 10 February 2007).

20 Cronon, "A Place for Stories," 1375.

21 The quotation drawn from *À la recherche du temps perdu* (*Remembrance of Things Past*, more recently translated and published as *In Search of Lost Time*) is widely quoted in slightly variant forms. For use in this context, see Nigel J.R. Allan, "Having New Eyes," *Geographical Review* 91, 1-2 (2001): 487-95.

PREFACE

1 Hoof prints: David M. Shackleton, *Hoofed Mammals of British Columbia*, Royal British Columbia Museum Handbook (Vancouver: UBC Press, 1999), 68. Forensics: Joe Nickell and John F. Fischer, *Crime Science: Methods of Forensic Detection* (Lexington: University Press of Kentucky, 1998), 150-54.

2 Shoe prints: Nickell and Fischer, *Crime Science,* 150-51. Historian's dictum: Edward Hallett Carr, *What Is History?* (New York: Vintage, 1961), 26.

3 Nationalists: Stephen Hume, "Canadian Explorers Blazed a Trail; Lewis and Clark Also-Rans," *Edmonton Journal,* 18 May 2003. There is also at least one Aboriginal person who may have made such a journey before the much-better-publicized voyages of Mackenzie and Lewis and Clark. Around 1700, a Yazoo named Moncacht-Apé left his home on the lower Mississippi River in search of the origins of his people. He travelled first to the northeast, where he encountered tidewater and saw Niagara Falls. After returning home, he decided to travel to the northwest and followed the Mississippi, Missouri, and Columbia rivers to the Pacific. He later told his story to the French, who published versions of it in the 1750s. See Antoine-Simon Le Page du Pratz, *Histoire de la Louisiane* (Paris, 1758), vol. 3, chaps. 6-8; Jonathan Carver, *Voyage dans les Parties Intérieures de l'Amérique Septentrionale, pendant les Années 1766, 1767 et 1768* (Yverdon, Switzerland, 1784), 404-5 (available from the Canadiana.org, formerly the Canadian Institute for Historical Microreproductions, CIHM 90454); Richard M. Kolbet, "Narratives of North American Exploration," *Books at Iowa* [University of Iowa Libraries] 6 (1967): 3-12; Scott Byram and David G. Lewis, "Ourigan: Wealth of the Northwest Coast," *Oregon Historical Quarterly* 102, 2 (2001): 126-57.

4 "Disk of the world": This phrase was used by Wallace Stegner to describe another North American place in *Wolf Willow: A History, a Story and a Memory of the Last Plains Frontier* (New York: Penguin, 2000), 6.

5 Clues: Carlo Ginzburg, "Clues: Roots of an Evidential Paradigm," in *Clues, Myths and the Historical Method* (Baltimore: Johns Hopkins University Press, 1989), 96-125; Edward Muir, "Observing Trifles," in *Microhistory and the Lost Peoples of Europe,* ed. Edward Muir and Guido Ruggiero (Baltimore: Johns Hopkins University Press,

1991), vii-xxviii; Carlo Ginzburg and Carlo Ponti, "The Name and the Game: Unequal Exchange and the Historiographic Marketplace," in Muir and Ruggiero, *Microhistory and the Lost Peoples,* 1-10; Giovanni Levi, "On Microhistory," in *New Perspectives on Historical Writing,* ed. Peter Burke (University Park, PA: Penn State University Press, 1991), 93-113; Jill Lepore, "Historians Who Love Too Much: Reflections on Microhistory and Biography," *Journal of American History* 88, 1 (2001): 129-44.

CHAPTER 1: FISH LAKE

1 Time travel: See, for example, Carolyn Foltz, *Voyagers of the Chilcotin* (Winnipeg: Hignell Printing, 1996), 13, 162. General stores: Gerry Bracewell, "You Want It They Have It: Long and Colorful History in West Chilcotin Country Stores," *Williams Lake Tribune,* 10 June 1980, BC Archives (hereafter cited as BCA) D19/027.

2 "Three hundred miles": Diana French, *The Road Runs West: A Century along the Bella Coola/Chilcotin Road* (Madeira Park, BC: Harbour Publishing, 1994), ix. "The Hill": Betty Funke, "Chilcotin Country ... It's No Sunday Drive," *Victoria Colonist Magazine,* 17 February 1980; Isobel Nanton, "Chilcotin: British Columbia's Last Western Frontier," *Hamilton (Ontario) Spectator,* 7 November 1998; Brett Johnson, "Rewards Are Great on 'Freedom Road': Going over the Hill Is a Rite of Passage in British Columbia," *Ventura County (California) Star,* 30 June 2000. "Loonshit": Paul H. St. Pierre, *Smith and Other Events: Tales of the Chilcotin* (New York: Penguin, 1985), 18.

3 Cf. David Lowenthal, *The Past Is a Foreign Country* (Cambridge: Cambridge University Press, 1985), xxiii.

4 Zoogeography: E.C. Pielou, *After the Ice Age: The Return of Life to Glaciated North America* (Chicago: University of Chicago Press, 1991), 111, 125, 263; C. Richard Harington, "Quaternary Animals: Vertebrates of the Ice Age," in *Life in Stone: A Natural History of British Columbia Fossils,* ed. R. Ludvigsen (Vancouver: UBC Press, 1996), 259-73. Fur trade records: William McBean, 30 October 1837, Fort Chilcotin Post Journals and Correspondence, Hudson's Bay Company Archives/Provincial Archives of Manitoba B-37/a/1-2, 1M20.

5 Charlotte Lake: Richmond Pearson Hobson Jr., *Grass beyond the Mountains: Discovering the Last Great Cattle Frontier on the North American Continent* (Toronto: McClelland and Stewart, 1987), 43. Riske Creek: Eric Collier, *Three against the Wilderness* (Toronto: Clarke, Irwin, 1959), 146-49. Mid-1920s: J. Hatter, "The Moose of Central British Columbia" (PhD dissertation, State College of Washington, 1950); Ian McTaggart Cowan and Charles J. Guiget, *The Mammals of British Columbia* (Victoria: BC Provincial Museum, Department of Recreation and Conservation, 1965), 376-81; David J. Spalding, "The Early History of Moose *(Alces alces)*: Distribution and Relative Abundance in British Columbia," *Contributions to Natural Science* [Royal BC Museum] 11 (1990): 1-12; David Nagorsen, *Mammals of British Columbia: A Taxonomic Catalogue* (Victoria: Royal BC Museum, 1990), 98-99; David M. Shackleton, *Hoofed Mammals of British Columbia,* Royal British Columbia Museum Handbook (Vancouver: UBC Press, 1999), 120-35. Tame enough to pet: Hazel Henry, "The Moose Came Back Again," in *Chilcotin: Preserving Pioneer Memories,* ed. Veera Bonner, Irene E. Bliss, and Hazel Henry Litterick (Surrey, BC: Heritage House, 1995), 407-9.

6 Paleobotany: W.H. Mathews, "Late Quaternary Environmental History Affecting

Human Habitation of the Pacific Northwest," *Canadian Journal of Archaeology* 3 (1979): 147-52; Richard J. Hebda, "Interior Grasslands Past and Future," *Cordillera* (1996): 344-46.

7 Climate: J.E. Kutzbach, "Model Simulations of the Climatic Patterns during the Deglaciation of North America," in *North America and Adjacent Oceans during the Last Deglaciation,* ed. William F. Ruddiman and H.E. Wright Jr. (Boulder, CO: Geological Society of American, 1987), 425-46; Hebda, "Interior Grasslands"; Paul L. Hancock and Brian J. Skinner, eds., *The Oxford Companion to the Earth* (Oxford: Oxford University Press, 2000) (hereafter cited as *OCE*), s.v., "climate models." Zoned by altitude: Hebda, "Interior Grasslands." Today: BC Ministry of Forests, Research Branch, "Biogeoclimatic Zones of British Columbia" [Map, 1:2,000,000] (Victoria: Government of BC, 1999); Idem, "The Ecology of the Bunchgrass Zone" (Victoria: Government of BC, 1998); Idem, "The Ecology of the Interior Douglas-fir Zone" (Victoria: Government of BC, n.d.); Dellis Vern Meidinger and Jim Pojar, eds., *Ecosystems of British Columbia,* Special Report Series No. 6 (Victoria: BC Ministry of Forests, 1991).

8 Wisconsin glaciation: John Imbrie and Katherine Palmer Imbrie, *Ice Ages: Solving the Mystery* (Cambridge, MA: Harvard University Press, 1986); Neil Roberts, *The Holocene: An Environmental History* (Oxford: Blackwell, 1989), 42-61; Pielou, *After the Ice Age;* N.F.G. Davis and W.H. Mathews, "Four Phases of Glaciation with Illustrations from Southwestern British Columbia," *Journal of Geology* 52 (1944): 404-6.

9 Glacial landforms of Chilcotin: David H. Huntley and Bruce E. Broster, "Glacial Lake Camelsfoot: A Late Wisconsinan Advance Stage Proglacial Lake in the Fraser River Valley, Gang Ranch Area, BC," *Canadian Journal of Earth Sciences* 31 (1994): 798-807; Stuart S. Holland, *Landforms of British Columbia: A Physiographic Outline* (Victoria: BC Department of Mines and Petroleum Resources, 1964); Nurettin Keser, *Interpretation of Landforms from Aerial Photographs: With Illustrations from British Columbia* (Victoria: BC Ministry of Forests, 1990). Coalescence of glaciers: Davis and Mathews, "Four Phases of Glaciation"; John Joseph Clague and John L. Luternauer, "Late Quaternary Sedimentary Environments, Southwestern British Columbia," in *Field Excursion Guide Book 30A* (St. Johns, NL: Geological Association of Canada), 5-6. Relative depression of land: Clague et al., "Late Quaternary Sea Levels and Crustal Movements, Coastal British Columbia," *Canadian Journal of Earth Sciences* 19 (1982): 597-618; John Joseph Clague and Thomas S. James, "History and Isostatic Effects of the Last Ice Sheet in Southern British Columbia," *Quaternary Science Reviews* 21, nos. 1-3 (2002): 71-87. Dynamic ice sheets: Paul A. Mayewski, George H. Denton, and Terrence J. Hughes, "Late Wisconsin Ice Sheets in North America," in *The Last Great Ice Sheets,* ed. George H. Denton and Terrence J. Hughes (New York: Wiley, 1981), 138; Pielou, *After the Ice Age.*

10 Pangaea: P.J. Coney, D.L. Jones, and J.W.H. Monger, "Cordilleran Suspect Terranes," *Nature* 288 (1980): 329; H. Gabrielse and C.J. Yorath, "DNAG #4. The Cordilleran Orogen in Canada," *Geoscience Canada* 16, 2 (1989): 71; James W.H. Monger, "The Origin and Evolution of Canada's Western Mountains," in Ludvigsen, *Life in Stone,* 38-40; Sydney Graham Cannings and Richard James Cannings, *Geology of British Columbia: A Journey through Time* (Vancouver: Greystone Books, 1999), 11-12; John McPhee, *Annals of the Former World* (New York: Farrar, Straus and Giroux, 1998), 27. Marine life, trapped carbon, and extinctions: *OCE,* s.vv., "Carboniferous," "carbon cycles," "coal," "enhanced greenhouse effect," "extinctions and mass extinctions," "Permian."

11 Subduction and plate tectonics: Coney, Jones, and Monger, "Cordilleran Suspect Terranes," 329; Monger, "Origin and Evolution," 30-33, 40-41; *OCE*, s.vv., "subduction
   zones," "plate tectonics, principles," "mantle convection, plumes, viscosity, and dynamics," "convergent plate margins."

12 Mosaic of terranes: Coney, Jones and Monger, "Cordilleran Suspect Terranes," 329-
   30; Gabrielse and Yorath, "DNAG #4," 71-72, 75, 83; W.H. White, "Cordilleran Tectonics in British Columbia," *Bulletin of the American Association of Petroleum Geologists*
   43, 1 (1959): 70-72, 78; J.W.H. Monger, "Upper Paleozoic Rocks of the Western Canadian Cordillera and Their Bearing on Cordilleran Evolution," *Canadian Journal of
   Earth Sciences* 14 (1977): 1832-59; Monger, "Origin and Evolution"; Cannings and
   Cannings, *Geology of British Columbia*, 15-22. Tectonic activity: *OCE*, s.vv., "moun-
   tain-building (orogenesis)," "Jurassic," "metamorphism, metamorphic facies, and
   metamorphic rocks." Broad plateau: Holland, *Landforms.*

13 Plants: James F. Basinger, Elisabeth McIver, and and Wesley C. Wehr, "Plant Life," in
   Ludvigsen, *Life in Stone,* 187-201. Extinction of dinosaurs: *OCE*, s.vv., "Cretaceous,"
   "extinctions and mass extinctions."

14 New ecological niches: Tim Flannery, *The Eternal Frontier: An Ecological History of
   North America and Its Peoples* (New York: Grove, 2001). Hoofed mammals: M.C. Maas
   and D.W. Krause, "Mammalian Turnover and Community Structure in the Paleocene of North America," *Historical Biology* 8 (1994): 91-128. BC mammals: Lee
   McKenzie McAnally, "Paleogene Mammals on Land and at Sea," in Ludvigsen, *Life
   in Stone,* 202-11.

15 Volcanic activity; Monger, "Origin and Evolution"; Cannings and Cannings, *Geology
   of British Columbia,* 30. Reconstructed ecology: Ted M. Cavender, "Review of the
   Fossil History of North American Freshwater Fishes," in *The Zoogeography of North
   American Freshwater Fishes,* ed. C.H. Hocutt and E.O. Wiley (New York: Wiley-
   Interscience, 1986), 699-724; Mark V.H. Wilson, "Fishes from Eocene Lakes of the
   Interior" and "Insects near Eocene Lakes of the Interior," in Ludvigsen, *Life in Stone,*
   212-24 and 225-33; Ruth A. Stockey and Wesley C. Wehr, "Flowering Plants in and
   around Eocene Lakes of the Interior," in Ludvigsen, *Life in Stone,* 234-47; James F.
   Basinger, Elisabeth McIver, and Wesley C. Wehr, "Eocene Conifers of the Interior,"
   in Ludvigsen, *Life in Stone,* 248-58. Temperate climate: Glenn E. Rouse and W.H.
   Mathews, "Radioactive Dating of Tertiary Plant-Bearing Deposits," *Science* 133, 3458
   (1961): 1079. Relaxation of the crust: Holland, *Landforms,* 14-15, 22, 38; *OCE*, s.v.,
   "subsidence and uplift."

16 Erosion: Rouse and Mathews, "Radioactive Dating"; Holland, *Landforms,* 22-23.
   Lava flows: W.H. Mathews, "Neogene Chilcotin Basalts in South-Central British
   Columbia: Geology, Ages, and Geomorphic History," *Canadian Journal of Earth Sci-
   ences* 26, 5 (1989): 969-82. Hot spots: M.L. Bevier, R.L. Armstrong, and J.G. Souther,
   "Miocene Peralkaline Volcanism in West-Central British Columbia, Its Temporal
   Plate and Tectonics Setting," *Geology* 7 (1979): 389-92; J.G. Souther, "The Western
   Anahim Belt: Root Zone of a Peralkaline Magma System," *Canadian Journal of Earth
   Sciences* 23 (1986): 895-908; Gabrielse and Yorath, "DNAG #4," 81; Cannings and
   Cannings, *Geology of BC,* 30-31; *OCE*, s.v., "plate tectonics, principles"; W.H. Mathews
   and Glenn E. Rouse, "Late Tertiary Volcanic Rocks and Plant-Bearing Deposits in
   British Columbia," *Geological Society of America Bulletin* 74 (1963): 55-60.

17 Episodes of glaciation: *OCE*, s.vv., "ice-age theories," "ice ages"; Pielou, *After the Ice*

Age. Human colonists: Knut R. Fladmark, *British Columbia Prehistory* (Ottawa: National Museum of Man, 1986); Roy L. Carlson and Luke Dalla Bona, eds., *Early Human Occupation in British Columbia* (Vancouver: UBC Press, 1996).

18 Dennis Teskey et al., "High-Resolution Regional Aeromagnetic Survey: Interior Plateau British Columbia," in *Interior Plateau Geoscience Project: Summary of Geological, Geochemical and Geophysical Studies,* ed. L.J. Diakow, J.M. Newell, and Paul Metcalfe (Victoria: BC Geological Survey, 1997), 221-222.

19 Obstructions: Teskey et al., "High-Res," 221; L.J. Diakow, P. van der Heyden, and Paul Metcalfe, "Introduction," in Diakow, Newell, and Metcalfe, *Interior Plateau Geoscience Project,* 1. Magnetic anomalies: *OCE,* s.vv., "aeromagnetic surveying," "geomagnetic measurement: techniques and surveys."

20 Magnetization: *OCE,* s.vv., "rock," "Curie temperature," "geomagnetic measurement: techniques and surveys," "palaeomagnetism: techniques and remanent magnetization"; Charles W. Chesterman, *National Audubon Society Field Guide to North American Rocks and Minerals* (New York: Knopf, 1979), s.vv., "hematite," "magnetite." Magnetometer: Teskey et al., "High-Res," 221; G. Bartington, "Sensors for Low Level, Low Frequency Magnetic Fields" (paper presented at the IEE Colloquium on Low-Level Low-Frequency Magnetic Fields, London, 14 April 1994), 2/4; S. Foner, "Review of Magnetometry," *IEEE Transactions on Magnetics* MAG-17, 6 (1981): 3358-63; W.F. Stuart, "Earth's Field Magnetometry," *Report on Progress in Physics* 35 (1972): 803-81.

21 Magnetic anomaly mapping: Dennis Teskey et al., "The Aeromagnetic Survey Program of the Geological Survey of Canada: Contribution to Regional Geological Mapping and Mineral Exploration," *Canadian Journal of Earth Sciences* 30, 2 (1993): 252, fig. 6a; Teskey et al., "High-Res," 222. Faults: P.J. Umhoefer and H.W. Tipper, *Stratigraphy, Depositional Environment, and Tectonic Setting of the Upper Triassic to Middle Jurassic Rocks of the Chilcotin Ranges, Southwestern British Columbia* (Ottawa: Geological Survey of Canada, Bulletin 519, 1998), 6; Paul Schiarizza et al., "Geology and Mineral Occurrences of the Yalakom River Area (92O/1, 2, 92J/15, 16)," in *Geological Fieldwork 1989: A Summary of Field Activity and Current Research* (Victoria: BC Ministry of Energy, Mines and Petroleum Resources, 1990), 53-72; *OCE,* s.v. "faults and faulting." Lineament: Holland cites air photo BC 498:41 in *Landforms,* 123.

22 Dating: Peter S. Mustard and P. van der Heyden, "Geology of Tatla Lake (92N/15) and the East Half of Bussel Creek (92N/14) Map Areas," in Diakow, Newell, and Metcalfe, *Interior Plateau Geoscience Project,* 104-7, 111; Paul Schiarizza and Janet Riddell, "Geology of the Tatlayoko Lake – Beece Creek Area (92N/8, 9, 10; 92O/5, 6, 12)," in Diakow, Newell, and Metcalfe, *Interior Plateau Geoscience Project,* 88-89; Umhoefer and Tipper, *Stratigraphy,* 6; *OCE,* s.v. "isotopic dating."

23 Teskey et al., "Aeromagnetic Survey Program," 244-45.

24 Flight altitude: Stuart, "Earth's Field," 807-8. Economic significance: Teskey et al., "High-Res," 223; Schiarizza and Riddell, "Geology of Tatlayoko Lake," 97; Taseko Mines Limited (hereafter cited as TML), Form 20-F for US Securities and Exchange Commission, 17 February 1998 (available from System for Electronic Document Analysis and Retrieval [hereafter cited as SEDAR], operated for Canadian Securities Administrators by the Canadian Depository for Securities).

25 Colin E. Dunn, "Biogeochemical Surveys in the Interior Plateau of British Columbia," in Diakow, Newell, and Metcalfe, *Interior Plateau Geoscience Project,* 205-18.

26 Geological inferences: *OCE,* s.v., "geological maps" and map-making"; Martin J.S.

Rudwick, "The Emergence of a Visual Language for Geological Science," *History of Science* 14 (1976): 149-95. Porphyry deposit: BC Department of Mines and Petroleum Resources, *The Identification of Common Rocks* (Victoria: Author, 1970), 9; Chesterman, *Field Guide*, 598; BC Ministry of Energy and Mines, Geological Survey Branch, Mineral Inventory Database site description number (hereafter cited as MINFILE) 092O 041.

27 Porphyries: *OCE*, s.vv., "hydrothermal solutions," "plutonic rocks," "porphyry copper deposits," "subduction zones," "volcanoes and volcanic rock." Fish Lake: Michael R. Wolfhard, "Fish Lake," in *Porphyry Deposits of the Canadian Cordillera: A Volume Dedicated to Charles S. Ney*, ed. A. Sutherland Brown (n.p.: Canadian Institute of Mining and Metallurgy, 1976), 317-22; MINFILE 092O 041; Monger, "Origin and Evolution"; Schiarizza and Riddell, "Geology of Tatlayoko Lake," 88-89, 93-95; W.J. McMillan, "Porphyry Deposits in Volcanic Arcs with Deposits on the Canadian Cordillera," in *The Metallogeny of Volcanic Arcs (1998-8)*, ed. D.V. Lefebure (Victoria: BC Ministry of Energy and Mines, Geological Survey Branch, 1998), F.

28 Gold rush: Gordon R. Elliot, *Barkerville, Quesnel and the Cariboo Gold Rush* (Vancouver: Douglas and McIntyre, 1978); Netta Sterne, *Fraser Gold 1858! The Founding of British Columbia* (Pullman: Washington State University Press, 1998); Jean Barman, *The West beyond the West: A History of British Columbia* (Toronto: University of Toronto Press, 1991). Subsequent mining activity: Jo Harris, "Mineral Development," in *British Columbia, the Pacific Province: Geographical Essays*, ed. Colin J.B. Wood (Victoria: Western Geographical Press, 2001), 261-67.

29 1930s: B.T. O'Grady, "Western Mineral Survey District (No. 6)," in *Annual Report of the Minister of Mines of the Province of British Columbia for the Year Ended 31st December 1935* (Victoria: Legislative Assembly, 1936), F28. 1950s: TML, Form 20-F, 17 February 1998 (available from SEDAR). 1960s: Wolfhard, "Fish Lake"; MINFILE 092O 041. 1970s: BC Ministry of Energy and Mines, "British Columbia Producer Prices – Annual Averages – 1901 to 2000," news release, 2000, http://www.em.gov.bc.ca/Mining/MiningStats/22priceprodr.htm; R.H. Seraphim, "Geophysical Induced Polarization Report – Fish Lake Project," 1970. Available through Ministry of Energy, Mines and Petroleum Resources' Assessment Report Indexing System (hereafter cited as ARIS) 02483.

30 Copper prices: BC Ministry of Energy and Mines, "British Columbia Producer Prices." History of company surveying: Wolfhard, "Fish Lake"; William A. Howell, "Diamond drilling report on the Fish Lake property (TK claims), Fish lake, Chilco lake area," 1974, ARIS 04966; W.J. McMillan, "Taseko Lakes Area," in *Geological Fieldwork 1976: A Summary of Field Activities of the Geological Division, Mineral Resources Branch* (Victoria: BC Ministry of Mines and Petroleum Resources, 1977), 47-53; John Schreiner, "'Sleeping' BC Mining Firm Roused," *Financial Post* (Toronto), 10 June 1991; TML, Form 20-F, 17 February 1998 (available from SEDAR); A.M. Pauwels, "Drilling Report on the TK Claims and FIS Placer Claim," 1989, ARIS 19378; N. Caira and Darwin W. Piroshco, "Diamond Drilling Report on the Fish Lake Property," 1991, ARIS 22060.

31 Expanded field program: BC Ministry of Energy, Mines and Petroleum Resources, *Annual Report 1988/89* (Victoria: Author, 1989), 19, 22. Hickson quote: "Geological History Mapped," *Williams Lake Tribune*, 1991, Cariboo-Chilcotin Archives, vertical files on Fish Lake, gold/copper mining, Mining, Taseko, Prosperity (hereafter cited as

CCA-M). Promising deposits: BC Ministry of Energy, Mines and Petroleum Resources, *Annual Report 1990/91* (Victoria: Author, 1991), 42-43, 47-48, 55.

32 Yoram Barzel, *Economic Analysis of Property Rights* (Cambridge: Cambridge University Press, 1989).

33 Schreiner, "'Sleeping'"; TML, Form 20-F, 17 February 1998 (available from SEDAR). The agreement allowed Taseko Mines to develop or sell Fish Lake in a minimum of three years or be taken over by Cominco. Under the terms of the new contract, Cominco stood to make between $20 million and $48 million if Taseko Mines was successful. According to Schreiner, if Taseko Mines failed, Cominco would get the Fish Lake property in 1994, "with Taseko retaining a 20% net profits interest and a right of first refusal, should Cominco then offer Fish Lake for sale."

34 Estimates: Schreiner, "'Sleeping'"; "Exploration Firm Hoping for a Big Find," *Williams Lake Tribune*, 17 September 1991, CCA-M. Mining characteristics of deposit: "Fish Lake Results," *Mining Magazine,* December 1991, 115.

35 Hydroelectric surveys: Corporation of BC Land Surveyors, "Richard Preston Bishop B.C.L.S., F.R.G.S. 1884-1954," in *Report of Proceedings of the 50th Annual General Meeting* (n.p.: Author, 1955), 47, Philip and Helen Akrigg Fonds 5-52, University of BC Special Collections; Victor Dolmage, "Chilko Lake and Vicinity," in *Summary Report 1924, Part A* ([Ottawa]: Geological Survey of Canada, 1925); Richard Charles Farrow, Surveyor, papers, 1929, BCA MS1977; MINFILE 092N. Imagined potential: "Huge Power Source Is Found in Canada: Engineers Say Potential British Columbia Developments Would Surpass Those on St. Lawrence," *New York Times,* 28 July 1930. Salmon: Bruce Hutchinson, *The Fraser* (New York: Rinehart and Co., 1950), 340-41.

36 "This large stretch of country": Dolmage, "Chilko Lake." More mineral deposits: D.F. VanDine, H.W. Nasmith, and C.F. Ripley, "The Emergence of Engineering Geology in British Columbia: 'An Engineering Geologist Knows a Dam Site Better!'" in *Pioneering Geology in the Canadian Cordillera*, BC Geological Survey Branch, Open File 1992-19 (Victoria: BC Geological Survey Branch, 1992). Park proposal: Federation of Mountain Clubs of BC, "Chilcotin Wild and Gentle: The Chilcotin Wilderness," in *Educational Report* (Vancouver: Author, 1991), University of BC Special Collections, Pamphlet Collection (hereafter cited as SPAM) 21676. Nation of porters: Victor Dolmage, "First Things First," *Mining and Industrial Record,* July 1931.

37 Class A park: Federation of Mountain Clubs of BC, "Chilcotin Wild and Gentle"; *Park Act, Revised Statutes of BC,* 1996, c. 344, s. 8 (2); Moira Farrow, "Chilcotin Park Plans Studied by Government," *Vancouver Sun,* 18 January 1977, BCA D19/027. 1982 team: Quoted in SPAM 21676. 1991 team: BC Parks, Cariboo District, *Tŝ'il?os Provincial Park Master Plan* (Victoria: BC Parks, 1997).

38 Graeme Peter McLaren, "Geology and Mineral Potential of the Chilko Lake Area (92N/1, 8; 92O4)" in *Geological Fieldwork 1986: A Summary of Field Activities and Current Research* (Victoria: BC Ministry of Energy, Mines and Petroleum Resources, 1987), 231-43; Graeme Peter McLaren, *A Mineral Resource Assessment of the Chilko Lake Planning Area* (Victoria: BC Ministry of Energy, Mines and Petroleum Resources, 1990); *OCE,* s.v., "elemental associations and ore minerals and allied deposits."

39 Federation of Mountain Clubs of BC, "Chilcotin Wild and Gentle," SPAM 21676; Julie Taub, "The Raw Beauty of BC," *Ottawa Citizen,* 29 August 1992.

40 Copper prices: BC Ministry of Energy and Mines, "British Columbia Producer Prices," Pioneer Metals (hereafter cited as PMC): Oscar Rojo, "Pioneer Metals Starts

with Clean Slate," *Toronto Star,* 3 January 1992; PMC, "Pioneer Metals Corporation Completes Restructuring," *Canada NewsWire,* 2 January 1992. Quotation from PMC: "Pioneer Metals Corporation Announces Induced Polarization Anomaly Discovered on Task Claims Adjoining Taseko Mines' Fish Lake Property – Amended News Release," *Canada NewsWire,* 1 December 1992. Verdstone: "Gold Values Intersected at Newton," *Northern Miner,* 27 January 1992; "Trenching on Newton Hill," *Mining Magazine,* February 1992; Verdstone Gold Corporation, "Encouraging Diamond Drill Results Received on Newton Hill Property," *Canada NewsWire,* 6 April 1992.

41 Mount Milligan: "Mount Milligan Decision Threatens Property Market (Placer Dome Writes Off BC Gold Project)," *Northern Miner,* 17 February 1992. Taseko: TML, "$7.14 Million Financing Obtained – Fish Lake Program Begins," *Canada NewsWire,* 9 March 1992. Quotation from TML, "Taseko Begins Trading on NASDAQ with Symbol TKO:CF," *Canada NewsWire,* 25 March 1992; TML, "Taseko Mines Limited Deposit Width Doubles – Drilling Continues at Fish lake," *Canada NewsWire,* 9 June 1992; "Taseko's Drilling Doubles Width of Fish Lake Deposit," *Northern Miner,* 15 June 1992; TML, "Taseko Mines Limited Announces Final Closing of Private Placement," *Canada NewsWire,* 23 June 1992; TML, "Drilling Continues to Delineate Immense Gold-Copper Deposit," *Canada NewsWire,* 17 July 1992; TML, Form 20-F, 17 February 1998 (available from SEDAR).

42 "Public Visits New Minesite," *Williams Lake Tribune,* July 1991, CCA-M. Questionnaire: "Drilling Continues to Delineate Immense Gold-Copper Deposit."

43 "Rapidly depleting metal reserve" quotation from TML, "Taseko Mines Limited – Drilling Continues – Reserve Calculation Commences for Giant Gold-Copper Deposit," *Canada NewsWire,* 15 September 1992; "Fish Lake Update," *Mining Journal,* 16 October 1992; TML, "Taseko Warrants Exercised to Raise an Additional $7.24 Million," *Canada NewsWire,* 19 October 1992; TML, "Taseko Mines – Rebuilding Canada's Mineral Inventory," *Canada NewsWire,* 18 November 1992. Ongoing exploration: "New BC Mining Projects in Works," *Northern Miner,* 25 January 1993; TML, "Independent Engineering Studies Confirm Copper-Gold Deposit as World Class," *Canada NewsWire,* 10 March 1993.

44 Sustainable development: World Commission on Environment and Development, *Our Common Future* (Oxford: Oxford University Press, 1987), 43. Canadian Wilderness Charter: "WWF Hails Chilko Lake Park as Model for Establishment of New Protected Areas," *Canada NewsWire,* 13 January 1994.

45 Economic history: Douglass Cecil North, *Institutions, Institutional Change, and Economic Performance* (Cambridge: Cambridge University Press, 1990); Kenneth Pomeranz and Steven Topik, *The World that Trade Created: Society, Culture, and the World Economy 1400 to the Present* (Armonk, NY: M.E. Sharpe, 1999), chap. 6; cf. James C. Scott, *Seeing Like a State: How Certain Schemes to Improve the Human Condition Have Failed* (New Haven, CT: Yale University Press, 1998). History of science: Bruno Latour, *Science in Action: How to Follow Scientists and Engineers through Society* (Cambridge, MA: Harvard University Press, 1987); Joan H. Fujimura, "Crafting Science: Standardized Packages, Boundary Objects, and 'Translation,'" in *Science as Practice and Culture,* ed. Andrew Pickering (Chicago: University of Chicago Press, 1992), 168-211; Joseph O'Connell, "Metrology: The Creation of Universality by the Circulation of Particulars," *Social Studies of Science* 23 (1993): 129-73.

46 Bruce Batchelor, "The Resource Inventory Committee," *BC Environmental Report* 4, 1 (1993): 19.

47 Nadine Schuurman, *GIS: A Short Introduction* (Malden, MA: Blackwell, 2004), 12 (quote), 68-75, 86.

48 CORE: Mark Roseland, J.C. Day, and Robert W. Penrose, "Shared Decision Making in Public Land Planning: An Evaluation of the Cariboo-Chilcotin CORE Process," *Environments* 25, 2/3 (1998): 27-47; Colin J.B. Wood, Cimarron Corpé, and Laurie Jackson, "Land Use Planning," in Wood, *British Columbia, the Pacific Province*, 229-59; "Victoria Now Recognizing Mining Industry Problems," *Williams Lake Tribune*, 8 April 1993, CCA-M.

49 Rod Nutt, "Peace Proposal Offers Fitness Plan," *Vancouver Sun*, 11 March 1993.

50 Difficulties: "Taseko Advances Fish Lake Project," *Northern Miner*, 12 April 1993; TML, "Taseko Mines Limited Quality – Long Life – Low Cost Deposit Confirmed," *Canada NewsWire*, 3 May 1993; "Fish Lake Found Viable," *Williams Lake Tribune*, 13 May 1993, CCA-M. Price slump: Peter Kennedy, "Taseko News Dampened by Low Copper Price," *Financial Post* (Toronto), 5 May 1993; "Copper Price Dips," *Williams Lake Tribune*, 6 May 1993, CCA-M; "Fish Lake Doubts," *Mining Journal*, 14 May 1993; "Copper Prices Stalls [sic] Mining," *Williams Lake Tribune*, 25 May 1993, CCA-M. City councillors: "Use Taseko as Model – City," *Williams Lake Tribune*, 27 May 1993, CCA-M. Fall in funding: "BC Exploration in a Trough," *Northern Miner*, 31 May 1993.

51 Planning: TML, "Taseko Mines Limited Announces Giant Fish Lake Gold-Copper Deposit Enters Mine Development Permitting Process," *Canada NewsWire*, 25 August 1993. Enrolling stakeholders: MINFILE 092O 041; "Taseko Filings," *Financial Post*, 26 August 1993; "Taseko Mines Progressing," *Weekender*, 29 August 1993, CCA-M; "Taseko Mines Project Progressing," *Williams Lake Tribune*, 31 August 1993, CCA-M. Prefeasibility: TML, "Taseko Mines Limited Announces Contract Awarded for Detailed Prefeasibility Study," *Canada NewsWire*, 13 September 1993.

52 "BC Endangered Spaces Local Action Projects Underway," *BC Environmental Report* 3, 2 (1992): 4; "BC Improves on National Wilderness Report Card," *Canada NewsWire*, 30 September 1993; "World Wildlife Fund's Endangered Spaces Campaign Update," *BC Environmental Report* 4, 4 (1993): 16.

53 To establish the date, take the land area of Canada (9,093,507 square kilometres) and multiply by 247 to get the number of acres of Canadian land (over 2.2 billion). This is the most "wilderness" that there could be in Canada. The rate of disappearance is given at 4 acres per minute, or 2,102,400 acres per year. Dividing the acres of land by the rate of disappearance gives the number of years it will take to disappear, about 1069. Add that number to 1993 to get the year 3062. The figure for the land area of Canada comes from Energy, Mines and Resources Canada's *National Atlas of Canada*, 5th ed. (Ottawa: Energy Mines and Resources Canada, 1985).

54 Regional implementation of CORE: Susan Rautio, "Endangered Spaces Campaign Update," *BC Environmental Report* 3, 3 (1992): 19; "A Guide to the Protected Areas Strategy," *BC Environmental Report* 3, 3 (1992): 21; "World Wildlife Fund Report Reveals Temperate Forest Severely Threatened," *BC Environmental Report* 3, 4 (1992): 29. Chilko Lake preservation: Dave Neads, "Chilko Lake Park Now One Step Closer to Reality," *BC Environmental Report* 4, 2 (1993): 29; BC Parks, Cariboo District, *Tŝʼilʔos Provincial Park Master Plan*.

55 "Taseko Mines Project Closer," *Williams Lake Tribune*, 9 November 1993, CCA-M; TML, "Taseko Acquires Right to Purchase Cominco's Remaining Interest in Fish Lake Property," *Canada NewsWire*, 15 December 1993; Peter Kennedy, "Taseko, Cominco

Alter Pact on Fish Lake Find," *Financial Post* (Toronto), 17 December 1993; "Taseko Mines Has Solidified Hold on Fish Lake Property," *Williams Lake Tribune,* 21 December 1993, CCA-M.

56 "WWF Hails Chilko Lake Park as Model for Establishment of New Protected Areas," *Canada NewsWire,* 13 January 1994; "Wilderness Park Created," *Rocky Mountain News* (Denver), 18 January 1994; "Tš'yl-os Park, BC's Newest," *BC Environmental Report* 5, 1 (1994): 23; BC Parks, Cariboo District, *Tš'il?os Provincial Park Master Plan.*

57 TML, "Taseko Completes $25 Million Buyout of Fish Lake Gold-Copper Deposit," *Canada NewsWire,* 7 March 1993; "Mine Land Secure," *Williams Lake Tribune,* 10 March 1994, CCA-M; "Mining Mood Gets Better," *Williams Lake Tribune,* 24 May 1994, CCA-M; Energy, Mines and Petroleum Resources, "Upswing in the BC Mining Scene," news release, 1994.

58 Judy Smith, "Victoria Making Mining Nearly Impossible," *Williams Lake Tribune,* 24 May 1994, CCA-M.

59 PMC, "Pioneer Metals Corporation Advises Shareholders," *Canada NewsWire,* 25 November 1993; PMC, "Pioneer Metals Corporation Update," *Canada NewsWire,* 17 March 1994; PMC, "Pioneer Metals – Drilling Results," *Canada NewsWire,* 4 May 1994; PMC, "Pioneer Metals Corp. Announces Results," *Canada NewsWire,* 30 September 1994; "Pioneer Metals Plans Drilling, Restructures (BC)," *Northern Miner,* 17 October 1994.

60 Energy, Mines and Petroleum Resources, "Upswing in the BC Mining Scene."

61 Bill Phillips, "Fish Lake Looks Good," *Williams Lake Tribune,* 24 May 1994, CCA-M; "Kilborn Studies Confirm Major Gold-Copper Mine at Fish Lake," *Canada NewsWire,* 6 July 1994; "Taseko Fleshes Out Fish Lake Option (BC)," *Northern Miner,* 25 July 1994. Ministry of Environment, Lands and Parks objection: Letter from Toby Vigod, Ministry of Environment, Lands and Parks, to Bruce McRae, Ministry of Energy, Mines and Petroleum Resources, 25 July 1994, cited in Sierra Legal Defence Fund, *Digging up Trouble: The Legacy of Mining in British Columbia* (Vancouver: Sierra Legal Defence Fund, 1998) (hereafter cited as *DuT*). Drainage of Fish Lake: Letter from Lee Nikl, Department of Fisheries and Oceans, to Stephen Sheehan, Environment Canada, 19 November 1993, cited in *DuT.* No way to mitigate impacts: Vigod to McRae, 25 July 1994. Federal law: *Fisheries Act, Revised Statutes of Canada,* 1985, c. F-14, s. 35 (1). Permanent loss of habitat: Nikl to Sheehan, 19 November 1993.

62 Jarvis quotation: "Mining Critic Blasts Process," *Williams Lake Tribune,* 1 November 1994, CCA-M; see also "Mining Projects Get Thumbs Up," *Williams Lake Advocate,* 2 November 1994, CCA-M. TML vs. federal fisheries department: "Fish Concerns Impact Mine," *Williams Lake Tribune,* 1 December 1994, CCA-M.

63 Kemano II: Peter Kennedy and John Schreiner, "Resource Firms Slam BC: Province's Decision to Cancel $1.3-Billion Alcan Project Leaves Many Resource Companies Re-Evaluating Plans for Major Investments," *Financial Post* (Toronto), 25 January 1995; Ross Howard, "BC Liable for Dam Compensation, Ottawa Says," *Globe and Mail* (Toronto), 25 January 1995; Greg McDade, "Fair Compensation for Alcan?" *BC Environmental Report* 6, 1 (1995): 18. Resource companies band together: "Brown Coalition of Coalitions," *BC Environmental Report* 6, 4 (1995): 10.

64 Commendation: "BC Gets Canada's Top Grade for Wilderness Protection," *Canada NewsWire,* 19 April 1995. Banner quotation: Bill Phillips, "Taseko Mines Plays Waiting Game," *Williams Lake Tribune,* 30 May 1995, CCA-M; see also Bal Russell, [Title

Missing], *Williams Lake Advocate,* July 1995, CCA-M. TML looking for buyer: Bloomberg Business News, "TSE Logs Another Gain," *Montreal Gazette,* 30 May 1995; Dow Jones, "Taseko Shops Fish Lake Deposit," *Financial Post* (Toronto), 30 May 1995.

65 Mining Council activities: "The Environmental Mining Council," *BC Environmental Report* 6, 1 (1995): 14. Active network: Alan Young, "The Environmental Effects of Mining," *BC Environmental Report* 6, 2 (1995): 27. Voter's guide: Alan Young, "Where Is the Modern in Modern Mining?" *BC Environmental Report* 6, 3 (1995): 35.

66 Standardized process: Harris, "Mineral Development," 270-73. New review process: Energy, Mines and Petroleum Resources, "British Columbia Mineral Exploration Review 1996 – Advanced Exploration and Development," news release (see also the dates on which various application documents for the project were posted to the Electronic Project Information Centre (e-PIC) of the BC Environmental Assessment Office). Internal e-mail: Doug Dryden to Norm Ringstad, Environmental Assessment Office, 24 July 1995, cited in *DuT.* Definitive answer: Bal Russell, [Title Missing], *Williams Lake Advocate,* July 1995, CCA-M; TML, "Taseko Mines Ltd. Retains Toronto Dominion Securities as Financial Advisor," *Canada NewsWire,* 6 July 1995.

67 Bal Russell, "Mine's Impact under Review," *Williams Lake Advocate,* 19 July 1995, CCA-M.

68 Jurisdiction: *DuT,* 58. No reasonable grounds: Letter from D. Griggs, Department of Fisheries and Oceans, to D.J. Copeland, Taseko Mines, 10 July 1996, cited in *DuT,* 59. Without approval: *DuT,* 58.

69 Nuntsi Lakes: Russell, "Mine's Impact under Review." Feds not persuaded: *DuT,* 59.

70 Letter: "Scientists Call for Action on Endangered Species," *BC Environmental Report* 6, 4 (1995): 10. Scientific literature: See, for example, Sinclair et al., "Biodiversity and the Need for Habitat Renewal," *Ecological Applications* 5, 3 (1995): 579-87.

71 *DuT,* 59.

CHAPTER 2: PROSPERITY GOLD

1 Property renamed: Sierra Legal Defence Fund, *Digging up Trouble: The Legacy of Mining in British Columbia* (Vancouver: Sierra Legal Defence Fund, 1998) (hereafter cited as *DuT*), 60n1. Ministry of Environment, Lands and Parks view: E-mail from Susan Pollard, fish geneticist, to Ted Down, Ministry of Environment, Lands and Parks, 6 June 1996, cited in *DuT.*

2 Unpleasant news: Susan Pollard, "re: Review of Chilcotin Rainbow Trout Genetics Study (R. Leary and G. Sage) and Attached Letter from Triton (B. Ford)," 6 September 1996, cited in *DuT.* Lake buried under ice: David H. Huntley, "Late Wisconsinan Glaciation of East-Central Taseko Lakes, British Columbia" (PhD dissertation, University of New Brunswick, 1997). Nematode parasite: E.C. Pielou, *After the Ice Age: The Return of Life to Glaciated North America* (Chicago: University of Chicago Press, 1991), 70. Proglacial lakes and streams: H.W. Tipper, *Glacial Geomorphology and Pleistocene History of Central British Columbia,* Bulletin 196 (Ottawa: Geological Survey of Canada, 1971); J.D. McPhail and C.C. Lindsey, "Zoogeography of the Freshwater Fishes of Cascadia (the Columbia System and Rivers North to the Stikine)," in *The Zoogeography of North American Freshwater Fishes,* ed. C.H. Hocutt and E.O. Wiley (New York: Wiley-Interscience, 1986), 615-37; John C. Briggs, "Introduction to the

Zoogeography of North American Fishes," in Hocutt and Wiley, *Zoogeography*, 1-16;
David H. Huntley and Bruce E. Broster, "The Late Wisconsinan Deglacial History
of the East-Central Taseko Lakes Area, British Columbia," *Canadian Journal of Earth
Sciences* 34 (1997): 1510-20; Bert Brink, "Glacial Lakes in British Columbia," *Cordillera*
(1997): 3-6.

3 Bal Russell, "Elders Oppose Mine," *Williams Lake Advocate,* 17 January 1996, Cari-
boo-Chilcotin Archives, vertical files on Fish Lake, gold/copper mining, Mining,
Taseko, Prosperity (hereafter cited as CCA-M). Quotations from Jim Swanson, T.N.G.
Rejects Taseko," *Williams Lake Tribune,* 23 January 1996, CCA-M.

4 Descendents: Knut R. Fladmark, *British Columbia Prehistory* (Ottawa: National
Museum of Man, 1986). British settle with French: Wilbur R. Jacobs, "British Indian
Policies to 1783," in *Handbook of North American Indians,* vol. 4, *History of Indian-
White Relations,* ed. Wilcomb E. Washburn (Washington, DC: Smithsonian Institu-
tion, 1988), 10. Treaties: Robert J. Surtees, "Canadian Indian Policies," in Washburn,
Handbook, vol. 4, 81-95; Douglas Sanders, "Government Indian Agencies in Canada,"
in Washburn, *Handbook,* vol. 4, 276-83; BC Treaty Commission, "Why Treaties?"
(Vancouver: Author, 2000).

5 Interactions with Tsilhqot'in: See, for example, Ross Cox, *Adventures on the Colum-
bia River: Including the Narrative of a Residence of Six Years on the Western Side of the
Rocky Mountains among Various Tribes of Indians hitherto Unknown: Together with a
Journey across the American Continent* (New York: J. and J. Harper, 1832), available from
Canadiana.org (formerly the Canadian Institute for Historical Microreproductions),
CIHM 33317; Henry Spencer Palmer, *Report of a Journey of a Survey from Victoria to
Fort Alexander, via North Bentinck Arm* (New Westminster, BC: Royal Engineer Press,
1863), BC Archives (hereafter cited as BCA) Library, NW971.MP174; Adrien Gabriel
Morice, *The History of the Northern Interior of British Columbia* (Fairfield, WA: Ye
Galleon Press, 1971); Victor Dolmage, "Chilko Lake and Vicinity," in *Summary Report
1924, Part A* ([Ottawa]: Geological Survey of Canada, 1925). Social Credit: Jean Bar-
man, *The West beyond the West: A History of British Columbia* (Toronto: University of
Toronto Press, 1991), 280-83 (Bennett quoted on 283). Outsiders: Robert Lane, "Chil-
cotin," in *Handbook of North American Indians,* vol. 6, *Subarctic,* ed. June Helm
(Washington, DC: Smithsonian Institution, 1981), 412.

6 Terry Glavin and People of Nemiah, *Nemiah: The Unconquered Country* (Vancouver:
New Star, 1992), 4-5. For an analysis of the bilingual Tsilhqot'in / English document,
see David W. Dinwoodie, *Reserve Memories: The Power of the Past in a Chilcotin Community* (Lincoln: University of Nebraska Press, 2002), chap. 4.

7 Support for declaration: Glavin, *Nemiah,* 12; Federation of Mountain Clubs of BC,
"Chilcotin Wild and Gentle: The Chilcotin Wilderness," in *Educational Report* (Vancouver: Author, 1991), University of BC Special Collections, Pamphlet Collection
21676. Park name: G.P.V. Akrigg and Helen B. Akrigg, *British Columbia Place Names,*
3rd ed.(Vancouver: UBC Press, 1997), s.v., "Tatlow"; BC Parks, Cariboo District,
Tŝ'il?os Provincial Park Master Plan (Victoria: BC Parks, 1997); Dinwoodie, *Reserve
Memories.* Park plan: BC Parks, Cariboo District, *Tŝ'il?os Provincial Park Master Plan.*

8 "Taseko Completes Financing," *Canada NewsWire,* 5 March 1996; "Taseko Deal Is
Finalized," *Williams Lake Tribune,* 21 March 1996, CCA-M; "Mining Faces Some
Critical Issues," *Williams Lake Tribune,* 7 March 1996, CCA-M.

9 Anglers: Don Robertson, "Time to Make Deal with Taseko Mines," *Williams Lake*

Advocate, 3 April 1996, CCA-M. Support in Williams Lake: "Lakecity is B.C.'s Mining Capital," *Williams Lake Tribune,* 14 May 1996, CCA-M. Fish habitat: Bill Phillips, "Taseko Goes for Gold at Fish Lake Location," *Williams Lake Tribune,* 25 July 1996, CCA-M. Fish vs. jobs: Jessica Whiteside, "Miners Fishing for Gold: But DFO Isn't Biting," *Williams Lake Advocate,* 31 July 1996, CCA-M; "Feds 'Refuse' to Look at Project," *Williams Lake Tribune,* 6 August 1996, CCA-M.

10 Tsilhqot'in opposition: "Natives Seek Trust with Company," *Williams Lake Advocate,* 31 July 1996, CCA-M; "Mine 'Will Bring Problems,'" *Williams Lake Tribune,* 30 August 1996, CCA-M; "Chiefs Want Taseko Gone," *Williams Lake Tribune,* 5 September 1996, CCA-M; "Natives Make Moose Priority over Mining," *Vancouver Sun,* 9 September 1996. Legal basis: "Deadline Near for Prosperity," *Williams Lake Tribune,* 26 September 1996, CCA-M.

11 *Sparrow v. The Queen,* [1990] 1 S.C.R. 1075; Michael Hudson, "The Fiduciary Obligations of the Crown towards Aboriginal People," in *Aboriginal Title in British Columbia: Delgamuukw v. The Queen,* ed. Frank Cassidy (Lantzville, BC: Oolichan Books, 1992), 44-50.

12 *Delgamuukw v. The Queen* (1991), 79 D.L.R. (4th) 185 (B.C.S.C.); Frank Cassidy, ed., *Aboriginal Title in British Columbia: Delgamuukw v. The Queen* (Lantzville, BC: Oolichan Books, 1992); *Delgamuukw v. British Columbia,* [1997] 3 S.C.R. 1010 (Supreme Court of Canada); BC Treaty Commission, "A Lay Person's Guide to Delgamuukw" (Vancouver: Author, 1999); Canada, Department of Indian and Northern Affairs, "Fact Sheet: Aboriginal Rights in BC," news release, 2002.

13 "Taseko Mines Limited – Feasibility Program Confirming a Large, High Quality Gold-Copper Mine," *Canada NewsWire,* 6 February 1997; BC Ministry of Energy and Mines, Geological Survey Branch, Mineral Inventory Database site description number (hereafter cited as MINFILE) 092O 041; Taseko Mines Limited (hereafter cited as TML), "Annual Report 1996: The Road to Prosperity," 14 February 1997 (available from System for Electronic Document Analysis and Retrieval [hereafter cited as SEDAR], operated for Canadian Securities Administrators by the Canadian Depository for Securities).

14 BC Environmental Network, Environmental Assessment Caucus, "Comments on the Implementation of the BC Environmental Assessment Process, news release, 12 May 1997; TML, "Annual Report 1996," 14 February 1997 (available from SEDAR).

15 Storefront office: "Mine to Get Another Look," *Williams Lake Tribune,* 3 July 1997, CCA-M; "Taseko Invites Input," *Williams Lake Tribune,* 9 September 1997, CCA-M; Daniel Wall, "Prosperity One Step Closer," *Williams Lake Advocate,* 16 September 1997, CCA-M. DFO letter and quotation from Jenkins, "Mine to Get Another Look."

16 Plans: TML, "Taseko Mines Limited – Major Project Milestones Nearing Completion for Prosperity," 24 September 1997 (available from SEDAR); TML, "Taseko Mines Limited – Excellent Results Received from Prosperity Pilot Plant Program," 17 November 1997 (available from SEDAR); "Ore in 2001," *Williams Lake Tribune,* 7 October 1997, CCA-M. Deans quotation: "Mine Locations Studied," *Williams Lake Tribune,* 20 November 1997, CCA-M. Seminars: "Public Update on Mine," *Williams Lake Tribune,* 6 November 1997, CCA-M; "Taseko Mines Puts on Public Info Sessions," *Williams Lake Advocate,* 11 November 1997, CCA-M; "Taseko Hosts Open House," *Williams Lake Advocate,* 2 December 1997, CCA-M; "Seminar Set," *Williams Lake Tribune,* 9 December 1997, CCA-M.

17 "First Nations Oppose Taseko," *Williams Lake Advocate,* 18 November 1997, CCA-M; "Natives Oppose Taseko Project," *Williams Lake Tribune,* 20 November 1997, CCA-M.

18 "Prices Hurting Mines," *Williams Lake Tribune,* 18 December 1997, CCA-M; Jo Harris, "Mineral Development," in *British Columbia, the Pacific Province: Geographical Essays,* ed. Colin J.B. Wood (Victoria: Western Geographical Press, 2001), 261-62. Worldwide threat: Environmental Mining Council of BC, "More Precious than Gold: Mineral Development and the Protection of Biological Diversity in Canada" (Victoria: Author, 1998), 16.

19 *Delgamuukw v. British Columbia,* [1997] 3 S.C.R. 1010; BC Treaty Commission, "Lay Person's Guide."

20 Stephen Hume, "Crown Land Lawsuits Loom," *Vancouver Sun,* 17 January 1998.

21 Tsilhqot'in: "TNG Responds to Mine Review," *Williams Lake Advocate,* 10 February 1998, CCA-M. Report to US SEC: TML, Form 20-F, 17 February 1998 (available from SEDAR).

22 "Proposed Mine Could Impact Area," *Williams Lake Tribune,* 20 January 1998, CCA-M; Sven McGirr, "Taseko Undertakes Study," *Williams Lake Advocate,* 3 February 1998, CCA-M; "Wildlife Inventory Near Finish," *Williams Lake Tribune,* 5 February 1998, CCA-M; TML, Form 20-F, 17 February 1998 (available from SEDAR); Dellis Vern Meidinger and Jim Pojar, eds., *Ecosystems of British Columbia,* Special Report Series No. 6 (Victoria: BC Ministry of Forests, 1991); Roberta Parish, Ray Coupé, and Dennis Lloyd, eds., *Plants of Southern Interior British Columbia and the Inland Northwest* (Vancouver: Lone Pine, 1999); Daniel Wall, "Taseko Mines Gathers Input," *Williams Lake Advocate,* 10 February 1998, CCA-M; "Open House on Proposed Mine," *Williams Lake Tribune,* 24 February 1998, CCA-M; "Taseko Looking for Input on Mine Project," *Williams Lake Advocate,* 24 February 1998, CCA-M.

23 Environmental group initiatives: *DuT;* Environmental Mining Council of BC, "Annual Report 1997." Williams Lake: "Draft Report Viewed," *Williams Lake Tribune,* 3 March 1998, CCA-M; quotation from "Lobby for Mine," *Williams Lake Tribune,* 5 March 1998, CCA-M; "Doors Closed in Review," *Williams Lake Tribune,* 5 March 1998, CCA-M.

24 Public letters: Public comments/submissions posted to the Electronic Project Information Centre of the BC Environmental Assessment Office (hereafter cited as e-PIC). Federal department: "Taseko Review Still Open," *Williams Lake Tribune,* 19 March 1998, CCA-M. Williams Lake: Local government comments/submissions posted to e-PIC; Daniel Wall, "Taseko Mine Hearings Biased Says Councillor," *Williams Lake Advocate,* 24 March 1998, CCA-M; "Chamber Calls for Open Hearings," *Williams Lake Advocate,* 24 March 1998, CCA-M. Agreeing to disagree: "Mine Plan at Fish Lake Seen as Stumbling Block," *Williams Lake Tribune,* 7 April 1998, CCA-M; "Mine Review Goes On," *Williams Lake Tribune,* 16 April 1998, CCA-M; Sven McGirr, "Taseko Gets Good News," *Williams Lake Advocate,* 21 April 1998, CCA-M. Blaming the feds: "Rare Chance at Economic Upswing," *Advisor,* 25 November 1998, CCA-M; "Mine Boss Lays Blame," *Williams Lake Tribune,* 26 November 1998, CCA-M.

25 TML, "Prosperity Project Update," *Weekender,* 28 March 1999, CCA-M; TML, "Form 20-F," 17 February 1999 (available from SEDAR); Prosperity Project Committee, "Prosperity Gold-Copper Project: Project Report Specifications," (report prepared for Environmental Assessment Office), April 1998, posted to e-PIC.

26 Design of mine/mill complex: TML, "Form 20-F," 17 February 1999 (available from SEDAR).

27 Power: "Power Cheaper in the States," *Williams Lake Tribune,* 17 March 1998, CCA-M; quotation from "Taseko Mines and BC Government Sign Cooperative Resource Development Protocol," 15 December 1998, SEDAR; Ken Fisher, "Power Agreement Will Help Prosperity Project Proposal," *Williams Lake Tribune,* 31 December 1998, CCA-M.

28 Multiple account evaluation: TML, "Prosperity Project Update," *Weekender,* 28 March 1999, CCA-M; TML, "Form 20-F," 17 February 1999 (available from SEDAR).

29 Claims of Tsilhqot'in: "New Compensation Guidelines Are Concern for Taseko Mines," *Williams Lake Tribune,* 6 April 1999, CCA-M; "William on Committee," *Williams Lake Tribune,* 6 April 1999, CCA-M; Roger William, "Taseko Story is Clarified," *Williams Lake Tribune,* 22 April 1999, CCA-M. TML chooses original design: Louisa Chapman, "Prosperity Project Option Identified," *Mining Week,* 11 May 1999, CCA-M.

30 Environmental Mining Council of BC, "Acid Mine Drainage: Ming and Water Pollution Issues in BC" (Victoria: Environmental Council of BC, 1997); Environmental Mining Council of BC, "Mining in Remote Areas: Issues and Impacts," (Victoria: Author, 1998); Environmental Mining Council of BC, "More Precious than Gold"; Environmental Mining Council of BC, "Undermining the Law: Addressing the Crisis in Compliance with Environmental Mining Laws in BC" (Victoria: Author, 2001); E.C. Pielou, *Fresh Water* (Chicago: University of Chicago Press, 1998); TML, "Form 20-F," 17 February 1999 (available from SEDAR).

31 Turner quote: "WWF Canada Withdraws Court Action on BHP Diamond Mine," *Canada NewsWire,* 13 January 1997. The website for the museum is http://www.bcmuseumofmining.org. Acid mine discharge: *DuT,* 2-3, 24-26.

32 Rethinking government: Sierra Legal Defence Fund, "False Economy: The Hidden Future Costs of Cuts in Regulatory Services" (Vancouver: Sierra Legal Defence Fund, 2002). Additional information: Sheila Wynn, "Transition Order #02-12," 30 December 2002, posted on e-PIC.

33 TML, "Annual Information Form," 17 February 2003 (available from SEDAR).

34 C.S. Peirce, "Logic as Semiotic: The Theory of Signs," in *Philosophical Writings of Peirce,* ed. Justus Buchler (New York: Dover, 1955), 105-6; Daniel Defoe, *Robinson Crusoe* (New York: W.W. Norton, 1994), 74 (grapes), 112 (footprint).

35 Karl Marx, *Capital* (New York: Penguin, 1990), 1:169-72. Division of labour: Adam Smith, *An Inquiry into the Nature and Causes of the Wealth of Nations* (Chicago: University of Chicago Press, 1976).

36 Symptoms and spoor: Carlo Ginzburg, "Clues: Roots of an Evidential Paradigm," in *Clues, Myths and the Historical Method* (Baltimore: Johns Hopkins University Press, 1989).

37 Cf. Bruno Latour, *Science in Action: How to Follow Scientists and Engineers through Society* (Cambridge, MA: Harvard University Press, 1987) and Bruno Latour, "Visualization and Cognition: Thinking with Eyes and Hands," *Knowledge and Society: Studies in the Sociology of Culture Past and Present* 6 (1986): 1-40.

38 Academic funding: Natural Sciences and Engineering Research Council of Canada, "Discovery Grants Awarded by Grant Selection Committee," 2002, http://www.nserc.ca/about/stats/2001-2002/en/tables/table_42e.htm. $1.25 phone call: Bill Phillips, "Taseko Mines Plays Waiting Game," *Williams Lake Tribune,* 30 May 1995, CCA-M.

39 John W. Dower, "Three Narratives of Our Humanity," in *History Wars: The Enola Gay and Other Battles for the American Past,* ed. Edward T. Linenthal and Tom Engelhardt (New York: Henry Holt, 1996), 90.

40 The original paper is Ronald H. Coase, "The Problem of Social Cost," *Journal of Law and Economics* 3 (1960): 1-44. For explorations of the idea, see Yoram Barzel, *Economic Analysis of Property Rights* (Cambridge: Cambridge University Press, 1989); Ronald H. Coase, "The Institutional Structure of Production (1991 Alfred Nobel Memorial Lecture in Economic Sciences)," in *Essays on Economics and Economists* (Chicago: University of Chicago Press, 1994), 3-14; Nicholas Mercuro and Steven G. Medema, "Chicago Law and Economics," chap. 2 in *Economics and the Law: From Posner to Post-Modernism* (Princeton, NJ: Princeton University Press, 1997), 51-83; Eirik G. Furubotn and Rudolf Richter, "Absolute Property Rights: Ownership of Physical Objects," chap. 3 in *Institutions and Economic Theory: The Contribution of the New Institutional Economics* (Ann Arbor: University of Michigan Press, 1997), 69-120.

41 Definition of environmental history: See, for example, Richard White, *Land Use, Environment, and Social Change: The Shaping of Island County, Washington* (Seattle: University of Washington Press, 1992), 5-7; William Cronon, *Changes in the Land: Indians, Colonists, and the Ecology of New England* (New York: Hill and Wang, 1983), 13-14. The activities of archaeologists and the oral traditions of Aboriginal people are the subject of Part 2.

42 The adjustment of scale as an analytical procedure is one characteristic of microhistory: Giovanni Levi, "On Microhistory," in *New Perspectives on Historical Writing,* ed. Peter Burke (University Park, PA: Penn State University Press, 1991), 93-113. "World in general": Clifford Geertz, "Afterword," in *Senses of Place,* ed., Steven Feld and Keith H. Basso (Santa Fe, NM: School of American Research Press, 1996), 262.

CHAPTER 3: MACKENZIE

1 Dog Husband: Livingston Farrand, *Publications of the Jesup North Pacific Expedition,* vol. 2(1), *Traditions of the Chilcotin Indians,* ed. Franz Boas (New York: American Museum of Natural History, 1990); Robert Lane, "Cultural Relations of the Chilcotin Indians of West Central British Columbia" (PhD dissertation, University of Washington, 1953); David W. Dinwoodie, *Reserve Memories: The Power of the Past in a Chilcotin Community* (Lincoln: University of Nebraska Press, 2002); Claude Lévi-Strauss, *The Story of Lynx* (Chicago: University of Chicago Press, 1995), chap. 14. According to Xeni Gwet'in elders: BC Parks, Cariboo District, *Tŝ'il?os Provincial Park Master Plan* (Victoria: BC Parks, 1997). Transformers and myth time in the oral traditions of interior people: Andrea Laforet and Annie York, *Spuzzum: Fraser Canyon Histories, 1809-1939* (Vancouver: UBC Press, 1998); Darwin Hanna and Mamie Henry, eds., *Our Tellings: Interior Salish Stories of the Nlha7kapmx People* (Vancouver: UBC Press, 1995). Traces in the landscape: cf. Keith H. Basso, *Wisdom Sits in Places: Landscape and Language among the Western Apache* (Albuquerque: University of New Mexico Press, 1996); Hugh Brody, *Maps and Dreams* (New York: Pantheon, 1981).

2 Tractor-style steam engine: Franz Klingender, "Tractors: From Unfamiliar Oddity to Commonplace Tool" (Ottawa: Canada Agriculture Museum, 2002). Arthur Knoll: Terry George, comp., *History and Legends of the Chilcotin* (Williams Lake, BC: Cariboo Press, [1958]), 5; Veera Bonner, Irene E. Bliss, and Hazel Henry Litterick, eds., *Chilcotin: Preserving Pioneer Memories* (Surrey, BC: Heritage House, 1995), 213, 242 (picture), 320. Material culture of log buildings and fences in interior BC: Donovan

Clemson, *Living with Logs: British Columbia's Log Buildings and Rail Fences* (Saanich-ton, BC: Hancock House, 1974); Donovan Clemson "Pioneer Fences," in *Pioneer Days in British Columbia,* ed. Art Downs (Surrey, BC: Heritage House, 1975), 26-31. Cattle drive: Norman Lee, *Klondike Cattle Drive: The Journal of Norman Lee* (Van-couver: Mitchell Press, 1960), 23 (illustration of the brand). Brands: Richard William Blacklaws and Diana French, *Ranchland: British Columbia's Cattle Country* (Madeira Park, BC: Harbour, 2001), 30; Ownership Identification Incorporated, "How to Read a Brand," http://www.ownership-id.com/article_reading_brands.php. Plaque: Bonner, Bliss, and Litterick, *Chilcotin,* 137 (photograph).

3 Fladmark, *British Columbia Prehistory,* 11; Elizabeth Furniss, "The Early Culture of the Southern Carrier" (manuscript, X̱wi7x̱wa Library, UBC, 1991), 7. Ranching industry: John Lutz, "Interlude or Industry? Ranching in British Columbia, 1859-1885," *BC Historical News* 13, 4 (1980): 2-11; Blacklaws and French, *Ranchland.*

4 William Lyon Mackenzie King, speech to the Canadian House of Commons, 18 June 1936.

5 Alexander Mackenzie, *Journal of a Voyage to the Pacific* (New York: Dover, 1995), 159-69; Ethelbert Olaf Stuart Scholefield, "Sir Alexander Mackenzie," chap. 9 of *British Columbia from the Earliest Times* (Vancouver: S.J. Clarke, 1914), 1:199-233; Walter Sheppe, "Mackenzie's Route," appendix 2 of Mackenzie, *Journal,* 314-36. Favourite project: Alexander Mackenzie, *Voyages from Montreal: On the River St. Laurence, through the Continent of North America, to the Frozen and Pacific Oceans, in the Years 1789 and 1793* (London, 1801), iv (available from Canadiana.org, formerly the Canad-ian Institute for Historical Microreproductions, CIHM 33950). Fur-trading concern: Barry M. Gough, *Distant Dominion: Britain and the Northwest Coast of North Amer-ica, 1579-1809* (Vancouver: UBC Press, 1980), 135-45; Barry M. Gough, *First across the Continent: Sir Alexander Mackenzie* (Norman: University of Oklahoma Press, 1997), 171-72.

6 Advantages and drawbacks: Gough, *First across the Continent,* 123. Aboriginal groups along the river were Secwepemc (Shuswap), Stl'atl'imx (Lillooet), and Nlaka'pamux (Thompson): M. Dale Kinkade et al., "Languages," in *Handbook of North American Indians,* vol. 12, *Plateau,* ed. Deward E. Walker Jr. (Washington, DC: Smithsonian Institution, 1988), 49-72. State of geographical knowledge in Mackenzie's time: William H. Goetzmann and Glyndwr Williams, *The Atlas of North American Exploration: From the Norse Voyages to the Race to the Pole* (Norman: University of Oklahoma Press, 1992); Derek Hayes, *Historical Atlas of British Columbia and the Pacific Northwest: Maps of Exploration; British Columbia, Washington, Oregon, Alaska, Yukon* (Vancouver: Cavendish, 1998); Richard I. Ruggles, *A Country So Interesting: The Hudson's Bay Com-pany and Two Centuries of Mapping, 1670-1870* (Montreal and Kingston: McGill-Queen's University Press, 1991). Retrograde motion: Mackenzie, *Journal,* 163, 164. The Tacoutche Tesse did not turn out to be the river that we now know as the Columbia but rather the one that we call the Fraser. Its mouth is a little north of the 49th parallel.

7 Unsure of position: Mackenzie, *Journal,* 160; Frank C. Swannell, "Mackenzie's Expe-dition to the Pacific Ocean, 1793," in *Report of Proceedings of the 23rd Annual General Meeting* ([Victoria?]: Corporation of BC Land Surveyors, 1928), 42-47. Principal cir-cumstances: Mackenzie, *Journal,* 166; Gough, *First across the Continent,* 139.

8 The analysis of the encounter between Mackenzie and the Aboriginal people closely follows Bruno Latour's analysis of the meeting between La Pérouse and the Chinese

of Sakhalin in his "Visualization and Cognition: Thinking with Eyes and Hands," *Knowledge and Society: Studies in the Sociology of Culture Past and Present* 6 (1986): 3-4, and in chap. 6 of Latour's *Science in Action: How to Follow Scientists and Engineers through Society* (Cambridge, MA: Harvard University Press, 1987). Aboriginal mapmaking abilities and the importance of Aboriginal maps to the newcomers: G. Malcolm Lewis, "Indian Maps," in *Old Trails and New Directions: Papers of the Third North American Fur Trade Conference,* ed. Carol M. Judd and Arthur J. Ray (Toronto: University of Toronto Press, 1978); D. Wayne Moodie, "Indian Maps," plate 59 of R. Cole Harris, ed., *Historical Atlas of Canada,* vol. 1, *From the Beginning to 1800* (Toronto: University of Toronto Press, 1987); Ruggles, *A Country So Interesting;* Theodore Binnema, *Common and Contested Ground: A Human and Environmental History of the Northwestern Plains* (Norman: University of Oklahoma Press, 2001). Geographical knowledge of Dene: Robin Ridington, "Technology, World View and Adaptive Strategy in a Northern Hunting Society," in *Little Bit Know Something: Stories in a Language of Anthropology* (Iowa City: University of Iowa Press, 1990), 84-99; Brody, *Maps and Dreams;* Basso, *Wisdom Sits in Places;* Renée Fossett, "Mapping Inuktut: Inuit Views of the Real World," in *Reading beyond Words: Contexts for Native History,* ed. Jennifer S.H. Brown and Elizabeth Vibert (Peterborough, ON: Broadview, 1996), 74-94. Mackenzie's training in surveying: Gough, *First across the Continent,* 99-102; Swannell, "Mackenzie's Expedition."

9   Practices of reading, writing, and calculating among the fur traders: Arthur J. Ray and Donald Freeman, "The Early Hudson's Bay Company Account Books," chap. 9 in *"Give Us Good Measure": An Economic Analysis of Relations between Indians and the Hudson's Bay Company before 1763* (Toronto: University of Toronto Press, 1978), 81-119; Michael Payne and Gregory Thomas, "Literacy, Literature and Libraries in the Fur Trade," *The Beaver* 63 (1983): 46-53. Celestial navigation in Mackenzie's time: Robert Mentzer, "Jupiter's Moons and the Longitude Problem," *Mercury* 31, 3 (2002): 34; Richard Sorrenson, "The Ship as a Scientific Instrument in the Eighteenth Century," *Osiris,* 2nd ser., 11 (1996): 221-36. Maps as immutable mobiles: Latour, *Science in Action.*

10 Biases of maps: Mark Monmonier, *How to Lie with Maps* (Chicago: University of Chicago Press, 1996); J. Brian Harley, "Rereading Maps of the Columbian Encounter," *Annals of the Association of American Geographers* 82, 3 (1992): 522-36; Ken G. Brealey, "Mapping Them 'Out': Euro-Canadian Cartography and the Appropriation of the Nuxalk and Tŝ'ilhqot'in First Nations' Territories, 1793-1916," *Canadian Geographer* 39, 2 (1995): 140-56.

11 Mackenzie, *Journal,* 160-62.

12 Lieutenant: Mackenzie, *Journal,* 169; Ramsay Cook et al., eds., *Dictionary of Canadian Biography,* 14 vols. (Toronto: University of Toronto Press, 1966-98), s.v., "MacKay, Alexander" (available online at http://www.biographi.ca/EN/index.html). Headed back: Mackenzie, *Journal,* 179-80, 183, 185-86.

13 Arrowsmith map, editions of 1790s: Aaron Arrowsmith, *Chart of the World on Mercator's Projection, Exhibiting All the New Discoveries to the Present Time ...* (London: A. Arrowsmith, 1790), BC Archives (hereafter cited as BCA) CM/X12; Hayes, *Historical Atlas,* 57 (reproduction of Northwest Coast portion), 97 (reproduction of a portion); Aaron Arrowsmith, [Untitled map], 1794, updated to 1798, BCA. Later editions: A. Farley, "The Historical Cartography of British Columbia" (PhD dissertation, University of Wisconsin, 1960); Ruggles, *A Country So Interesting;* C. Verner, "The Arrowsmith

Firm and the Cartography of Canada," in *Explorations in the History of Canadian Mapping*, ed. B. Farrell and A. Desbarats (Ottawa: Association of Canadian Map Libraries and Archives, 1988), 47-54. Symbolic assertion of sovereignty: Brealey, "Mapping Them 'Out'" (includes reproduction of portions of 1801 and 1824 editions).

14 Douglas Cole and Bradley Lockner, eds., *The Journals of George M. Dawson: British Columbia, 1875-1876* (Vancouver: UBC Press, 1989), 1:32-40.

15 Sandford Fleming, *Report on Surveys and Preliminary Operations on the Canadian Pacific Railway up to January 1877* (Ottawa: MacLean, Roger and Company, 1877), 12-35. Later surveyors: Richard Preston Bishop, *Mackenzie's Rock* (Ottawa: Department of the Interior, 1924); Swannell, "Mackenzie's Expedition"; Frank C. Swannell, "On Mackenzie's Trail," *The Beaver* Outfit 289, 18 (1958): 9-14; Parks Canada, ARC Branch, Planning Division, "Alexander Mackenzie Historic Trail: Preliminary Development Concept" (Ottawa: Department of Indian and Northern Affairs, 1976), note 14, Cariboo-Chilcotin Archives, box on the Mackenzie Grease Trail (hereafter cited as CCA-G). Sheppe: Sheppe, "Mackenzie's Route," 319-36.

16 Parks Canada, "Preliminary Development Concept," 3, 5, CCA-G.

17 John Woodworth: "Seven Year Lobby Effort Pays Off," *Central Okanagan Capital News*, 22 November 1980, BCA D19-002; Brian Bergman, "A River of Destiny: Mackenzie's Arctic Voyage Still Disturbs Natives," *Maclean's*, 6 July 1992; Flygares: John Woodworth and Hälle Flygare, *In the Steps of Alexander Mackenzie*, 2nd ed. (Kelowna, BC: Alexander Mackenzie Trail Association, 1987), 191; John Woodworth, "Show Us Where Mackenzie Walked," *BC Historical News* 26, 2 (1993): 2-4.

18 Woodworth and Flygare, *In the Steps*, 37. Walter Sheppe could not find the beginning of Mackenzie's trail in 1959 either. See Sheppe, "Mackenzie's Route," 333.

19 Mackenzie, *Journal*, 186-88. Pièces: Grace Lee Nute, *The Voyageur* (St. Paul: Minnesota Historical Society, 1955), 38; Eric Ross, *Beyond the River and the Bay: Some Observations on the State of the Canadian Northwest in 1811 with a View to Providing the Intending Settler with an Intimate Knowledge of That Country* (Toronto: University of Toronto Press, 1970), 56. Voyageur status: Carolyn Podruchny, *Making the Voyageur World: Travelers and Traders in the North American Fur Trade* (Toronto: University of Toronto Press, 2006), 13, 153, 184-87.

20 Signs of extensive trade: Mackenzie, *Journal*, 188-190. Captain Cook: Philip Edwards, ed., *The Journals of Captain Cook* (London: Penguin, 1999), 538-47; Nicholas Thomas, *Cook: The Extraordinary Voyages of Captain James Cook* (New York: Walker and Company, 2004). Maritime fur trade: James R. Gibson, *Otter Skins, Boston Ships, and China Goods: The Maritime Fur Trade of the Northwest Coast, 1785-1841* (Montreal and Kingston: McGill-Queen's University Press, 1991); Robin Fisher, *Contact and Conflict: Indian-European Relations in British Columbia, 1774-1890*, 2nd ed. (Vancouver: UBC Press, 1992), 1-23.

21 Looting: F.W. Howay, "An Outline Sketch of the Maritime Fur Trade," in *Canadian Historical Association, Annual Report, 1932* (Toronto: Canadian Historical Association, 1932), 14. Aboriginal trading skill: Fisher, *Contact and Conflict*, chap. 1. Products: Gibson, *Otter Skins*, 9. Slavery: Leland Donald, *Aboriginal Slavery on the Northwest Coast of North America* (Berkeley: University of California Press, 1997). No one has yet made a really good map of the trade routes and products of the interior Aboriginal trails, but the complexity of the system can be readily inferred from archaeological evidence and Aboriginal oral tradition. Some partial maps of the relevant trade routes

are Harris, *Historical Atlas*, plates 13, 14; Helen Hornbeck Tanner, ed., *The Settling of North America: The Atlas of the Great Migrations into North America from the Ice Age to the Present* (New York: Macmillan, 1995), 28-29; William R. Swagerty, "Indian Trade in the Trans-Mississippi West to 1870," in *Handbook of North American Indians*, vol. 4, *History of Indian-White Relations*, ed. Wilcomb E. Washburn (Washington, DC: Smithsonian Institution, 1988), 352, fig. 1; Arnould H. Stryd and Mike K. Rousseau, "Early Prehistory of the Mid Fraser-Thompson River Area," in *Early Human Occupation in British Columbia*, ed. Roy L. Carlson and Luke Dalla Bona (Vancouver: UBC Press, 1996), 178, fig. 1; Sage Birchwater, *Ulkatcho: Stories of the Grease Trail* (Anahim Lake, BC: Ulkatcho Indian Band, 1993), 3.

22 Further Aboriginal products: Harris, *Historical Atlas*, plate 13; Gibson, *Otter Skins*, 10. Products of newcomers: Gibson, *Otter Skins*, chap. 8. Hawaiian feather caps and cloaks: Mary Malloy, *Souvenirs of the Fur Trade: Northwest Coast Indian Art and Artifacts Collected by American Mariners, 1788-1844* (Cambridge, MA: Peabody Museum of Harvard University, 2000), 48. Changing supply, demand, and fashions in the fur trade: Arthur J. Ray, *Indians in the Fur Trade: Their Role as Trappers, Hunters, and Middlemen in the Lands Southwest of Hudson Bay, 1660-1870* (Toronto: University of Toronto Press, 1998); Arthur J. Ray, "Indians as Consumers in the Eighteenth Century," in *Old Trails and New Directions: Papers of the Third North American Fur Trade Conference*, ed. Carol M. Judd and Arthur J. Ray (Toronto: University of Toronto Press, 1978), 255-71; Shepard Krech III, ed., *The Subarctic Fur Trade: Native Social and Economic Adaptations* (Vancouver: UBC Press, 1984). Art objects created for trade: Malloy, *Souvenirs*.

23 Kenneth F. Kiple, ed., *The Cambridge World History of Human Disease* (Cambridge: Cambridge University Press, 1993); Robert Boyd, *The Coming of the Spirit of Pestilence: Introduced Infectious Diseases and Population Decline among Northwest Coast Indians, 1774-1874* (Vancouver: UBC Press, 1999); Robert Boyd, "Demographic History, 1774-1874," in *Handbook of North American Indians*, vol. 7, *Northwest Coast*, ed. Wayne Suttles (Washington, DC: Smithsonian Institution, 1990), 135-48; Alfred W. Crosby, "Virgin Soil Epidemics as a Factor in the Aboriginal Depopulation of America," *William and Mary Quarterly* 33, 2 (1976): 290-99; Alfred W. Crosby, *Ecological Imperialism: The Biological Expansion of Europe, 900-1900* (Cambridge: Cambridge University Press, 1993).

24 Sickly appearance: Mackenzie, *Journal*, 193-94. Indolence: Elizabeth Vibert, *Traders' Tales: Narratives of Cultural Encounter on the Columbia Plateau, 1807-1846* (Norman: University of Oklahoma Press, 1997), 120-31 (quote from 120). Carrying old woman: Mackenzie, *Journal*, 193.

25 BC Forest Service, "Hiking Trails: Blackwater Canyon" (brochure).

26 Wagon road and mileposts: Richmond Pearson Hobson Jr., *Grass beyond the Mountains: Discovering the Last Great Cattle Frontier on the North American Continent* (Toronto: McClelland and Stewart, 1987), 127; Woodworth and Flygare, *In the Steps*, 21, 29, 42, 44, 58; Birchwater, *Ulkatcho*, 21; Woodworth, "Show Us." Telegraph news of gold rush: "Telegraph Line to the Yukon," *New York Times*, 10 August 1897; *New York Times*, 7 March 1899; "Telegraph Line to Dawson," *Canadian Telegraphic*, 18 March 1899; "Yukon Telegraph Circuit Completed," *Canadian Telegraphic*, 25 September 1901. Pack trains: Lee, *Klondike Cattle Drive*, 4.

27 CPR survey: Cole and Lockner, *Journals of George M. Dawson*, 1:92; Marcus Smith,

"Report on the Surveys in British Columbia during the Year 1875," in Fleming, *Report on Surveys,* appendix I, 162-76. Dr. Alfred R.C. Selwyn, director of the Geological Survey and Dawson's superior, also visited Blackwater Bridge in 1875 and made some photographs of the bridge and the canyon: Library and Archives Canada PA-051022, PA-037525, and PA-037524. Dawson: Cole and Lockner, *Journals of George M. Dawson,* 1:200-2 (quote from 202). Collins telegraph: Jean Barman, *The West beyond the West: A History of British Columbia* (Toronto: University of Toronto Press, 1991), 86-87.

28 Woodworth and Flygare, *In the Steps,* 46-47, 53, 55, 57-60; Parks Canada, "Preliminary Development Concept," 18, CCA-G.

29 Basins: Mackenzie, *Journal,* 196. Glacial kettles: Woodworth, "Show Us"; Centre for Topographic Information, Pelican Lake [Map 1:50,000], 2nd ed., NTS 093G05 (Ottawa: Natural Resources Canada, 1984); E.C. Pielou, *After the Ice Age: The Return of Life to Glaciated North America* (Chicago: University of Chicago Press, 1991), 23, 109. Wagon roads: Woodworth and Flygare, *In the Steps,* 21, 58, 63. Population: Parks Canada, "Preliminary Development Concept," 20, CCA-G.

30 Woodworth and Flygare, *In the Steps,* 64; Mackenzie, *Journal,* 196, 197.

31 Re-live travels: Alexander Mackenzie Heritage Trail Coordinating Committee, "Alexander Mackenzie Heritage Trail: Management Plan for Trail Portions on Public Forest Lands" (Williams Lake, BC: Author, 1993), 28. Regional ecology: BC Ministry of Forests, Research Branch, "Biogeoclimatic Zones of British Columbia" [Map, 1:2,000,000] (Victoria: Government of BC, 1999); Idem, "The Ecology of the Sub-Boreal Spruce Zone" (Victoria: Government of BC, 1998); Idem, "The Ecology of the Engelmann Spruce – Subalpine Fir Zone" (Victoria: Government of BC, 1998); Idem, "The Ecology of the Sub-Boreal Pine – Spruce Zone" (Victoria: Government of BC, 1998); Dellis Vern Meidinger and Jim Pojar, eds., *Ecosystems of British Columbia,* Special Report Series No. 6 (Victoria: BC Ministry of Forests, 1991). Flooding: Woodworth and Flygare, *In the Steps,* 91. Cattle and horses: Parks Canada, "Preliminary Development Concept," 17, CCA-G. The introduction of horses and cattle to the region is discussed in Part 3.

32 Woodworth and Flygare, *In the Steps,* 66-67, 72, 74, 75, 79.

33 Mackenzie, *Journal,* 196-99.

34 Mackenzie, *Journal,* 199. More recent signs of forest fires: Woodworth and Flygare, *In the Steps,* 97, 111. Fire ecology: E.C. Pielou, *The World of the Northern Evergreens* (Ithaca, NY: Cornell University Press, 1998), 116-23; BC Ministry of Forests, Research Branch, "Ecology of the Sub-Boreal Spruce Zone"; Idem, "Ecology of the Sub-Boreal Pine – Spruce Zone." Aboriginal burning practices: Carmen Wong, "Natural Disturbance Regimes in the Cariboo Region: What Is Known to Guide Forest Management?" (Williams Lake, BC: Lignum Ltd., 2000); Applied Ecosystem Management, "Characterising Fire Regimes in Sub-Boreal Landscapes: Fire History Research in SBPS and SBS Biogeoclimatic Zones of the Cariboo Forest Region" (Williams Lake, BC: Lignum Ltd., 2002); Kristi E. Iverson et al., "Past Fire Regimes in the Interior Douglas-fir, Dry Cool Subzone, Fraser Variant (IDFdk3)" (Williams Lake, BC: Lignum Ltd., 2002); H.T. Lewis and Theresa A. Ferguson, "Yards, Corridors and Mosaics: How to Burn a Boreal Forest," *Human Ecology* 16 (1988): 57-77; Stephen J. Pyne, *Fire in America: A Cultural History of Wildland and Rural Fire* (Seattle: University of Washington Press, 1997).

35 Mackenzie, *Journal,* 200-1; Woodworth and Flygare, *In the Steps,* 94-96, 101. There's

a photograph of the airstrip signs on the cover of Jack Brown and Darlene Brown's *The Legend of Pan Phillips* (Victoria: Morriss Publishing, 1988). View from float plane: Tom Stienstra, "Floatplane Venture Affords Wondrous Vision of Nature," *Examiner* (San Francisco), 21 August 1994. View from ground: Woodworth and Flygare, *In the Steps*, 16.

36 Hobson, *Grass beyond the Mountains*, 15-16.

37 Cattle ranching: BC Department of Lands, "Grazing Possibilities of British Columbia," Land Series Bulletin 4 (Victoria: BC Department of Lands, 1924), University of BC Koerner Library, Microfilm AW1.R7550; Thomas R. Weir, "The Winter Feeding Period in the Southern Interior Plateau of British Columbia," *Annals of the Association of American Geographers* 44, 2 (1954): 194-204; BC Ministry of Agriculture and Food, "Agriculture in the Cariboo-Chilcotin" (Victoria: BC Ministry of Agriculture and Food, 1999); Clayton W. Campbell and Alfred H. Bawtree, eds., *Rangeland Handbook for BC* (Kamloops: BC Cattlemen's Association, 1998); Blacklaws and French, *Ranchland*. Phillips ranch: Woodworth and Flygare, *In the Steps*, 103-6; Brown and Brown, *Legend of Pan Phillips;* Hobson, *Grass beyond the Mountains*.

38 Woodworth and Flygare, *In the Steps*, 97, 106-8.

39 Puzzling direction: Mackenzie, *Journal*, 201-5; Dawson, "Report on Explorations in BC, Chiefly in the Basins of the Blackwater, Salmon, and Nechacco Rivers, and on Francois Lake" (n.p.: Geological Survey of Canada, 1877), 25; Centre for Topographic Information, Bella Coola [Map 1:250,000], 2nd ed., NTS 93D (Ottawa: Natural Resources Canada, 1989), and Anahim Lake [Map 1:250,000], 3rd ed., NTS 93C (Ottawa: Natural Resources Canada, 1989); Alexander Mackenzie Heritage Trail Coordinating Committee, "Management Plan"; Woodworth and Flygare, *In the Steps*, 9.

40 Mackenzie, *Journal*, 205-11; Gough, *First across the Continent*, 141; Woodworth and Flygare, *In the Steps*, 9.

41 Mackenzie, *Journal*, 212-13; Gough, *First across the Continent*, 143. Dangerous for hikers: Woodworth and Flygare, *In the Steps*, 21, 124, 157, 162.

42 Mackenzie, *Journal*, 213-39.

43 Bishop, *Mackenzie's Rock*. Early twentieth century uncertainty about rock's exact location: John T. Walbran, *British Columbia Coast Names: Their Origin and History* (Vancouver: Douglas and McIntyre, 1971), s.v., "Cascade Inlet."

44 Plaque: M.H. Long, "The Historic Sites and Monuments Board of Canada (Presidential Address)," in *Canadian Historical Association Report of the Annual Meeting* (n.p.: Canadian Historical Association, 1954), 1-11; Woodworth and Flygare, *In the Steps*, 6 (photo). Call for creation of monument: M.S. Wade, *Mackenzie of Canada: The Life and Adventure of Alexander Mackenzie, Discoverer* (Edinburgh: W. Blackwood, 1927). Correspondence: Letter from B.F. Jacobsen to Judge Howay, 6 April 1926, Philip and Helen Akrigg Fonds, Box 3, File 37, Xerox 213, University of BC Special Collections; Gough, *First across the Continent*, 153-54. Photographs: Gough, *First across the Continent*, 38; BCA A-02313 (ca. 1927); NA-04372 (1930); NA-13124 (1952); and I-05474 through I-05478 (1980).

45 Woodworth, "Show Us." Canadian coat of arms: Canadian Heritage, "Ceremonial and Canadian Symbols Promotion," http://www.pch.gc.ca/progs/cpsc-ccsp/index_e.cfm.

46 "Cause of Canadian unity": Alexander Mackenzie Voyageur Route Association, http://www.amvr.org; "John Woodworth to Receive Gabrielle Leger Award," *Canada News Wire*, 18 September 1995; Heritage Canada, "Heritage Day," http://www.heritagecanada.org/eng/h_day.html; David Crary, "By a Whisker Canada Survives, but Quebec Faces

Divisive Days," Associated Press, 31 October 1995. Phoning: "Perseverance Pays Off for Heritage-Award Winner," *Canadian Press Newswire,* 8 October 1995.

47 Tracey Tyler, "Forty Students to Relive Adventures of Explorer," *Toronto Star,* 19 February 1988; Lynn Hancock, "Bicentennial Recreates Voyages of Mackenzie," *Toronto Star,* 8 July 1989.

48 Pierre Berton, "May We Only Celebrate History's Nice Guys?" *Toronto Star,* 16 November 1991.

49 Oolichan Festival: "Column One," *Vancouver Sun,* 10 April 1993. Cattle drive: Bev Christensen, "BC Cattle Drive Will Be Rugged for Horses, Riders," *Calgary Herald,* 4 April 1992.

50 Blocked at Alexandria: Jerry Macdonald, "Second Coming of Mackenzie a Dream Come True," *Vancouver Sun,* 24 July 1993. Durieu system: Margaret Mary Whitehead, *The Cariboo Mission: A History of the Oblates* (Victoria: Sono Nis, 1981); Margaret Mary Whitehead, *Sound Heritage,* vol. 34, *Now You Are My Brother: Missionaries in British Columbia* (Victoria: Provincial Archives of BC, 1981); Margaret Mary Whitehead, ed., *They Call Me Father: Memoirs of Father Nicholas Coccola* (Vancouver: UBC Press, 1988); David Mulhall, *Will to Power: The Missionary Career of Father Morice* (Vancouver: UBC Press, 1986); J.R. Miller, "Reading Photographs, Reading Voices: Documenting the History of Native Residential Schools," in Brown and Vibert, *Reading beyond Words,* 461-81; Elizabeth Furniss, *Victims of Benevolence: The Dark Legacy of the Williams Lake Residential School* (Vancouver: Arsenal Pulp, 1995). The Durieu system is discussed in more detail in Chapter 6. Alexandria band: G.P.V. Akrigg and Helen B. Akrigg, *British Columbia Place Names,* 3rd ed.(Vancouver: UBC Press, 1997), 4; Canada, Department of Indian Affairs and Northern Development, "First Nation Profiles: Alexandria," http://pse2-esd2.ainc-inac.gc.ca/FNProfiles/ FNProfiles_home.htm. Highway 20: Jerry Macdonald, "True Patriot Shove," *Vancouver Sun,* 11 August 1993.

51 Macdonald, "True Patriot Shove."

52 Other commemorative flops: Peter E. Pope, *The Many Landfalls of John Cabot* (Toronto: University of Toronto Press, 1997); Norman Knowles, *Inventing the Loyalists: The Ontario Loyalist Tradition and the Creation of Usable Pasts* (Toronto: University of Toronto Press, 1997). Oolichan Festival: Macdonald, "Second Coming" and "True Patriot Shove."

53 BC, Legislative Assembly, *Official Report of the Debates of the Legislative Assembly (Hansard),* vol. 10, 12 (28 May 1993), 6603-5 (Paul Ramsey and Cliff Serwa, MLAs); [John Woodworth], "After the Re-enactments," *BC Historical News* 27, 1 (1993/94): 15-17.

54 National anthem: Canadian Heritage, "Ceremonial and Canadian Symbols Promotion." The corresponding line in the (original) French version of the national anthem refers to "terre de nos aïeux" (literally "land of our forefathers / ancestors"), which doesn't have the same connotations of naturalness, innateness, or indigenousness as "native land." Standard tablet design: Long, "Historic Sites and Monuments Board of Canada." "Principal races" quote: Bishop, *Mackenzie's Rock,* 31.

55 Changing sensibilities: Anthony H. Richmond, "Immigration and Pluralism in Canada," *International Migration Review* 4, 1 (1969): 7; Canada, *The Charter of Rights and Freedoms: A Guide for Canadians* (Ottawa: Supply and Services, 1982). Change in census categories: K.G. Basavarajappa and Dali Ram, "Origins of the Population,

Census Dates, 1871 to 1971," in *Historical Statistics of Canada,* Section A, *Population and Migration,* ed. F.H. Leacy (Ottawa: Statistics Canada, 1999), A125-163; Statistics Canada, "1996 Census: Ethnic Origin, Visible Minorities" (Ottawa: Author, 1998).

56 Bishop, *Mackenzie's Rock,* 8-9.

57 Correcting Ambrose: John Woodworth, "Across the Great Divide," *Newsweek,* 28 October 1996. Lakehead students misidentified: Macdonald, "True Patriot Shove." More extreme comparisons: Donald Jones, "He Was the First to Cross the Rockies to the Pacific," *Toronto Star,* 10 June 1989; Bruce Cole, "On the Trail with Lewis and Clark: A Conversation with Gary Moulton," *Humanities* (National Endowment for the Humanities) (November-December 2002): http://www.neh.gov/news/humanities/2002-11/contents.html; Stephen Hume, "Lionized US Explorers Were Also-Rans at Charting the Continent," *Vancouver Sun,* 10 May 2003; Stephen Hume, "Canadian Explorers Blazed a Trail: Lewis and Clark Also-Rans," *Edmonton Journal,* 18 May 2003; Stephen Hume, "Lewis and Clark Were Latecomers," *Ottawa Citizen,* 18 May 2003.

58 On reification: "Alterations to the past ... affect those who make them. They run counter to desires for a fixed and stable heritage and undermine our role as its continuators." David Lowenthal, *The Past Is a Foreign Country* (Cambridge: Cambridge University Press, 1985), xxiv.

CHAPTER 4: GREASE TRAILS

1 Sage Birchwater, *Ulkatcho: Stories of the Grease Trail* (Anahim Lake, BC: Ulkatcho Indian Band, 1993), 1.

2 Robert Lane, "Cultural Relations of the Chilcotin Indians of West Central British Columbia" (PhD dissertation, University of Washington, 1953), 219; Birchwater, *Ulkatcho;* Sage Birchwater, *'Ulkatchot'en: The People of Ulkatcho* (Anahim Lake, BC: Uklatcho Indian Band, 1991); Diana Alexander, "A Cultural Heritage Overview of the Cariboo Forest Region" (Victoria: BC Ministry of Forests, Cariboo Forest Region, 1997), 55-60, 219.

3 Birchwater, *Ulkatcho,* 2, 5 (quote). As the quote indicates, Aboriginal people differ in the extent to which they espouse creationist views, as do non-Aboriginals.

4 E.C. Pielou, *After the Ice Age: The Return of Life to Glaciated North America* (Chicago: University of Chicago Press, 1991), 12; K.O. Emery and Louis E. Garrison, "Sea Levels 7,000 to 20,000 Years Ago," *Science* 157 (1967): 684-91.

5 Roy L. Carlson, "The Early Period on the Central Coast of British Columbia," *Canadian Journal of Archaeology* 3 (1979): 211. According to Donald W. Clark, "the coast was envisioned as too rugged for Early Man to traverse, and too marginal in terms of subsistence for him to have survived. Everyone knew that early people were supposed to eat elephants and bison, and this steep, rocky, forested region was never elephant nor bison country. The arts of fishing, watercraft and navigation were considered to be too advanced for early migrants." See Clark, *Western Subarctic Prehistory* (Ottawa: Canadian Museum of Civilization, 1991). Challenges to traditional view: E. James Dixon, "Human Colonization of the Americas: Timing, Technology and Process," *Quaternary Science Reviews* 20, nos. 1-3 (2001): 277-99.

6 Chain of refugia: Knut Fladmark, "Routes: Alternate Migration Corridors for Early Man in North America," *American Antiquity* 44 (1979): 64; Helen Hornbeck Tanner,

ed., *The Settling of North America: The Atlas of the Great Migrations into North America from the Ice Age to the Present* (New York: Macmillan, 1995), 20-21. Generalized foragers: Richard B. Lee and Irven DeVore, eds., *Man the Hunter* (Chicago: Aldine, 1969); B. Isaac, "Economy, Ecology and Analogy: The !Kung San and the Generalized Foraging Model," in *Early Paleoindian Economies of Eastern North America,* ed. B. Isaac and K. Tankersley (Greenwich, CT: Jai Press, 1990). Robert L. Kelly argues that the most serious critique of the generalized forager model comes from the fact that "living foragers are not isolated from the world system." The first colonists of the Americas probably were relatively isolated from the Old World, although not from one another. See Kelly, *The Foraging Spectrum: Diversity in Hunter-Gatherer Lifeways* (Washington, DC: Smithsonian Institution, 1995), 23. Timing of colonization: Dixon, "Human Colonization," 294; Robert McGhee, *Ancient People of the Arctic* (Vancouver: UBC Press, 1996).

7 W.H. Mathews, "Late Quaternary Environmental History Affecting Human Habitation of the Pacific Northwest," *Canadian Journal of Archaeology* 3 (1979): 147-52; Knut R. Fladmark, *British Columbia Prehistory* (Ottawa: National Museum of Man, 1986); Sydney Graham Cannings and Richard James Cannings, *Geology of British Columbia: A Journey through Time* (Vancouver: Greystone Books, 1999), 65; Richard J. Hebda, "Interior Grasslands Past and Future," *Cordillera* (1996): 344-46; G. Clifford Carl, W.A. Clemens, and C.C. Lindsey, "The Salmon, Trout, and Char – Family Salmonidae," in *Fresh-Water Fishes of British Columbia* (Victoria: BC Provincial Museum, Department of Recreation and Conservation, 1967), 52-83.

8 Obsidian on trail: John Woodworth and Hälle Flygare, *In the Steps of Alexander Mackenzie,* 2nd ed. (Kelowna, BC: Alexander Mackenzie Trail Association, 1987), 131, 149. Geology: Charles W. Chesterman, *National Audubon Society Field Guide to North American Rocks and Minerals* (New York: Knopf, 1979), s.v., "Obsidian," 690-91. Source of obsidian: Douglas Cole and Bradley Lockner, eds., *The Journals of George M. Dawson: British Columbia, 1875-1876* (Vancouver: UBC Press, 1989), 1:206-7, 214.

9 BC obsidian: Roscoe Wilmeth, "Distribution of Several Types of Obsidian from Archaeological Sites in British Columbia," *Canadian Archaeological Association Bulletin* 5 (1973): 27-60; W. Karl Hutchings, "The Namu Obsidian Industry," in *Early Human Occupation in British Columbia,* ed. Roy L. Carlson and Luke Dalla Bona (Vancouver: UBC Press, 1996). Fingerprinting obsidian: J.R. Cann, J.E. Dixon, and Colin Renfrew, "Obsidian Analysis and the Obsidian Trade," in *Science in Archaeology,* ed. D. Brothwell and E. Higgs (London: Thames and Hudson, 1969), 578-91; George Rapp Jr. and Christopher L. Hill, *Geoarchaeology: The Earth-Science Approach to Archaeological Investigation* (New Haven, CT: Yale University Press, 1998), 137-38, 148-49.

10 Distribution map: Wilmeth, "Distribution," 41 (see also G.F. MacDonald's comment on 46). Reciprocal trade: See Paul F. Donahue's comments in Wilmeth, "Distribution," 44. There is also some evidence that the Tsilhqot'in, Ulkatcho Carrier, and Kluskus Carrier fought one another for control of obsidian sources in relatively recent times: Alexander, "Cultural Heritage Overview," 105. Controlled access: Squinas to Clark Davis, quoted in Wilmeth, "Distribution," 49. Thomas Squinas had been a cowboy on Arthur Knoll's 1939 cattle drive from Chezacut to Bella Coola that followed grease trails through the Coast Mountains. He later helped Lester Dorsey blaze the route that Highway 20 now takes from Anahim Lake through Heckman Pass. See Veera Bonner, Irene E. Bliss, and Hazel Henry Litterick, eds., *Chilcotin: Preserving*

Pioneer Memories (Surrey, BC: Heritage House, 1995), 324-25; Diana French, *The Road Runs West: A Century along the Bella Coola/Chilcotin Road* (Madeira Park, BC: Harbour Publishing, 1994), 187.

11 Database of samples: Brian Apland, "Reconnaissance Survey in the Rainbow Mountains Region of West-Central British Columbia," in *Annual Report for the Year 1976: Activities of the Provincial Archaeologist's Office of British Columbia and Selected Research Reports* (Victoria: BC Ministry of Provincial Secretary and Government Services, 1979). Trade networks: Roy L. Carlson, "Trade and Exchange in Prehistoric British Columbia," in Prehistoric Exchange Systems in North America, ed. Timothy G. Baugh and Jonathon E. Ericson (New York: Plenum, 1994), 307-61 (quote at 318).

12 Efflorescence: Brian Hayden, "Research and Development in the Stone Age: Technological Transitions among Hunter-Gatherers," *Current Anthropology* 22, 5 (1981): 519-48. Namu: Carlson, "Early Period"; Roy L. Carlson, "Early Namu," in Carlson and Bona, *Early Human Occupation,* 83-102; Aubrey Cannon, "The Early Namu Archaeofauna," in Carlson and Bona, *Early Human Occupation,* 103-10; Fladmark, *BC Prehistory;* David L. Pokotylo, *Blood from Stone: Making and Using Stone Tools in Prehistoric British Columbia* (Vancouver: UBC Museum of Anthropology, 1988); John C. Whittaker, *Flintknapping: Making and Understanding Stone Tools* (Austin: University of Texas Press, 1994).

13 Cobble tools: R. Cole Harris, ed., *Historical Atlas of Canada,* vol. 1, *From the Beginning to 1800* (Toronto: University of Toronto Press, 1987), 2, plates 4, 6, 14; Charles E. Borden, "A Late Pleistocene Pebble Tool Industry of Southwestern British Columbia," in *Early Man in Western North America,* ed. C. Irwin-Williams (Portales, NM: Eastern New Mexico University Press, 1968), 55-69; Roy L. Carlson, "C.E. Borden's Archaeological Legacy," *BC Studies* 42 (1979): 3-12. Basalt quarries: Alexander, "Cultural Heritage Overview," 105-6.

14 Innovations in tool use and stone boiling: Hayden, "Research and Development," 519-20 (quote). Faunal assemblages: Mike K. Rousseau, "Early Prehistoric Occupation of South-Central British Columbia: A Review of the Evidence and Recommendations for Further Research," *BC Studies* 99 (1993): 166; Arnould H. Stryd and Mike K. Rousseau, "Early Prehistory of the Mid Fraser-Thompson River Area," in Carlson and Bona, *Early Human Occupation,* 184, 187-88, 198; Jonathan C. Driver, "Zooarchaeology in British Columbia," *BC Studies* 99 (1993): 77-105; David Sanger, "7,000 Years of Prehistory in British Columbia," *The Beaver* Outfit 198 (1968): 34-40, and David Sanger, "Prehistory of the Pacific Northwest Plateau as seen from the Interior of British Columbia," *American Antiquity* 32 (1967): 186-97. Gore Creek man: J.S. Cybulski et al., "An Early Human Skeleton from Southcentral British Columbia: Dating and Bioarchaeological Inference," *Canadian Journal of Archaeology* 5 (1981): 59-60; Stryd and Rousseau, "Early Prehistory," 184. Freshwater shellfish: Stryd and Rousseau, "Early Prehistory," 186, 196; Alexander, "Cultural Heritage Overview," 80.

15 Watape kettles: Nancy J. Turner, *Plant Technology of First Peoples of British Columbia* (Vancouver: UBC Press, 1998), 85-86. Fish roe dish: Alexander Mackenzie, *Journal of a Voyage to the Pacific* (New York: Dover, 1995), 210; Harlan I. Smith, "A Semi-Subterranean House Site in the Bella Coola Indian Area on the Coast of British Columbia," *Man* 25 (1925): 176-77; Cole and Lockner, eds. *Journals of George M. Dawson,* 1:212. Inferences about impermanent technologies: Stryd and Rousseau, "Early Prehistory," 191; Fladmark, *BC Prehistory.*

16 Pit houses: Mackenzie, *Journal,* 155, 156. Pit house depressions: Woodworth and Fly-gare, *In the Steps,* 46-47, 87. The most intensively studied pit house village site in the interior is at Keatley Creek, about 20 kilometres up the Fraser River from Lillooet, which contains over 115 pit house depressions. See Brian Hayden, ed., *A Complex Culture of the British Columbia Plateau: Traditional Stl'átl'imx Resource Use* (Vancouver: UBC Press, 1992); Brian Hayden, ed., *The Ancient Past of Keatley Creek,* 2 vols. (Burnaby, BC: Simon Fraser University Archaeology Press, 2000); Brian Hayden and June M. Ryder, "Prehistoric Cultural Collapse in the Lillooet Area," *American Antiquity* 56, 1 (1991): 50-65. Dating: Roy L. Carlson, "The Later Prehistory of British Columbia," in Carlson and Bona, *Early Human Occupation,* 225. Tezli: Paul F. Donahue, "4500 Years of Cultural Continuity on the Central Interior Plateau of British Columbia" (PhD dissertation, University of Wisconsin, 1977). Climate change: Richard J. Hebda, "Postglacial History of Grasslands of Southern British Columbia and Adjacent Regions," in *Grassland Ecology and Classification Symposium Proceedings,* ed. A.C. Nicholson, A. McLean, and T.E. Baker (Victoria: BC Ministry of Forests, 1982), 442-54; Richard J. Hebda, "British Columbia Vegetation and Climate History with Focus on 6 KA BP," *Géographie Physique et Quaternaire* 49 (1995): 55-79. Pit house design: James Alexander Teit, "The Thompson Indians of British Columbia," in *Jesup North Pacific Expedition,* edited by Franz Boas, vol. 1(4) (New York: Knickerbocker Press, 1900), 163-392; Marian W. Smith, "House Types of the Middle Fraser River," *American Antiquity* 4 (1947): 255-67; Fladmark, *BC Prehistory,* 124-29; Kenneth M. Ames and Herbert D.G. Maschner, *Peoples of the Northwest Coast: Their Archaeology and Prehistory* (London: Thames and Hudson, 1999), 151-52, 155-57.
17 Carlson, "Later Prehistory"; Thomas H. Richards and Michael K. Rousseau, *Late Prehistoric Cultural Horizons on the Canadian Plateau* (Burnaby, BC: Simon Fraser University Department of Archaeology, 1987); Alexander, "Cultural Heritage Overview," 68. There is also archaeological evidence for the keeping of domestic dogs at interior pit house sites. See Stryd and Rousseau, "Early Prehistory," 196. Dogs were common among indigenous peoples of the interior when they were observed by newcomers in the eighteenth and nineteenth centuries, and their ancestors probably accompanied the first human groups to enter the Americas. See Marion Schwartz, *A History of Dogs in the Early Americas* (New Haven, CT: Yale University Press, 1997).
18 Carl, Clemens, and Lindsey, *Fresh-Water Fishes of British Columbia,* 52-83; Richard James Cannings and Sydney Graham Cannings, *British Columbia: A Natural History* (Vancouver: Greystone Books, 2000), 256-60; Colin J.B. Wood and Cimarron Corpé, "Fisheries," in *British Columbia, the Pacific Province: Geographical Essays,* ed. Colin J.B. Wood (Victoria: Western Geographical Press, 2001), 329-44.
19 Spatial gradient: Alexander, "Cultural Heritage Overview," 68-69; cf. Richard White, *The Organic Machine* (New York: Hill and Wang, 1995). Legal aspects of salmon capture including property rights: Douglas C. Harris, *Fish, Law and Colonialism: The Legal Capture of Salmon in British Columbia* (Toronto: University of Toronto Press, 2001). Strategic placement of houses: Hayden and Ryder, "Prehistoric Cultural Collapse," 55 (quote). Trade fairs: Fladmark, *BC Prehistory,* 51-53, 137-139; Harris, *Historical Atlas,* 3, plates 4, 7.
20 Surplus: Carlson, "Later Prehistory," 218-19, 226 (quote); Fladmark, *BC Prehistory,* 51-53, 137-39. Relative advantages of a larger, sedentary population over smaller, nomadic ones: William McNeill, *Plagues and Peoples* (New York: Anchor Books, 1989); Jared

M. Diamond, *Guns, Germs and Steel: The Fates of Human Societies* (New York: W.W. Norton, 1997); Hugh Brody, *The Other Side of Eden: Hunters, Farmers, and the Shaping of the World* (New York: North Point, 2000); J.R. McNeill and William H. McNeill, *The Human Web: A Bird's-Eye View of World History* (New York: W.W. Norton, 2003); Charles L. Redman, *Human Impact on Ancient Environments* (Tucson: University of Arizona Press, 1999).

21 Plant foods: Turner, *Plant Technology;* Nancy J. Turner, *Food Plants of Interior First Peoples* (Vancouver: UBC Press, 1997); Hebda, "Interior Grasslands." Women's production: Eugene S. Hunn, Nancy J. Turner, and David H. French, "Ethnobiology and Subsistence," in *Handbook of North American Indians,* vol. 12, *Plateau,* ed. Deward E. Walker Jr. (Washington, DC: Smithsonian Institution, 1998), 526 (quote). Burning practices: Nancy J. Turner, "Burning Mountain Sides for Better Crops: Aboriginal Landscape Burning in British Columbia," *Archaeology in Montana* 32, 2 (1991): 57-73. Aboriginal cultivation in BC: Douglas Eugene Deur, "A Domesticated Landscape: Native American Plant Cultivation on the Northwest Coast of North America" (PhD dissertation, Louisiana State University and Agricultural and Mechanical College, 2001); L.M. Gottesfeld-Johnson, *Plants That We Use: Traditional Plant Uses of the Wet'suwet'en People* (Moricetown, BC: Kyah Wiget Education Society, 1991); L.M. Gottesfeld-Johnson, "Aboriginal Burning for Vegetation Management in Northwest British Columbia," *Human Ecology* 22 (1994): 171-88; Nancy J. Turner et al., *Thompson Ethnobotany: Knowledge and Usage of Plants by the Thompson Indians of British Columbia* (Victoria: Royal BC Museum, 1990), 25-28; Roberta Parish, Ray Coupé, and Dennis Lloyd, eds., *Plants of Southern Interior British Columbia and the Inland Northwest* (Vancouver: Lone Pine, 1999), 22.

22 C.J. Hickson, J.K. Russell, and M.V. Stasiuk, "Volcanology of the 2350 BP Eruption of Mount Meager Volcanic Complex, BC, Canada: Implications for Hazards from Eruptions in Topographically Complex Terrain," *Bulletin of Volcanology* 60, 7 (1999): 489-507.

23 Alan Daniel McMillan and Ian Hutchinson, "When the Mountain Dwarfs Danced: Aboriginal Traditions of Paleoseismic Events along the Cascadia Subduction Zone of Western North America," *Ethnohistory* 49, 1 (2002).

24 L. Siebert and T. Simkin, *Volcanoes of the World: An Illustrated Catalog of Holocene Volcanoes and Their Eruptions* (Washington, DC: Smithsonian Institution, Global Volcanism Program Digital Information Series, GVP-3, 2002). Available at http://www.volcano.si.edu/gvp/world/.

25 Michael E. Krauss and Victor K. Golla, "Northern Athapaskan Languages," in *Handbook of North American Indians,* vol. 6, *Subarctic,* ed. June Helm (Washington, DC: Smithsonian Institution, 1981), 67-85; William B. Workman, "The Significance of Volcanism in the Prehistory of Subarctic Northwest North America," in *Volcanic Activity and Human Ecology,* ed. Payson D. Sheets and Donald K. Grayson (New York: Academic, 1979), 339-71.

26 Shift in weaponry: P. Gregory Hare et al., "Ethnographic and Archaeological Investigations of Alpine Patches in Southwest Yukon, Canada," *Arctic* 57, 3 (2004): 260-72. Continuity of cultural elements in interior: Paul F. Donahue, "Concerning Athapaskan Prehistory in British Columbia," *Western Canadian Journal of Anthropology* 5, nos. 3-4 (1975): 21-63. General critique of anthropological studies of cultural distributions that presuppose migration: William Y. Adams, Dennis P. Van Gerven, and Richard S. Levy, "The Retreat from Migrationism," *Annual Review of Anthropology* 7 (1978): 483-532.

27 Athapaskan intergroup communication: Krauss and Golla, "Northern Athapaskan Languages," 68-69. So-called trade diasporas: Kenneth Pomeranz and Steven Topik, *The World that Trade Created: Society, Culture, and the World Economy 1400 to the Present* (Armonk, NY: M.E. Sharpe, 1999). No traditions of migration: Robert Lane, "Chilcotin," in Helm, *Handbook*, vol. 6, 402; Elizabeth Furniss, "The Early Culture of the Southern Carrier" (manuscript, X̱wi7x̱wa Library, UBC, 1991), 7.

28 Hayden and Ryder, "Prehistoric Cultural Collapse" (quote from 61). Archaeological overview of human-environmental relations: Redman, *Human Impact*.

29 Mackenzie, *Journal*, 210; Lyn Harrington, "On the Trail of the Candlefish," *The Beaver* Outfit 283 (1953): 41, 44; Terry Glavin, *This Ragged Place: Travels across the Landscape* (Vancouver: New Star, 1996), 202; Birchwater, *Ulkatcho*, 7.

30 Birchwater, *Ulkatcho*, 6; Harrington, "On the Trail"; Erna Gunther, *Indian Life on the Northwest Coast of North America, as Seen by the Early Explorers and Fur Traders during the Last Decades of the Eighteenth Century*,(Chicago: University of Chicago Press, 1972), 34-36; Hilary Stewart, *Indian Fishing: Early Methods on the Northwest Coast* (Vancouver: Douglas and McIntyre, 1996); Ron Sutherland, "The Oolichan Fishery of Northern British Columbia," *BC Historical News* 34, 3 (2001): 8-13; Scott Byram and David G. Lewis, "Ourigan: Wealth of the Northwest Coast," *Oregon Historical Quarterly* 102, 2 (2001): 126-57.

31 Drying: Harrington, "On the Trail," 42; P.N. Compton, "Forts and Fort Life in New Caledonia under the Hudson's Bay Company Regime," (Victoria, 1878), Philip and Helen Akrigg Fonds (hereafter cited as AKR) Box 4, File 49, Xerox 339, University of BC Special Collections (original in the Public Archives of Canada, MG29 B.35, vol. 4). Nutritious: H.V. Kuhnlein et al., "Ooligan Grease: A Nutritious Fat Used by Native People of Coastal British Columbia," *Journal of Ethnobiology* 2, 2 (1982): 154-61.

32 Grease: Harrington, "On the Trail," 42-43; Sutherland, "Oolichan Fishery," 9. "Stink boxes": Birchwater, *Ulkatcho*, 6-7. Disgusting smell: T.F. McIlwraith, *The Bella Coola Indians* (Toronto: University of Toronto Press, 1948), 2:537.

33 Gradient in oiliness: James G. Swan, "The Surf-Smelt of the Northwest Coast, and the Method of Taking Them by the Quillehute Indians, West Coast of Washington Territory," *Proceedings of the United States National Museum for 1880* 3 (1881): 43-46. Importance of spring freshets: Sutherland, "Oolichan Fishery," 8. Aboriginal monopolies: Richard Somerset Mackie, *Trading beyond the Mountains: The British Fur Trade on the Pacific, 1793-1843* (Vancouver: UBC Press, 1996), 127. Fort Simpson: James R. Gibson, *Otter Skins, Boston Ships, and China Goods: The Maritime Fur Trade of the Northwest Coast, 1785-1841* (Montreal and Kingston: McGill-Queen's University Press, 1991), 231-33; Mackie, *Trading beyond the Mountains*, 132-33, 242-43, 287.

34 "Grand mart": George Simpson to William Smith, 17 November 1828, reprinted in Frederick Merk, ed., *Fur Trade and Empire: George Simpson's Journal, 1824-25* (Cambridge, MA: Belknap Press of Harvard, 1968), 300; Marjorie M. Halpin and Margaret Seguin, "Tsimshian Peoples: Southern Tsimshian, Coast Tsimshian, Nishga, and Gitksan," in *Handbook of North American Indians*, vol. 7, *Northwest Coast*, ed. Wayne Suttles (Washington, DC: Smithsonian Institution, 1990), 267-84. Trade routes: George F. Macdonald, Gary Coupland, and David Archer, "The Coast Tsimshian, ca 1750," in Harris, *Historical Atlas*, plate 13; Harrington, "On the Trail," 43. Surveyor: Frank C. Swannell, "On Mackenzie's Trail," *The Beaver* Outfit 289, 18 (1958): 12 (quote); "Frank Cyril Swannell," *Annual Report* (n.p.: Corporation of BC Land Surveyors, 1970), 117-19,

162-65, AKR, Box 6, File 54, Xerox 554. Haisla trail: Charles Hamori-Torok, "Haisla," in Suttles, *Handbook,* vol. 7, 306-11. Nuxalk trail: Birchwater, *Ulkatcho,* 6, 9.

35 Swannell, "On Mackenzie's Trail," 12, 13; Cole and Lockner, *Journals of George M. Dawson,* 1:223; Mackenzie, *Journal,* 207-8.

36 Ulkatcho: Paul F. Donahue, "Ulkatcho: An Archaeological Outline," *Syesis* 6 (1973): 153-78; Donald W. Clark, "Prehistory of the Western Subarctic," in Helm, *Handbook,* vol. 6, 126; Mackenzie, *Journal,* 205; George M. Dawson, "Report on Explorations in BC, Chiefly in the Basins of the Blackwater, Salmon, and Nechacco Rivers, and on Francois Lake" (n.p.: Geological Survey of Canada, 1877), 27; Cole and Lockner, *Journals of George M. Dawson,* 1:213 (long quote). Chinook Jargon: George Gibbs, *Dictionary of the Chinook Jargon, or Trade Language of Oregon* (New York: Cramoisy Press, 1863), 7. Cole and Lockner suggest that Culla Culla House was constructed between 1780 and 1790, *Journals of George M. Dawson,* 1:213 n. 606.

37 Recent definition: Thomas J. Barfield, ed., *The Dictionary of Anthropology* (Oxford: Blackwell, 1997), s.v., "potlatch." Alternate definition: Douglas Cole and Ira Chaikin, *An Iron Hand upon the People: The Law against Potlatch on the Northwest Coast* (Vancouver: Douglas and McIntyre, 1990), 5.

38 Anthropological explanations: Helen Codere, *Fighting with Property: A Study of Kwakiutl Potlatching and Warfare, 1792-1930* (New York: J.J. Augustus, 1950); Marcel Mauss, *The Gift: The Form and Reason for Exchange in Archaic Societies* (New York: W.W. Norton, 1990); Abraham Rosman and Paula G. Rubel, *Feasting with Mine Enemy: Rank and Exchange among Northwest Coast Societies* (New York: Columbia University Press, 1971); Philip Drucker and Robert F. Heizer, *To Make My Name Good: A Reexamination of the Southern Kwakiutl Potlatch* (Berkeley: University of California Press, 1967); Sergei Kan, *Symbolic Immortality: The Tlingit Potlatch of the Nineteenth Century* (Washington, DC: Smithsonian Institution, 1989). Experience-near concepts: Clifford Geertz, *Local Knowledge: Further Essays in Interpretive Anthropology* (New York: Basic Books, 1983), 57. Discussing potlatch with outsiders: Cole and Chaikin, *Iron Hand,* 6. In a recent analysis that draws heavily on Heidegger and Derrida, Christopher Bracken suggests that the potlatch was a fiction invented by the colonial officials to use against indigenous people, and that it is more informative on the subject of colonial anxieties about property than it is about Aboriginal life. See Bracken, *The Potlatch Papers: A Colonial Case History* (Chicago: University of Chicago Press, 1997).

39 Donahue, "Ulkatcho." Horizons: Gordon R. Willey and Philip Phillips, *Method and Theory in American Archaeology* (Chicago: University of Chicago Press, 1958), 33 (cultural traits or complexes); Richards and Rousseau, *Late Prehistoric Cultural Horizons* (whole cultures). "Horizon" used to denote distinct layers of soil: Rapp and Hill, *Geoarchaeology,* 30-38, 50-85 (quote from 50); Dina F. Dincauze, *Environmental Archaeology: Principles and Practice* (Cambridge: Cambridge University Press, 2000), 282-88.

40 Donahue, "Ulkatcho," 155-58; Richard William Blacklaws, *Mackenzie Grease Trail Heritage Inventory and Assessment Project: Kluskus-Ulkatcho* (Victoria: BC Heritage Conservation Branch, 1979), Cariboo-Chilcotin Archives, box on the Mackenzie Grease Trail (hereafter cited as CCA-G). A.W. Vowell: R. Cole Harris, *Making Native Space: Colonialism, Resistance, and Reserves in British Columbia* (Vancouver: UBC Press, 2002), 220. Ulkatcho elders: Birchwater, *Ulkatcho.* Irving Goldman (ethnographer) did fieldwork at Ulkatcho village in 1935: Irving Goldman, "The Alkatcho Carrier of British Columbia," in *Acculturation in Seven American Indian Tribes,* ed. R. Linton

(New York: D. Appleton-Century, 1940); Catharine McClellan, "History of Research in the Subarctic Cordillera," in Helm, *Handbook,* vol. 6, 35-42.

41 Parks Canada and BC Ministry of Lands, Parks and Housing, "Canada – BC Agreement for Recreation and Conservation on the Alexander Mackenzie Heritage Trail: Master Development Plan" (Ottawa: Parks Canada, 1985). The potential for human-bear interaction in the interior is pretty high wherever there are humans. Local papers like the *Williams Lake Tribune* publish accounts of bear maulings, warnings, and sightings, and the provincial environment and parks ministry created a "Bear Information Kit" for the public (Cariboo-Chilcotin Archives, box on the Environment). To take a single mishap as an example, Russell Walker, a science teacher at Sir Alexander Mackenzie High School in Bella Coola, was mountain biking on a logging road in the summer of 2001 when he encountered a grizzly bear sow and her cubs. "I could hear it crunching away, biting me," he later told reporters from his hospital bed as they inspected the damage to the back of his head and neck. Somehow Walker managed to stop screaming and go limp long enough for the bear and her cubs to leave. Then he mounted his bike for the seven-kilometre ride back to the main road. See Frank Luba, "'She Was Big and Mangy': Mountain Biker Jumped by Mother Bear Guarding Cubs," *Province* (Vancouver), 4 June 2001.

42 Parks Canada and BC Ministry of Lands, Parks and Housing, "Canada – BC Agreement."

43 Representations in history: Marc Bloch, *The Historian's Craft* (New York: Vintage, 1953); Edward Hallett Carr, *What Is History?* (New York: Vintage, 1961); G.R. Elton, *The Practice of History* (New York: Thomas Y. Crowell, 1967); E.P. Thompson, *The Poverty of Theory and Other Essays* (New York: Monthly Review Press, 1978); David Hackett Fischer, *Historians' Fallacies: Toward a Logic of Historical Thought* (New York: Harper and Row, 1970); Keith Jenkins, *Re-Thinking History* (London: Routledge, 2003); Peter Burke, *What Is Cultural History?* (Cambridge: Polity, 2004). Particularity: Elton, *Practice of History,* 11-12. Caroline Walker Bynum says that "surely what characterizes historians above all else is the capacity to be shocked by the singularity of events in a way that stimulates the search for 'significance.'" See Bynum, "Wonder," *American Historical Review* 102, 1 (1997): 1-17.

44 Collective memory: Maurice Halbwachs, *On Collective Memory* (Chicago: University of Chicago Press, 1992); Paul Connerton, *How Societies Remember* (Cambridge: Cambridge University Press, 1989). Re-enactments: David Lowenthal, *The Past Is a Foreign Country* (Cambridge: Cambridge University Press, 1985), 295-301. No untainted passages: In the forensic sciences, this idea is known as Locard's Exchange Principle, formulated by one of the early students of criminalistics who was also, not surprisingly, a devotee of Sherlock Holmes. See Joe Nickell and John F. Fischer, *Crime Science: Methods of Forensic Detection* (Lexington: University Press of Kentucky, 1998), 9-10.

CHAPTER 5: CONVERGING TOWARDS "BANSHEE"

1 Edward S. Casey, "How to Get from Space to Place in a Fairly Short Stretch of Time: Phenomenological Prolegomena," in *Senses of Place,* ed. Steven Feld and Keith H. Basso (Santa Fe, NM: School of American Research Press, 1996), 24, 25.

2 Stance: John Phillip Reid, *Patterns of Vengeance: Crosscultural Homicide in the North*

American Fur Trade (Pasadena, CA: Ninth Judicial Circuit Historical Society, 1999), 26. Perpetrators: R.C. Lundin Brown, *Klatsassan, and Other Reminiscences of Missionary Life in British Columbia* (London: Society for Promoting Christian Knowledge, 1873), 100.

3 Landscapes where violent or tragic events occurred: Kenneth E. Foote, *Shadowed Ground: America's Landscapes of Violence and Tragedy* (Austin: University of Texas Press, 1997). Place fetishism is analogous to Marx's idea of commodity fetishism – "nothing but the definite social relation between men themselves which assumes here, for them, the fantastic form of a relation between things." The consequence is "personification of things and reification of persons." See Karl Marx, *Capital* (New York: Penguin, 1990), 1:163-77 (quotes on 165 and 209); Isaak Illich Rubin, *Essays on Marx's Theory of Value* (Detroit, MI: Black and Red Press, 1972), chap. 3.

4 "Local Sites Had a Story to Tell," *Williams Lake Tribune,* 24 August 1976, Cariboo-Chilcotin Archives, vertical file on archaeology (hereafter cited as CCA-A).

5 Jonathan Desbarats, "Burial Site Discovered near Bridge," *Williams Lake Tribune,* 17 October 1996, CCA-A.

6 Ibid.

7 Ibid.

8 "'Land Attack' Irks Rancher," *Williams Lake Tribune,* 1 July 1997, CCA-A.

9 Tsilhqot'in National Government, "Tsilhqot'in Declaration of Sovereignty" (Williams Lake, BC: Author, 1997).

10 Ibid.

11 "Bones to Be Reburied," *Williams Lake Tribune,* 14 October 1997, CCA-A.

12 Zirnhelt's opponents: "Talks to Start Soon," *Williams Lake Tribune,* 28 October 1997, CCA-A. Origin of bones: Doug Sabiston, "Chilcotin Confrontation Looms," *Williams Lake Tribune,* 11 November 1997, CCA-A.

13 Doug Sabiston, "Dispute Bones to Stay Put for Now," *Williams Lake Tribune,* 13 November 1997, CCA-A.

14 Need for written agreement: "Tentative Agreement on Bone Reburial," *Williams Lake Tribune,* 18 November 1997, CCA-A. Talks stall: "Agreement Gone Sour," *Williams Lake Tribune,* 20 November 1997, CCA-A. Treaty process: Daniel Wall, "Talks Continue on Burial Site," *Williams Lake Tribune,* 6 January 1998, CCA-A.

15 Ken Fisher, "Skeletons Finally Put to Rest," *Williams Lake Tribune,* 6 January 1998, CCA-A.

16 Popular history: Mel Rothenburger, *The Chilcotin War* (Langley, BC: Mr. Paperback, 1978), 8. Opting out of the trade: Robin Fisher, *Contact and Conflict: Indian-European Relations in British Columbia, 1774-1890,* 2nd ed. (Vancouver: UBC Press, 1992), 35. The first edition was published in 1977.

17 Simon Fraser, "Journal of a Voyage from the Rocky Mountains to the Pacific Coast," in *Les Bourgeois de la Compagnie du Nord-Ouest,* ed. Louis Rodrigue Masson (Quebec, 1808), 156-221; Ramsay Cook et al., eds., *Dictionary of Canadian Biography,* 14 vols. (hereafter cited as *DCB*) (Toronto: University of Toronto Press, 1966-98), s.v., "Fraser, Simon" (available online at http://www.biographi.ca/EN/index.html). NWC posts: Arthur J. Ray, "The Hudson's Bay Company and Native People," in *Handbook of North American Indians,* vol. 4, *History of Indian-White Relations,* ed. Wilcomb E. Washburn (Washington, DC: Smithsonian Institution, 1988), 335-50.

18 James R. Gibson, *The Lifeline of the Oregon Country: The Fraser-Columbia Brigade System, 1811-1847* (Vancouver: UBC Press, 1997), 3-18 (quote on 15).

19 George McDougall, 18 January 1822, Fort St. James Correspondence Books, Hudson's Bay Company Archives/Provincial Archives of Manitoba (hereafter cited as HBCA/ PAM) B.188/b/1, fo. 34-34d, 1M223 (quoted in HBCA/PAM Fort Chilcotin post history and search file). There is also a copy of the HBCA's post history for Fort Chilcotin in the BC Archives (hereafter cited as BCA), MM/C43.

20 Ibid. Joseph McGillivray described the Tsilhqot'in that he met on the same trip as "cleanly in their persons, and remarkably hospitable." See Ross Cox, *Adventures on the Columbia River: Including the Narrative of a Residence of Six Years on the Western Side of the Rocky Mountains among Various Tribes of Indians hitherto Unknown: Together with a Journey across the American Continent* (New York: J. and J. Harper, 1832), 322 (available from Canadiana.org, formerly the Canadian Institute for Historical Micro-reproductions, CIHM 33317); cf. Elizabeth Vibert, *Traders' Tales: Narratives of Cultural Encounter on the Columbia Plateau, 1807-1846* (Norman: University of Oklahoma Press, 1997).

21 Decision to establish post: R. Harvey Fleming, ed. *Minutes of Council, Northern Department of Rupert Land, 1821-31* (Toronto: Champlain Society, 1940), 45. 1823-24 killings: Reid, *Patterns of Vengeance,* 129 (these were the killings James Douglas was avenging when he ran afoul of the Carrier in 1828). Disputes: William Connolly to Sir George Simpson, Correspondence Inward, HBCA/PAM D.4/119, fo. 65-65d, 3M52 (quoted in HBCA/PAM Fort Chilcotin post history and search file).

22 William Connolly, "Report of New Caledonia District, 1826-27," HBCA/PAM B.188/e/4, 1M782. I'm grateful to Al Grove for sharing the Connolly report with me.

23 Disputes between Tsilhqot'in and Carrier in the 1820s: Connolly HBCA/PAM B.188/e/4, 1M782; Joseph McGillivray's account is from George Simpson, *Part of Dispatch from George Simpson Esquire, Governor of Ruperts Land to the Governor & Committee of the Hudson's Bay Company, London, March 1, 1829, Continued and Completed March 24 and June 5, 1829,* ed. E.E. Rich (Toronto: Champlain Society, 1947), 211-15, parts of which are reprinted in Cox, *Adventures,* 321-22; HBCA/PAM Fort Chilcotin post history and search file; Robert Lane, "Chilcotin," in *Handbook of North American Indians,* vol. 6, *Subarctic,* ed. June Helm (Washington, DC: Smithsonian Institution, 1981), 410-11; Catharine McClellan, "Intercultural Relations and Cultural Change in the Cordilleras," in Helm, *Handbook,* vol. 6, 388; Katherine L. Reedy-Maschner and Herbert D.G. Maschner, "Marauding Middlemen: Western Expansion and Violent Conflict in the Subarctic," *Ethnohistory* 46, 4 (1999): 721-22. Intercultural aspects of the law of vengeance: Reid, *Patterns of Vengeance.*

24 HBC food supply: McGillivray in Cox, *Adventures,* 316-31. Emergency plant foods in the interior: Nancy J. Turner *Food Plants of Interior First Peoples* (Vancouver: UBC Press, 1997), 28, 33-36; Roberta Parish, Ray Coupé, and Dennis Lloyd, eds., *Plants of Southern Interior British Columbia and the Inland Northwest* (Vancouver: Lone Pine, 1999), 20, 439. Another trip to Chilcotin: William Connolly, 4 March 1830, in Sir George Simpson, Correspondence Inward, HBCA/PAM D.4/123, fos. 80d-81d, 3M53 (quoted in HBCA/PAM Fort Chilcotin post history and search file).

25 Food supply networks: Arthur J. Ray, *Indians in the Fur Trade: Their Role as Trappers, Hunters, and Middlemen in the Lands Southwest of Hudson Bay, 1660-1870* (Toronto: University of Toronto Press, 1998), 126-32. Dérouines: Grace Lee Nute, *The Voyageur* (St. Paul: Minnesota Historical Society, 1955), 92-93; Robert Vézina, "Les mauvais renards et la garce: description et origine du terme *drouine,*" in *Le passage du Détroit:*

300 ans de présence francophone/Passages: Three Centuries of Francophone Presence at Le Détroit, ed. M. Bénéteau (Windsor, ON: Humanities Research Group, University of Windsor, 2003), 127-47; Carolyn Podruchny, *Making the Voyageur World: Travelers and Traders in the North American Fur Trade* (Toronto: University of Toronto Press, 2006), 201-3, 222-23.

26 Interrelation of fur trade and fur cycle: Ian McTaggart Cowan, "The Fur Trade and the Fur Cycle: 1825-1857," *BC Historical Quarterly* (1938): 19-30. Working of God's will: John McLean, *Notes of a Twenty-Five Year's Service in the Hudson's Bay Territories* (London: R. Bentley, 1849), 253-54.

27 Provisioning trade: Ray, *Indians in the Fur Trade,* 126-32. Intercultural misunderstandings occasioned by trades in food: Vibert, *Traders' Tales,* 119-204; George W. Colpitts, *Game in the Garden: A Human History of Wildlife in Western Canada to 1940* (Vancouver: UBC Press, 2003), 14-37. Different perspectives: Arthur J. Ray, "Periodic Shortages, Native Welfare, and the Hudson's Bay Company 1670-1930," in *The Subarctic Fur Trade: Native Social and Economic Adaptations,* ed. Shepard Krech III (Vancouver: UBC Press, 1984), 1-20. Semantics: Mary Black-Rogers, "Varieties of 'Starving': Semantics and Survival in the Subarctic Fur Trade, 1750-1850," *Ethnohistory* 33, 4 (1986): 353-83. Case of syncretism: Carolyn Podruchny, "Werewolves and Windigos: Narratives of Cannibal Monsters in French-Canadian Voyageur Oral Tradition," *Ethnohistory* 51, 4 (2004): 677-700. Oatmeal: Daniel Francis and Toby Morantz, *Partners in Furs: A History of the Fur Trade in Eastern James Bay 1600-1870* (Montreal and Kingston: McGill-Queen's University Press, 1983), 93-94. Actual deaths: Vibert, *Traders' Tales,* 186-87.

28 Ray, "Periodic Shortages."

29 William Connolly, 1 October 1829, Fort St. James Correspondence Books, HBCA/PAM B.188/b/7, fos. 6d-9d, 1M224 (quoted in HBCA/PAM Fort Chilcotin post history and search file); George McDougall, 10 October 1829, HBCA/PAM B.188/b/7, fos. 24d-25, 1M224 (quoted in HBCA/PAM Fort Chilcotin post history and search file) (emphasis in original).

30 George McDougall, 18 October 1829, HBCA/PAM B.188/b/7, fos. 25d-26, 1M224 (quoted in HBCA/PAM Fort Chilcotin post history and search file).

31 William Connolly, 28 January 1830, HBCA/PAM B.188/b/7, fos. 19-20, 1M224; see also William Connolly, 4 March 1830, in Sir George Simpson, Correspondence Inward, HBCA/PAM D.4/123, fo. 81d, 3M53 (both quoted in HBCA/PAM Fort Chilcotin post history and search file); Peter Warren Dease, 19 April 1831, HBCA/PAM D.4/125, fo. 24-24d, 3M54 (quoted in HBCA/PAM Fort Chilcotin post history and search file). Simpson on McDougall, "The 'Character Book' of Governor George Simpson 1832," in *Hudson's Bay Miscellany 1670-1870,* ed. Glyndwr Williams (Winnipeg: Hudson's Bay Record Society, 1975), 219-20.

32 Peter Warren Dease, 14 May 1831, 9 October 1831, 23 February 1832, Fort St. James Post Journals, HBCA/PAM B.188/a/15, fo. 24-24d, 1M130 (quoted in HBCA/PAM Fort Chilcotin post history and search file).

33 Fort St. James Post Journals, HBCA/PAM B.188/a/5, 1M129; Fort Alexandria Post Journals, HBCA/PAM B.5/a/3, 1M14; and York Factory Minutes of Council, HBCA/PAM B.239/k/2, 1M814 (all cited in HBCA/PAM Fort Chilcotin post history and search file); George Simpson to the governor and committee, 21 July 1834, HBCA/PAM D.4/100, fo. 9, 3M46 (quoted in HBCA/PAM Fort Chilcotin post history and

search file); George Simpson to Peter Skene Ogden, 27 June 1836, HBCA/PAM D.4/22, fo. 36, 3M7 (quoted in HBCA/PAM Fort Chilcotin post history and search file); Fort Alexandria Post Journals, HBCA/PAM B.5/a/4, 1M14 (cited in HBCA/PAM Fort Chilcotin post history and search file). See also Fort Chilcotin Post Journals, HBCA/PAM B.37/a/1, fo. 3, 1M20. Trading links with Nuxalk: Lane, "Chilcotin," 411.

34 Fort Chilcotin Post Journals, HBCA/PAM B.37/a/1, fos. 1, 1d, 1M20. Subsistence activities: James R. Gibson, *Farming the Frontier: The Agricultural Opening of the Oregon Country 1786-1846* (Vancouver: UBC Press, 1985). Searching for horses: Paul H. St. Pierre, "Looking for Horses" and "Looking for Horses Again," in *Tell Me a Good Lie: Tales from the Chilcotin Country* (Vancouver: Douglas and McIntyre, 2001), 114-19. Winter feeding: Thomas R. Weir, "The Winter Feeding Period in the Southern Interior Plateau of British Columbia," *Annals of the Association of American Geographers* 44, 2 (1954): 194-204.

35 Brigade: Gibson, *Lifeline;* Clayton W. Campbell and Alfred H. Bawtree, eds., *Rangeland Handbook for BC* (Kamloops: BC Cattlemen's Association, 1998); Richard William Blacklaws and Diana French, *Ranchland: British Columbia's Cattle Country* (Madeira Park, BC: Harbour, 2001). What animals eat: Elliot West, *The Contested Plains: Indians, Goldseekers, and the Rush to Colorado* (Lawrence: University of Kansas Press, 1998), 50-51.

36 HBCA/PAM B.37/a/1, fo. 2d, 1M20. Glacial extent: Stanton Tuller, "Climate," in *British Columbia, the Pacific Province: Geographical Essays,* ed. Colin J.B. Wood (Victoria: Western Geographical Press, 2001), 45-63. For the stresses faced by posts on the margins of trade and transportation routes, cf. Lloyd Keith, ed., *North of Athabasca: Slave Lake and Mackenzie River Documents of the North West Company, 1800-1821* (Montreal and Kingston: McGill-Queen's University Press, 2001).

37 HBCA/PAM B.37/a/1, fos. 3d-4, 5, 1M20. McBean's wife and child survived: HBCA/PAM B.37/a/2, fo. 5, 1M20.

38 HBCA/PAM B.37/a/1, fo. 7, 1M20.

39 HBCA/PAM B.37/a/1, fo. 7d, 1M20. Tsilhqot'in not interested in trade: e.g., Fisher, *Contact and Conflict,* 35. On fur trade forts as "power containers," see R. Cole Harris, "Strategies of Power in the Cordilleran Fur Trade," in *The Resettlement of British Columbia: Essays on Colonialism and Geographic Change* (Vancouver: UBC Press, 1996), 31-67.

40 HBCA/PAM B.37/a/2, fos. 2, 4, 1M20. Aboriginal fishing law: Diana Alexander, "A Cultural Heritage Overview of the Cariboo Forest Region" (Victoria: BC Ministry of Forests, Cariboo Forest Region, 1997), 68-75; Douglas C. Harris, *Fish, Law and Colonialism: The Legal Capture of Salmon in British Columbia* (Toronto: University of Toronto Press, 2001), 18-27; William McBean to John Tod, 20 June 1840, HBCA/PAM B.37/a/2, fos. 28d-29, 1M20 (quoted in HBCA/PAM Fort Chilcotin post history and search file). There isn't an entry for "Atnahyews" in the indices of the relevant volumes of the *Handbook of North American Indians,* so it is not clear which Aboriginal group this was. Both Alexander Mackenzie and Simon Fraser learned to call the Secwepemc "Atnahs," from the Carrier word for "foreigner"; this may be who was meant. See Marianne Boelscher Ignace, "Shuswap," in *Handbook of North American Indians,* vol. 12, *Plateau,* ed. Deward E. Walker Jr. (Washington, DC: Smithsonian Institution, 1988), 216.

41 *DCB* s.v. "McLean, Donald," (quote); Reid, *Patterns of Vengeance,* 116-17.

42 Donald McLean: Fort Alexandria Post Journals, HBCA/PAM B.5/a/5, 1M14 (quoted

in HBCA/PAM Fort Chilcotin post history and search file); Alexander Caulfield Anderson to George Simpson, 21 January 1843, HBCA/PAM D.5/8, fo. 40-40d, 3M62 (quoted in HBCA/PAM Fort Chilcotin post history and search file). Fort Chilcotin maintained: HBCA/PAM Fort Chilcotin post history and search file. Withdrawal: Anderson to Simpson, 13 February 1845, HBCA/PAM D.5/13, fo. 129, 3M69 (quoted in HBCA/PAM Fort Chilcotin post history and search file).

43 Position of Tsilhqot'in vis-à-vis their Aboriginal neighbours: Robert Lane, "Cultural Relations of the Chilcotin Indians of West Central British Columbia" (PhD dissertation, University of Washington, 1953).

44 Aboriginal languages: UBC Museum of Anthropology, "First Nations Languages of BC" [map], http://www.moa.ubc.ca/pdf/FN_Lang_map.pdf; Laurence C. Thompson and M. Dale Kinkade, "Languages," in *Handbook of North American Indians,* vol. 7, *Northwest Coast,* ed. Wayne Suttles (Washington, DC: Smithsonian Institution, 1990), 30-51; Michael E. Krauss and Victor K. Golla, "Northern Athapaskan Languages," in Helm, *Handbook,* vol. 6, 67-85; M. Dale Kinkade et al., "Languages," in Walker, *Handbook,* vol. 12, 49-72. Explorers' use of interpreters: Alexander Mackenzie, *Journal of a Voyage to the Pacific* (New York: Dover, 1995), 153, 154, 160 (and for his attempt to collect Aboriginal vocabularies, 164-65); Fraser, "Journal," 159, 160, 162, 169; W. Kaye Lamb, ed., *Sixteen Years in the Indian Country: The Journals of Daniel Williams Harmon* (Toronto: Macmillan, 1957), 137 (30 January and 18 March 1811), 155 (23 January 1813), 180 (30 September 1815). Simpson: Frederick Merk, ed., *Fur Trade and Empire: George Simpson's Journal, 1824-25* (Cambridge, MA: Belknap Press of Harvard, 1968), 27, 47 (for the Blackfoot language), 127, 137 (for "Mr. Deases Interpreter"). Brigade interpreters: Gibson, *Lifeline,* 207, 222 (Connolly), 230-31 (Dease). Marrying into Aboriginal families: Sylvia van Kirk, *"Many Tender Ties": Women in Fur-Trade Society in Western Canada, 1670-1870* (Winnipeg: Watson and Dwyer, 1980); Jennifer S.H. Brown, *Strangers in Blood: Fur Trade Company Families in Indian Country* (Norman: University of Oklahoma Press, 1996).

45 Reid, *Patterns of Vengeance.* Reid also argued that since the HBC had a monopoly (after 1821), it was able to use Aboriginal dependence on the company to avoid direct conflict by simply withdrawing the source of trade, 152-53. This was not true in the Chilcotin, as will be shown below. Carrier warning: Fisher, *Contact and Conflict,* 37. James Douglas: There are a wide range of stories about this event, both written and oral. In some, Douglas was saved by the women of the post; in others, by the interpreter's Aboriginal wife or by his own wife, who was the Métis daughter of another fur trader and a Cree woman. See Frieda Esau Klippenstein, "The Challenge of James Douglas and Carrier Chief Kwah," in *Reading beyond Words: Contexts for Native History,* ed. Jennifer S.H. Brown and Elizabeth Vibert (Peterborough, ON: Broadview, 1996), 124-51; Reid, *Patterns of Vengeance,* 90-91, 98, 112, 129. For a similar account of the negotiation of intercultural violence, see Richard White, *The Middle Ground: Indians, Empires, and Republics in the Great Lakes Region, 1650-1815* (Cambridge: Cambridge University Press, 1991), 75-82.

46 Response to crisis: Deward E. Walker Jr. and Helen H. Schuster, "Religious Movements," in Walker, *Handbook,* vol. 12, 499-514; Christopher L. Miller, *Prophetic Worlds: Indians and Whites on the Columbia Plateau* (New Brunswick, NJ: Rutgers University Press, 1985), 35 (quote). "A sort of religion": McLean, *Notes of a Twenty-Five Year's Service,* 263-64. Carrier prophets: Margaret L. Tobey, "Carrier," in Helm, *Handbook,* vol. 6,

429; Diamond Jenness, "The Carrier Indians of the Bulkley River: Their Social and Religious Life," in *Anthropoloical Papers,* no. 25, 469-586 (Washington, DC: Smithsonian Institution, Bureau of American Ethnology, Bulletin 133, 1943).

47 Demers, letter to the Bishop of Quebec, 20 December 1842, reprinted in Quebec Mission, *Notices and Voyages of the Famed Quebec Mission to the Pacific Northwest* (Portland: Oregon Historical Society, 1956), 152-65; Alexandria post journal quoted in HBCA/PAM Fort Chilcotin post history and search file. Surprised missionary: Quebec Mission, *Notices and Voyages,* 139; Margaret Mary Whitehead, *The Cariboo Mission: A History of the Oblates* (Victoria: Sono Nis, 1981); *DCB,* s.v., "Demers, Modeste."

48 *DCB,* s.v., "Nobili, John"; Adrien Gabriel Morice, *The History of the Northern Interior of British Columbia* (Fairfield, WA: Ye Galleon Press, 1971), 236-38. The judgments of Nobili's stature and character are Morice's, 237; his quote about the Prophet Dance is on 238. Adrian Morice didn't believe that Nobili actually visited the Tsilhqot'in, but rather that the missionary had meant to say that he visited the Babines. See Morice, *History,* 335 n. 1. Howay, who accepted Nobili's claim that he did visit the Tsilhqot'in, describes Nobili's twelve-day visit as follows: "Those were busy days. His time was fully occupied as he relates converting, marrying, baptising, blessing, burying, and abolishing polygamy everywhere." See Howay, *British Columbia from the Earliest Times to the Present* (Vancouver: S.J. Clarke, 1914), vol. 2, 609. Brown, *Klatsassan,* 5-7; Whitehead, *Cariboo Mission,* 35.

49 Columbia district population: Merk, ed., *Fur Trade and Empire,* 66. First census: Jean Barman, *The West beyond the West: A History of British Columbia* (Toronto: University of Toronto Press, 1991), 61. Aboriginal populations: Robert Boyd, *The Coming of the Spirit of Pestilence: Introduced Infectious Diseases and Population Decline among Northwest Coast Indians, 1774-1874* (Vancouver: UBC Press, 1999), 3; Wilson Duff, *The Indian History of British Columbia: The Impact of the White Man* (Victoria: Royal BC Museum, 1997), 55, table 3.

50 Derek Hayes, *Historical Atlas of British Columbia and the Pacific Northwest: Maps of Exploration; British Columbia, Washington, Oregon, Alaska, Yukon* (Vancouver: Cavendish, 1998); Barman, *West beyond the West,* 47-49.

51 Dorothy Johansen, *Empire of the Columbia: A History of the Pacific Northwest,* 2nd ed. (New York: Harper & Row, 1967), 151; Barman, *West beyond the West,* 52-54, 63-66.

52 Robert Boyd, "Demographic History, 1774-1874," in Suttles, *Handbook,* vol. 7, 135-48.

53 "The 'Eliza Anderson'" and "Arrival of the Eliza Anderson," *Daily British Colonist,* 5 June 1861. Alexander Selkirk (1676-1721) was a Scottish sailor who quarrelled with the captain of his ship during a privateering voyage and was marooned on an uninhabited island in 1704. He was rescued in 1709, and published accounts of his life provided some of the impetus for Defoe's *Robinson Crusoe.* Repeal of liquor law: Letter from Ephraim Evans to the editor, *British Columbian,* 20 August 1861.

54 Importance of metropolis and hinterland in historiography of Canada: D.C. Masters, "Toronto vs. Montreal: The Struggle for Financial Hegemony, 1860-1875," *Canadian Historical Review* 22 (June 1941): 133-46; J.M.S. Careless, "The Toronto *Globe* and Agrarian Radicalism," *Canadian Historical Review* 29 (March 1948): 15-16, 39; J.M.S. Careless, "Frontierism, Metropolitanism, and Canadian History," *Canadian Historical Review* 35 (March 1954): 1-21; J.M.S. Careless, *Frontier and Metropolis: Regions, Cities, and Identities in Canada before 1914* (Toronto: University of Toronto Press, 1989). In environmental history: William Cronon, *Nature's Metropolis: Chicago and the Great*

West (New York: W.W. Norton, 1991). Victoria vs. New Westminster: Ethelbert Olaf Stuart Scholefield, *British Columbia from Earliest Times to the Present* (Vancouver: S.J. Clarke, 1914), vol. 1, chap. 14; John S. Galbraith, *The Hudson's Bay Company as an Imperial Factor, 1821-1869* (Berkeley: University of California Press, 1957), 222-23; Edwin Ernest Rich, *The History of the Hudson's Bay Company, 1763-1870* (London: Hudson's Bay Record Society, 1959), 2:749; Howay, *BC from Earliest Times,* 2:65-68. Barkerville: Barman, *West beyond the West,* 72-73, 78-79; Dorothy Blakey Smith, *James Douglas: Father of British Columbia* (Oxford: Oxford University Press, 1971), 96-100; Gordon R. Elliot, *Barkerville, Quesnel and the Cariboo Gold Rush* (Vancouver: Douglas and McIntyre, 1978), 112-25.

55 W. Champness, *To Cariboo and Back in 1862* (Fairfield, WA: Ye Galleon Press, 1972). Fort Berens: G.P.V. Akrigg and Helen B. Akrigg, *British Columbia Place Names,* 3rd ed. (Vancouver: UBC Press, 1997) (hereafter cited as *BCPN*), s.v., "Lillooet." Construction of the wagon roads: Howay, *BC from Earliest Times,* 2:87-107. Part of the route the Champness followed had been surveyed by Lt. Henry Spencer Palmer in 1859.

56 Ranald Macdonald and John G. Barnston, letter to James Douglas from Bonaparte River, Reporting on a Trip from Alexandria to North Bentinck Arm, 24 July 1861, Howay Papers 21-18, Philip and Helen Akrigg Fonds (hereafter cited as AKR) Box 3, File 61, Xerox 237, University of BC Special Collections; *DCB,* s.v., "Macdonald, Ranald."

57 Venables: "Route from Alexandria to North Bentinck Arm," *British Colonist,* 28 October 1861. Unreliable route: "Important from the Coast Route – Destitution and Suffering," *British Colonist,* 22 July 1862. Apparently the "tender mercies of the savages" were tender after all. In January of the following year, a Canadian named Linn was alive and well, cutting hay in the Chilcotin for the packer Mr. Hood. See "The Bentinck Arm Route," *British Colonist,* 3 January 1863. That raises the question, however, of why the Aboriginal people were willing to take care of people suffering from smallpox in the first place.

58 Palmer and Moody: *DCB,* s.vv., "Palmer, Henry Spencer," "Moody, Richard Clement"; Woodward, "Influence."

59 Henry Spencer Palmer, letters of 17 July and 13 August 1862 to Col. Moody, AKR Box 2, File 25, Xerox 125. For the Chinook Jargon, see George Gibbs, *Dictionary of the Chinook Jargon, or Trade Language of Oregon* (New York: Cramoisy Press, 1863), 10, 18, 28. The expression "kloshe nanitsh" is given the imperative meaning of "look out!" or "take care!" by Gibbs. Palmer's use of the same phrase for the English "a good look," which is a literal translation, may be a sign that he wasn't fluent in the jargon. On the other hand, since constant improvisation is necessary in the use of a pidgin language, this may be a sign of his fluency. Certainly he expected Moody to understand what he meant. A considerably revised version of Palmer's account was published the following year in New Westminster. See Henry Spencer Palmer, *Report of a Journey of a Survey from Victoria to Fort Alexander, via North Bentinck Arm* (New Westminster, BC: Royal Engineer Press, 1863), BCA Library NW971.MP174re.

60 James Douglas, letter to the Duke of Newcastle, 13 November 1863, and Arthur Johnstone Blackwood both quoted in *DCB,* s.v., "Palmer, Henry Spencer."

61 Bentinck Arm route: "Four Days Later from Bentinck Arm," *British Colonist,* 27 August 1862; "The Bentinck Arm Route," *British Colonist,* 3 January 1863. Waddington's remarks: "Coast Route Meeting," *British Colonist,* 5 June 1861. Details about the committee members: *DCB;* Dorothy Blakey Smith, ed., "The Journal of Arthur Thomas

Bushby, 1858-59," *BC Historical Quarterly* 21, nos. 1-4 (1957-58): 164-65, 190. All the members of the committee subsequently had places in BC named after them. See under specific names in the BC Geographical Names Information System (http://ilmbwww.gov.bc.ca/bcnames/); *BCPN;* Canadian Geographical Names Database (http://geonames.nrcan.gc.ca/); John T. Walbran, *British Columbia Coast Names: Their Origin and History* (Vancouver: Douglas and McIntyre, 1971). Subscription: "Coast Route Meeting," *British Colonist,* 11 June 1861.

62 "Major Downie's Meeting," *British Colonist,* 20 August 1861; Rich Mole, "Homathco: The Stubborn wilderness (and the Men Who Tried to Tame It)," *Western Living* (September 1978): 83-90; Anonymous, *Cariboo: The Newly Discovered Gold Fields of British Columbia* (Fairfield, WA: Ye Galleon Press, 1975), 51-53.

63 "Return of the 'Henrietta' from Bute Inlet," *British Colonist,* 1 October 1861; Mole, "Homathco"; "The Bute Inlet Surveying Party," *British Colonist,* 21 December 1861.

64 "Bute Inlet," *British Colonist,* 7 May 1862. Identity of "Euclutaus": Helen Codere, "Kwakiutl: Traditional Culture," in Suttles, *Handbook,* vol. 7, 359-77.

65 *DCB,* s.v., "Tiedemann, Hermann Otto"; Mole, "Homathco" (Tiedemann quote reprinted in both sources); "The Bute Inlet Explorers," *British Colonist,* 25 July 1862. Palmer's quotes about Tiedemann: Frank C. Swannell, "Lieutenant Palmer Makes a Survey," *The Beaver* Outfit 292, 20 (1961): 33-38.

66 Alfred Waddington, "The Bute Inlet Route," *British Colonist,* 1 August 1862; "The Bute Inlet Meeting," *British Colonist,* 27 August 1862; "Bute Inlet Stock," *British Colonist,* 29 August 1862.

67 "Arrival from Bute Inlet," *British Colonist,* 7 November 1862.

68 "Latest from Bute Inlet," *British Colonist,* 6 July 1863.

CHAPTER 6: CHILCOTIN WAR

1 Edward Sleigh Hewlett, "The Chilcotin Uprising of 1864," *BC Studies* 19 (1973): 50-72; Ramsay Cook et al., eds., *Dictionary of Canadian Biography,* 14 vols.(hereafter cited as *DCB*) (Toronto: University of Toronto Press, 1966-98), s.v., "Whymper, Frederick" (available online at http://www.biographi.ca/EN/index.html); Frederick Whymper, *Travel and Adventure in the Territory of Alaska ... and in Various Other Parts of the North Pacific* (London: John Murray, 1868), 29 (quote); "The Last Indian Atrocity," *British Colonist,* 12 May 1864. Whymper's use of the term "murder" presupposed that the killings were unlawful. John Phillip Reid, *Patterns of Vengeance: Crosscultural Homicide in the North American Fur Trade* (Pasadena, CA: Ninth Judicial Circuit Historical Society, 1999), 24.

2 "The Last Indian Atrocity."

3 Hewlett, "Chilcotin Uprising of 1864."

4 Ibid.

5 Ibid.; Admiral Kingcome to the Secretary of the Admiralty, 21 June 1864, Philip and Helen Akrigg Fonds (hereafter cited as AKR) Box 4, File 18, Xerox 307, University of BC Special Collections [Copied from Public Record Office ADM 1/5878, x/8688].

6 Hewlett, "Chilcotin Uprising of 1864"; *DCB,* s.v., "Cox, William George,"; Chartres Brew, letter to Colonial Secretary, 23 May 1864, in Colonial Correspondence: Originals, 1857-1872, BC Archives (hereafter cited as BCA) GR1372, File 193; *DCB,* s.v., "Brew, Chartres"; "News from the Bute Expedition," *British Columbian,* 28 May

1864; "Proclamation: Bute Inlet Massacre!" *British Columbian,* 25 May 1864 (same proclamation also in edition of 1 June 1864); "Another Indian Massacre," *British Columbian,* 28 May 1864. Role of Royal Navy in constitution of colonial authority: Barry M. Gough, *Gunboat Frontier: British Maritime Authority and Northwest Coast Indians, 1846-1890* (Vancouver: UBC Press, 1984).

7 "The Bute Inlet Route," *British Columbian,* 1 June 1864.

8 Failure of Bute Inlet expedition: Governor Frederick Seymour to Admiral Kingcome, 1 June 1864, AKR Box 4, File 18, Xerox 307 [Copied from Public Record Office ADM 1/5878, x/8688]. Alexandria expedition: Hewlett, "Chilcotin Uprising of 1864"; Governor Frederick Seymour to Sir Frederic Rogers, 1 June 1864, AKR Box 4, File 18, Xerox 307 [Copied from Public Record Office ADM 1/5878, x/8688]. Fear of Aboriginal war: Seymour to Kingcome, 1 June 1864. Vigilante justice: Robin Fisher, *Contact and Conflict: Indian-European Relations in British Columbia, 1774-1890,* 2nd ed. (Vancouver: UBC Press, 1992), 108-9.

9 William George Cox to Colonial Secretary, 19 June 1864, AKR Box 4, File 18, Xerox 307 [Copied from Public Record Office ADM 1/5878, x/8688]; Hewlett, "Chilcotin Uprising of 1864." Collective liability: Reid, *Patterns of Vengeance.*

10 A.H. Wallace, "Letter from Bentinck Arm," *British Colonist,* 27 June 1864; A.H. Wallace, "The Bentinck Arm Tragedy," *British Colonist,* 15 July 1864.

11 *DCB,* s.v., "McLean, Donald"; Hewlett, "Chilcotin Uprising of 1864"; "News from the Chilacoten Country!" *British Columbian,* 6 August 1864.

12 R.C. Lundin Brown, *Klatsassan, and Other Reminiscences of Missionary Life in British Columbia* (London: Society for Promoting Christian Knowledge, 1873); Hewlett, "Chilcotin Uprising of 1864"; Hewlett, "The Chilcotin Uprising: A Study of Indian-European Relations in Nineteenth Century British Columbia" (master's thesis, University of British Columbia, 1972). Role of compensation in Aboriginal law: Reid, *Patterns of Vengeance.*

13 *DCB,* s.v., "Waddington, Alfred Pendrell," "Cox, William George," "Brew, Chartres," "Seymour, Frederick," "Begbie, Sir Matthew Baillie," "Tod, John."

14 John Tod, letter to Edward Ermatinger, 1 June 1864, AKR Box 9, File 6.

15 Tina Loo, "Bute Inlet Stories," in *Making Law, Order, and Authority in British Columbia, 1821-1871* (Toronto: Toronto University Press, 1994), chap. 7 (quotes from 134-35). Loo cites the *Colonist* for use of the term "impelled." Of course, as she notes, these characterizations were not fixed: "In emphasizing the Indians' otherness they became self-conscious and reflective about their own behaviour, and discovered, quite to their dismay, that despite their best efforts to distance themselves from the Indians the gulf between them was not as wide as they wished" (ibid., 147). There is a vast literature on the "savage" in western thought, see, for example, Robert F. Berkhofer, *The White Man's Indian: Images of the American Indian from Columbus to the Present* (New York: Vintage, 1979); Anthony Pagden, *The Fall of Natural Man: The American Indian and the Origins of Comparative Ethnology* (Cambridge: Cambridge University Press, 1987); Roger Bartra, *The Artificial Savage: Modern Myths of the Wild Man* (Ann Arbor: University of Michigan Press, 1997); Shepard Krech III, *The Ecological Indian: Myth and History* (New York: W.W. Norton, 2000); Ter Ellingson, *The Myth of the Noble Savage* (Berkeley: University of California Press, 2001).

16 Loo, "Bute Inlet Stories," 150, 151, 156 (quotes). "Californization": M.B. Begbie, letter to Governor Douglas, 18 May 1859, BCA GR1372, reel B1307, item 142b.

17 Jill Lepore, *The Name of War: King Philip's War and the Origins of American Identity* (New York: Random House, 1999), xxi.

18 Trutch's policy: Fisher, *Contact and Conflict*, 164-66; *DCB*, s.v., "Trutch, Sir Joseph William." Federal responsibility: Robert J. Surtees, "Canadian Indian Policies," in *Handbook of North American Indians*, vol. 4, *History of Indian-White Relations*, ed. Wilcomb E. Washburn (Washington, DC: Smithsonian Institution, 1988), 89; Douglas Sanders, "Government Indian Agencies in Canada," in Washburn, *Handbook*, vol. 4, 276. Continuing importance of Aboriginal people: John Lutz, "After the Fur Trade: The Aboriginal Labouring Class of British Columbia, 1849-1890," *Journal of the Canadian Historical Association* (1992): 69-93 (federal minister quoted on 71). Tsilhqot'in fears: Fisher, *Contact and Conflict*, 184-85. The definitive work on the history of reserves in BC is R. Cole Harris, *Making Native Space: Colonialism, Resistance, and Reserves in British Columbia* (Vancouver: UBC Press, 2002).

19 Manuscript account of O'Reilly's trip to the Chilcotin via Bute Inlet: BCA A/E/ Or3/Or3.1. Quarrel with John Salmon: George Walkem, Chief Commission of Lands and Works, letter to Israel Wood Powell, 5 December 1872, Library and Archives Canada, Archival Records from Department of Indian Affairs, RG-10, Vol. 3583, File 1102. Peter O'Reilly: *DCB*, s.v., "O'Reilly, Peter." Killing of Chinese man: BCA GR0429, Box 1, File 12, no folio. Powell's policies: *DCB*, s.v., "Powell, Israel Wood."

20 Walkem, letter to Powell, 5 December 1872; Powell, 15 January 1873, BCA GR0868, Original 32/73; *DCB*, s.v., "Walkem, George Anthony"; Powell, Letter, BCA GR0983, File 2, Original 430/72; Powell, letter to Walkem, December 1872, Library and Archives Canada, Archival Records from Department of Indian Affairs, RG-10, Vol. 3583, File 1102.

21 Situation at Kamloops: Fisher, *Contact and Conflict*, 185, 191-94. McLean Gang: *DCB*, s.v., "McLean, Allen," "McLean, Donald."

22 L.W. Riske, Samuel Withrow, Silas Fields, Benjamin F. English, and Donald McIntyre to J.W. Powell, 19 March 1883, BCA GR0429, Box 1, File 12.

23 Telegram: BCA GR0429, Box 1, File 12, fo. 121/83.

24 Daniel Francis, *The Encyclopedia of British Columbia* (Madeira Park, BC: Harbour Publishing, 2000), s.v., "Chinese."

25 BCA GR0429, Box 1, File 12, fo. 122/83.

26 BCA GR0429, Box 1, File 12, fo. 141/83.

27 BCA GR0429, Box 2, File 4, fo. 377/91; BCA GR0429, Box 2, File 4, fo. 636/91.

28 Local ranchers supporting Tsilhqot'in: Edward Penrose Lee in BCA MS0364, Box 10, File 12 (1957 typescript). Reply to ranchers: BCA C/D/30.7/R24. Government pamphlets: BC Department of Lands, "How to Pre-Empt Land," Land Series Bulletin (LSB) 1 (Victoria: Author, 1918); BC Department of Lands, "Some Questions and Answers Regarding British Columbia Canada," LSB 2 (Victoria: Author, 1920); BC Bureau of Provincial Information, "BC Land Recording Divisions, North and Central Interior," LSB 3 (Victoria: Author, 1928); BC Department of Lands, "Grazing Possibilities of British Columbia," LSB 4 (Victoria: Author, 1924); BC Bureau of Provincial Information, "Purchase and Lease of Crown Lands," LSB 10 (Victoria: Author, 1925); BC Department of Lands, "Tatla, Chilko, and Anahim Lakes; Chilanko, Chilcotin, Euchiniko, Dean, Bellakula and Toba Rivers and Vicinities," LSB 22 (Victoria: Author, 1919). Copies of all these pamphlets are in University of BC Koerner Library, Microfilm AW1.R7550. BC Department of Lands, "The Chilcotin

Plateau," LSB 34 (Victoria: Author, 1921), University of BC Special Collections, Pamphlet Collection 6821. Game warden's correspondence: Wm. Drayton Jr., C.H. Clark, and Norman S. Mackie, Hotel Ryan, St. Paul, Minnesota, to A. Bryan Williams, 23 September 1907, BCA GR0446; BCA GR0446 (quotations from 7, 8, 14). For the history of recreational hunting in western Canada, see George W. Colpitts, *Game in the Garden: A Human History of Wildlife in Western Canada to 1940* (Vancouver: UBC Press, 2003); Tina Loo, *States of Nature: Conserving Canada's Wildlife in the Twentieth Century* (Vancouver: UBC Press, 2006).

29 David Mulhall, *Will to Power: The Missionary Career of Father Morice* (Vancouver: UBC Press, 1986), 19. Morice believed that Fouquet did visit the Tsilhqot'in and was the first Catholic missionary to do so. Adrien Gabriel Morice, *The History of the Northern Interior of British Columbia* (Fairfield, WA: Ye Galleon Press, 1971), 335 n. 1; Margaret Mary Whitehead, *The Cariboo Mission: A History of the Oblates* (Victoria: Sono Nis, 1981), 46-47, 51-52 (McGuckin quotes).

30 Mulhall, *Will to Power,* 19-20; *DCB,* s.v., "Durieu, Paul"; Wilson Duff, *The Indian History of British Columbia: The Impact of the White Man* (Victoria: Royal BC Museum, 1997), 134; E.M. Lemert, "The Life and Death of an Indian State," *Human Organization* 13, 3 (1955): 23-27; Robert Lane, "Chilcotin," in *Handbook of North American Indians,* vol. 6, *Subarctic,* ed. June Helm (Washington, DC: Smithsonian Institution, 1981), 411-12. Housing reform: Mary-Ellen Kelm, *Colonizing Bodies: Aboriginal Health and Healing in British Columbia, 1900-50* (Vancouver: UBC Press, 1998); Adele Perry, "From 'the Hot-Bed of Vice' to the 'Good and Well-Ordered Christian Home': First Nations Housing and Reform in Nineteenth-Century British Columbia," *Ethnohistory* 50, 4 (2003): 587-610; Susan Neylan, *The Heavens Are Changing: Nineteenth-Century Protestant Missions and Tsimshian Christianity* (Montreal and Kingston: McGill-Queen's University Press, 2003). The "modern" cabin not only dismantled multi-family living, reducing the sharing of household tasks, but also caused a shift from semi-nomadic to permanent housing that interfered with subsistence cycles and pushed these groups into wage work and affected a whole way of life. Most houses, furthermore, did not have indoor plumbing, which meant that the water supply was constantly at risk of contamination.

31 Killings: Attorney general's correspondence, BCA GR0429. Reassignment of Morice: Mulhall, *Will to Power,* 21-33. Durieu system: Margaret Mary Whitehead, *Sound Heritage,* vol. 34, *Now You Are My Brother: Missionaries in British Columbia* (Victoria: Provincial Archives of BC, 1981), 26-39; Whitehead, *Cariboo Mission,* 131. Tsilhqot'in in villages: Lane, "Chilcotin," 411-12; Diana Alexander, "A Cultural Heritage Overview of the Cariboo Forest Region" (Victoria: BC Ministry of Forests, Cariboo Forest Region, 1997), 42; cf. Neylan, *Heavens Are Changing.*

32 Jean Barman, *The West beyond the West: A History of British Columbia* (Toronto: University of Toronto Press, 1991), 159-60.

33 Brown, *Klatsassan,* 3, 4, 10.

34 Ibid., 114-17.

35 Morice, *History,* 4-6. "Dene" is the name by which anthropologists refer to Canadian Athapaskans, and the name by which many refer to themselves. Beryl C. Gillespie, "Territorial Groups before 1821: Athapaskans of the Shield and the Mackenzie Drainage," in Helm, *Handbook,* vol. 6, 168.

36 Morice, *History,* 7, 209, 313-20; Mullhall, *Will to Power,* 25; Adrien Gabriel Morice, "The Western Denes," *Proceedings of the Canadian Institute,* 3rd ser., vol. 7 (1889): 118.
37 Morice, *History,* 9, 14, 16, 19.
38 Magazine article: Richard Thomas Wright, "The Chinlac Massacre," *BC Outdoors* (March 1986): 54-55, 63-64. Archaeology: Charles E. Borden, "Results of Archaeological Investigations in Central British Columbia," *Anthropology in BC* 3 (1952): 34.
39 Morice, *History,* 76, 123-24, 193; Simon Fraser, "Journal of a Voyage from the Rocky Mountains to the Pacific Coast," in *Les Bourgeois de la Compagnie du Nord-Ouest,* ed. Louis Rodrigue Masson (Quebec, 1808), 165. In his article "Some Early Historians of British Columbia" (*BC Historical Quarterly* 21, nos. 1-4 [1957-58]), Walter N. Sage notes that Morice "was no admirer of H.H. Bancroft."
40 Morice, *History,* 314, 338.
41 F.W. Howay, *British Columbia from the Earliest Times to the Present* (Vancouver: S.J. Clarke, 1914), 2:181, 188.
42 Forgetting: Theodore W. Adorno and Max Horkheimer, "all reification is a forgetting," in *Dialectic of Enlightenment* (London: Verso, 1979), 230. Mythical frontier: Elizabeth Furniss, *The Burden of History: Colonialism and the Frontier Myth in a Rural Canadian Community* (Vancouver: UBC Press, 1999). Role of colonial photography: Carol J. Williams, *Framing the West: Race, Gender, and the Photographic Frontier in the Pacific Northwest* (Oxford: Oxford University Press, 2003).
43 Skirmish: Terry George, comp., *History and Legends of the Chilcotin* (Williams Lake, BC: Cariboo Press, [1958]), 36. Battle Mountains: Teit, *The Shuswap,* quoted in G.P.V. Akrigg and Helen B. Akrigg, *British Columbia Place Names,* 3rd ed.(Vancouver: UBC Press, 1997), 15.
44 Richmond Pearson Hobson Jr., *Grass beyond the Mountains: Discovering the Last Great Cattle Frontier on the North American Continent* (Toronto: McClelland and Stewart, 1987), 35, 124; Eric Collier, *Three against the Wilderness* (Toronto: Clarke, Irwin, 1959), 3.
45 "Mountain Ranges Guard Isolated Anahim Country," *Vancouver Sun,* 19 October 1953, BCA D19-003; Richard Andre Ramme, "Cow-Town People," *Vancouver Sun Magazine Supplement,* 27 January 1951, BCA D19-002.
46 Copy of RCMP Division file 51-X-16, forwarded to Archives on 30 October 1951, BCA D19-002.
47 BCA MS-0364, Box 10, File 12. Article reprinted with the permission of the Williams Lake *Tribune.*
48 Hance and Quilt: Veera Bonner, Irene E. Bliss, and Hazel Henry Litterick, eds., *Chilcotin: Preserving Pioneer Memories* (Surrey, BC: Heritage House, 1995). Quilt accused of perjury: BCA GR0429, Box 2, File 4, fos. 689/91, 709/91, 805/91, 831/91 and 876/91.
49 E.P. Lee, "Out of the Horse's Mouth," BCA MS0364, Box 10, File 12; "Ancient Way of Life Continues on Isolated B.C. Reserve," *Kelowna Courier,* 15 October 1959, BCA D19-003; "Taming the Chilcotin," *Cariboo Nugget* 1, 3 (July 1968) [special edition published by *News of Williams Lake and the Cariboo*], BCA microfilmed newspapers; *Big Country Adventurer* (Williams Lake), 1, 1 (1 June 1970), BCA MS0364, Box 10, File 13; "The Big Country," special edition of the *Williams Lake Tribune,* Summer 1970, BCA MS0364, Box 10, File 9 ("raping" quote, 21).
50 Tim Cahill, "Death on Chilcotin Road," *Rolling Stone,* 4 January 1973, 45, 46.
51 Jes Odam, "Second Fied Quilt Inquest Opens," *Vancouver Sun,* 18 July 1972, BCA

MS0364, Box 10, File 8; Dave Stockand, "Death and Game Show Gap in Indian-White Relations," *Vancouver Sun,* 21 July 1972, BCA MS0364, Box 10, File 8; Jes Odam, "Mountie's Report Refused Quilt Jury," *Vancouver Sun,* 21 July 1972, BCA MS0364, Box 10, File 8; Jes Odam, "Nurse Told by Quilt That Police Kicked Him," *Vancouver Sun,* 25 July 1972, BCA MS0364, Box 10, File 8; Jes Odam, "Doctor Disputes Quilt Autopsy Finding," *Vancouver Sun,* 22 July 1972, BCA MS0364 Box 10, File 8.

52 Jes Odam, "Fred Quilt Fell Twice on Road, Mountie Tells Inquest Jury," *Vancouver Sun,* 26 July 1972, BCA MS0364 Box 10, File 8; Odam, "Mountie's Report Refused"; Jes Odam, "Mountie Denies Anyone Jumped on Fred Quilt," *Vancouver Sun,* 20 July 1972, BCA MS0364, Box 10, File 8.

53 Jes Odam, "Bloodstained Shirt Shown to Quilt Inquest Jury," *Vancouver Sun,* 19 July 1972, BCA MS0364, Box 10, File 8; Odam, "Nurse Told by Quilt"; Nate Smith, "Quilt Failed Rapidly Driver Tells Inquest," *Vancouver Sun,* n.d., BCA MS0364, Box 10, File 8.

54 Cahill, "Death," 48 (first quote Cahill, second Stockand); "Laker Acquitted, Two Fined," *News of Williams Lake and the Cariboo,* 20 September 1967; Harold Box, "Appeal Rose Roper Case," *News of WL and Cariboo,* 4 October 1967; Fr. Leo Casey, OMI, "An Open Letter to Rosemary Roper," *News of WL and Cariboo,* 13 March 1968; "Croft, Wilson Sentenced on Assault Charges," *News of WL and Cariboo,* 2 April 1968 (all in BCA microfilmed newspaper collection).

55 Cahill, "Death"; Terry Glavin, "Last Day in Alexis Creek" in *This Ragged Place: Travels across the Landscape* (Vancouver: New Star, 1996), 122-69.

56 Protests and demonstrations: Jes Odam, "New Quilt Inquest Opens in Kamloops," *Vancouver Sun,* 17 July 1972, BCA MS0364, Box 10, File 8. Fred Quilt Committee: Cahill, "Death," 50. LeCours as maverick MLA: *Hansard,* 4th sess., 32nd Parl. (22 June 1982), 8363. His defence of underdogs: *Hansard,* 2nd sess., 30th Parl. (6 February 1973), 260. Lecours on Fred Quilt: *Hansard,* 3rd sess., 29th Parl. (21 January 1972), 12-13. Hartley on Fred Quilt: *Hansard,* 3rd sess., 29th Parl. (27 January 1972), 105-6.

57 Chief coroner: Cahill, "Death." Nimsick: *Hansard,* 3rd sess., 29th Parl. (14 February 1972), 483. Widespread dissatisfaction: Cahill, "Death," 45, 50, 52.

58 Association between RCMP and coroner's jury: "BC Indian Death Still Unresolved," *Canadian News Facts* 6, 14 (1972): 864. Kamloops inquest: Odam, "New Quilt Inquest." Harry Rankin: Cahill, "Death," 52; "BC Indian Death Still Unresolved,"; Doug Ward, "'People's Champion' a Fighter to the End," *Vancouver Sun,* 27 February 2002; Allen Garr, "Harry Left Huge Imprint," *Vancouver Courier,* 11 March 2002. "Brutal racist police": "Indians Urged to Strive for Better Place in Life," *Vancouver Sun,* 17 July 1972, BCA MS0364, Box 10, File 8. Vigil: Dave Stockand, "2 MPs Rapped by Indians," *Vancouver Sun,* 18 July 1972, BCA MS0364, Box 10, File 8.

59 Odam, "Second Fred Quilt Inquest"; Odam, "Mountie Denies Anyone Jumped on Fred Quilt."

60 Odam, "Mountie's Report Refused"; Jes Odam, "Quilt Family Put Up a 'Wall of Silence' to Police after Death," *Vancouver Sun,* 28 July 1972, BCA MS0364, Box 10, File 8.

61 Cahill, "Death"; Odam, "Mountie's Report Refused"; Odam, "Doctor Disputes"; Odam, "Nurse Told by Quilt"; Odam, "Second Fred Quilt Inquest"; Odam, "Bloodstained Shirt."

62 "BC Indian Death Still Unresolved"; Cahill, "Death."

63 Best documented: Hewlett, "Chilcotin Uprising of 1864," 51. Thesis, articles, and books: Edward Sleigh Hewlett, "The Chilcotin Uprising: A Study of Indian-European

Relations in Nineteenth Century British Columbia" (master's thesis, University of British Columbia, 1972); Garnet Basque, "The Waddington Massacre," *Canadian Frontier* (1972): 11-16, BCA Library NW971.C225 v. 1; Sleigh, "Chilcotin Uprising of 1864"; Neville Langrell Barlee, "The Chilcotin War of 1864," *Canada West Magazine* (Fall 1976): 13-23, BCA Library NW971K.C212 v. 6; Mel Rothenburger, *The Chilcotin War* (Langley, BC: Mr. Paperback, 1978).

64 Judith Williams, *High Slack: Waddington's Gold Road and the Bute Inlet Massacre of 1864* (Vancouver: New Star, 1996), 107; Furniss, *Burden of History*, 64; Rothenburger, *Chilcotin War*, 7-8.

65 Both quotes are from the cover of the 1978 edition published by Mr. Paperback of Langley, BC. This edition seems to have been the most widely distributed: a World-Cat search (3 December 2003) showed that thirty-two libraries in the US and Canada hold a copy of the Mr. Paperback edition. There was also a 1976 edition published in Kamloops, BC, by Ryan, Mclean Alaric. The only publicly held copy of the earlier edition seems to be in Library and Archives Canada. The cover painting is attributed to "Manitoba artist Terry McLean."

66 Margaret Atwood, *Survival: A Thematic Guide to Canadian Literature* (Toronto: House of Anansi Press, 1972); Rothenburger, *Chilcotin War*, 18, 20, 48, 50, 55. Generalizations: Loo, "Bute Inlet Stories," 140.

67 Rothenburger, *Chilcotin War*, 58, 70-71, 129, 145, 155-58. Historian's duty to "make a special effort to achieve parity of treatment" when "study[ing] the clash of two societies": James Axtell, "A Moral History of Indian-White Relations Revisited" (quotes) and "Forked Tongues: Moral Judgments in Indian History," in *After Columbus: Essays in the Ethnohistory of Colonial North America* (New York: Oxford University Press, 1988).

68 Rothenburger, *Chilcotin War*, 14-16, 21-22, 25-26, 30-33, 43, 47, 68, 121-22, 131, 133, 142-43, 147-49, 150, 158.

69 Ibid., 23-24, 37, 40, 72, 91-92, 125, 141, 156, 159.

70 Barman, *West beyond the West;* Colin J.B. Wood, ed., *British Columbia, the Pacific Province: Geographical Essays,* ed. (Victoria: Western Geographical Press, 2001).

71 CBC Newsworld Flashback 1990, http://archives.cbc.ca/IDD-1-71-99/conflict_war/oka/; "The High Cost of Oka," *Edmonton Journal,* 6 May 1991.

72 "Natives and the Justice System: Shortcomings Revealed in the Cases of Five Natives," *Ottawa Citizen,* 3 August 1991; "Native Justice: Case Histories Leave Many Questions Unanswered," *Calgary Herald,* 11 August 1991.

73 Cariboo-Chilcotin Justice Inquiry (BC), and Anthony Sarich (hereafter cited as *CCJI*), *Report on the Cariboo-Chilcotin Justice Inquiry* (Victoria: Cariboo-Chilcotin Justice Inquiry, 1993), 5-8.

74 Ibid., 10-13 (quote on 12-13).

75 Ibid., 18-25.

76 Ibid., 13, 14, 56; Glavin, *This Ragged Place,* 163 (Barnett quote).

77 *CCJI*, 15, 16.

78 Ibid., 29-41.

79 Ibid., 30.

80 Williams, *High Slack,* 104-7 (Rothenburger quote on 106-7). The "High Slack" exhibit was on display at the museum from 21 June 1994 to 3 January 1995.

81 Glavin, "The Circus Comes to Gustafsen Lake" in *This Ragged Place,* 109-20 (quote on 109).

82 Glavin, "The Circus Comes to Gustafsen Lake"; Janice G.A.E. Switlo, *Gustafsen Lake under Siege: Exposing the Truth behind the Gustafsen Lake Stand-Off* (Peachland, BC: TIAC Communications, 1997); Francis, *Encyclopedia of British Columbia*, s.v., "Gustafsen Lake."

83 Cf. Paula Pryce, *'Keeping the Lakes' Way': Reburial and the Re-Creation of a Moral World among an Invisible People* (Toronto: University of Toronto Press, 1999), 11, 94-95, 106.

84 Canadian Heritage, Human Rights Program, "Thirteenth and Fourteenth Reports of Canada on the International Convention on the Elimination of All Forms of Racial Discrimination covering the Period June 1993 to May 1997," (Ottawa: Canadian Heritage, 2001), pt. 4, art. 5, http://www.pch.gc.ca/progs/pdp-hrp/docs/cerd/index13-14_e.cfm.

AFTERWORD

1 Paul H. St. Pierre, *Smith and Other Events: Tales of the Chilcotin* (New York: Penguin, 1985), 71.

2 The horse was domesticated around 4000 BC in the Ukraine. Jared M. Diamond, *Guns, Germs, and Steel: The Fates of Human Societies* (New York: W.W. Norton, 1997).

GLOSSARY

1 Charles Hartshorne, Paul Weiss, and Arthur W. Burks, eds., *Collected Papers of Charles Saunders Peirce* (Cambridge, MA: Harvard University Press, 1935-66), 2:623-25; Umberto Eco and Thomas A. Sebeok, eds., *The Sign of Three: Dupin, Holmes, Peirce* (Bloomington: Indiana University Press, 1984).

2 Information obtained from the BC Archival Union List at the BC Archival Information Network website (http://aabc.bc.ca/aabc/bcaul.html).

3 Nancy J. Turner, *Food Plants of Interior First Peoples* (Vancouver: UBC Press, 1997), 66.

4 University of Oxford Radiocarbon Accelerator Unit, OxCal v. 3.5, University of Oxford Radiocarbon Accelerator Unit. For more on dating, see Joseph W. Michels, "Dating Methods," *Annual Review of Anthropology* 1 (1972): 113-26; Neil Roberts, *The Holocene: An Environmental History* (Oxford: Blackwell, 1989); George Rapp Jr. and Christopher L. Hill, *Geoarchaeology: The Earth-Science Approach to Archaeological Investigation* (New Haven, CT: Yale University Press, 1998); Dina F. Dincauze, *Environmental Archaeology: Principles and Practice* (Cambridge: Cambridge University Press, 2000).

5 This usage is consistent with E.C. Pielou, *After the Ice Age: The Return of Life to Glaciated North America* (Chicago: University of Chicago Press, 1991); Richard J. Hebda, "Postglacial History of Grasslands of Southern British Columbia and Adjacent Regions," in *Grassland Ecology and Classification Symposium Proceedings*, ed. A.C. Nicholson, A. McLean, and T.E. Baker (Victoria: BC Ministry of Forests, 1982), 442-54; Mike K. Rousseau, "Early Prehistoric Occupation of South-Central British Columbia: A Review of the Evidence and Recommendations for Further Research," *BC Studies* 99 (1993), 140-83; Arnould H. Stryd and Mike K. Rousseau, "Early Prehistory of the Mid Fraser-Thompson River Area," in *Early Human Occupation in British Columbia*, ed. Roy L. Carlson and Luke Dalla Bona (Vancouver: UBC Press, 1996),

177-204; and other authors. It differs from the dates given by Edward S. Deevey and Richard Foster Flint in "Postglacial Hypsithermal Interval" (*Science* 125, 3240 [1957]: 182-84), which are 9500 to 2500 BP.

6 Nancy J. Turner, *Plant Technology of First Peoples of British Columbia* (Vancouver: UBC Press, 1998), 73-74.

7 David Tilman and Peter Kareiva, eds., *Spatial Ecology: The Role of Space in Population Dynamics and Interspecific Interactions* (Princeton, NJ: Princeton University Press, 1997).

Bibliography

ARCHIVAL SOURCES

University of British Columbia Special Collections, Vancouver

Philip and Helen Akrigg Fonds
Pamphlet Collection

British Columbia Archives, Victoria

BC Attorney General Records. 1872-1937, GR0429
BC Colonial Correspondence. 1857-72, GR1372
BC Department of Lands and Works Records. 1871-83, GR0868
BC Department of Lands and Works Records. 1871-72, GR0983
BC Provincial Game Warden Records. 1905-22, GR0446
Farrow, Richard Charles, 1892-1950. Surveyor. Papers. 1929, MS1977
Orchard, Imbert, 1910-. Broadcaster. Papers. 1961-72, MS0364
Vertical files, 1851-1982, D19

Cariboo-Chilcotin Archives, Williams Lake, British Columbia

Archaeology: Vertical file
Environment: Box
Fish Lake, Gold/Copper Mining, Mining, Taseko, Prosperity: Vertical files
Mackenzie Grease Trail: Box

**Hudson's Bay Company Archives/Provincial Archives
    of Manitoba, Winnipeg**

Fort Alexandria post history and search file
Fort Chilcotin post history and search file
Fort Chilcotin post journals, 1837-40, HBCA/PAM B.37/a/1-2

Library and Archives Canada

Department of Indian Affairs, RG-10

OTHER SOURCES

Adams, William Y., Dennis P. Van Gerven, and Richard S. Levy. "The Retreat from Migrationism." *Annual Review of Anthropology* 7 (1978): 483-532.

Adorno, Theodore W., and Max Horkheimer. *Dialectic of Enlightenment.* London: Verso, 1979.

Akrigg, G.P.V., and Helen B. Akrigg. *British Columbia Place Names.* 3rd ed. Vancouver: UBC Press, 1997.

Alexander, Diana. "A Cultural Heritage Overview of the Cariboo Forest Region." Victoria: BC Ministry of Forests, Cariboo Forest Region, 1997.

Alexander Mackenzie Heritage Trail Coordinating Committee. "Alexander Mackenzie Heritage Trail: Management Plan for Trail Portions on Public Forest Lands." Williams Lake, BC: Alexander Mackenzie Heritage Trail Coordinating Committee, 1993.

Alley, Richard B. *The Two-Mile Time Machine: Ice Cores, Abrupt Climate Change, and Our Future.* Princeton, NJ: Princeton University Press, 2000.

Ames, Kenneth M., and Herbert D.G. Maschner. *Peoples of the Northwest Coast: Their Archaeology and Prehistory.* London: Thames and Hudson, 1999.

Anonymous. *Cariboo: The Newly Discovered Gold Fields of British Columbia.* Fairfield, WA: Ye Galleon Press, 1975.

Anonymous. *Trapper's Companion.* Columbus, OH: A.R. Harding, 1946.

Apland, Brian. "Reconnaissance Survey in the Rainbow Mountains Region of West-Central British Columbia." In *Annual Report for the Year 1976: Activities of the Provincial Archaeologist's Office of British Columbia and Selected Research Reports.* Victoria: BC Ministry of Provincial Secretary and Government Services, 1979.

Applied Ecosystem Management Ltd. "Characterising Fire Regimes in Sub-Boreal Landscapes: Fire History Research in SBPS and SBS Biogeoclimatic Zones of the Cariboo Forest Region." Williams Lake, BC: Lignum Ltd., 2002.

Atwood, Margaret. *Survival: A Thematic Guide to Canadian Literature.* Toronto: House of Anansi Press, 1972.

Axtell, James. *After Columbus: Essays in the Ethnohistory of Colonial North America.* New York: Oxford University Press, 1988.

Barfield, Thomas J., ed. *The Dictionary of Anthropology.* Oxford: Blackwell, 1997.

Barlee, Neville Langrell. "The Chilcotin War of 1864." *Canada West Magazine,* Fall 1976, 13-23. BC Archives Library NW971K.C212 v. 6.

Barman, Jean. *The West beyond the West: A History of British Columbia.* Toronto: University of Toronto Press, 1991.

Bartington, G. "Sensors for Low Level, Low Frequency Magnetic Fields." Paper presented at the IEE Colloquium on Low Level Low Frequency Magnetic Fields, London, 14 April 1994.

Bartra, Roger. *The Artificial Savage: Modern Myths of the Wild Man.* Ann Arbor: University of Michigan Press, 1997.

Barzel, Yoram. *Economic Analysis of Property Rights.* Cambridge: Cambridge University Press, 1989.

Basavarajappa, K.G., and Bali Ram. "Origins of the Population, Census Dates, 1871 to 1971." In *Historical Statistics of Canada*, Section A, *Population and Migration*, edited by F.H. Leacy, A125-63. Ottawa: Statistics Canada, 1999.

Basinger, James F., Elisabeth McIver, and Wesley C. Wehr. "Eocene Conifers of the Interior." In *Life in Stone: A Natural History of British Columbia Fossils*, edited by R. Ludvigsen, 248-58. Vancouver: UBC Press, 1996.

Basque, Garnet. "The Waddington Massacre." *Canadian Frontier*, 1972, 11-16. BC Archives Library NW971.C225 v. 1.

Basso, Keith H. *Wisdom Sits in Places: Landscape and Language among the Western Apache*. Albuquerque: University of New Mexico, 1996.

BC Department of Mines and Petroleum Resources. *The Identification of Common Rocks*. Victoria: BC Department of Mines and Petroleum Resources, 1970.

BC Department of Recreation and Conservation. *British Columbia Recreational Atlas*. 1st ed. Victoria: BC Department of Recreation and Conservation, 1975.

BC Environmental Assessment Office. Project Information Centre (e-PIC). http://www.eao.gov.bc.ca/epic/output/html/deploy/epic_home.html (object name Prosperity Copper-Gold Project; accessed 5 July 2003).

BC Ministry of Agriculture and Food. "Agriculture in the Cariboo-Chilcotin." Victoria: BC Ministry of Agriculture and Food, 1999.

BC Ministry of Energy, Mines and Petroleum Resources. *Annual Report 1988/89*. Victoria: BC Ministry of Energy, Mines and Petroleum Resources, 1989.

–. *Annual Report 1990/91*. Victoria: BC Ministry of Energy, Mines and Petroleum Resources, 1991.

BC Ministry of Energy, Mines and Petroleum Resources. Assessment Report Indexing System (ARIS). http://www.em.gov.bc.ca/mining/Geolsurv/aris/default.htm (for assessment reports; accessed 11 June 2003).

BC Ministry of Energy, Mines and Petroleum Resources. Mineral Inventory (MINFILE). http://www.em.gov.bc.ca/Mining/Geolsurv/Minfile/ (object name MINFILE 092O 041; accessed 11 June 2003).

BC Ministry of Forests. "The Ecology of the Bunchgrass Zone." Victoria: BC Ministry of Forests, Research Branch, 1998.

–. "The Ecology of the Engelmann Spruce – Subalpine Fir Zone." Victoria: BC Ministry of Forests, Research Branch, 1998.

–. "The Ecology of the Interior Douglas-fir Zone." Victoria: BC Ministry of Forests, Research Branch, n.d.

–. "The Ecology of the Sub-Boreal Pine – Spruce Zone." Victoria: BC Ministry of Forests, Research Branch, 1998.

–. "The Ecology of the Sub-Boreal Spruce Zone." Victoria: BC Ministry of Forests, Research Branch, 1998.

BC Ministry of Forests. Research Branch. "Biogeoclimatic Zones of British Columbia." Victoria: Government of BC, 1999.

BC Ministry of Mines. *Annual Report of the Minister of Mines of the Province of British Columbia for the Year Ended 31st December 1935*. Victoria: BC Ministry of Mines, 1936.

BC Parks. Cariboo District. *Tŝ'il?os Provincial Park Master Plan*. Victoria: BC Parks, Cariboo District, 1997.

BC Treaty Commission. "A Lay Person's Guide to Delgamuukw." Vancouver: BC Treaty Commission, 1999.

—. "Why Treaties?" Vancouver: BC Treaty Commission, 2000.

Beck, M.E., Jr. "Discordant Paleomagnetic Pole Positions as Evidence of Regional Shear in the Western Cordillera of North America." *American Journal of Science* 276 (1976): 694-712.

Bergman, Brian. "A River of Destiny: Mackenzie's Arctic Voyage Still Disturbs Natives." *Maclean's*, 6 July 1992.

Berkhofer, Robert F. *The White Man's Indian: Images of the American Indian from Columbus to the Present.* New York: Vintage, 1979.

Bevier, M.L., R.L. Armstrong, and J.G. Souther. "Miocene Peralkaline Volcanism in West-Central British Columbia, Its Temporal and Plate Tectonics Setting." *Geology* 7 (1979): 389-92.

Binnema, Theodore. *Common and Contested Ground: A Human and Environmental History of the Northwestern Plains.* Norman: University of Oklahoma Press, 2001.

Birchwater, Sage. *Ulkatcho: Stories of the Grease Trail.* Anahim Lake, BC: Ulkatcho Indian Band, 1993.

—. *'Ulkatchot'en: The People of Ulkatcho.* Anahim Lake, BC: Ulkatcho Indian Band, 1991.

Bishop, Richard Preston. *Mackenzie's Rock.* Ottawa: Department of the Interior, 1924.

Black-Rogers, Mary. "Varieties of 'Starving': Semantics and Survival in the Subarctic Fur Trade, 1750-1850," *Ethnohistory* 33, 4 (1986): 353-83.

Blacklaws, Richard William. *Mackenzie Grease Trail Heritage Inventory and Assessment Project: Kluskus-Ulkatcho.* Victoria: BC Heritage Conservation Branch, 1979. Cariboo-Chilcotin Archives, box on the Mackenzie Grease Trail.

Blacklaws, Richard William, and Diana French. *Ranchland: British Columbia's Cattle Country.* Madeira Park, BC: Harbour, 2001.

Bloch, Marc. *The Historian's Craft.* New York: Vintage, 1953.

Bonner, Veera, Irene E. Bliss, and Hazel Henry Litterick. *Chilcotin: Preserving Pioneer Memories.* Surrey, BC: Heritage House, 1995.

Borden, Charles E. "A Late Pleistocene Pebble Tool Industry of Southwestern British Columbia." In *Early Man in Western North America,* edited by C. Irwin-Williams, 55-69. Portales, NM: Eastern New Mexico University Press, 1968.

—. "Results of Archaeological Investigations in Central British Columbia." *Anthropology in BC* 3 (1952): 31-43.

—. "A Uniform Site Designation Scheme for Canada." *Anthropology in BC* 3 (1952): 44-48.

Boyd, Robert. *The Coming of the Spirit of Pestilence: Introduced Infectious Diseases and Population Decline among Northwest Coast Indians, 1774-1874.* Vancouver: UBC Press, 1999.

—. "Demographic History, 1774-1874." In *Handbook of North American Indians.* Vol. 7, *Northwest Coast,* edited by Wayne Suttles, 135-48. Washington, DC: Smithsonian Institution, 1990.

Bracken, Christopher. *The Potlatch Papers: A Colonial Case History.* Chicago: University of Chicago Press, 1997.

Brealey, Ken G. "Mapping Them 'Out': Euro-Canadian Cartography and the Appropriation of the Nuxalk and Ts'ilhqot'in First Nations' Territories, 1793-1916." *Canadian Geographer* 39, 2 (1995): 140-56.

Briggs, John C. "Introduction to the Zoogeography of North American Fishes." In *The Zoogeography of North American Freshwater Fishes,* edited by C.H. Hocutt and E.O. Wiley, 1-16. New York: Wiley-Interscience, 1986.

Brink, Bert. "Glacial Lakes in British Columbia." *Cordillera* (1997): 3-6.

Brody, Hugh. *Maps and Dreams.* New York: Pantheon, 1981.

–. *The Other Side of Eden: Hunters, Farmers, and the Shaping of the World.* New York: North Point, 2000.

Brown, Jack, and Darlene Brown. *The Legend of Pan Philips.* Victoria: Morriss Publishing, 1988.

Brown, Jennifer S.H. *Strangers in Blood: Fur Trade Company Families in Indian Country.* Norman: University of Oklahoma Press, 1996.

Brown, R.C. Lundin. *Klatsassan, and Other Reminiscences of Missionary Life in British Columbia.* London: Society for Promoting Christian Knowledge, 1873.

Brunvand, Jan Harold. *The Vanishing Hitchhiker: American Urban Legends and Their Meanings.* New York: W.W. Norton, 1981.

Burke, Peter. *What is Cultural History?* Cambridge: Polity, 2004.

Bynum, Caroline Walker. "Wonder." *American Historical Review* 102, 1 (1997): 1-17.

Byram, Scott, and David G. Lewis. "Ourigan: Wealth of the Northwest Coast." *Oregon Historical Quarterly* 102, 2 (2001): 126-57.

Cahill, Tim. "Death on Chilcotin Road." *Rolling Stone,* 4 January 1973, 44-52.

Calder v. Attorney General of British Columbia, [1973] S.C.R. 313; 34 D.L.R. (3d) 145.

Campbell, Clayton W., and Alfred H. Bawtree, eds. *Rangeland Handbook for BC.* Kamloops: BC Cattlemen's Association, 1998.

Canada. *The Charter of Rights and Freedoms: A Guide for Canadians.* Ottawa: Supply and Services, 1982.

Canada. Department of Canadian Heritage. Human Rights Program. "Thirteenth and Fourteenth Reports of Canada on the International Convention on the Elimination of All Forms of Racial Discrimination covering the Period June 1993 to May 1997." Ottawa: Department of Canadian Heritage, Human Rights Program, 2001. http://www.pch.gc.ca/progs/pdp-hrp/docs/cerd/index13-14_e.cfm.

Canada. Energy, Mines and Resources Canada. *National Atlas of Canada.* 5th ed. Ottawa: Energy, Mines and Resources Canada, 1985.

Canada. Parks Canada, and BC Ministry of Lands, Parks and Housing. "Canada – British Columbia Agreement for Recreation and Conservation on the Alexander Mackenzie Heritage Trail: Master Development Plan." Ottawa: Parks Canada, 1985.

Canada. Parks Canada. ARC Branch. Planning Division. "Alexander Mackenzie Historic Trail: Preliminary Development Concept." Ottawa: Department of Indian and Northern Affairs, 1976. Cariboo-Chilcotin Archives, box on the Mackenzie Grease Trail.

Canadian Depository for Securities (for Canadian Securities Administrators). System for Electronic Document Analysis and Retrieval (SEDAR). http://www.sedar.com/homepage_en.htm (object name Taskeo Mines Ltd.; accessed 9 June 2003).

Canadian Oxford Dictionary. Don Mills, ON: Oxford University Press, 2001.

Cann, J.R., J.E. Dixon, and Colin Renfrew. "Obsidian Analysis and the Obsidian Trade." In *Science in Archaeology,* edited by D. Brothwell and E. Higgs, 578-91. London: Thames and Hudson, 1969.

Cannings, Richard James, and Sydney Graham Cannings. *British Columbia: A Natural History.* Vancouver: Greystone Books, 2000.

Cannings, Sydney Graham, and Richard James Cannings. *Geology of British Columbia: A Journey through Time.* Vancouver: Greystone Books, 1999.

Cannon, Aubrey. "The Early Namu Archaeofauna." In *Early Human Occupation in British Columbia,* edited by Roy L. Carlson and Luke Dalla Bona, 103-10. Vancouver: UBC Press, 1996.

Careless, J.M.S. *Frontier and Metropolis: Regions, Cities, and Identities in Canada before 1914.* Toronto: University of Toronto Press, 1989.

—. "Frontierism, Metropolitanism, and Canadian History." *Canadian Historical Review* 35 (March 1954): 1-21.

—. "The Toronto *Globe* and Agrarian Radicalism." *Canadian Historical Review* 29, (March 1948): 14-39.

Cariboo-Chilcotin Justice Inquiry (BC), and Anthony Sarich. *Report on the Cariboo-Chilcotin Justice Inquiry.* Victoria: Cariboo-Chilcotin Justice Inquiry, 1993.

Carl, G. Clifford, W.A. Clemens, and C.C. Lindsey. *Fresh-Water Fishes of British Columbia.* Victoria: BC Provincial Museum, Department of Recreation and Conservation, 1967.

Carlson, Roy L. "C.E. Borden's Archaeological Legacy." *BC Studies* 42 (1979): 3-12.

—. "Early Namu." In *Early Human Occupation in British Columbia,* edited by Roy L. Carlson and Luke Dalla Bona, 83-102. Vancouver: UBC Press, 1996.

—. "The Early Period on the Central Coast of British Columbia." *Canadian Journal of Archaeology* 3 (1979): 211-28.

—. "The Later Prehistory of British Columbia." In *Early Human Occupation in British Columbia,* edited by Roy L. Carlson and Luke Dalla Bona, 215-26. Vancouver: UBC Press, 1996.

—. "Trade and Exchange in Prehistoric British Columbia." In *Prehistoric Exchange Systems in North America,* edited by Timothy G. Baugh and Jonathon E. Ericson, 307-61. New York: Plenum, 1994.

Carlson, Roy L., and Luke Dalla Bona, eds. *Early Human Occupation in British Columbia.* Vancouver: UBC Press, 1996.

Carr, Edward Hallett. *What Is History?* New York: Vintage, 1961.

Carver, Jonathan. *Voyage dans les Parties Intérieures de l'Amérique Septentrionale, pendant les Années 1766, 1767 et 1768.* Yverdon Suisse, 1784. Available from Canadiana.org (formerly the Canadian Institute for Historical Microreproductions), CIHM 90454.

Casey, Edward S. "How to Get from Space to Place in a Fairly Short Stretch of Time: Phenomenological Prolegomena." In *Senses of Place,* edited by Steven Feld and Keith H. Basso, 13-52. Santa Fe, NM: School of American Research Press, 1996.

Cassidy, Frank, ed. *Aboriginal Title in British Columbia: Delgamuukw v. The Queen.* Lantzville, BC: Oolichan Books, 1992.

Cavender, Ted M. "Review of the Fossil History of North American Freshwater Fishes." In *The Zoogeography of North American Freshwater Fishes,* edited by C.H. Hocutt and E.O. Wiley, 699-724. New York: Wiley-Interscience, 1986.

Champness, W. *To Cariboo and Back in 1862.* Fairfield, WA: Ye Galleon Press, 1972.

Chesterman, Charles W. *National Audubon Society Field Guide to North American Rocks and Minerals.* New York: Knopf, 1979.

Chisholm, B.S., D.E. Nelson, and H.P. Schwarcz. "Stable-Carbon Isotope Ratios as a Measure of Marine versus Terrestrial Protein in Ancient Diets." *Science* 216 (1982): 1131-32.

Clague, John Joseph, John R. Harper, Richard J. Hebda, and D.E. Howes. "Late

Quaternary Sea Levels and Crustal Movements, Coastal British Columbia." *Canadian Journal of Earth Sciences* 19 (1982): 597-618.

Clague, John Joseph, and Thomas S. James. "History and Isostatic Effects of the Last Ice Sheet in Southern British Columbia." *Quaternary Science Reviews* 21, nos. 1-3 (2002): 71-87.

Clague, John Joseph, and John L. Luternauer. "Late Quaternary Sedimentary Environments, Southwestern British Columbia." In *Field Excursion Guide Book 30A.* St. Johns, NL: Geological Association of Canada, 1982.

Clark, Donald W. "Prehistory of the Western Subarctic." In *Handbook of North American Indians.* Vol. 6, *Subarctic,* edited by June Helm, 107-29. Washington, DC: Smithsonian Institution, 1981.

–. *Western Subarctic Prehistory.* Ottawa: Canadian Museum of Civilization, 1991.

Clemson, Donovan. *Living with Logs: British Columbia's Log Buildings and Rail Fences.* Saanichton, BC: Hancock House, 1974.

–. "Pioneer Fences." In *Pioneer Days in British Columbia,* edited by Art Downs, 26-31. Surrey, BC: Heritage House, 1975.

Coase, Ronald H. "The Institutional Structure of Production (1991 Alfred Nobel Memorial Lecture in Economic Sciences)." In *Essays on Economics and Economists,* 3-14. Chicago: University of Chicago Press, 1994.

–. "The Problem of Social Cost." *Journal of Law and Economics* 3 (1960): 1-44.

Codere, Helen. *Fighting with Property: A Study of Kwakiutl Potlatching and Warfare, 1792-1930.* New York: J.J. Augustus, 1950.

–. "Kwakiutl: Traditional Culture." In *Handbook of North American Indians.* Vol. 7, *Northwest Coast,* edited by Wayne Suttles, 359-77. Washington, DC: Smithsonian Institution, 1990.

Cole, Bruce. "On the Trail with Lewis and Clark: A Conversation with Gary Moulton." *Humanities* (National Endowment for the Humanities), November-December 2002.

Cole, Douglas, and Ira Chaikin. *An Iron Hand upon the People: The Law against Potlatch on the Northwest Coast.* Vancouver: Douglas and McIntyre, 1990.

Cole, Douglas, and Bradley Lockner, eds. *The Journals of George M. Dawson: British Columbia, 1875-1878.* 2 vols. Vancouver: UBC Press, 1989.

Collier, Eric. *Three against the Wilderness.* Toronto: Clarke, Irwin and Company, 1959.

Colpitts, George W. *Game in the Garden: A Human History of Wildlife in Western Canada to 1940.* Vancouver: UBC Press, 2003.

Compton, P.N. "Forts and Fort Life in New Caledonia under the Hudson's Bay Company Regime." Victoria, 1878. Philip and Helen Akrigg Fonds, Box 4, File 49, Xerox 339, University of BC Special Collections.

Coney, P.J., D.L. Jones, and J.W.H. Monger. "Cordilleran Suspect Terranes." *Nature* 288 (1980): 329-33.

Connerton, Paul. *How Societies Remember.* Cambridge: Cambridge University Press, 1989.

Cook, Ramsay, George W. Brown, Frances G. Halpenny, and David M. Hayne, eds. *Dictionary of Canadian Biography.* 14 vols. Toronto: University of Toronto Press, 1966-98. Available online at http://www.biographi.ca/EN/index.html.

Cook, Ramsay, John Saywell, and John Ricker. *Canada: A Modern Study.* Rev. ed. Toronto: Clarke, Irwin and Company, 1977.

Corporation of BC Land Surveyors. "Richard Preston Bishop B.C.L.S, F.R.G.S. 1884-1954." In *Report of Proceedings of the 50th Annual General Meeting,* 47-48. N.p.: Corporation of BC Land Surveyors, 1955. Philip and Helen Akrigg Fonds 5-52, University of BC Special Collections.

Cowan, Ian McTaggart. "The Fur Trade and the Fur Cycle: 1825-1857." *BC Historical Quarterly* (1938): 19-30.

Cowan, Ian McTaggart, and Charles J. Guiguet. *The Mammals of British Columbia.* Victoria: BC Provincial Museum. Department of Recreation and Conservation, 1965.

Cox, Ross. *Adventures on the Columbia River: Including the Narrative of a Residence of Six Years on the Western Side of the Rocky Mountains among Various Tribes of Indians hitherto Unknown: Together with a Journey across the American Continent.* New York: J. and J. Harper, 1832. Available from the Canadiana.org (formerly the Canadian Institute for Historical Microreproductions), CIHM 33317.

Cronon, William. *Changes in the Land: Indians, Colonists, and the Ecology of New England.* New York: Hill and Wang, 1983.

–. *Nature's Metropolis: Chicago and the Great West.* New York: W.W. Norton, 1991.

Crosby, Alfred W. *Ecological Imperialism: The Biological Expansion of Europe, 900-1900.* Cambridge: Cambridge University Press, 1993.

–. "Virgin Soil Epidemics as a Factor in the Aboriginal Depopulation of America." *William and Mary Quarterly* 33, 2 (1976): 290-99.

Cybulski, J.S., D.E. Howes, J.C. Haggarty, and M. Eldridge. "An Early Human Skeleton from Southcentral British Columbia: Dating and Bioarchaeological Inference." *Canadian Journal of Archaeology* 5 (1981): 59-60.

Davis, N.F.G., and W.H. Mathews. "Four Phases of Glaciation with Illustrations from Southwestern British Columbia." *Journal of Geology* 52 (1944): 403-13.

Dawson, George M. "Report on Explorations in British Columbia, Chiefly in the Basins of the Blackwater, Salmon, and Nechacco Rivers, and on François Lake." 17-49. [Ottawa?]: Geological Survey of Canada, 1877.

Deevey, Edward S., and Richard Foster Flint. "Postglacial Hypsithermal Interval." *Science* 125, 3240 (1957): 182-84.

Defoe, Daniel. *Robinson Crusoe.* New York: W.W. Norton, 1994.

Delgamuukw v. The Queen (1991), 79 D.L.R. (4th) 185 (B.C.S.C.).

Delgamuukw v. British Columbia, [1997] 3 S.C.R. 1010.

Deur, Douglas Eugene. "A Domesticated Landscape: Native American Plant Cultivation on the Northwest Coast of North America." PhD diss., Louisiana State University and Agricultural and Mechanical College, 2001.

Diakow, L.J., P. van der Heyden, and Paul Metcalfe. "Introduction." In *Interior Plateau Geoscience Project: Summary of Geological, Geochemical and Geophysical Studies,* edited by L.J. Diakow, J.M. Newell, and Paul Metcalfe, 1-3. Victoria: BC Geological Survey, 1997.

Diamond, Jared M. *Guns, Germs, and Steel: The Fates of Human Societies.* New York: W.W. Norton, 1997.

Dincauze, Dina F. *Environmental Archaeology: Principles and Practice.* Cambridge: Cambridge University Press, 2000.

Dinwoodie, David W. *Reserve Memories: The Power of the Past in a Chilcotin Community.* Lincoln: University of Nebraska Press, 2002.

Dixon, E. James. "Human Colonization of the Americas: Timing, Technology and Process." *Quaternary Science Reviews* 20, nos. 1-3 (2001): 277-99.

Dolmage, Victor. "Chilko Lake and Vicinity." In *Summary Report 1924, Part A,* 59-75. [Ottawa?]: Geological Survey of Canada, 1925.

–. "First Things First." *Mining and Industrial Record,* July 1931.

Donahue, Paul F. "Concerning Athapaskan Prehistory in British Columbia." *Western Canadian Journal of Anthropology* 5, nos. 3-4 (1975): 21-63.

–. "4500 Years of Cultural Continuity on the Central Interior Plateau of British Columbia." PhD diss., University of Wisconsin, 1977.

–. "Ulkatcho: An Archaeological Outline." *Syesis* 6 (1973): 153-78.

Donald, Leland. *Aboriginal Slavery on the Northwest Coast of North America.* Berkeley: University of California Press, 1997.

Dower, John W. "Three Narratives of Our Humanity." In *History Wars: The Enola Gay and Other Battles for the American Past,* edited by Edward T. Linenthal and Tom Engelhardt, 63-96. New York: Henry Holt, 1996.

Driver, Jonathan C. "Zooarchaeology in British Columbia." *BC Studies* 99 (1993): 77-105.

Drucker, Philip, and Robert F. Heizer. *To Make My Name Good: A Reexamination of the Southern Kwakiutl Potlatch.* Berkeley: University of California Press, 1967.

Duff, Wilson. *The Indian History of British Columbia: The Impact of the White Man.* Victoria: Royal BC Museum, 1997.

Dunn, Colin E. "Biogeochemical Surveys in the Interior Plateau of British Columbia." In *Interior Plateau Geoscience Project: Summary of Geological, Geochemical and Geophysical Studies,* edited by L.J. Diakow, J.M. Newell, and Paul Metcalfe, 205-18. Victoria: BC Geological Survey, 1997.

Eco, Umberto, and Thomas A. Sebeok, eds. *The Sign of Three: Dupin, Holmes, Peirce.* Bloomington: Indiana University Press, 1984.

Edwards, Philip, ed. *The Journals of Captain Cook.* London: Penguin, 1999.

Ellingson, Ter. *The Myth of the Noble Savage.* Berkeley: University of California Press, 2001.

Elliott, Gordon R. *Barkerville, Quesnel and the Cariboo Gold Rush.* Vancouver: Douglas and McIntyre, 1978.

Elton, G.R. *The Practice of History.* New York: Thomas Y. Crowell, 1967.

Emery, K.O., and Louis E. Garrison. "Sea Levels 7,000 to 20,000 Years Ago." *Science* 157 (1967): 684-91.

Emrich, Duncan. *Folklore on the American Land.* Boston: Little, Brown and Company, 1972.

Environmental Mining Council of BC. "Acid Mine Drainage: Mining and Water Pollution Issues in BC." Victoria: Environmental Mining Council of BC, 1997.

–. "Mining in Remote Areas: Issues and Impacts." Victoria: Environmental Mining Council of BC, 1998.

–. "More Precious than Gold: Mineral Development and the Protection of Biological Diversity in Canada." Victoria: Environmental Mining Council of BC, 1998.

–. "Undermining the Law: Addressing the Crisis in Compliance with Environmental Mining Laws in BC." Victoria: Environmental Mining Council of BC, 2001.

Farley, A. "The Historical Cartography of British Columbia." PhD diss., University of Wisconsin, 1960.

Farrand, Livingston. *Traditions of the Chilcotin Indians.* Edited by Franz Boas. Vol.

2(1), *Publications of the Jesup North Pacific Expedition.* New York: American Museum of Natural History, 1900.

Federation of Mountain Clubs of BC. "Chilcotin Wild and Gentle: The Chilcotin Wilderness." In *Educational Report.* Vancouver: Federation of Mountain Clubs of BC, 1991. University of BC Special Collections, Pamphlet Collection 21676.

Feld, Steven, and Keith H. Basso, eds. *Senses of Place.* Santa Fe, NM: School of American Research Press, 1996.

Fischer, David Hackett. *Historians' Fallacies: Toward a Logic of Historical Thought.* New York: Harper and Row, 1970.

Fisher, Robin. *Contact and Conflict: Indian-European Relations in British Columbia, 1774-1890.* 2nd ed. Vancouver: UBC Press, 1992.

Fladmark, Knut R. *British Columbia Prehistory.* Ottawa: National Museum of Man, 1986.

–. "Routes: Alternate Migration Corridors for Early Man in North America." *American Antiquity* 44 (1979): 55-69.

Flannery, Tim. *The Eternal Frontier: An Ecological History of North America and Its Peoples.* New York: Grove, 2001.

Fleming, R. Harvey, ed. *Minutes of Council, Northern Department of Rupert Land, 1821-31.* Toronto: Champlain Society, 1940.

Fleming, Sandford. *Report on Surveys and Preliminary Operations on the Canadian Pacific Railway up to January 1877.* Ottawa: MacLean, Roger and Company, 1877.

Foltz, Carolyn. *Voyagers of the Chilcotin.* Winnipeg: Hignell Printing, 1996.

Foner, S. "Review of Magnetometry." *IEEE Transactions on Magnetics* MAG-17, 6 (1981): 3358-63.

Foote, Kenneth E. *Shadowed Ground: America's Landscapes of Violence and Tragedy.* Austin: University of Texas Press, 1997.

Fossett, Renée. "Mapping Inuktut: Inuit Views of the Real World." In *Reading Beyond Words: Contexts for Native History,* edited by Jennifer S.H. Brown and Elizabeth Vibert, 74-94. Peterborough: Broadview, 1996.

Francis, Daniel, ed. *Encyclopedia of British Columbia.* Madeira Park, BC: Harbour Publishing, 2000.

Francis, Daniel, and Toby Morantz. *Partners in Furs: A History of the Fur Trade in Eastern James Bay 1600-1870.* Montreal and Kingston: McGill-Queen's University Press, 1983.

Fraser, Simon. "Journal of a Voyage from the Rocky Mountains to the Pacific Coast." In *Les Bourgeois de la Compagnie du Nord-Ouest,* edited by Louis Rodrigue Masson, 156-221. Quebec, 1808.

French, Diana. *The Road Runs West: A Century along the Bella Coola/Chilcotin Road.* Madeira Park, BC: Harbour, 1994.

Fujimura, Joan H. "Crafting Science: Standardized Packages, Boundary Objects, and 'Translation.'" In *Science as Practice and Culture,* edited by Andrew Pickering, 168-211. Chicago: University of Chicago Press, 1992.

Furniss, Elizabeth. *The Burden of History: Colonialism and the Frontier Myth in a Rural Canadian Community.* Vancouver: UBC Press, 1999.

–. "The Early Culture of the Southern Carrier." Manuscript. X̱wi7x̱wa Library, University of BC, 1991.

–. *Victims of Benevolence: The Dark Legacy of the Williams Lake Residential School.* Vancouver: Arsenal Pulp, 1995.

Furubotn, Eirik G., and Rudolf Richter. *Institutions and Economic Theory: The Contribution of the New Institutional Economics*. Ann Arbor: University of Michigan Press, 1997.

Gabrielse, H., and C.J. Yorath. "DNAG #4. The Cordilleran Orogen in Canada." *Geoscience Canada* 16, 2 (1989): 67-83.

Galbraith, John S. *The Hudson's Bay Company as an Imperial Factor, 1821-1869*. Berkeley: University of California Press, 1957.

Geertz, Clifford. *Local Knowledge: Further Essays in Interpretive Anthropology*. New York: Basic Books, 1983.

–. "Afterword." In *Senses of Place*, edited by Steven Feld and Keith H. Basso, 259-62. Santa Fe, NM: School of American Research Press, 1996.

George, Terry (compiler). *History and Legends of the Chilcotin*. Williams Lake, BC: Cariboo Press, [1958].

Gibbs, George. *Dictionary of the Chinook Jargon, or, Trade Language of Oregon*. New York: Cramoisy Press, 1863.

Gibson, James R. *Farming the Frontier: The Agricultural Opening of the Oregon Country 1786-1846*. Vancouver: UBC Press, 1985.

–. *The Lifeline of the Oregon Country: The Fraser-Columbia Brigade System, 1811-1847*. Vancouver: UBC Press, 1997.

–. *Otter Skins, Boston Ships, and China Goods: The Maritime Fur Trade of the Northwest Coast, 1785-1841*. Montreal and Kingston: McGill-Queen's University Press, 1991.

Gillespie, Beryl C. "Territorial Groups before 1821: Athapaskans of the Shield and the Mackenzie Drainage." In *Handbook of North American Indians*. Vol. 6, *Subarctic*, edited by June Helm, 161-68. Washington, DC: Smithsonian Institution, 1981.

Ginzburg, Carlo. "Clues: Roots of an Evidential Paradigm." In *Clues, Myths and the Historical Method*, 96-125. Baltimore: Johns Hopkins University Press, 1989.

Ginzburg, Carlo, and Carlo Ponti. "The Name and the Game: Unequal Exchange and the Historiographic Marketplace." In *Microhistory and the Lost Peoples of Europe*, edited by Edward Muir and Guido Ruggiero, 1-10. Baltimore: Johns Hopkins University Press, 1991.

Glavin, Terry. *This Ragged Place: Travels across the Landscape*. Vancouver: New Star, 1996.

Glavin, Terry, and People of Nemiah. *Nemiah: The Unconquered Country*. Vancouver: New Star, 1992.

Goetzmann, William H., and Glyndwr Williams. *The Atlas of North American Exploration: From the Norse Voyages to the Race to the Pole*. Norman: University of Oklahoma Press, 1992.

Goldman, Irving. "The Alkatcho Carrier of British Columbia." In *Acculturation in Seven American Indian Tribes*, edited by R. Linton. New York: D. Appleton-Century, 1940.

Gottesfeld-Johnson, L.M. "Aboriginal Burning for Vegetation Management in Northwest British Columbia." *Human Ecology* 22 (1994): 171-88.

–. *Plants That We Use: Traditional Plant Uses of the Wet'suwet'en People*. Moricetown, BC: Kyah Wiget Education Society, 1991.

Gough, Barry M. *Distant Dominion: Britain and the Northwest Coast of North America, 1579-1809*. Vancouver: UBC Press, 1980.

–. *First across the Continent: Sir Alexander Mackenzie*. Norman: University of Oklahoma Press, 1997.

–. *Gunboat Frontier: British Maritime Authority and Northwest Coast Indians, 1846-1890.* Vancouver: UBC Press, 1984.

Gunther, Erna. *Indian Life on the Northwest Coast of North America, As Seen by the Early Explorers and Fur Traders During the Last Decades of the Eighteenth Century.* Chicago: University of Chicago Press, 1972.

Halbwachs, Maurice. *On Collective Memory.* Chicago: University of Chicago Press, 1992.

Halpin, Marjorie M., and Margaret Seguin. "Tsimshian Peoples: Southern Tsimshian, Coast Tsimshian, Nishga, and Gitksan." In *Handbook of North American Indians.* Vol. 7, *Northwest Coast,* edited by Wayne Suttles, 267-84. Washington, DC: Smithsonian Institution, 1990.

Hamori-Torok, Charles. "Haisla." In *Handbook of North American Indians.* Vol. 7, *Northwest Coast,* edited by Wayne Suttles, 306-11. Washington, DC: Smithsonian Institution, 1990.

Hancock, Paul L., and Brian J. Skinner, eds. *The Oxford Companion to the Earth.* Oxford: Oxford University Press, 2000.

Hanna, Darwin, and Mamie Henry, eds. *Our Tellings: Interior Salish Stories of the Nlha7kapmx People.* Vancouver: UBC Press, 1995.

Hare, P. Gregory, Sheila Greer, Ruth Gotthardt, Richard Farnell, Vandy Bowyer, Charles Schweger, and Diane Strand. "Ethnographic and Archaeological Investigations of Alpine Patches in Southwest Yukon, Canada," *Arctic* 57, 3 (2004): 260-72.

Harington, C. Richard. "Quaternary Animals: Vertebrates of the Ice Age." In *Life in Stone: A Natural History of British Columbia Fossils,* edited by R. Ludvigsen, 259-73. Vancouver: UBC Press, 1996.

Harley, J. Brian. "Rereading Maps of the Columbian Encounter." *Annals of the Association of American Geographers* 82, 3 (1992): 522-36.

Harrington, Lyn. "On the Trail of the Candlefish." *The Beaver* Outfit 283 (1953): 40-44.

Harris, Douglas C. *Fish, Law and Colonialism: The Legal Capture of Salmon in British Columbia.* Toronto: University of Toronto Press, 2001.

Harris, Jo. "Mineral Development." In *British Columbia, the Pacific Province: Geographical Essays,* edited by Colin J.B. Wood, 260-75. Victoria: Western Geographical Press, 2001.

Harris, R. Cole, ed. *Historical Atlas of Canada.* Vol. 1, *From the Beginning to 1800.* Toronto: University of Toronto Press, 1987.

–. *Making Native Space: Colonialism, Resistance, and Reserves in British Columbia.* Vancouver: UBC Press, 2002.

–. "Strategies of Power in the Cordilleran Fur Trade." In *The Resettlement of British Columbia: Essays on Colonialism and Geographic Change,* 31-67. Vancouver: UBC Press, 1996.

Hartshorne, Charles, Paul Weiss, and Arthur W. Burks, eds. *Collected Papers of Charles Saunders Peirce.* 8 vols. Cambridge, MA: Harvard University Press, 1935-66.

Hatter, J. "The Moose of Central British Columbia." PhD, State College of Washington, 1950.

Hayden, Brian, ed. *The Ancient Past of Keatley Creek.* 2 vols. Burnaby: Simon Fraser University Archaeology Press, 2000.

–, ed. *A Complex Culture of the British Columbia Plateau: Traditional Stl'átl'imx Resource Use.* Vancouver: UBC Press, 1992.

–. "Research and Development in the Stone Age: Technological Transitions among Hunter-Gatherers." *Current Anthropology* 22, 5 (1981): 519-48.

Hayden, Brian, and June M. Ryder. "Prehistoric Cultural Collapse in the Lillooet Area." *American Antiquity* 56, 1 (1991): 50-65.

Hayes, Derek. *Historical Atlas of British Columbia and the Pacific Northwest: Maps of Exploration: British Columbia, Washington, Oregon, Alaska, Yukon.* Vancouver: Cavendish, 1998.

Hebda, Richard J. "British Columbia Vegetation and Climate History with Focus on 6 KA BP." *Géographie Physique et Quaternaire* 49 (1995): 55-79.

–. "Interior Grasslands Past and Future." *Cordillera* (1996): 344-46.

–. "Postglacial History of Grasslands of Southern British Columbia and Adjacent Regions." In *Grassland Ecology and Classification Symposium Proceedings,* edited by A.C. Nicholson, A. McLean, and T.E. Baker, 442-54. Victoria: BC Ministry of Forests, 1982.

Heilbron, J.L., ed. *The Oxford Companion to the History of Modern Science.* Oxford: Oxford University Press, 2003.

Helm, June, ed. *Handbook of North American Indians.* Vol. 6, *Subarctic.* Washington, DC: Smithsonian Institution, 1981.

Henry, Hazel. "The Moose Came Back Again." In *Chilcotin: Preserving Pioneer Memories,* edited by Veera Bonner, Irene E. Bliss, and Hazel Henry Litterick, 407-9. Surrey, BC: Heritage House, 1995.

Hewlett, Edward Sleigh. "The Chilcotin Uprising: A Study of Indian-European Relations in Nineteenth Century British Columbia." MA thesis, University of British Columbia, 1972.

–. "The Chilcotin Uprising of 1864." *BC Studies* 19 (1973): 50-72.

Hickson, C.J., J.K. Russell, and M.V. Stasiuk. "Volcanology of the 2350 BP Eruption of Mount Meager Volcanic Complex, BC, Canada: Implications for Hazards from Eruptions in Topographically Complex Terrain." *Bulletin of Volcanology* 60, 7 (1999): 489-507.

Hobson, Richmond Pearson, Jr. *Grass beyond the Mountains: Discovering the Last Great Cattle Frontier on the North American Continent.* Toronto: McClelland and Stewart, 1987.

Hocutt, C.H., and E.O. Wiley, eds. *The Zoogeography of North American Freshwater Fishes.* New York: Wiley-Interscience, 1986.

Hogg, Robert S. "Evaluating Historic Fertility Change in Small Reserve Populations." *BC Studies* 101 (1994): 79-95.

Holland, Stuart S. *Landforms of British Columbia: A Physiographic Outline.* Victoria: BC Department of Mines and Petroleum Resources, 1964.

Howay, F.W. *British Columbia from the Earliest Times to the Present.* Vol. 2. Vancouver: S.J. Clarke, 1914.

–. "An Outline Sketch of the Maritime Fur Trade." In *Canadian Historical Association, Annual Report, 1932,* 5-14. Toronto, 1932.

Hudson, Michael. "The Fiduciary Obligations of the Crown towards Aboriginal People." In *Aboriginal Title in British Columbia: Delgamuukw v. The Queen,* edited by Frank Cassidy, 44-50. Lantzville, BC: Oolichan Books, 1992.

Hunn, Eugene S., Nancy J. Turner, and David H. French. "Ethnobiology and Subsistence." In *Handbook of North American Indians.* Vol. 12, *Plateau,* edited by Deward E. Walker Jr., 525-45. Washington, DC: Smithsonian Institution, 1998.

Huntley, David H. "Late Wisconsinan Glaciation of East-Central Taseko Lakes, BC." PhD diss., University of New Brunswick, 1997.

Huntley, David H., and Bruce E. Broster. "Glacial Lake Camelsfoot: A Late Wisconsinan Advance Stage Proglacial Lake in the Fraser River Valley, Gang Ranch Area, BC." *Canadian Journal of Earth Sciences* 31 (1994): 798-807.

–. "The Late Wisconsinan Deglacial History of the East-Central Taseko Lakes Area, BC." *Canadian Journal of Earth Sciences* 34 (1997): 1510-20.

Hutchings, W. Karl. "The Namu Obsidian Industry." In *Early Human Occupation in British Columbia,* edited by Roy L. Carlson and Luke Dalla Bona, 167-76. Vancouver: UBC Press, 1996.

Hutchinson, Bruce. *The Fraser.* New York: Rinehart and Company, 1950.

Ignace, Marianne Boelscher. "Shuswap." In *Handbook of North American Indians.* Vol. 12, *Plateau,* edited by Deward E. Walker Jr., 203-19. Washington, DC: Smithsonian Institution, 1998.

Imbrie, John, and Katherine Palmer Imbrie. *Ice Ages: Solving the Mystery.* Cambridge, MA: Harvard University Press, 1986.

Irving, E. "Paleopoles and Paleolatitudes of North America and Speculations about Displaced Terrains." *Canadian Journal of Earth Sciences* 16 (1979): 669-94.

Irving, E., and P.J. Wynne. "Paleomagnetism: Review and Tectonic Implications." In *Geology of the Cordilleran Orogen in Canada,* edited by H. Gabrielse and C.J. Yorath, 61-86. Ottawa: Geological Survey of Canada, 1991.

Isaac, B. "Economy, Ecology and Analogy: The !Kung San and the Generalized Foraging Model." In *Early Paleoindian Economies of Eastern North America,* edited by B. Isaac and K. Tankersley. Greenwich, CT: Jai Press, 1990.

Iverson, Kristi E., Robert W. Gray, Bruce A. Blackwell, Carmen Wong, and Ken L. MacKenzie. "Past Fire Regimes in the Interior Douglas-fir, Dry Cool Subzone, Fraser Variant (IDFdk3)." Williams Lake, BC: Lignum Ltd., 2002.

Jacobs, Wilbur R. "British Indian Policies to 1783." In *Handbook of North American Indians.* Vol. 4, *History of Indian-White Relations,* edited by Wilcomb E. Washburn, 5-12. Washington, DC: Smithsonian Institution, 1988.

Jenkins, Keith. *Re-Thinking History.* London: Routledge, 2003.

Jenness, Diamond. "The Carrier Indians of the Bulkley River: Their Social and Religious Life." In *Anthropological Papers* no. 25, 469-586. Washington, DC: Smithsonian Institution, Bureau of American Ethnology, Bulletin 133, 1943.

Johansen, Dorothy. *Empire of the Columbia: A History of the Pacific Northwest.* 2nd ed. New York: Harper & Row, 1967.

Kan, Sergei. *Symbolic Immortality: The Tlingit Potlatch of the Nineteenth Century.* Washington, DC: Smithsonian Institution, 1989.

Keith, Lloyd, ed. *North of Athabasca: Slave Lake and Mackenzie River Documents of the North West Company, 1800-1821.* Montreal and Kingston: McGill-Queen's University Press, 2001.

Kelly, Robert L. *The Foraging Spectrum: Diversity in Hunter-Gatherer Lifeways.* Washington, DC: Smithsonian Institution, 1995.

Kelm, Mary-Ellen. *Colonizing Bodies: Aboriginal Health and Healing in British Columbia, 1900-50.* Vancouver: UBC Press, 1998.

Keser, Nurettin. *Interpretation of Landforms from Aerial Photographs: With Illustrations from British Columbia.* Victoria: BC Ministry of Forests, 1990.

Kinkade, M. Dale, William W. Elmendorf, Bruce Rigsby, and Haruo Aoki. "Languages." In *Handbook of North American Indians.* Vol. 12, *Plateau,* edited by Deward E. Walker Jr., 49-72. Washington, DC: Smithsonian Institution, 1998.

Kiple, Kenneth F., ed. *The Cambridge World History of Human Disease.* Cambridge: Cambridge University Press, 1993.

–. "The Ecology of Disease." In *Companion Encyclopedia to the History of Medicine,* edited by W.F. Bynum and Roy Porter, 357-81. London: Routledge, 1993.

Klingender, Franz. "Tractors: From Unfamiliar Oddity to Commonplace Tool." Ottawa: Canada Agriculture Museum, 2002.

Klippenstein, Frieda Esau. "The Challenge of James Douglas and Carrier Chief Kwah." In *Reading beyond Words: Contexts for Native History,* edited by Jennifer S.H. Brown and Elizabeth Vibert, 124-51. Peterborough, ON: Broadview, 1996.

Knowles, Norman. *Inventing the Loyalists: The Ontario Loyalist Tradition and the Creation of Usable Pasts.* Toronto: University of Toronto Press, 1997.

Kolbet, Richard M. "Narratives of North American Exploration." *Books at Iowa* 6 (1967).

Krauss, Michael E., and Victor K. Golla. "Northern Athapaskan Languages." In *Handbook of North American Indians.* Vol. 6, *Subarctic,* edited by June Helm, 67-85. Washington, DC: Smithsonian Institution, 1981.

Krech, Shepard, III. *The Ecological Indian: Myth and History.* New York: W.W. Norton, 2000.

–. *The Subarctic Fur Trade: Native Social and Economic Adaptations.* Vancouver: UBC Press, 1984.

Kuhnlein, H.V., A.C. Chan, J.N. Thompson, and S. Nakai. "Ooligan Grease: A Nutritious Fat Used by Native People of Coastal British Columbia." *Journal of Ethnobiology* 2, 2 (1982): 154-61.

Kutzbach, J.E. "Model Simulations of the Climatic Patterns during the Deglaciation of North America." In *North America and Adjacent Oceans during the Last Deglaciation,* edited by William F. Ruddiman and H.E. Wright Jr., 425-46. Boulder CO: Geological Society of America, 1987.

Laforet, Andrea, and Annie York. *Spuzzum: Fraser Canyon Histories, 1809-1939.* Vancouver: UBC Press, 1998.

Lamb, W. Kaye, ed. *Sixteen Years in the Indian Country: The Journals of Daniel Williams Harmon.* Toronto: Macmillan, 1957.

Lane, Robert. "Chilcotin." In *Handbook of North American Indians.* Vol. 6, *Subarctic,* edited by June Helm, 402-12. Washington, DC: Smithsonian Institution, 1981.

–. "Cultural Relations of the Chilcotin Indians of West Central British Columbia." PhD diss., University of Washington, 1953.

Larsen, Clark Spencer. *Skeletons in Our Closet: Revealing Our Past through Bioarchaeology.* Princeton, NJ: Princeton University Press, 2000.

Latour, Bruno. *Science in Action: How to Follow Scientists and Engineers through Society.* Cambridge, MA: Harvard University Press, 1987.

–. "Visualization and Cognition: Thinking with Eyes and Hands." *Knowledge and Society: Studies in the Sociology of Culture Past and Present* 6 (1986): 1-40.

Le Page du Pratz, Antoine-Simon. *Histoire de la Louisiane.* Vol. 3. Paris, 1758.

Lee, Norman. *Klondike Cattle Drive: The Journal of Norman Lee.* Vancouver: Mitchell Press, 1960.

Lee, Richard B., and Irven DeVore, eds. *Man the Hunter.* Chicago: Aldine, 1969.

Lemert, E.M. "The Life and Death of an Indian State." *Human Organization* 13, 3 (1955): 23-27.

Lepore, Jill. "Historians Who Love Too Much: Reflections on Microhistory and Biography." *Journal of American History* 88, 1 (2001): 129-44.

–. *The Name of War: King Philip's War and the Origins of American Identity.* New York: Random House, 1999.

Levi, Giovanni. "On Microhistory." In *New Perspectives on Historical Writing,* edited by Peter Burke, 93-113. University Park: Penn State University Press, 1991.

Lévi-Strauss, Claude. *The Savage Mind.* Chicago: University of Chicago Press, 1966.

–. *The Story of Lynx.* Chicago: University of Chicago Press, 1995.

Lewis, G. Malcolm. "Indian Maps." In *Old Trails and New Directions: Papers of the Third North American Fur Trade Conference,* edited by Carol M. Judd and Arthur J. Ray, 9-23. Toronto: University of Toronto Press, 1978.

Lewis, H.T., and Theresa A. Ferguson. "Yards, Corridors and Mosaics: How to Burn a Boreal Forest." *Human Ecology* 16 (1988): 57-77.

Long, M.H. "The Historic Sites and Monuments Board of Canada (Presidential Address)." In *Canadian Historical Association Report of the Annual Meeting,* 1-11. Ottawa: CHA, 1954.

Loo, Tina. "Bute Inlet Stories." In *Making Law, Order, and Authority in British Columbia, 1821-1871.* Vancouver: Toronto University Press, 1994.

–. *States of Nature: Conserving Canada's Wildlife in the Twentieth Century.* Vancouver: UBC Press, 2006.

Lowenthal, David. *The Past Is a Foreign Country.* Cambridge: Cambridge University Press, 1985.

Ludvigsen, R., ed. *Life in Stone: A Natural History of British Columbia's Fossils.* Vancouver: UBC Press, 1996.

Lutz, John. "After the Fur Trade: The Aboriginal Labouring Class of British Columbia 1849-1890." *Journal of Canadian Historical Association* (1992): 69-93.

–. "Interlude or Industry? Ranching in British Columbia, 1859-1885." *BC Historical News* 13, 4 (1980): 2-11.

Maas, M.C., and D.W. Krause. "Mammalian Turnover and Community Structure in the Paleocene of North America." *Historical Biology* 8 (1994): 91-128.

Macdonald, George F., Gary Coupland, and David Archer, "The Coast Tsimshian, ca. 1750." In *Historical Atlas of Canada.* Vol. 1, *From the Beginning to 1800,* edited by Harris, R. Cole, plate 13. Toronto: University of Toronto Press, 1987.

MacEwan, John Walter Grant. "Norman Lee, Chilcotin Pioneer." In *The Sodbusters,* 121-26. Edinburgh: Thomas Nelson and Sons, n.d.

Mackenzie, Alexander. *Journal of a Voyage to the Pacific.* New York: Dover, 1995.

–. *Voyages from Montreal: On the River St. Laurence, through the Continent of North America, to the Frozen and Pacific Oceans, in the Years 1789 and 1793.* London, 1801. Available from Canadiana.org (formerly the Canadian Institute for Historical Microreproductions), CIHM 33950.

Mackie, Richard Somerset. *Trading beyond the Mountains: The British Fur Trade on the Pacific, 1793-1843.* Vancouver: UBC Press, 1996.

Malloy, Mary. *Souvenirs of the Fur Trade: Northwest Coast Indian Art and Artifacts Collected by American Mariners 1788-1844.* Cambridge, MA: Peabody Museum of Harvard University, 2000.

Marx, Karl. *Capital.* Vol. 1. New York: Penguin, 1990.

Masters, D.C. "Toronto vs. Montreal: The Struggle for Financial Hegemony, 1860-1875." *Canadian Historical Review* 22 (June 1941): 133-46.

Mathews, W.H. "Late Quaternary Environmental History Affecting Human Habitation of the Pacific Northwest." *Canadian Journal of Archaeology* 3 (1979): 145-56.

–. "Neogene Chilcotin Basalts in South-Central British Columbia: Geology, Ages, and Geomorphic History." *Canadian Journal of Earth Sciences* 26, 5 (1989): 969-82.

Mathews, W.H., and Glenn E. Rouse. "Late Tertiary Volcanic Rocks and Plant-Bearing Deposits in British Columbia." *Geological Society of America Bulletin* 74 (1963): 55-60.

Mauss, Marcel. *The Gift: The Form and Reason for Exchange in Archaic Societies.* New York: W.W. Norton, 1990.

Mayewski, Paul A., George H. Denton, and Terrence J. Hughes. "Late Wisconsin Ice Sheets in North America." In *The Last Great Ice Sheets,* edited by George H. Denton and Terrence J. Hughes, 67-178. New York: Wiley, 1981.

McAnally, Lee McKenzie. "Paleogene Mammals on Land and at Sea." In *Life in Stone: A Natural History of British Columbia's Fossils,* edited by R. Ludvigsen, 202-11. Vancouver: UBC Press, 1996.

McClellan, Catharine. "History of Research in the Subarctic Cordillera." In *Handbook of North American Indians.* Vol. 6, *Subarctic,* edited by June Helm, 35-42. Washington, DC: Smithsonian Institution, 1981.

–. "Intercultural Relations and Cultural Change in the Cordillera." In *Handbook of North American Indians.* Vol. 6, *Subarctic,* edited by June Helm, 387-401. Washington, DC: Smithsonian Institution, 1981.

McGhee, Robert. *Ancient People of the Arctic.* Vancouver: UBC Press, 1996.

McIlwraith, T.F. *The Bella Coola Indians.* Toronto: University of Toronto Press, 1948.

McLaren, Graeme Peter. "Geology and Mineral Potential of the Chilko Lake Area (92N/1, 8; 92O4)." In *Geological Fieldwork 1986: A Summary of Field Activities and Current Research,* 231-43. Victoria: BC Ministry of Energy Mines and Petroleum Resources, 1987.

–. *A Mineral Resource Assessment of the Chilko Lake Planning Area.* Victoria: BC Ministry of Energy Mines and Petroleum Resources, 1990.

McLean, John. *Notes of a Twenty-Five Year's Service in the Hudson's Bay Territories.* London: R. Bentley, 1849.

McMillan, Alan Daniel, and Ian Hutchinson. "When the Mountain Dwarfs Danced: Aboriginal Traditions of Paleoseismic Events along the Cascadia Subduction Zone of Western North America." *Ethnohistory* 49, 1 (2002).

McMillan, W.J. "Porphyry Deposits in Volcanic Arcs with Deposits on the Canadian Cordillera." In *The Metallogeny of Volcanic Arcs,* edited by D.V. Lefebure, file 1998-8. Victoria: BC Ministry of Energy and Mines. Geological Survey Branch, 1998.

–. "Taseko Lakes Area." In *Geological Fieldwork 1976: A Summary of Field Activities of the Geological Division, Mineral Resources Branch,* 47-53. Victoria: BC Ministry of Mines and Petroleum Resources, 1977.

McMillan, W.J., J.F.H. Thompson, C.J.R. Hart, and S.T. Johnston. "Regional Geological and Tectonic Setting of Porphyry Deposits in British Columbia and Yukon Territory." In *Porphyry Deposits of the Northwestern Cordillera of North America,* edited by T.G. Schroeter, 40-57. Montreal: Canadian Institute of Mining, Metallurgy and Petroleum, 1995.

McNeill, J.R., and William H. McNeill. *The Human Web: A Bird's-Eye View of World History.* New York: W.W. Norton, 2003.

McNeill, William. *Plagues and Peoples.* New York: Anchor Books, 1989.

McPhail, J.D., and C.C. Lindsey. "Zoogeography of the Freshwater Fishes of Cascadia (the Columbia System and Rivers North to the Stikine)." In *The Zoogeography of North American Freshwater Fishes,* edited by C.H. Hocutt and E.O. Wiley, 615-37. New York: Wiley-Interscience, 1986.

McPhee, John. *Annals of the Former World.* New York: Farrar, Straus and Giroux, 1998.

Meidinger, Dellis Vern, and Jim Pojar, eds. *Ecosystems of British Columbia,* Special Report Series No. 6. Victoria: BC Ministry of Forests, 1991.

Mentzer, Robert. "Jupiter's Moons and the Longitude Problem." *Mercury* 31, 3 (2002): 34.

Mercuro, Nicholas, and Steven G. Medema. *Economics and the Law: From Posner to Post-Modernism.* Princeton, NJ: Princeton University Press, 1997.

Merk, Frederick, ed. *Fur Trade and Empire: George Simpson's Journal, 1824-25.* Cambridge, MA: Belknap Press of Harvard, 1968.

Michels, Joseph W. "Dating Methods." *Annual Review of Anthropology* 1 (1972): 113-26.

Miller, Christopher L. *Prophetic Worlds: Indians and Whites on the Columbia Plateau.* New Brunswick, NJ: Rutgers, 1985.

Miller, J.R. "Reading Photographs, Reading Voices: Documenting the History of Native Residential Schools." In *Reading beyond Words: Contexts for Native History,* edited by Jennifer S.H. Brown and Elizabeth Vibert, 461-81. Peterborough, ON: Broadview, 1996.

Mitchell, Donald H. "Archaeological Investigations on the Chilcotin Plateau, 1968." *Syesis* 3, 1/2 (1970): 45-65.

–. "Excavations on the Chilcotin Plateau: Three Sites, Three Phases." *Northwest Anthropological Research Notes* 4 (1970): 99-116.

Mole, Rich. "Homathco: The Stubborn Wilderness (and the Men Who Tried to Tame It)." *Western Living* (September 1978): 83-90.

Monger, James W.H. "The Origin and Evolution of Canada's Western Mountains." In *Life in Stone: A Natural History of British Columbia's Fossils,* edited by R. Ludvigsen, 25-44. Vancouver: UBC Press, 1996.

–. "Upper Paleozoic Rocks of the Western Canadian Cordillera and Their Bearing on Cordilleran Evolution." *Canadian Journal of Earth Sciences* 14 (1977): 1832-59.

Monmonier, Mark. *How to Lie with Maps.* Chicago: University of Chicago Press, 1996.

Morice, Adrien Gabriel. *The History of the Northern Interior of British Columbia.* Fairfield, WA: Ye Galleon Press, 1971.

–. "The Western Denes." *Proceedings of the Canadian Institute,* 3rd ser., 7 (1889): 109-80.

Muir, Edward. "Observing Trifles." In *Microhistory and the Lost Peoples of Europe,* edited by Edward Muir and Guido Ruggiero, vii-xxviii. Baltimore: Johns Hopkins University Press, 1991.

Mulhall, David. *Will to Power: The Missionary Career of Father Morice.* Vancouver: UBC Press, 1986.

Mustard, Peter S., and P. van der Heyden. "Geology of Tatla Lake (92N/15) and the East Half of Bussel Creek (92N/14) Map Areas." In *Interior Plateau Geoscience Project: Summary of Geological, Geochemical and Geophysical Studies,* edited by L.J. Diakow, J.M. Newell, and Paul Metcalfe, 103-18. Victoria: BC Geological Survey, 1997.

Nagorsen, David. *The Mammals of British Columbia: A Taxonomic Catalogue.* Victoria: Royal BC Museum, 1990.

Neylan, Susan. *The Heavens Are Changing: Nineteenth-Century Protestant Missions and Tsimshian Christianity.* Montreal and Kingston: McGill-Queen's University Press, 2003.

Nickell, Joe, and John F. Fischer. *Crime Science: Methods of Forensic Detection.* Lexington: University Press of Kentucky, 1998.

North, Douglass Cecil. *Institutions, Institutional Change, and Economic Performance.* Cambridge: Cambridge University Press, 1990.

Nute, Grace Lee. *The Voyageur.* St. Paul: Minnesota Historical Society, 1955.

O'Connell, Joseph. "Metrology: The Creation of Universality by the Circulation of Particulars." *Social Studies of Science* 23 (1993): 129-73.

O'Grady, B.T. "Western Mineral Survey District (No. 6)." In *Annual Report of the Minister of Mines of the Province of British Columbia for the Year Ended 31st December 1935,* F1-F58. Victoria: Legislative Assembly, 1936.

P.T.C. Phototype Composing. *British Columbia Recreational Atlas.* 4th ed. Victoria: P.T.C. Phototype Composing, 1997.

–. *British Columbia Road and Recreational Atlas.* 5th ed. Victoria: P.T.C. Phototype Composing, 2001.

Pagden, Anthony. *The Fall of Natural Man: The American Indian and the Origins of Comparative Ethnology.* Cambridge: Cambridge University Press, 1987.

Palmer, Henry Spencer. *Report of a Journey of a Survey from Victoria to Fort Alexander, via North Bentinck Arm.* New Westminster: Royal Engineer Press, 1863. BC Archives NW971.MP174re.

Parish, Roberta, Ray Coupé, and Dennis Lloyd, eds. *Plants of Southern Interior British Columbia and the Inland Northwest.* Vancouver: Lone Pine, 1999.

Payne, Michael, and Gregory Thomas. "Literacy, Literature and Libraries in the Fur Trade." *The Beaver* 63 (1983): 46-53.

Peirce, C.S. "Logic as Semiotic: The Theory of Signs." In *Philosophical Writings of Peirce,* edited by Justus Buchler. New York: Dover, 1955.

Perry, Adele. "From 'the Hot-Bed of Vice' to the 'Good and Well-Ordered Christian Home': First Nations Housing and Reform in Nineteenth-Century British Columbia," *Ethnohistory* 50, 4 (2003): 587-610.

Pielou, E.C. *After the Ice Age: The Return of Life to Glaciated North America.* Chicago: University of Chicago Press, 1991.

–. *Fresh Water.* Chicago: University of Chicago Press, 1998.

–. *The World of the Northern Evergreens.* Ithaca, NY: Cornell University Press, 1998.

Podruchny, Carolyn. *Making the Voyageur World: Travelers and Traders in the North American Fur Trade.* Toronto: University of Toronto Press, 2006.

–. "Werewolves and Windigos: Narratives of Cannibal Monsters in French-Canadian Voyageur Oral Tradition," *Ethnohistory* 51, 4 (2004): 677-700.

Pokotylo, David L. *Blood from Stone: Making and Using Stone Tools in Prehistoric British Columbia.* Vancouver: UBC. Museum of Anthropology, 1988.

Pomeranz, Kenneth, and Steven Topik. *The World that Trade Created: Society, Culture, and the World Economy 1400 to the Present.* Armonk, NY: M.E. Sharpe, 1999.

Pope, Peter E. *The Many Landfalls of John Cabot.* Toronto: University of Toronto Press, 1997.

Prosperity Project Committee. "Prosperity Gold-Copper Project: Project Report Specifications." BC Environmental Assessment Office 1998.

Pryce, Paula. *"Keping the Lakes' Way": Reburial and the Re-creation of a Moral World among an Invisible People.* Toronto: University of Toronto Press, 1999.

Pyne, Stephen J. *Fire in America: A Cultural History of Wildland and Rural Fire.* Seattle: University of Washington Press, 1997.

Quebec Mission. *Notices and Voyages of the Famed Quebec Mission to the Pacific Northwest.* Portland: Oregon Historical Society, 1956.

Rapp, George (Rip), Jr., and Christopher L. Hill. *Geoarchaeology: The Earth-Science Approach to Archaeological Investigation.* New Haven, CT: Yale University Press, 1998.

Ray, Arthur J. "The Hudson's Bay Company and Native People." In *Handbook of North American Indians.* Vol. 4, *History of Indian-White Relations,* edited by Wilcomb E. Washburn, 335-50. Washington, DC: Smithsonian Institution, 1988.

–. "Indians as Consumers in the Eighteenth Century." In *Old Trails and New Directions: Papers of the Third North American Fur Trade Conference,* edited by Carol M. Judd and Arthur J. Ray, 255-71. Toronto: University of Toronto Press, 1978.

–. *Indians in the Fur Trade: Their Role as Trappers, Hunters, and Middlemen in the Lands Southwest of Hudson Bay, 1660-1870.* Toronto: University of Toronto Press, 1998.

–. "Periodic Shortages, Native Welfare, and the Hudson's Bay Company 1670-1930." In *The Subarctic Fur Trade: Native Social and Economic Adaptations,* edited by Shepard Krech, III, 1-20. Vancouver: UBC Press, 1984.

Ray, Arthur J., and Donald Freeman. *'Give Us Good Measure': An Economic Analysis of Relations between the Indians and the Hudson's Bay Company before 1763.* Toronto: University of Toronto Press, 1978.

Redman, Charles L. *Human Impact on Ancient Environments.* Tucson: University of Arizona, 1999.

Reedy-Maschner, Katherine L., and Herbert D.G. Maschner. "Marauding Middlemen: Western Expansion and Violent Conflict in the Subarctic." *Ethnohistory* 46, 4 (1999): 703-43.

Reid, John Phillip. *Patterns of Vengeance: Crosscultural Homicide in the North American Fur Trade.* Pasadena, CA: Ninth Judicial Circuit Historical Society, 1999.

Rich, Edwin Ernest. *The History of the Hudson's Bay Company.* 2 vols. London: Hudson's Bay Record Society, 1959.

Richards, Thomas H., and Michael K. Rousseau. *Late Prehistoric Cultural Horizons on the Canadian Plateau.* Burnaby: Simon Fraser University Department of Archaeology, 1987.

Richmond, Anthony H. "Immigration and Pluralism in Canada." *International Migration Review* 4, 1 (1969): 5-24.

Riddington, Robin. *Little Bit Know Something: Stories in a Language of Anthropology.* Iowa City: University of Iowa, 1990.

Roberts, Neil. *The Holocene: An Environmental History.* Oxford: Blackwell, 1989.

Roseland, Mark, J.C. Day, and Robert W. Penrose. "Shared Decision Making in Public Land Planning: An Evaluation of the Cariboo-Chilcotin CORE Process." *Environments* 25, 2/3 (1998): 27-47.

Rosman, Abraham, and Paula G. Rubel. *Feasting with Mine Enemy: Rank and Exchange among Northwest Coast Societies.* New York: Columbia University, 1971.

Ross, Eric. *Beyond the River and the Bay: Some Observations on the State of the Canadian*

Northwest in 1811 with a View to Providing the Intending Settler with an Intimate Knowledge of That Country. Toronto: University of Toronto Press, 1970.

Rothenburger, Mel. *The Chilcotin War.* Langley, BC: Mr. Paperback, 1978.

Rouse, Glenn E., and W.H. Mathews. "Radioactive Dating of Tertiary Plant-Bearing Deposits." *Science* 133, 3458 (1961): 1079-80.

Rousseau, Mike K. "Early Prehistoric Occupation of South-Central British Columbia: A Review of the Evidence and Recommendations for Further Research." *BC Studies* 99 (1993): 140-83.

Rubin, Isaak Illlich. *Essays on Marx's Theory of Value.* Detroit, MI: Black and Red Press, 1972.

Rudwick, Martin J.S. "The Emergence of a Visual Language for Geological Science." *History of Science* 14 (1976): 149-95.

Ruggles, Richard I. *A Country So Interesting: The Hudson's Bay Company and Two Centuries of Mapping, 1670-1870.* Montreal and Kingston: McGill-Queen's University Press, 1991.

Sage, Walter N. "Some Early Historians of British Columbia." *BC Historical Quarterly* 21, 1-4 (1957-58).

Sanders, Douglas. "Government Indian Agencies in Canada." In *Handbook of North American Indians.* Vol. 4, *History of Indian-White Relations,* edited by Wilcomb E. Washburn, 276-83. Washington, DC: Smithsonian Institution, 1988.

Sanger, David. "Prehistory of the Pacific Northwest Plateau as Seen from the Interior of British Columbia," *American Antiquity* 32 (1967): 186-97.

–. "7,000 Years of Prehistory in British Columbia," *The Beaver* Outfit 298 (1968): 34-40.

Schiarizza, Paul, R.G. Gaba, M. Coleman, J.I. Garver, and J.K. Glover. "Geology and Mineral Occurrences of the Yalakom River Area (92O/1, 2, 92J/15, 16)." In *Geological Fieldwork 1989: A Summary of Field Activity and Current Research,* 53-72. Victoria: BC Ministry of Energy, Mines and Petroleum Resources. Mineral Resources Division. Geological Survey Branch, 1990.

Schiarizza, Paul, and Janet Riddell. "Geology of the Tatlayoko Lake – Beece Creek Area (92N/8, 9, 10; 92O/5, 6, 12)." In *Interior Plateau Geoscience Project: Summary of Geological, Geochemical and Geophysical Studies,* edited by L.J. Diakow, J.M. Newell, and Paul Metcalfe, 63-101. Victoria: BC Geological Survey, 1997.

Scholefield, Ethelbert Olaf Stuart. *British Columbia from the Earliest Times to the Present.* Vol. 1. Vancouver: S.J. Clarke, 1914.

Schuurman, Nadine. *GIS: A Short Introduction.* Malden, MA: Blackwell, 2004.

Schwartz, Marion. *A History of Dogs in the Early Americas.* New Haven, CT: Yale University Press, 1997.

Scott, James C. *Seeing Like a State: How Certain Schemes to Improve the Human Condition Have Failed.* New Haven, CT: Yale University Press, 1998.

Shackleton, David M. *Hoofed Mammals of British Columbia.* Vancouver: Royal BC Museum, 1999.

Sheppe, Walter. "Mackenzie's Route." Appendix 2 of *Journal of a Voyage to the Pacific,* by Alexander Mackenzie, 314-36. New York: Dover, 1995.

Siebert, L., and T. Simkin. *Volcanoes of the World: An Illustrated Catalog of Holocene Volcanoes and their Eruptions.* Global Volcanism Program Digital Information Series, GVP-3. Washington, DC: Smithsonian Institution, 2002. Available at http://www.volcano.si.edu/gvp/world/.

Sierra Legal Defence Fund. *Digging up Trouble: The Legacy of Mining in British Columbia*. Vancouver: Sierra Legal Defence Fund, 1998.

–. "False Economy: The Hidden Future Costs of Cuts in Regulatory Services." Vancouver: Sierra Legal Defence Fund, 2002.

Simpson, George. "The 'Character Book' of Governor George Simpson 1832," in *Hudson's Bay Miscellany 1670-1870*, ed. Glyndwr Williams, 151-236. Winnipeg: Hudson's Bay Record Society, 1975.

–. *Part of Dispatch from George Simpson Esquire, Governor of Ruperts Land to the Governor & Committee of the Hudson's Bay Company, London, March 1, 1829, Continued and Completed March 24 and June 5, 1829*, ed. E.E. Rich. Toronto: Champlain Society, 1947.

Sinclair, A.R.E., D.S. Hik, O.J. Schmitz, G.G.E. Scudder, D.H. Turpin, and N.C. Larter. "Biodiversity and the Need for Habitat Renewal." *Ecological Applications* 5, 3 (1995): 579-87.

Smith, Adam. *An Inquiry into the Nature and Causes of the Wealth of Nations*. Chicago: University of Chicago Press, 1976.

Smith, Dorothy Blakey. *James Douglas: Father of British Columbia*. Oxford: Oxford University Press, 1971.

–, ed. "The Journal of Arthur Thomas Bushby, 1858-59." *BC Historical Quarterly* 21, 1-4 (1957-58): 83-160.

Smith, Harlan I. "A Semi-Subterranean House Site in the Bella Coola Indian Area on the Coast of British Columbia." *Man* 25 (1925): 176-77.

Smith, Marcus. "Report on the Surveys in British Columbia during the Year 1875." Appendix 1 in *Report on Surveys and Preliminary Operations on the Canadian Pacific Railway up to January 1877*, by Sandford Fleming, 162-76. Ottawa: MacLean, Roger and Company, 1877.

Smith, Marian W. "House Types of the Middle Fraser River." *American Antiquity* 4 (1947): 255-67.

Sorrenson, Richard. "The Ship as a Scientific Instrument in the Eighteenth Century." *Osiris*, 2nd ser., 11 (1996): 221-36.

Souther, J.G. "The Western Anahim Belt: Root Zone of a Peralkaline Magma System." *Canadian Journal of Earth Sciences* 23 (1986): 895-908.

Spalding, David J. "The Early History of Moose (Alces alces): Distribution and Relative Abundance in British Columbia." *Contributions to Natural Science* [Royal BC Museum] 11 (1990): 1-12.

Sparrow v. The Queen, [1990] 1 S.C.R. 1075.

St. Pierre, Paul H. *Smith and Other Events: Tales of the Chilcotin*. New York: Penguin, 1985.

–. *Tell Me a Good Lie: Tales from the Chilcotin Country*. Vancouver: Douglas and McIntyre, 2001.

Statistics Canada. "1996 Census: Ethnic Origin, Visible Minorities." Ottawa: Statistics Canada, 1998.

Stegner, Wallace. *Wolf Willow: A History, A Story, and a Memory of the Last Plains Frontier*. New York: Penguin, 2000.

Sterne, Netta. *Fraser Gold 1858! The Founding of British Columbia*. Pullman: Washington State University Press, 1998.

Stewart, Hilary. *Indian Fishing: Early Methods on the Northwest Coast*. Vancouver: Douglas and McIntyre, 1996.

Stienstra, Tom. "Floatplane Venture Affords Wondrous Vision of Nature." *Examiner* (San Francisco), 21 August 1994.

Stockey, Ruth A., and Wesley C. Wehr. "Flowering Plants in and around Eocene Lakes of the Interior." In *Life in Stone: A Natural History of British Columbia Fossils,* edited by R. Ludvigsen, 234-47. Vancouver: UBC Press, 1996.

Stryd, Arnould H., and Mike K. Rousseau. "The Early Prehistory of the Mid Fraser-Thompson River Area." In *Early Human Occupation in British Columbia,* edited by Roy L. Carlson and Luke Dalla Bona, 177-204. Vancouver: UBC Press, 1996.

Stuart, W.F. "Earth's Field Magnetometry." *Report on Progress in Physics* 35 (1972): 803-81.

Surtees, Robert J. "Canadian Indian Policies." In *Handbook of North American Indians.* Vol. 4, *History of Indian-White Relations,* edited by Wilcomb E. Washburn, 81-95. Washington, DC: Smithsonian Institution, 1988.

Sutherland, Ron. "The Oolichan Fishery of Northern British Columbia." *BC Historical News* 34, 3 (2001): 8-13.

Suttles, Wayne, ed. *Handbook of North American Indians.* Vol. 7, *Northwest Coast.* Washington, DC: Smithsonian Institution, 1990.

Swagerty, William R. "Indian Trade in the Trans-Mississippi West to 1870." In *Handbook of North American Indians.* Vol. 4, *History of Indian-White Relations,* edited by Wilcomb E. Washburn, 351-74. Washington, DC: Smithsonian Institution, 1988.

Swan, James G. "The Surf-smelt of the Northwest Coast, and the Method of Taking Them by the Quillehute Indians, West Coast of Washington Territory." *Proceedings of the United States National Museum for 1880* 3 (1881): 43-46.

Swannell, Frank C. "Lieutenant Palmer Makes a Survey." *The Beaver* Outfit 292, 20 (1961): 33-38.

–. "Mackenzie's Expedition to the Pacific Ocean, 1793." In *Report of Proceedings of the 23rd Annual General Meeting,* 42-47. N.p.: Corporation of BC Land Surveyors, 1928.

–. "On Mackenzie's Trail." *The Beaver* Outfit 289, 18 (1958): 9-14.

Switlo, Janice G.A.E. *Gustafsen Lake under Siege: Exposing the Truth behind the Gustafsen Lake Stand-Off.* Peachland, BC: TIAC Communications, 1997.

Symons, D.T.A. "Paleomagnetism of the Triassic Guichon Batholith and Rotation in the Interior Plateau, British Columbia." *Canadian Journal of Earth Sciences* 8 (1971): 1388-96.

Tanner, Helen Hornbeck, ed. *The Settling of North America: The Atlas of the Great Migrations into North America from the Ice Age to the Present.* New York: Macmillan, 1995.

Teit, James Alexander. "The Thompson Indians of British Columbia." In *Jesup North Pacific Expedition,* edited by Franz Boas. Vol. 1, Part 4, 163-392. New York: Knickerbocker Press, 1900.

Teskey, Dennis, P.J. Hood, L.W. Morley, R.A. Gibb, P. Sawatzky, M. Bower, and E.E. Ready. "The Aeromagnetic Survey Program of the Geological Survey of Canada: Contribution to Regional Geological Mapping and Mineral Exploration." *Canadian Journal of Earth Sciences* 30, 2 (1993): 243-60.

Teskey, Dennis, Peter Stone, Peter S. Mustard, and Paul Metcalfe. "High-Resolution Regional Aeromagnetic Survey: Interior Plateau British Columbia." In *Interior Plateau Geoscience Project: Summary of Geological, Geochemical and Geophysical Studies,* edited by L.J. Diakow, J.M. Newell, and Paul Metcalfe, 221-24. Victoria: BC Geological Survey, 1997.

Thomas, Nicholas. *Cook: The Extraordinary Voyages of Captain James Cook.* New York: Walker and Company, 2004.

Thompson, E.P. *The Poverty of Theory and Other Essays.* New York: Monthly Review Press, 1978.

Thompson, Laurence C., and M. Dale Kinkade. "Languages." In *Handbook of North American Indians.* Vol. 7, *Northwest Coast,* edited by Wayne Suttles, 30-51. Washington, DC: Smithsonian Institution, 1990.

Tilman, David, and Peter Kareiva, eds. *Spatial Ecology: The Role of Space in Population Dynamics and Interspecific Interactions.* Princeton: Princeton University Press, 1997.

Tipper, H.W. *Glacial Geomorphology and Pleistocene History of Central British Columbia.* Bulletin 196. Ottawa: Geological Survey of Canada, 1971.

Tobey, Margaret L. "Carrier." In *Handbook of North American Indians.* Vol. 6, *Subarctic,* edited by June Helm, 413-32. Washington, DC: Smithsonian Institution, 1981.

Tsilhqot'in National Government. "Tsilhqot'in Sovereignty Declaration." Williams Lake, BC, 1997.

Tuller, Stanton. "Climate." In *British Columbia, the Pacific Province: Geographical Essays,* edited by Colin J.B. Wood, 45-63. Victoria: Western Geographical Press, 2001.

Turner, Nancy J. "Burning Mountain Sides for Better Crops: Aboriginal Landscape Burning in British Columbia." *Archaeology in Montana* 32, 2 (1991): 57-73.

–. *Food Plants of Interior First Peoples.* Vancouver: UBC Press, 1997.

–. *Plant Technology of First Peoples of British Columbia.* Vancouver: UBC Press, 1998.

Turner, Nancy J., Laurence C. Thompson, M. Terry Thompson, and Annie York. *Thompson Ethnobotany: Knowledge and Usage of Plants by the Thompson Indians of British Columbia.* Victoria: Royal BC Museum, 1990.

UBC Museum of Anthropology. "First Nations Languages of British Columbia." [Map], Vancouver: UBC Press, 1994. http://www.moa.ubc.ca/pdf/FN_Lang_map.pdf.

Umhoefer, P.J., and H.W. Tipper. *Stratigraphy, Depositional Environment, and Tectonic Setting of the Upper Triassic to Middle Jurassic Rocks of the Chilcotin Ranges, Southwestern British Columbia.* Ottawa: Geological Survey of Canada, Bulletin 519, 1998.

University of Oxford Radiocarbon Accelerator Unit. OxCal Version 3.5. http://c14.arch.ox.ac.uk/.

van Kirk, Sylvia. *"Many Tender Ties": Women in Fur-Trade Society in Western Canada, 1670-1870.* Winnipeg: Watson and Dwyer, 1980.

VanDine, D.F., H.W. Nasmith, and C.F. Ripley. "The Emergence of Engineering Geology in British Columbia: "An Engineering Geologist Knows a Dam Site Better"!" In *Pioneering Geology in the Canadian Cordillera.* BC Geological Survey Branch, Open File 1992-19. Victoria: BC Geological Survey Branch, 1992.

Verner, C. "The Arrowsmith Firm and the Cartography of Canada." In *Explorations in the History of Canadian Mapping,* edited by B. Farrell and A. Desbarats, 47-54. Ottawa: Association of Canadian Map Libraries and Archives, 1988.

Vézina, Robert. "Les mauvais renards et la garce: description et origine du terme drouine." In *Le passage du Détroit: 300 ans de présence francophone / Passages: Three Centuries of Francophone Presence at Le Détroit,* edited by M. Bénéteau, 127-47. Windsor: Humanities Research Group, University of Windsor, 2003.

Vibert, Elizabeth. *Traders' Tales: Narratives of Cultural Encounter on the Columbia Plateau, 1807-1846.* Norman: University of Oklahoma Press, 1997.

Wade, M.S. *Mackenzie of Canada: The Life and Adventure of Alexander Mackenzie, Discoverer.* Edinburgh: W. Blackwood, 1927.

Walbran, John T. *British Columbia Coast Names: Their Origin and History.* Vancouver: Douglas and McIntyre, 1971.

Walker, Deward E., Jr., ed. *Handbook of North American Indians.* Vol. 12, *Plateau.* Washington, DC: Smithsonian Institution, 1998.

–. "Introduction." In *Handbook of North American Indians.* Vol. 12, *Plateau,* edited by Deward E. Walker, Jr., 1-7. Washington, DC: Smithsonian Institution, 1998.

Walker, Deward E., Jr., and Helen H. Schuster. "Religious Movements." In *Handbook of North American Indians.* Vol. 12, *Plateau,* edited by Deward E. Walker, Jr., 499-514. Washington, DC: Smithsonian Institution, 1998.

Washburn, Wilcomb E., ed. *Handbook of North American Indians.* Vol. 4, *History of Indian-White Relations.* Washington, DC: Smithsonian Institution, 1988.

Weir, Thomas R. "The Winter Feeding Period in the Southern Interior Plateau of British Columbia." *Annals of the Association of American Geographers* 44, 2 (1954): 194-204.

West, Elliot. *The Contested Plains: Indians, Goldseekers, and the Rush to Colorado.* Lawrence: University of Kansas, 1998.

White, Richard. *Land Use, Environment, and Social Change: The Shaping of Island County, Washington.* Seattle: University of Washington Press, 1992.

–. *The Middle Ground: Indians, Empires, and Republics in the Great Lakes Region, 1650-1815.* Cambridge: Cambridge University Press, 1991.

–. *The Organic Machine.* New York: Hill and Wang, 1995.

White, W.H. "Cordilleran Tectonics in British Columbia." *Bulletin of the American Association of Petroleum Geologists* 43, 1 (1959): 60-100.

Whitehead, Margaret Mary. *The Cariboo Mission: A History of the Oblates.* Victoria: Sono Nis, 1981.

–. *Sound Heritage.* Vol. 34, *Now You Are My Brother: Missionaries in British Columbia.* Victoria: Provincial Archives of BC, 1981.

–, ed. *They Call Me Father: Memoirs of Father Nicholas Coccola.* Vancouver: UBC Press, 1988.

Whittaker, John C. *Flintknapping: Making and Understanding Stone Tools.* Austin: University of Texas, 1994.

Whymper, Frederick. *Travel and Adventure in the Territory of Alaska ... and in Various Other Parts of the North Pacific.* London: John Murray, 1868.

Willey, Gordon R., and Philip Phillips. *Method and Theory in American Archaeology.* Chicago: University of Chicago Press, 1958.

Williams, Carol J. *Framing the West: Race, Gender, and the Photographic Frontier in the Pacific Northwest.* Oxford: Oxford University Press, 2003.

Williams, Judith. *High Slack: Waddington's Gold Road and the Bute Inlet Massacre of 1864.* Vancouver: New Star, 1996.

Wilmeth, Roscoe. "Distribution of Several Types of Obsidian from Archaeological Sites in British Columbia." *Canadian Archaeological Association Bulletin* 5 (1973): 27-60.

Wilson, Mark V.H. "Fishes from Eocene Lakes of the Interior." In *Life in Stone: A Natural History of British Columbia Fossils,* edited by R. Ludvigsen, 212-24. Vancouver: UBC Press, 1996.

–. "Insects near Eocene Lakes of the Interior." In *Life in Stone: A Natural History of British Columbia Fossils,* edited by R. Ludvigsen, 225-33. Vancouver: UBC Press, 1996.

Wolfhard, Michael R. "Fish Lake." In *Porphyry Deposits of the Canadian Cordillera: A Volume Dedicated to Charles S. Ney,* edited by A. Sutherland Brown, 317-22. N.p.: Canadian Institute of Mining and Metallurgy, 1976.

Wong, Carmen. "Natural Disturbance Regimes in the Cariboo Region: What is Known to Guide Forest Management?" Williams Lake, BC: Lignum Ltd., 2000.

Wood, Colin J.B., and Cimarron Corpé. "Fisheries." In *British Columbia, the Pacific Province: Geographical Essays,* edited by Colin J.B. Wood, 329-44. Victoria: Western Geographical Press, 2001.

Wood, Colin J.B., Cimarron Corpé, and Laurie Jackson. "Land Use Planning." In *British Columbia, the Pacific Province: Geographical Essays,* edited by Colin J.B. Wood, 229-59. Victoria: Western Geographical Press, 2001.

Woodward, Frances M. "The Influence of the Royal Engineers on the Development of British Columbia." *BC Studies* 24 (1974): 3-51.

Woodworth, John. "Show Us Where Mackenzie Walked." *BC Historical News* 26, 2 (1993): 2-4.

[Woodworth, John]. "After the Re-enactments." *BC Historical News* 27, 1 (1993/94): 15-17.

Woodworth, John, and Hälle Flygare. *In the Steps of Alexander Mackenzie.* 2nd ed. Kelowna, BC: Alexander Mackenzie Trail Association, 1987.

Workman, William B. "The Significance of Volcanism in the Prehistory of Subarctic Northwest North America." In *Volcanic Activity and Human Ecology,* edited by Payson D. Sheets and Donald K. Grayson, 339-71. New York: Academic, 1979.

World Commission on Environment and Development. *Our Common Future.* Oxford: Oxford University Press, 1987.

Wright, Richard Thomas. "The Chinlac Massacre." *BC Outdoors,* March 1986, 54-55, 63-64.

Toponymic Index

General Index

Aboriginal groups: Athapaskan (*see* Dene); Babine, 196; Cree, 152; Dene, 122-23, 142, 152, 195-97, 216; Dene migrations, 123; Gitxsan, 51, 114; Haisla, 127-28; Kwakwaka'wakw, 175; Mohawk, 217; Musqueam Indian Band, 50-51; Nuxalk, 103, 108, 122, 128-29, 155, 160, 171, 199, 215; Secwepemc, 55, 57, 144-45, 160, 164, 199, 222-24; Sekani, 195; Stl'atl'imx, 81, 121; Tsimshian, 127; Ulkatcho Indian Band, 108-9, 114, 131; Wet'suwet'en, 51, 123; Xeni Gwet'in (*see* Tsilhqot'in). *See also* Aboriginals; Carrier; Tsilhqot'in

Aboriginals: agency of Aboriginal people, xv; alcohol, 167, 192, 204-05, 210-11, 214, 222; Assembly of First Nations, 216; *British North America Act,* 187; *Calder v. Attorney General of British Columbia,* 216; Cariboo-Chilcotin Justice Inquiry, xv, 218-21, 224; contact: against notion of contact as rupture, 81-82; *Contact and Conflict* (Robin Fisher), 146; *Delgamuukw v. British Columbia* (1997), 50-52, 56, 71; Dene Declaration, 216; fishing rights, 50-51, 158-59; "Fourth World," emergence of, 143, 216; Fred Quilt Committee, 206-09; Gustafsen Lake, 222-23; *Indian Act* (1880), 193,

216; indolence, Aboriginal people accused of, 89; land policy and title, xii, 46, 51-52, 56, 133, 187, 191, 217; law, Aboriginal, 162, 182; literacy, 194-95; National Indian Brotherhood, 215; Oka, 217; outsiders' views of Aboriginal people, 169, 184-85, 195-96, 216-17; potlatch, 130; racism, xiv, 194, 226; rights, xv, 110; Royal Canadian Mounted Police (RCMP), xv, 201, 204-05, 207-11, 217, 219-22; *Royal Proclamation* (1763), 46; Sarich commission (*see* Cariboo-Chilcotin Justice Inquiry); *Sparrow v. The Queen* (1990), 50-52, 71, 216; status, 193, 216; treaties, lack of, 46; *Treaty of Paris* (1763), 46. *See also* war

anglers and fishing, xii, 26, 89-90, 93, 109, 116-17, 125-26, 133, 141, 158-59; conflict over Fish Lake, 38, 42-44, 47-52, 54-56, 61, 70-71; *Fisheries Act,* 50; Pan Phillips Fishing Resort, 95; salmon fishing, 38, 70, 109-10, 117, 119-21, 127-28, 148, 151-54, 158

anthropology: ethnobiology, 121; ethnohistory, xv, xvi; ethnology, xvi, 133; folklore, 5; generalized foragers, 112; nomadism and sedentism, 120-21, 151; oral tradition, 5, 197; subsistence cycles,

314